HANDBOOK ON DATA PROTECTION IN HUMANITARIAN ACTION

This handbook is a foundational text which offers a comprehensive, accessible analysis of personal data protection law, and its significance to humanitarian organizations. Bringing together years of research on personal data protection principles, it outlines how humanitarian organizations can use these principles to uphold the rights and dignity of the most vulnerable. Reflecting the rapid evolution of new technologies, the handbook provides an in-depth analysis of the impacts of using specific technologies in humanitarian contexts. It raises awareness of the importance of data protection and suggests practical steps that humanitarian organizations can implement to process the personal data that they hold in a responsible manner that complies with personal data protection principles and requirements. With tailored advice and extensive, up-to-date research, this is a vital resource for humanitarian practitioners and lawyers, data protection authorities and researchers working on humanitarian affairs and personal data protection. This title is also available as Open Access on Cambridge Core.

Massimo Marelli is the Head of Data Protection Office at the International Committee of the Red Cross (ICRC), and a member of the Advisory Board and a Fellow of the European Centre on Privacy and Cybersecurity at the University of Maastricht.

HANDBOOK ON DATA PROTECTION IN HUMANITARIAN ACTION

MASSIMO MARELLI (Ed.)

THIRD EDITION

This Handbook has been endorsed by:

GPA
Global Privacy Assembly

IFRC

UNHCR
The UN Refugee Agency

World Food Programme

CAMBRIDGE UNIVERSITY PRESS

CAMBRIDGE UNIVERSITY PRESS

Shaftesbury Road, Cambridge CB2 8EA, United Kingdom

One Liberty Plaza, 20th Floor, New York, NY 10006, USA

477 Williamstown Road, Port Melbourne, VIC 3207, Australia

314–321, 3rd Floor, Plot 3, Splendor Forum, Jasola District Centre, New Delhi – 110025, India

103 Penang Road, #05–06/07, Visioncrest Commercial, Singapore 238467

Cambridge University Press is part of Cambridge University Press & Assessment, a department of the University of Cambridge.

We share the University's mission to contribute to society through the pursuit of education, learning and research at the highest international levels of excellence.

www.cambridge.org
Information on this title: www.cambridge.org/9781009414623

DOI: 10.1017/9781009414630

© Cambridge University Press & Assessment 2024

This work is in copyright. It is subject to statutory exceptions and to the provisions of relevant licensing agreements; with the exception of the Creative Commons version the link for which is provided below, no reproduction of any part of this work may take place without the written permission of Cambridge University Press.

An online version of this work is published at doi.org/10.1017/9781009414630 under a Creative Commons Open Access license CC-BY-NC-ND 4.0 which permits re-use, distribution and reproduction in any medium for non-commercial purposes providing appropriate credit to the original work is given. You may not distribute derivative works without permission. To view a copy of this license, visit https://creativecommons.org/licenses/by-nc-nd/4.0

All versions of this work may contain content reproduced under license from third parties.
Permission to reproduce this third-party content must be obtained from these third-parties directly.

When citing this work, please include a reference to the DOI 10.1017/9781009414630

First published 2024

A catalogue record for this publication is available from the British Library

Library of Congress Cataloging-in-Publication Data
Names: Marelli, Massimo, 1979– editor.
Title: Handbook on data protection in humanitarian action / Massimo Marelli (ed.).
Description: Third edition. | Cambridge, United Kingdom ; New York, NY : Cambridge University Press, [2023?] | Includes bibliographical references and index.
Identifiers: LCCN 2023016257 (print) | LCCN 2023016258 (ebook) | ISBN 9781009414623 (hardback) | ISBN 9781009414654 (paperback) | ISBN 9781009414630 (epub)
Subjects: LCSH: Data protection–Law and legislation. | Computer networks–Security measures. | Privacy, Right of. | Humanitarian assistance–Data processing.
Classification: LCC K3560 .H36 2023 (print) | LCC K3560 (ebook) | DDC 342.08/58–dc23/eng/20230712
LC record available at https://lccn.loc.gov/2023016257
LC ebook record available at https://lccn.loc.gov/2023016258

ISBN 978-1-009-41462-3 Hardback
ISBN 978-1-009-41465-4 Paperback

Cambridge University Press & Assessment has no responsibility for the persistence or accuracy of URLs for external or third-party internet websites referred to in this publication and does not guarantee that any content on such websites is, or will remain, accurate or appropriate.

CONTENTS

LIST OF CONTRIBUTORS XIV

FOREWORD TO THE THIRD EDITION XVIII
by Christopher Kuner

FOREWORD TO THE FIRST AND SECOND EDITIONS XIX
by Jean-Philippe Walter

ACKNOWLEDGEMENTS XXI

GLOSSARY OF DEFINED TERMS AND ABBREVIATIONS XXIV

1   INTRODUCTION 3
    1.1   Background 4
    1.2   Objective 4
    1.3   Structure and approach 8
    1.4   Target audience 9

PART I: DATA PROTECTION PRINCIPLES IN HUMANITARIAN ACTION 11
Massimo Marelli

2   BASIC PRINCIPLES OF DATA PROTECTION 13
    2.1   Introduction 14
    2.2   Basic data protection concepts 16
    2.3   Aggregate, Pseudonymized and Anonymized data sets 18
    2.4   Applicable law and International Organizations 20
    2.5   Data Processing principles 21
        2.5.1   The principle of the fairness and lawfulness of Processing 21
        2.5.2   The purpose limitation principle 22
        2.5.3   The principle of proportionality 24
        2.5.4   The principle of data minimization 26
        2.5.5   The principle of data quality 27
    2.6   Special Data Processing situations 27
        2.6.1   Health purposes 27
        2.6.2   Administrative activities 28
    2.7   Data retention 28
    2.8   Data security and Processing security 29
        2.8.1   Introduction 29
        2.8.2   Physical security 31

		2.8.3	IT security 31

      2.8.3   IT security 31
      2.8.4   Duty of discretion and staff conduct 32
      2.8.5   Contingency planning 33
      2.8.6   Destruction methods 33
      2.8.7   Other measures 34
  2.9   The principle of accountability 35
  2.10 Information 35
      2.10.1 Data collected from the Data Subject 36
      2.10.2 Information notices 36
      2.10.3 Data not collected from the Data Subject 37
  2.11 Rights of Data Subjects 38
      2.11.1 Introduction 38
      2.11.2 Access 38
      2.11.3 Correction 40
      2.11.4 Right to erasure 40
      2.11.5 Right to object 41
  2.12 Data sharing and International Data Sharing 41

3 LEGAL BASES FOR PERSONAL DATA PROCESSING 43
  3.1   Introduction 44
  3.2   Consent 45
      3.2.1   Unambiguous 46
      3.2.2   Timing 46
      3.2.3   Validity 46
      3.2.4   Vulnerability 46
      3.2.5   Children 47
      3.2.6   Informed 48
      3.2.7   Documented 48
      3.2.8   Withholding/Withdrawing Consent 48
  3.3   Vital interest 49
  3.4   Important grounds of public interest 50
  3.5   Legitimate interest 51
  3.6   Performance of a contract 52
  3.7   Compliance with a legal obligation 53
      3.7.1   The disclosure of Personal Data to authorities 54

4 INTERNATIONAL DATA SHARING 57
  4.1   Introduction 58
  4.2   Basic rules for International Data Sharing 59
  4.3   Providing a legal basis for International Data Sharing 60
      4.3.1   Introduction 60
      4.3.2   Legal bases for International Data Sharing 60

4.4	Mitigating the risks to the individual		61
	4.4.1	Appropriate safeguards/Contractual clauses	61
	4.4.2	Accountability	63
4.5	Data Controller/Data Processor relationship		63

5 DATA PROTECTION IMPACT ASSESSMENTS (DPIAS) 65

5.1	Introduction		66
5.2	The DPIA process		67
	5.2.1	Is a DPIA necessary?	67
	5.2.2	The DPIA team	67
	5.2.3	Describing the Processing of Personal Data	68
	5.2.4	Consulting stakeholders	68
	5.2.5	Identify risks	69
	5.2.6	Assess the risks	69
	5.2.7	Identify solutions	70
	5.2.8	Propose recommendations	72
	5.2.9	Implement the agreed recommendations	72
	5.2.10	Provide expert review and/or audit of the DPIA	73
	5.2.11	Update the DPIA if there are changes in the project	73

PART II: SPECIFIC PROCESSING SITUATIONS, TECHNOLOGIES AND TECHNOLOGY AREAS 75

6 DESIGNING FOR DATA PROTECTION 77
Carmela Troncoso and Wouter Lueks

6.1	Introduction		78
	6.1.1	What is a system?	79
6.2	Case study: Privacy-preserving contact-tracing apps		79
	6.2.1	Decentralized privacy-preserving proximity tracing	81
6.3	Protection of individuals and their dignity and rights through purpose limitation		82
	6.3.1	Why determining purpose matters	84
	6.3.2	Determining purpose	87
	6.3.3	Analysing purpose limitation	88
6.4	The role of data minimization		93
6.5	Challenges to purpose limitation		94

7 DRONES/UAVS AND REMOTE SENSING 97
Massimo Marelli

7.1	Introduction		98
7.2	Application of basic data protection principles		101
	7.2.1	Legal bases for Personal Data Processing	102
	7.2.2	Transparency/Information	104

	7.2.3	Purpose limitation and Further Processing	105
	7.2.4	Data minimization	105
	7.2.5	Data retention	106
	7.2.6	Data security	106
7.3	Rights of Data Subjects		106
7.4	Data sharing		108
7.5	International Data Sharing		109
7.6	Data Controller/Data Processor relationship		109
7.7	Data Protection Impact Assessments		110

8 BIOMETRICS 113
Massimo Marelli

	8.1	Introduction	114
	8.2	Application of basic data protection principles	116
	8.2.1	Legal bases for Personal Data Processing	118
	8.2.2	Fair and lawful Processing	120
	8.2.3	Purpose limitation and Further Processing	121
	8.2.4	Data minimization	122
	8.2.5	Data retention	123
	8.2.6	Data security	123
	8.2.7	Excessiveness by nature	124
8.3	Rights of Data Subjects		124
8.4	Data sharing		125
8.5	International Data Sharing		125
8.6	Data Controller/Data Processor relationship		126
8.7	Data Protection Impact Assessments		126

9 CASH AND VOUCHER ASSISTANCE 129
Massimo Marelli

	9.1	Introduction	130
	9.2	Application of basic data protection principles	134
	9.3	Basic principles of data protection	135
	9.3.1	Legal bases for Personal Data Processing	136
	9.3.2	Purpose limitation and Further Processing	137
	9.3.3	Data minimization	139
	9.3.4	Data retention	140
	9.3.5	Data security	140
9.4	Rights of Data Subjects		141
9.5	Data sharing		141
9.6	International Data Sharing		142
9.7	Data Controller/Data Processor relationship		143
9.8	Data Protection Impact Assessments		143

10 CLOUD SERVICES 147
Paolo Balboni

    10.1 Introduction 148
    10.2 Data Controller/Data Processor relationship 151
    10.3 Responsibility and accountability in the cloud 151
    10.4 Application of basic data protection principles 152
        10.4.1 Legal bases for Personal Data Processing 152
        10.4.2 Fair and lawful Processing 153
        10.4.3 Purpose limitation and Further Processing 153
        10.4.4 Transparency 154
        10.4.5 Data retention 155
    10.5 Data security 156
        10.5.1 Data in transit protection 160
        10.5.2 Asset protection 160
        10.5.3 Separation between users 162
        10.5.4 Governance 162
        10.5.5 Operational security 162
        10.5.6 Personnel 163
        10.5.7 Development 163
        10.5.8 Supply chain 163
        10.5.9 User management 163
        10.5.10 Identity and authentication 164
        10.5.11 External interfaces 164
        10.5.12 Service administration 164
        10.5.13 Audits 164
        10.5.14 Service usage 164
    10.6 Rights of Data Subjects 165
    10.7 International Data Sharing 165
    10.8 Data Protection Impact Assessments 165
    10.9 Privileges and immunities and the cloud 166
        10.9.1 Legal measures 166
        10.9.2 Organizational measures 167
        10.9.3 Technical measures 167
    10.10 Codes of conduct 167

11 CLOUD AND GOVERNMENT ACCESS 171
Andrea Raab-Gray

    11.1 Mapping legislations allowing governments to require service providers to
         disclose Humanitarian Data 173
        11.1.1 Legal frameworks allowing governments to compel service providers
            to disclose humanitarian data for purposes of national security 174

11.1.2 Legal frameworks allowing governments to compel service
providers to disclose data for purposes of criminal proceedings 178
11.2 Impacts of compelled disclosure on Humanitarian Action and persons
benefiting from it 184
11.3 Mitigating the risk of disclosure of Humanitarian Data processed in a public
cloud environment 186
11.3.1 Ensuring the effectiveness of privileges and immunities 186
11.3.2 Sensitizing States to the importance of not using or requesting
Humanitarian Data for purposes incompatible with the work of
Humanitarian Organizations 189

12 MOBILE MESSAGING APPS 191
Lina Jasmontaite-Zaniewicz

12.1 Introduction 192
12.1.1 Mobile messaging apps in Humanitarian Action 194
12.2 Application of basic data protection principles 195
12.2.1 Processing of Personal Data through mobile messaging apps 196
12.2.2 What kind of data do messaging apps collect or store? 197
12.2.3 How could other parties access data shared on messaging apps? 200
12.2.4 Messaging app features related to privacy and security 202
12.2.5 Processing of Personal Data collected through mobile
messaging apps 205
12.3 Legal bases for Personal Data Processing 206
12.4 Data retention 207
12.5 Data Subject rights to rectification and deletion 207
12.6 Data minimization 208
12.7 Purpose limitation and Further Processing 209
12.8 Managing, analysing and verifying data 209
12.9 Data protection by design 210
12.10 International Data Sharing 211

13 DIGITAL IDENTITY 213
Vincent Graf Narbel

13.1 Introduction 214
13.1.1 Authentication, identification and verification: Who are you and
how can you prove it? 216
13.1.2 Digital Identity 217
13.1.3 System design and governance 218
13.1.4 Digital Identity in the humanitarian sector: Possible scenarios 220
13.1.5 Digital Identity as foundational identity 221
13.2 Data Protection Impact Assessments 222
13.3 Data protection by design and by default 222

13.4 Data Controller/Data Processor relationship 223
13.5 Rights of Data Subjects 224
      13.5.1 Right of access 225
      13.5.2 Rights to rectification and erasure 226
13.6 Application of basic data protection principles 226
      13.6.1 Legal bases for Personal Data Processing 226
      13.6.2 Purpose limitation and Further Processing 227
      13.6.3 Proportionality 227
      13.6.4 Data minimization 228
      13.6.5 Data security 228
      13.6.6 Data retention 229
13.7 International Data Sharing 229

14 SOCIAL MEDIA 231
Júlia Zomignani Barboza and Lina Jasmontaite-Zaniewicz

14.1 Introduction 232
      14.1.1 Social media in the humanitarian sector 232
      14.1.2 Social media and data 234
14.2 Data Protection Impact Assessments 239
14.3 Ethical issues and other challenges 241
14.4 Data Controller/Data Processor relationship 243
14.5 Basic data protection principles 244
      14.5.1 Legal bases for Personal Data Processing 244
      14.5.2 Information 245
      14.5.3 Data retention 246
      14.5.4 Data security 247
14.6 International Data Sharing 247

15 BLOCKCHAIN 249
Vincent Graf Narbel

15.1 Introduction 250
      15.1.1 What is Blockchain? 250
      15.1.2 Types of Blockchain 253
      15.1.3 Blockchain in practice 255
      15.1.4 Humanitarian use cases 256
15.2 Data Protection Impact Assessments 258
15.3 Data Protection by design and by default 260
15.4 Data Controller/Data Processor relationship 261
15.5 Basic data protection principles 263
      15.5.1 Data minimization 263
      15.5.2 Data retention 264

15.5.3 Proportionality 264
15.5.4 Data security 264
15.6 Rights of Data Subjects 265
    15.6.1 Right of access 266
    15.6.2 Right to rectification 266
    15.6.3 Right to erasure 267
    15.6.4 Restrictions of Data Subjects' rights 267
15.7 International Data Sharing 268
15.8 Annex: Decision-making framework for Blockchain in Humanitarian Action . . . 269

16 CONNECTIVITY AS AID 275
Aaron Martin and John Warnes

16.1 Introduction 276
    16.1.1 Overview of connectivity as aid interventions 277
    16.1.2 Operational context 278
    16.1.3 Multiple stakeholders and partnerships 279
16.2 Data Protection Impact Assessments 281
16.3 Data Controller/Data Processor relationship 282
16.4 Basic data protection principles 283
    16.4.1 Legal bases for Personal Data Processing 283
    16.4.2 Data security 284
    16.4.3 Data retention 286
    16.4.4 Information 286
16.5 International Data Sharing 287

17 ARTIFICIAL INTELLIGENCE 289
Alessandro Mantelero

17.1 Introduction 290
    17.1.1 What Artificial Intelligence is and how it works 290
    17.1.2 Artificial Intelligence in the humanitarian sector 294
    17.1.3 Challenges and risks of using Artificial Intelligence 299
17.2 Application of basic data protection principles 301
    17.2.1 Legal bases for Personal Data Processing 302
    17.2.2 Purpose limitation and Further Processing 305
    17.2.3 Fair and lawful Processing 308
    17.2.4 Transparency 311
    17.2.5 Data minimization 312
    17.2.6 Data retention 314
    17.2.7 Data security 315
17.3 Rights of Data Subjects 316
    17.3.1 Rights related to automated decision making 316

17.4 Data Controller/Data Processor relationship 319
       17.4.1 Accountability 319
       17.4.2 Liability 320
17.5 International Data Sharing 321
17.6 Data Protection Impact Assessment and Human Rights Impact Assessment . . . 322
       17.6.1 Human Rights Impact Assessment for Artificial Intelligence 324
       17.6.2 Human Rights Impact Assessment: phases and procedure 325
17.7 Data Protection by design and by default 329
17.8 Ethical issues and challenges 329

APPENDIX 1: TEMPLATE FOR A DPIA REPORT 333

APPENDIX 2: WORKSHOP PARTICIPANTS 339

INDEX 343

CONTRIBUTORS

Massimo Marelli is the Head of the Data Protection Office at the International Committee of the Red Cross (ICRC). Massimo is a member of the Advisory Board and a Visiting Fellow at the European Centre on Privacy and Cybersecurity at Maastricht University, and a member of the Brussels Privacy Hub Advisory Board at the Vrije Universiteit Brussel. Massimo has been a Visiting Fellow at the Lauterpacht Centre for International Law at the University of Cambridge, and a member of the Data Protection Commission of the European Organization for Nuclear Research (CERN). Before taking the role of Head of Data Protection Office at the ICRC, Massimo worked in the field as an ICRC Delegate, as a Référendaire at the General Court of the European Union, and as a lawyer in private practice in London and Brussels specializing in antitrust and EU law.

Carmela Troncoso is an Assistant Professor at the Swiss Federal Institute of Technology Lausanne (EPFL) (Switzerland) where she heads the SPRING Lab. She holds a Master's degree in Telecommunication Engineering from the University of Vigo (2006) and a PhD in Engineering from KU Leuven (2011). Before joining EPFL she was a faculty member at the IMDEA Software Institute (Spain) for two years; the Security and Privacy Technical Lead at Gradiant, working closely with industry to deliver secure and privacy-friendly solutions to the market, for four years; and a postdoctoral researcher at the COSIC Group. Carmela's research focuses on security and privacy. Her thesis, "Design and Analysis Methods for Privacy Technologies", received the European Research Consortium for Informatics and Mathematics Security and Trust Management Best PhD Thesis Award, and her work on privacy engineering received the CNIL-INRIA Privacy Protection Award 2017. She regularly publishes in the most prestigious venues in security (e.g. ACM Conference on Computer Security; USENIX Security Symposium) and privacy (Privacy Enhancing Technologies).

Wouter Lueks is a tenure-track faculty member at the CISPA Helmholtz Center for Information Security in Saarbrücken, Germany, which he joined in late 2022. Before that he was a postdoctoral researcher at EPFL in Lausanne, Switzerland, where he worked with Carmela Troncoso in the SPRING lab. He is interested in solving real-world problems by designing end-to-end privacy-friendly systems. To do so he combines privacy, applied cryptography and systems research. His designs for privacy-friendly contact tracing have been deployed in millions of phones around the world, and his secure document search system is being deployed by a large organization for investigative journalists.

Paolo Balboni (PhD) is a Professor of Privacy, Cybersecurity and IT Contract Law at the European Centre on Privacy and Cybersecurity (ECPC) within the Maastricht

University Faculty of Law. He is also the Chairman of the European Patent Office (EPO) Data Protection Board and a member of the EUMETSAT Data Protection Supervisory Authority. As a qualified lawyer specializing in ICT, privacy and cyber security and intellectual property, he is admitted to the Milan Bar and also registered to the Amsterdam Bar. He is a Founding Partner of ICT Legal Consulting (ICTLC), an international law firm, and ICT Cyber Consulting, a company specializing in information/data security. Prof. Dr Balboni is a Recommended Lawyer ranked by *The Legal 500 EMEA 2021* in the areas of Data Privacy and Data Protection and Industry Focus: Telecom, Media and Technology. His main research focus is Data Protection as a Corporate Social Responsibility, which can be used to help organizations responsibly further their economic targets and at the same time positively contribute to the development of a fair data-centric society. Prof. Dr Balboni furthermore advises governments on national matters concerning cyber security and privacy, and in 2018 he drafted the national Surinamese Privacy and Data Protection Law.

Andrea Raab-Gray is currently working as a legal expert in the Office of the Legal Adviser at the Federal Ministry of European and International Affairs of the Republic of Austria. Prior to joining the Foreign Ministry, she worked as a legal adviser with the ICRC both in Geneva and London. She also worked with Judge Theodor Meron at the International Residual Mechanism for Criminal Tribunals, and Women's Initiatives for Gender Justice, a non-governmental organization based in The Hague combatting sexual and gender-based violence. Andrea graduated with distinction from the University of Oxford, where she read the MJur, and holds a law degree from the University of Vienna. For her academic achievements she received a number of scholarships and awards, including the Oxford Global Justice Internship Fund and the Volterra Fietta Prize in International Dispute Settlement.

Lina Jasmontaite-Zaniewicz is a doctoral candidate at the Vrije Universiteit Brussel. She is a contributing fellow and the Education Coordinator at the Brussels Privacy Hub, where she explores topics such as the legal implications of new legislative initiatives on individuals' rights to privacy and data protection. Her PhD research primarily concerns the Personal Data Breach notification obligations foreseen in the General Data Protection Regulation. She publishes on topics concerning the protection of human rights, regulation of new technologies (e.g. Digital Identity wallets and Artificial Intelligence (AI)) and cyber security.

Vincent Graf Narbel joined the ICRC in 2015 as an ICT Innovation Officer after more than 15 years in the private sector, where he held various positions in ICT from software developer to solutions architect and service manager. Vincent is currently working as a Strategic Technology Adviser in the ICRC Data Protection Office. He focuses on the adoption of new technology in the humanitarian sector with a strong emphasis on privacy, security, and ethics in general. He actively participated in the Data Protection in Humanitarian Action working series and in particular to the area of Biometrics, Digital Identity, Artificial Intelligence and Blockchain. He is also co-leading several research projects in these areas. Vincent holds a Master's in Mathematics from the EPFL (Switzerland).

Júlia Zomignani Barboza graduated in law in 2012 in Brazil, where she completed different internships and volunteer positions in varied fields of law. She holds an LLM in International Humanitarian Law and Human Rights from the Geneva Academy. In Geneva, she worked as a legal researcher at the human rights non-governmental organization (NGO) Alkarama and as an associate at the ICRC. Before joining the Vrije Universiteit Brussel (VUB; Free University of Brussels), she also worked as a legal advocate for asylum seekers and refugees in Bangkok and as a legal assistant working with asylum cases in Sydney. Júlia became a PhD candidate at the VUB in October 2018. Her PhD research focuses on the treatment of migrants who are (suspected) criminals but who cannot be returned to their country of origin without violating non-refoulement. At the same time, she contributes to multiple research projects on the topics of migration, humanitarian issues and data protection.

Aaron Martin is an Assistant Professor of Media Studies and Data Science at the University of Virginia. Prior to this, he was an Assistant Professor of International and European Law at Maastricht University and a postdoctoral researcher at the Tilburg Institute for Law, Technology, and Society (TILT), and he worked in the financial services sector in the area of cyber- governance and technology regulation. He has also worked in technology policy roles at the Organization for European Cooperation and Development (OECD), European Commission, and Vodafone Group. He is an Oxford Martin Associate at the Global Cyber Security Capacity Centre. He has a PhD in Information Systems and Innovation from the London School of Economics and Political Science.

John Warnes leads the Office of the United Nations High Commissioner for Refugees' (UNHCR's) Digital Inclusion programme within the agency's Innovation Service, where he focuses on brokering strong partnerships and facilitating solutions to ensure that all refugees and the communities that host them have the right and the choice to be included in a connected society. Prior to this, John was engaged in designing and implementing technology solutions to support UNHCR's activities around communicating with communities in emergencies and supporting the agency's Connectivity for Refugees efforts. Previously he worked with the Communicating with Disaster Affected Communities (CDAC) Network, exploring sector-wide issues relating to community engagement and accountability to affected people. He has also spent time working in the private sector for a telecommunications company and working for transparency and accountability NGO Transparency International in Berlin. He holds a BA in Politics from the University of Bath and an LLM in IT and Telecommunications Law from the University of Southampton.

Alessandro Mantelero is an Associate Professor of Private Law and Law & Technology at the Polytechnic University of Turin. He is a Council of Europe scientific expert on AI, data protection and human rights (Ad Hoc Committee on Artificial

Intelligence – CAHAI; Convention 108 – Consultative Committee) and has served as an expert on data regulation for several national and International Organizations, including the United Nations, the EU Agency for Fundamental Rights, and the European Commission. He has held visiting appointments in several universities, including the Berkman Klein Center for Internet & Society at Harvard University, Nanjing University of Information Science (NUIST), Universitat Oberta de Catalunya and Universidad de Murcia, and he joined the University of Oxford as a visiting research fellow at the Oxford Internet Institute in 2013 and 2014 working on data protection and big data. He is an associate editor of the *Computer Law & Security Review* and a member of the Editorial Board of the *European Data Protection Law Review*. His latest book is *Beyond Data: Human Rights, Ethical and Social Impact Assessment in AI* (T.M.C. Asser Press – Springer, 2022). In 2022 he was awarded the Jean Monnet Chair in Mediterranean Digital Societies and Law, in recognition of excellence in European Union studies, by the European Commission.

FOREWORD TO THE THIRD EDITION

The work of humanitarian organizations requires the processing of Personal Data. They must work as effectively and efficiently as possible to assist individuals faced with persecution or natural disasters, so protecting the processing of their Personal Data can literally be a matter of life and death. Despite its great benefits, Data Processing (particularly that carried out online) also brings risks, such as the potential for data misuse and threats to cyber security. This is why data protection has become essential for humanitarian organizations to fulfil their mandates, and why it is increasingly expected by their stakeholders.

The International Committee of the Red Cross (ICRC) and the Brussels Privacy Hub have already published jointly two editions of their *Handbook on Data Protection in Humanitarian Action*, of which I was proud to be co-editor. They provide guidance for organizations working in the humanitarian sector to implement data protection in their operations. However, since then the risks of data misuse, security breaches and unauthorized Data Processing have continued to grow, new legal issues surrounding Data Processing have emerged and the challenges for humanitarian organizations have increased correspondingly.

I am thus very happy that Massimo Marelli of the ICRC has edited this third edition of the *Handbook*, which is needed given the growing legal and practical complexity of implementing data protection. It goes beyond the first two editions by covering additional topics such as risk mitigation, digital contact tracing and government access, among others. It also provides further elucidation of both the relevant legal issues and the practical challenges that humanitarian organizations face.

Data protection must constantly evolve to meet threats to Data Processing. This third edition of the *Handbook* will be a key tool for humanitarian organizations to protect the data of vulnerable individuals and to fulfil their mandates.

Prof. Christopher Kuner
Former Co-Director, Brussels Privacy Hub, Vrije Universiteit Brussel,
Brussels, Belgium

Co-Editor, first and second editions of the
Handbook on Data Protection in Humanitarian Action
February 2022

FOREWORD TO THE FIRST AND SECOND EDITIONS

Jean-Philippe Walter

It is a pleasure to introduce the *Handbook on Data Protection in Humanitarian Action*, which is the result of a very fruitful collaboration between the International Committee of the Red Cross (ICRC) and the Brussels Privacy Hub (BPH).

Personal data protection is of fundamental importance for humanitarian organizations as it is an integral part of protecting the life, integrity and dignity of their beneficiaries.

In 2015, the 37th International Conference of Data Protection and Privacy Commissioners adopted the Resolution on Privacy and International Humanitarian Action. One of the resolution's aims was to meet the demand among humanitarian actors for cooperation to develop guidance on data protection. A working group was set up and became involved in the Data Protection in Humanitarian Action project, run jointly by the BPH and the ICRC, whose objectives were to explore the relationship between data protection laws and humanitarian action, to understand the impact of new technologies on data protection in the humanitarian sector and to formulate appropriate guidance.

The project brought together humanitarian organizations, data protection authorities and technology experts in a series of workshops covering a range of topics, including data analytics, drones, biometrics, cash transfer programming, cloud-based computing and messaging apps, all of which have become increasingly important in the humanitarian sector.

The Handbook is one of the outputs of this project; it will be a useful tool to raise awareness and assist humanitarian organizations in complying with personal data protection standards. It also addresses the need for specific guidance on the interpretation of data protection principles as applicable to humanitarian action, especially when new technologies are employed. I believe the Handbook will prove helpful to humanitarian actors, data protection authorities and private companies alike. It clearly demonstrates that data protection legislation does not prohibit the collection and sharing of personal data, but rather provides the framework in which personal data can be used in the knowledge and confidence that individuals' right to privacy is respected.

Jean-Philippe Walter is the Data Protection Commissioner of the Council of Europe, and a member of the Data Protection Commission of the ICRC. He is the former Deputy Swiss Federal Data Protection and Information Commissioner and has also been President of the French-speaking Association of Personal Data Protection Authorities and Coordinator of the International Conference of Data Protection and Privacy Commissioners (now Global Privacy Assembly) Working Group on the Resolution on Privacy and International Humanitarian Action.

ACKNOWLEDGEMENTS

This publication is the third edition of what has been, until the second edition, a joint publication I curated together with Prof. Christopher Kuner of the Brussels Privacy Hub, an academic research centre of the Vrije Universiteit Brussel (VUB; Free University of Brussels) in Brussels, Belgium.

Therefore, first and foremost I would like to thank Christopher for his key role and contribution as co-convener of the Data Protection in Humanitarian Action working series and as co-editor of the resulting first and second editions. His guidance, knowledge, expertise and mentorship over the years constitute strong foundations for the Handbook and continue to guide the spirit of this publication.

This third edition includes two new chapters which meet an important need for guidance that has clearly emerged since the second edition was published. In the first of these new chapters, Carmela Troncoso and Wouter Lueks provide guidance on how to approach data protection by design, and how to design programmes and systems in ways that integrate data protection from the outset. This chapter is a pivotal contribution that is relevant for all the technology areas discussed in Part II. In the second new chapter, Andrea Raab-Gray looks more closely at the challenges faced by humanitarian organizations using cloud-based tools vis-à-vis their capacity to keep the data they collect under their exclusive control and ensure their use for exclusively humanitarian purposes. More specifically, it provides guidance on how to analyse possible sources of "lawful" access to humanitarian data by governments through Third Party processors such as cloud service providers.

For all other pre-existing chapters, authors who primarily or significantly contributed to those chapters curated their update to ensure they are up to date with the latest trends, developments and analyses. The text of this edition is up to date as at the date of submission of the manuscript, 10 December 2022.

I would therefore also like to thank my co-authors who curated chapters in this third edition: Carmela Troncoso, Wouter Lueks, Paolo Balboni, Andrea Raab-Gray, Lina Jasmontaite-Zaniewicz, Júlia Zomignani Barboza, Vincent Graf Narbel, Alessandro Mantelero, Aaron Martin and John Warnes. It was a great privilege to work together both on this edition of the Handbook and on the many initiatives and projects that fed into it.

Like the previous editions, this one has benefited greatly from the insights provided through consultations, workshops, interviews, panels and conferences – including the DigitHarium working series that took place throughout 2021[1] – that brought

---

1   ICRC, "DigitHarium", ICRC, 2021, www.icrc.org/en/digitharium.

together a wide multi-stakeholder group of experts from academia, data protection authorities and privacy commissioners, humanitarian practitioners, donors, civil society and the private sector. And as with the previous editions, the work in progress was peer-reviewed by the Advisory Group for this edition, with plenty of lively debates along the way. The Advisory Group for this edition comprised:

- Christopher Kuner, formerly VUB
- Cosimo Monda and Herke Kranenborg, European Centre on Privacy and Cybersecurity, Maastricht University
- Michèle Finck, University of Tübingen
- Nathaniel Raymond, Yale University
- Carmela Troncoso, École Polytechnique Fédérale de Lausanne (EPFL)
- Catherine Lennman, Swiss Data Protection Authority, Global Privacy Assembly Working Group on Privacy and International Humanitarian Aid, and International Development
- Claire-Agnes Marnier, Olivier Matter and Petra Candellier, European Data Protection Supervisor
- Marine Revel, French-speaking Association of Personal Data Protection Authorities
- Irina Conovali and Abtin Kronold, Office of the United Nations High Commissioner for Refugees (UNHCR)
- Christina Vasala Kokkinaki, formerly International Organization for Migration (IOM) and currently International Telecommunication Union (ITU)
- Lucie Laplante and James de France, International Federation of Red Cross and Red Crescent Societies (IFRC)
- Stuart Campo, formerly United Nations Office for the Coordination of Humanitarian Affairs (OCHA)
- Alexandrine Pirlot de Corbion and Gus Hosein, Privacy International
- Mary Nunn, formerly Médecins Sans Frontières (MSF) and currently Global Survivors Fund
- Max Lamesch and Catherine Kayser, *Luxembourg Ministry of Foreign Affairs, Directorate for Development Cooperation and Humanitarian Affairs*
- Gilles Cerutti and Jonas Belina, Swiss Federal Department of Foreign Affairs.

Many thanks too to Cambridge University Press, who helped bring this third edition to fruition, especially Marianne Nield, and to my colleagues Silvia Pelucchi and Chloe Jensen for their dedication and very skilful management of the Handbook project.

For many years now our work in the area of data protection in humanitarian action has thrived thanks to generous support from the Luxembourg Ministry of Foreign Affairs and the Swiss Federal Department of Foreign Affairs, and the third edition of this Handbook is one of the concrete manifestations of this work.

I am very thankful for the continued engagement and contribution of a number of extraordinary communities which, together, continue to provide the knowledge and insights necessary to detect, anticipate and navigate new trends and dilemmas facing the humanitarian sector in digital transformation. First, the community of humanitarian practitioners: dedicated colleagues at the International Committee of the Red Cross, National Societies of the Red Cross and the Red Crescent, the International Federation of Red Cross and Red Crescent Societies, UN Agencies, and other organizations on the front line of humanitarian action. Driven by a relentless commitment to maximize the benefit of new technologies for vulnerable communities affected by humanitarian emergencies while ensuring their protection, dignity and agency, these practitioners provide the necessary field "reality check" to ensure that the guidance provided is meaningful and realistic in the extraordinary circumstances presented by humanitarian crises. Second, the community of data protection supervisory authorities and experts within the framework of the Global Privacy Assembly and the Council of Europe Consultative Committee for the Protection of Individuals with regard to Automatic Processing of Personal Data Convention 108 (T-PD) provide an extremely insightful space for exchange, reflection, and development of guidance on the application of key data protection rules to new technologies and technology areas. Third, the academic community of the European Centre on Privacy and Cybersecurity at Maastricht University and the Lausanne and Zurich Polytechnics, with unparalleled cutting-edge expertise in law and computer science respectively. These partnerships provide the type of forward-thinking environment, free of constraints, that academia can offer.

Specific credits and acknowledgements relating to the previous editions are reported therein.

Massimo Marelli
Geneva, November 2022

GLOSSARY OF DEFINED TERMS AND ABBREVIATIONS

Anonymization encompasses techniques that can be used to ensure that data sets containing Personal Data are fully and irreversibly anonymized so that they do not relate to an identified or identifiable natural person, or that the Data Subject is not or no longer identifiable.

Artificial Intelligence refers to "[a] set of sciences, theories and techniques whose purpose is to reproduce by a machine the cognitive abilities of a human being".[1] In its current form, it aims to allow technology developers "to entrust a machine with complex tasks previously delegated to a human".[2]

Biometrics or biometric recognition means the automated recognition of individuals based on their biological and behavioural characteristics.

Blockchain is "in essence an append-only decentralized database that is maintained by a consensus algorithm and stored on multiple nodes (computers)".[3]

Cash and Voucher Assistance, Cash Transfer Programming, cash-based interventions and cash-based assistance are terms in the humanitarian sector to describe the delivery of humanitarian aid in the form of vouchers or cash.

CERT – Computer Emergency Response Team

CISO – Chief Information Security Officer

Cloud Services most commonly refers to "a model for enabling ubiquitous, convenient, on-demand network access to a shared pool of configurable computing resources (e.g. networks, servers, storage, applications, and services) that can be rapidly provisioned and released with minimal management effort or service provider interaction".[4]

Consent means the freely given, specific and informed indication of a Data Subject's wishes by which the Data Subject signifies agreement to Personal Data relating to him or her being processed.

CSIRT – Computer Security Incident Response Team

CSO – Chief Security Officer

---

[1] Council of Europe (CoE), *Glossary on Artificial Intelligence*, Artificial Intelligence, accessed 6 January 2022: www.coe.int/en/web/artificial-intelligence/glossary.
[2] Ibid.
[3] Michèle Finck, "Blockchains and data protection in the European Union", *European Data Protection Law Review*, Vol. 4, No. 1, 2018, p. 17: https://doi.org/10.21552/edpl/2018/1/6.
[4] Peter Mell and Timothy Grance, *The NIST Definition of Cloud Computing*, NIST Special Publication 800-145, National Institute of Standards and Technology, US Department of Commerce, Gaithersburg, MD, September 2011: http://nvlpubs.nist.gov/nistpubs/Legacy/SP/nistspecialpublication800-145.pdf.

CTO – Chief Technology Officer

Data Analytics denotes the practice of combining very large volumes of diversely sourced information (big data) and analysing them, using sophisticated algorithms to inform decisions.

Data Breach means the unauthorized modification, copying, unlawful destruction, accidental loss, improper disclosure, or undue transfer of, or tampering with, Personal Data.

Data Controller means the person or organization who alone or jointly with others determines the purposes and means of the Processing of Personal Data.

Data Processor means the person or organization who processes Personal Data on behalf of the Data Controller.

Data Protection Impact Assessment or DPIA means an assessment that identifies, evaluates and addresses the risks to Personal Data arising from a project, policy, programme or other initiative.

Data Subject means a natural person (i.e. an individual) who can be identified, directly or indirectly, in particular by reference to Personal Data.

Digital Identity refers to "a collection of electronically captured and stored identity attributes that uniquely describe a person within a given context and are used for electronic transactions".[5]

DPO in the context of this Handbook means a Humanitarian Organization's internal data protection office or Data Protection Officer.

Drones are small aerial or non-aerial units that are remotely controlled or operate autonomously. They are also known as Unmanned Aerial Vehicles (UAVs) or Remotely Piloted Aircraft Systems (RPAS).

Further Processing means additional Processing of Personal Data that goes beyond the purposes originally specified at the time the data were collected.

Health Data means data related to the physical or mental health of an individual, which reveal information about their health status.

Humanitarian Action means any activity undertaken on an impartial basis to carry out assistance, relief and protection operations in response to a Humanitarian Emergency. Humanitarian Action may include "humanitarian assistance", "humanitarian aid" and "protection".

Humanitarian Emergency means an event or series of events (in particular arising out of armed conflicts or natural disasters) that poses a critical threat to the health, safety, security or well-being of a community or other large group of people, usually over a wide area.

---

[5] GSMA, World Bank Group, & Security Identity Alliance, *Digital Identity: Towards Shared Principles for Public and Private Sector Cooperation*, 2016, p. 11: www.gsma.com/mobilefordevelopment/resources/digital-identity-towards-shared-principles-public-private-sector-cooperation/.

Humanitarian Organization means an organization that provides aid to alleviate human suffering, and/or protects life and health, and upholds human dignity during Humanitarian Emergencies in accordance with its mandate and/or mission.

IaaS stands for Infrastructure as a Service.

International Data Sharing includes any act of transferring or making Personal Data accessible outside the country or International Organization where they were originally collected or processed, including to a different entity within the same Humanitarian Organization or to a Third Party, via electronic means, the Internet or other means.

International Organization means an organization and its subordinate bodies governed by public international law, or any other body which is set up by, or on the basis of, an agreement between two or more countries.

Know Your Customer (KYC) is a process enabling businesses to check the identity of their customers in order to comply with regulations and legislation on money laundering and corruption.[6]

Machine Learning is a specific form of Artificial Intelligence that can be defined as the study of algorithms that improve their performance when completing a certain task with experience in the form of machine-readable data.

PaaS – Platform as a Service

Personal Data means any information relating to an identified or identifiable natural person.

Processing means any operation or set of operations which is performed on Personal Data or sets of Personal Data, whether or not by automated means, such as collection, recording, organization, structuring, storage, adaptation or alteration, retrieval, consultation, use, disclosure by transmission, dissemination or otherwise making available, alignment, combination, or erasure.

Pseudonymization, as distinct from Anonymization, means the Processing of Personal Data in such a manner that the Personal Data can no longer be attributed to a specific Data Subject without the use of additional information, provided that such additional information is kept separately and is subject to technical and organizational measures to ensure that the Personal Data are not attributed to an identified or identifiable natural person.

Reidentification describes the process of turning allegedly Anonymized or Pseudonymized data back into Personal Data through the use of data matching or similar techniques. If the risk of Reidentification is deemed to be reasonably likely, the information should be considered to be Personal Data and subject to all the data

---

6   PwC, *Know Your Customer: Quick Reference Guide*, January 2016: www.pwc.lu/en/anti-money-laundering/docs/pwc-kyc-qrg-final-interactive-2016.pdf.

protection principles. It can be very difficult to assess the risk of Reidentification with absolute certainty.

SaaS – Software as a Service

Sensitive Data means Personal Data which, if disclosed, may result in discrimination against or the repression of the individual concerned. Typically, data relating to health, race or ethnicity, religious/political/armed group affiliation, or genetic and biometric data are considered to be Sensitive Data. All Sensitive Data require augmented protection even though different types of data falling under the scope of Sensitive Data (e.g. different types of biometric data) may present different levels of sensitivity. Given the specific situations in which Humanitarian Organizations work and the possibility that some data elements could give rise to discrimination, setting out a definitive list of Sensitive Data categories in Humanitarian Action is not meaningful. Sensitivity of data as well as appropriate safeguards (e.g. technical and organizational security measures) have to be considered on a case-by-case basis.

SLA – A service-level agreement is an official commitment between a service provider and a client, particularly for the provision of reliable telecommunications and Internet services.

Sought Person is a person unaccounted for, for whom a tracing operation has been launched.

Sub-Processor is a person or organization that is engaged by a Data Processor to process Personal Data on its behalf.

Third Party is any natural or legal person, public authority, agency, or any other body other than the Data Subject, the Data Controller or the Data Processor.

TLS – Transport Layer Security is a cryptographic protocol to provide privacy and data integrity between a client and a server over an Internet connection.

DATA
ANALYTICS
CLOUD SERVICES
CASH TRANSF
PROGRAMMIN
DIGITAL
IDENTITY
ROAD CLOSED
OPEN
MESSAGING
APPS
BIOMETRICS

DRONES

CONNECTIVITY AS AID

SOCIAL MEDIA

BLOCKCHAIN

ARTIFICIAL INTELLIGENCE

CHAPTER 1
INTRODUCTION
Massimo Marelli

1.1 BACKGROUND

In recent years, the development of new technologies allowing for easier and faster Processing of ever-increasing quantities of Personal Data in an interconnected world has given rise to concerns about possible intrusion into the private sphere of individuals. Regulatory efforts around the globe are ongoing to respond to these concerns.

Protecting individuals' Personal Data is an integral part of protecting their life, integrity and dignity. This is why Personal Data protection is of fundamental importance for Humanitarian Organizations.

In suggesting how data protection principles should be applied by Humanitarian Organizations, this Handbook builds on existing guidelines, working procedures and practices that have been established in Humanitarian Action in the most volatile environments and for the benefit of the most vulnerable victims of armed conflicts, other situations of violence, natural disasters, pandemics and other Humanitarian Emergencies (together 'Humanitarian Emergencies'). Some of these guidelines, procedures and practices predate the advent and development of data protection laws, but they all are based on the principle of human dignity and the same concept of protection which underpins data protection laws. These guidelines have been set out, notably, in the Professional Standards for Protection Work.[1]

1.2 OBJECTIVE

This Handbook aims to further the discussion launched by the Global Privacy Assembly (GPA) – previously known as the International Conference of Data Protection and Privacy Commissioners (ICDPPC) – with its Resolution on Privacy and International Humanitarian Action[2] adopted in Amsterdam in 2015. This discussion was relaunched and continued through the GPA Resolution on the Role of Personal Data Protection in International Development Aid, International Humanitarian Aid and Crisis Management[3] adopted in 2020, which makes specific reference to the development and publication of the previous editions of this

---

1 ICRC, *Professional Standards for Protection Work*, 3rd ed., ICRC, Geneva, 2018: https://shop.icrc.org/professional-standards-for-protection-work.html.
2 International Conference of Data Protection and Privacy Commissioners, Resolution on Privacy and International Humanitarian Action, 37th International Conference of Data Protection and Privacy Commissioners, Amsterdam, 27 October 2015: http://globalprivacyassembly.org/wp-content/uploads/2015/02/Resolution-on-Privacy-and-International-Humanitarian-Action.pdf.
3 Global Privacy Assembly, Resolution on the Role of Personal Data Protection in International Development Aid, International Humanitarian Aid and Crisis Management, 42nd Closed Session of the Global Privacy Assembly, October 2020: https://globalprivacyassembly.org/wp-content/uploads/2020/10/FINAL-GPA-Resolution-International-Aid-EN.pdf.

Handbook as one of the main achievements of the cooperation between humanitarian actors and the GPA.

It is not intended to replace compliance with applicable legal norms, or with data protection rules, policies and procedures that a particular organization may have adopted. Rather, the Handbook seeks to raise awareness and assist Humanitarian Organizations in ensuring that they comply with Personal Data protection standards in carrying out humanitarian activities, by providing specific guidance on the interpretation of data protection principles in the context of Humanitarian Action, particularly when new technologies are employed.

This Handbook is designed to assist in the integration of data protection principles and rights in the humanitarian environment. It does not, however, replace or provide advice in relation to the application of domestic legislation on data protection, where this is applicable to a Humanitarian Organization not benefiting from the privileges and immunities generally associated with an International Organization.

Compliance with Personal Data protection standards requires taking into account the specific scope and purpose of humanitarian activities to provide for the urgent and basic needs of vulnerable individuals. Data protection and Humanitarian Action should be seen as compatible, complementary to, and supporting each other. Thus, data protection should not be seen as hampering the work of Humanitarian Organizations; on the contrary, it should be of service to their work. Equally, data protection principles should never be interpreted in a way that hampers essential humanitarian work, and should always be interpreted in a way that furthers the ultimate objective of Humanitarian Action, namely safeguarding the life, integrity and dignity of victims of Humanitarian Emergencies.

The recommendations and guidelines contained in this Handbook are based on some of the most important international instruments dealing with data protection, in particular the following:

- UN General Assembly Resolution 45/95 of 14 December 1990[4] adopting the *Guidelines for the Regulation of Computerized Personal Data Files*,[5] which includes the "humanitarian clause" calling for particular care and flexibility when applying data protection principles in the humanitarian sector;
- the *UN Principles on Personal Data Protection and Privacy*, adopted by the UN High-Level Committee on Management (HLCM) at its 36th Session on 11 October 2018;[6]

---

[4] UN General Assembly, *Resolution 45/95 of 14 December 1990*, A/RES/45/95, 14 December 1990.
[5] UN General Assembly, *Guidelines for the Regulation of Computerized Personal Data Files*, 14 December 1990: www.refworld.org/docid/3ddcafaac.html.
[6] UN High-Level Committee on Management (HLCM), *UN Principles on Personal Data Protection and Privacy*, 11 December 2018: https://archives.un.org/sites/archives.un.org/files/_un-principles-on-personal-data-protection-privacy-hlcm-2018.pdf.

- the *International Standards on the Protection of Personal Data and Privacy* (The Madrid Resolution) adopted by the ICDPPC in Madrid in 2009;[7]
- *The OECD Privacy Guidelines* (2013);[8]
- the Council of Europe *Convention for the Protection of Individuals with regard to Automatic Processing of Personal Data* (Convention 108),[9] including *Protocol CETS No. 223* amending the Convention (known as Convention 108+).[10]

Other important standards have also been taken into account, in particular:
- recent regulatory developments, insofar as they reflect further development of data protection concepts and principles in light of their application over the years and the challenges generated by new technologies (this includes the updating of Convention 108, as well as the EU General Data Protection Regulation 2016/679 (GDPR));[11]
- the Resolution on Data Protection and Major Natural Disasters[12] adopted by the ICDPPC in Mexico City in 2011;
- the Resolution on Privacy and International Humanitarian Action adopted by the ICDPPC in Amsterdam in 2015;[13]
- The Resolution on the Role of Personal Data Protection in International Development Aid, International Humanitarian Aid and Crisis Management;[14]

---

[7] International Conference of Data Protection and Privacy Commissioners, *International Standards on the Protection of Personal Data and Privacy*, Resolution, Madrid, 5 November 2009: https://globalprivacyassembly.org/wp-content/uploads/2015/02/The-Madrid-Resolution.pdf.

[8] OECD, *OECD Privacy Guidelines*, 2013: https://legalinstruments.oecd.org/en/instruments/OECD-LEGAL-0188.

[9] Council of Europe (CoE), *Convention for the Protection of Individuals with Regard to Automatic Processing of Personal Data*, Treaty, Council of Europe Treaty Series (CETS) – No. 108, Strasbourg, 28 January 1981: www.coe.int/en/web/conventions/full-list?module=treaty-detail&treatynum=223.

[10] Council of Europe (CoE), *Protocol Amending the Convention for the Protection of Individuals with Regard to Automatic Processing of Personal Data*, Treaty, Council of Europe Treaty Series (CETS) – No. 223, Strasbourg, 10 October 2018: https://rm.coe.int/16808ac918.

[11] EU Regulation 2016/679 of the European Parliament and of the Council of 27 April 2016 on the protection of natural persons with regard to the Processing of personal data and on the free movement of such data, and repealing Directive 95/46/EC (EU General Data Protection Regulation), [2016] OJ L119/1.

[12] International Conference of Data Protection and Privacy Commissioners, *Resolution on Data Protection and Major Natural Disasters*, Resolution, 33rd International Conference of Data Protection and Privacy Commissioners, Mexico City, 2011: http://globalprivacyassembly.org/wp-content/uploads/2015/02/Resolution-on-Data-Protection-and-Major-Natural-Disasters.pdf.

[13] International Conference of Data Protection and Privacy Commissioners, *International Humanitarian Action*, Resolution, 37th International Conference of Data Protection and Privacy Commissioners, Amsterdam, 27 October 2015: http://globalprivacyassembly.org/wp-content/uploads/2015/02/Resolution-on-Privacy-and-International-Humanitarian-Action.pdf.

[14] *Global Privacy Assembly, Resolution on Personal Data Protection in International Development Aid*, Resolution, 42nd Closed Session of the Global Privacy Assembly, October 2020: https://globalprivacyassembly.org/wp-content/uploads/2020/10/FINAL-GPA-Resolution-International-Aid-EN.pdf.

- the ICRC *Rules on Personal Data Protection* (2015, updated and adopted by the ICRC Assembly on 19 December 2019);[15]
- the ICRC *Professional Standards for Protection Work* (2013);[16]
- the UNHCR *Policy on the Protection of Personal Data of Persons of Concern to UNHCR* (2015);[17]
- the *IOM Data Protection Manual* (2010).[18]

This Handbook provides recommended minimum standards for the Processing of Personal Data. Humanitarian Organizations may provide for stricter data protection requirements, should they deem it appropriate or be subject to stricter laws at the domestic or regional level.

A few important considerations should be highlighted from the outset:
- The right to privacy has long been recognized globally as a human right,[19] while the right to Personal Data protection is a relatively recent human right that is closely connected to the right to privacy and sets forth conditions for the Processing of data of an identified or identifiable individual. Specific data protection or privacy-related laws and norms have been adopted at national and regional levels in recent years in almost 150 countries,[20] and Personal Data protection as a fundamental right is gaining wider acceptance around the world. Accordingly, implementation of Personal Data protection standards, even where not a legal obligation given the privileges and immunities enjoyed by certain Humanitarian Organizations, should be a priority for all Humanitarian Organizations, considering that the main objective of their activities is to work for the safety and dignity of individuals.
- Some Humanitarian Organizations, having a status of International Organizations, enjoy privileges and immunities and do not follow national legislation on Personal Data protection.[21] Respect for privacy and data protection rules is nevertheless, in

---

15   ICRC, *Rules on Personal Data Protection*, Publication, ICRC, Geneva, 2015: www.icrc.org/en/publication/4261-icrc-rules-on-personal-data-protection.
16   ICRC, *Professional Standards for Protection Work*.
17   UN High Commissioner for Refugees (UNHCR), *Policy on the Protection of Personal Data of Persons of Concern to UNHCR*, May 2015, www.refworld.org/docid/55643c1d4.html.
18   International Organization for Migration (IOM), *IOM Data Protection Manual*, Geneva, 2010: https://publications.iom.int/books/iom-data-protection-manual.
19   See Article 12 of the Universal Declaration of Human Rights and Article 17 of the International Covenant on Civil and Political Rights.
20   See UN Conference on Trade and Development (UNCTAD), "Data Protection and Privacy Legislation Worldwide | Register", UNCTAD, accessed 6 January 2022: https://unctad.org/page/data-protection-and-privacy-legislation-worldwide.
21   Massimo Marelli, "The law and practice of international organizations' interactions with personal data protection domestic regulation: At the crossroads between the international and domestic legal orders", Computer Law and Security Review, Vol. 50, 2023, 105849: https://doi.org/10.1016/j.clsr.2023.105849.

- many cases, a prerequisite for them to receive Personal Data from other entities, and, therefore, to do their work.
- The exceptional emergency circumstances in which Humanitarian Organizations operate create special challenges regarding data protection. Accordingly, particular care and flexibility is required when applying data protection principles in the humanitarian sector. This need is also reflected in many of the international instruments and standards mentioned above, which include stricter rules for the Processing of Sensitive Data.[22]
- The lack of a uniform approach in data protection law to the Personal Data of deceased individuals means that Humanitarian Organizations should adopt their own policies on this matter (for example, by applying the rules applicable to the Personal Data of natural persons to the deceased, insofar as this makes sense). For organizations that do not enjoy immunity from jurisdiction, this question may be regulated by the applicable law.
- The focus of this Handbook is on Personal Data protection, and the application of this area of law to Humanitarian Action. Yet, in armed conflicts and other situations of violence, many threats are collective rather than individual – a village, a community, a specific group of men and women may share the same threats. So just focusing on the proper management of Personal Data may not be sufficient. In some cases, Processing of non-Personal Data may raise specific threats at the collective level. In this respect, a number of initiatives in the humanitarian sector have been focusing on the implications of Processing data more generally for communities and referring, for example, to 'demographically identifiable information',[23] or 'Community Identifiable Information'.[24]
- Humanitarian Organizations process the Personal Data of different categories of individuals in Humanitarian Emergencies, such as data of affected people and contacts involved in their activities, as well as data of staff and goods/service providers, or even data of donors. While the focus of this Handbook is the Processing of the Personal Data of the beneficiaries of humanitarian programmes, similar considerations apply to the handling of Personal Data of other categories of individuals.

1.3 STRUCTURE AND APPROACH

Part I of this Handbook applies to all types of Personal Data Processing in Humanitarian Emergencies and provides a detailed analysis of Personal Data

---

22 See Section 2.2: Basic data protection concepts.
23 See: "The Signal Code: A Rights Based Approach to Information during Crisis", The Signal Code, accessed 6 January 2022: https://signalcode.org.
24 See: Humanitarian Data Exchange Initiative, "Terms of Service", HDX, accessed 6 January 2022: https://data.humdata.org/faqs/terms.

protection principles and requirements contextualized in Humanitarian Emergencies. Part II deals with specific types of technologies, technology areas and data Processing situations, and contains a more specific discussion of the relevant data protection issues. The specific Processing scenarios outlined in Part II should always be read with Part I in mind. Defined terms are capitalized throughout this Handbook; the definitions are contained in the Glossary at the beginning of the Handbook.

1.4 TARGET AUDIENCE

This Handbook is aimed at legal professionals and staff of Humanitarian Organizations involved in Processing Personal Data for the humanitarian operations of their organization, particularly those in charge of advising on and applying data protection standards. It is also addressed to other parties involved in Humanitarian Action or data protection, such as data protection authorities, researchers and academics, private companies wishing to engage in partnerships with Humanitarian Organizations, and any others involved in these activities.

PART I
DATA PROTECTION PRINCIPLES IN HUMANITARIAN ACTION
Massimo Marelli

CHAPTER 2

BASIC PRINCIPLES OF DATA PROTECTION

2.1 INTRODUCTION

Humanitarian Organizations collect and process the Personal Data of individuals affected by Humanitarian Emergencies in order to perform humanitarian activities. Working primarily in Humanitarian Emergencies, they operate in situations where the rule of law may not be fully in force. In such situations, there may be limited, if any, access to justice and respect of the international human rights framework. In addition, Personal Data protection legislation may be embryonic or non-existent, or not entirely enforceable.

An individual's right to Personal Data protection is not an absolute right. It should be considered in relation to the overall objective of protecting human dignity, and be balanced with other fundamental rights and freedoms, in accordance with the principle of proportionality.[1]

As the activities of Humanitarian Organizations are carried out primarily in Humanitarian Emergencies, they operate in situations where the protection of the Personal Data of affected populations and staff is often necessary to safeguard their security, lives and work. Accordingly, Personal Data protection and Humanitarian Action are complementary and reinforce each other. However, there may also be instances of friction where a balance between different rights and freedoms needs to be struck (e.g. between the freedom of expression and information and the right to data protection, or between the right to liberty and security of a person and the right to data protection). The human rights framework aims to ensure respect for all human rights and fundamental freedoms by balancing different rights and freedoms on a case-by-case basis. This approach often requires a teleological interpretation of rights,[2] i.e. one that prioritizes the purposes the rights serve.

EXAMPLE:
Data protection law requires that individuals be given basic information about the Processing of their Personal Data. However, in a Humanitarian Emergency it is necessary to balance this right against other rights, and in particular the rights of all affected individuals. It would therefore not be necessary to inform all individuals of the conditions of data collection prior to receiving aid, if this would seriously hamper, delay or prevent the distribution of aid. Rather, the Humanitarian

---

1 The principle of proportionality in this context should not be confused with the principle of proportionality under international humanitarian law (IHL). The principle of proportionality as discussed here requires that Humanitarian Organizations take the least intrusive measures available when limiting the right of data protection and access to Personal Data in order to give effect to their mandate and to operate in emergencies.
2 In line with the humanitarian clause in the *UN Guidelines for the regulation of computerized personal data files* adopted by General Assembly Resolution 45/95 of 14 December 1990.

Organizations involved could provide such information in a less targeted and individualized way with public notices, or individually at a later stage.

Some Humanitarian Organizations with a mandate under international law need to rely on specific working procedures, in order to be in a position to fulfil their mandate. Under international law these mandates can justify derogations from the principles and rights recognized in Personal Data Processing.

For example, it may be necessary to balance, on the one hand, data protection rights with, on the other hand, the objective of ensuring the historical and humanitarian accountability of stakeholders in Humanitarian Emergencies. Indeed, in Humanitarian Emergencies, Humanitarian Organizations may be the only external entities present, and may be the only possibility for future generations to have an external account of history as well as to provide a voice to victims.[3] Furthermore, data from Humanitarian Organizations may also be needed to support the victims of armed conflicts and other situations of violence or their descendants, for example in documenting their identity and legal status, submitting claims of reparations, etc. Data retention by Humanitarian Organizations may be of fundamental importance particularly considering that in Humanitarian Emergencies few or no other records may be available.

Confidentiality may also be of fundamental importance for some Humanitarian Organizations, as it may be an essential precondition for the ongoing viability of Humanitarian Action in volatile environments, to ensure acceptance by parties to a conflict and people involved in other situations of violence, proximity to people in need and the safety of their staff. This may have an impact, for example, on the extent to which Data Subject access rights may be exercised.[4]

The boxed checklist sets out the main points explained in detail in this Handbook, which should be considered when dealing with data protection, in relation to the purpose or purposes for which data are processed.

- Is there Processing of Personal Data?
- Are individuals likely to be identified by the data processed?
- Does the information require protection even if it is not considered to be Personal Data?

---

3   See ICRC, "ICRC WWI Prisoner Archives Join UNESCO Memory of the World", 15 November 2007: www.icrc.org/en/doc/resources/documents/feature/2007/ww1-feature-151107.htm.

4   See Els Debuf, "Tools to do the job: The ICRC's legal status, privileges and immunities', *International Review of the Red Cross*, Vol. 97, No. 897-898, 2015, pp. 319-344: https://doi.org/10.1017/S181638311500051X.

- Have (if applicable) local data protection and privacy laws been complied with?
- For what purpose are the data being collected and processed? Is the Processing strictly limited to this purpose? Does this purpose justify the interference with the privacy of the Data Subject?
- What is the legal basis for Processing? How will it be ensured that the data are processed fairly and lawfully?
- Is the Processing of Personal Data proportionate? Could the same purpose be achieved in a less intrusive way?
- Which parties are Data Controllers and Data Processors? What is the relationship between them?
- Are the data accurate and up to date?
- Will the smallest amount of data possible be collected and processed?
- How long will Personal Data be retained? How will it be ensured that data are only retained as long as necessary to achieve the purpose of the Processing?
- Have adequate security measures been implemented to protect the data?
- Has it been made clear to individuals who is accountable and responsible for the Processing of Personal Data?
- Has information been provided to individuals about how their Personal Data are processed and with whom they will be shared?
- Are procedures in place to ensure that Data Subjects can assert their rights with regard to the Processing of Personal Data?
- Will it be necessary to share data with Third Parties? Under what circumstances will Personal Data be shared with or made accessible to Third Parties? How will individuals be informed of this?
- Will Personal Data be made accessible outside the country where they were originally collected or processed? What is the legal basis for doing so?
- Have Data Protection Impact Assessments been prepared to identify, evaluate, and address the risks to Personal Data arising from a project, policy, programme, or other initiative?

2.2 BASIC DATA PROTECTION CONCEPTS[5]

Data protection law and practice limit the **Processing of Personal Data of Data Subjects**, in order to protect individuals' rights.

Processing means any operation or set of operations which is performed upon Personal Data or sets of Personal Data, whether or not by automated means, such

---

5   The terms defined below are also given in the Glossary at the beginning of the Handbook.

as collection, recording, organization, structuring, storage, adaptation or alteration, retrieval, consultation, use, disclosure by transmission, dissemination or otherwise making available, alignment, combination or erasure.

Personal Data means any information relating to an identified or identifiable natural person.

A **Data Subject** is a natural person (i.e. an individual) who can be identified, directly or indirectly, in particular by reference to Personal Data.

Some data protection laws include the additional category of **Sensitive Data** in the concept of Personal Data. For the purposes of the present Handbook, Sensitive Data means Personal Data, which if disclosed may result in discrimination against, or repression of, an individual. Typically, data relating to health, race or ethnicity, religious/political/armed group affiliation, or genetic and biometric data are considered to be Sensitive Data. All Sensitive Data require augmented protection even though different types of data falling under the scope of Sensitive Data (e.g. different types of biometric data) may present different levels of sensitivity. Given the specific environments in which Humanitarian Organizations work and the possibility that various data elements may give rise to discrimination, setting out a definitive list of Sensitive Data categories for Humanitarian Action is not meaningful. For example, in some situations, a simple list of names may be very sensitive, if it puts the individuals on the list and/or their families at risk of persecution. Equally, in other situations, data collected to respond to Humanitarian Emergencies may need to include data that in a regular data protection context would be considered to be Sensitive Data and the Processing of such data would be, in principle, prohibited, but in the local culture and the specific circumstances may be relatively harmless. Therefore, it is necessary to consider the sensitivity of data and the appropriate safeguards to protect Sensitive Data (e.g. technical and organizational security measures) on a case-by-case basis.

It is important to remember that during Humanitarian Emergencies, Processing data can cause severe harm even when the data cannot be considered Personal Data. Humanitarian Organizations should therefore be prepared to apply the protections described in this Handbook to other types of data as well, when failing to do so in a particular case would create risks to individuals.

EXAMPLE:
A Humanitarian Organization inadvertently reveals the number of individuals in a stream of people who are fleeing a situation of armed violence and publishes online aerial imagery related to this. One of the armed actors involved in the violence, which is the reason people are fleeing, then uses this information to locate the displaced population and targets them with reprisals. The number of individuals in a group and

the aerial imagery (subject to the resolution and other factors potentially making it possible to identify individuals) is not by itself Personal Data, but such data can be extremely sensitive in certain circumstances. The Humanitarian Organization should have protected this data and not revealed it.

It is also important to understand the distinction between **Data Controller** and **Data Processor**. A Data Controller is the person or organization who alone or jointly with others determines the purposes and means of the Processing of Personal Data, whereas a Data Processor is the person or organization who processes Personal Data on behalf of the Data Controller. Finally, a Third Party is any natural or legal person, public authority, agency, or any entity other than the Data Subject, the Data Controller or the Data Processor.

EXAMPLE:
An International Humanitarian Organization collects information about the identity of individuals in a Humanitarian Emergency in order to provide them with aid. In order to do this, it engages the services of a local non-governmental organization (NGO) to help deliver the aid, which needs to use the identification information originally collected by the Humanitarian Organization. The two organizations sign a contract governing the use of the data, under which the International Humanitarian Organization has the power to direct how the NGO uses the data and the NGO commits to respect the data protection safeguards required by the Humanitarian Organization. The NGO also engages an IT consulting company in order to perform routine maintenance on its IT system in which the data are stored.

In the above situation, the International Humanitarian Organization, the NGO and the IT consulting company are Processing the Personal Data of the individuals, who are the Data Subjects. The International Humanitarian Organization is a Data Controller, and the NGO is a Data Processor, while the IT consulting company is a Sub-Processor.

2.3 AGGREGATE, PSEUDONYMIZED AND ANONYMIZED DATA SETS

As mentioned above, it is outside the scope of this Handbook to discuss the Processing of data that does not relate to individual persons, such as data that have been rendered anonymous in such a way that a Data Subject is no longer identifiable.

Where aggregate data are derived from Personal Data, and could in certain circumstances pose risks to persons of concern, it is important to ensure that the Processing, including sharing and/or publication, of such data cannot lead to the Reidentification of individuals.[6]

The Anonymization of Personal Data can help meet the protection and assistance needs of vulnerable individuals in a privacy-friendly way. The term Anonymization encompasses techniques that can be used to convert Personal Data into anonymized data. When aiming to anonymize data, it is essential to ensure that data sets containing Personal Data are fully and *irreversibly* anonymized, i.e. that Reidentification is not possible. Anonymization processes are challenging, especially where large data sets containing a wide range of Personal Data are concerned and may pose a greater risk of Reidentification.[7]

"Pseudonymization", as distinct from Anonymization, means the Processing of Personal Data in such a manner that the Personal Data can no longer be attributed to a specific Data Subject *without the use of additional information*, provided that such additional information is kept separately and is subject to technical and organizational measures to ensure that the Personal Data are not attributed to an identified or identifiable natural person. This may involve replacing the anagraphic[8] data in a data set with a number. Sharing registration/identification numbers instead of names is good practice, but does not amount to Anonymization.

The application of Pseudonymization to personal data can reduce the risks to the Data Subjects concerned by reducing the likelihood that they will be reidentified. The term "Reidentification" describes the process of turning allegedly anonymized or pseudonymized data back into Personal Data through the use of data matching or similar techniques.[9] Pseudonymization can also help controllers and processors meet their data protection obligations. Nevertheless, not every Pseudonymization technique fulfils data protection requirements on its own, and Pseudonymization techniques that may work in one specific case may not be sufficient to protect Personal Data in other cases.[10]

---

6   See UK Statistics Authority, *National Statistician's Guidance: Confidentiality of Official Statistics – GSS*, accessed 6 January 2022: https://gss.civilservice.gov.uk/policy-store/national-statisticians-guidance-confidentiality-of-official-statistics.
7   See UK Information Commissioner's Office (ICO), *Anonymisation: Managing Data Protection Risk Code of Practice*, ICO, Wilmslow, Cheshire, November 2012: https://ico.org.uk/media/1061/anonymisation-code.pdf.; see also EU Article 29 Working Party Opinion 05/2014 on Anonymisation Techniques: https://ec.europa.eu/justice/article-29/documentation/opinion-recommendation/files/2014/wp216_en.pdf.
8   "Anagraphic", in *Wiktionary*, 14 November 2020: https://en.wiktionary.org/w/index.php?title=anagraphic&oldid=61117548.
9   Note, "identified" does not necessarily mean "named"; it can be enough to be able to establish a reliable connection between particular data and a known individual.
10 See: Athena Bourka and Prokopios Drogkaris, eds., *Data Pseudonymisation: Advanced Techniques and Use Cases*, European Union Agency for Cybersecurity (ENISA), 28 January 2021: www.enisa.europa.eu/publications/data-pseudonymisation-advanced-techniques-and-use-cases.

Data protection principles have to be applied carefully when assessing these techniques, and risk analysis tools have to be apt to evaluate whether the mitigation techniques applied are effective. Principles such as purpose limitation and retention are of particular importance here, as they can help ensure that existing pseudonymized databases are not repurposed for new projects or combined with newer ones. Additionally, there will always be a trade-off between adding confidentiality to a data set and reducing its utility. Many privacy-preserving techniques work by perturbing (i.e. altering or obfuscating) the data to be released, resulting in data that, depending on scope, might be less useful for the purposes of the sharing or research.[11]

Prior to sharing or publicizing anonymized data, it is important to ensure that no Personal Data are included in the data set and that individuals cannot be re-identified. If the risk of Reidentification is deemed to be reasonably likely, the information should be considered to be Personal Data and subject to all the principles and guidance set out in this Handbook. It can be very difficult to assess the risk of Reidentification with absolute certainty. Generally speaking, Reidentification becomes significantly more likely where no mitigation measure is taken to protect Personal Data. This can be possible, for instance, where an entity holds certain data sets concerning the affected populations, which can then be combined with the Processed Data to generate new information about Data Subjects or the groups to which they belong.

For example, prior to sharing or publishing aggregate data, it is important to ensure that the data sets do not divulge the actual location of small, at-risk groups, such as by mapping data like country of origin, religion, or specific vulnerabilities to the geographical coordinates of persons of concern.

2.4 APPLICABLE LAW AND INTERNATIONAL ORGANIZATIONS

Humanitarian Action involves a large number of actors, such as Humanitarian Organizations, local authorities and private entities. As far as Humanitarian Organizations are concerned, some of them are NGOs subject to the jurisdiction of the country in which they operate, while others are International Organizations with privileges and immunities allowing them to perform the mandate attributed them by the community of states under international law in full independence.

---

[11] Gregory J. Matthews and Ofer Harel, "Data confidentiality: A review of methods for statistical disclosure limitation and methods for assessing privacy", *Statistics Surveys*, Vol. 5, 1 January 2011, pp. 1-29: https://doi.org/10.1214/11-SS074.

As far as NGOs are concerned, the rules for determining applicable data protection law depend on a number of different factual elements. This Handbook does not deal with issues of applicable law; any questions in this regard should be directed to the NGO's legal department or data protection office (DPO).[12]

In addition to any law that the NGO may be subject to, Personal Data Processing is controlled by its own internal data protection policy or rules, any contractual commitments and any other relevant applicable rules. The guidance contained in this Handbook should always be applied without prejudice to these rules and obligations. This guidance is based on recognized best practices and standards and it is recommended that International Organizations take this into consideration when designing or interpreting their data protection rules and policies for Humanitarian Action.

International Organizations enjoy privileges and immunities, in particular, to ensure they can perform the mandate attributed to them by the international community under international law in full independence, and are not covered by the jurisdiction of the countries in which they work. They can therefore process Personal Data according to their own rules, subject to the internal monitoring and enforcement of their own compliance systems; in this regard they constitute their own "jurisdiction".[13] This aspect of International Organizations has specific implications, in particular for International Data Sharing, which will be discussed in detail in Chapter 4: International Data Sharing.

2.5 DATA PROCESSING PRINCIPLES

Personal Data Processing undertaken by Humanitarian Organizations should comply with the following principles.

2.5.1 THE PRINCIPLE OF THE FAIRNESS AND LAWFULNESS OF PROCESSING

Personal Data should be processed fairly and lawfully. The lawfulness of the Processing requires a legal basis for Processing operations to take place, as detailed in Chapter 3: Legal bases for Personal Data Processing. The other crucial component of fairness of the Processing is transparency.

Any Processing of Personal Data should be transparent for the Data Subjects involved. The principle of transparency requires that at least a minimum amount of

---

12 See Section 1.2 – Objective.
13 For more on this matter, see Massimo Marelli, "The law and practice of international organizations' interactions with personal data protection domestic regulation: At the crossroads between the international and domestic legal orders", Computer Law and Security Review, Vol. 50, 2023, 105849: https://doi.org/10.1016/j.clsr.2023.105849.

information concerning the Processing be provided to the Data Subjects at the moment of collection, albeit subject to the prevailing security and logistical conditions, as well as with regard to the possible urgent nature of the Processing. Any information and communication relating to the Processing of Personal Data should be easily accessible and easy to understand, which implies providing translations where necessary, and clear and plain language should be used. More detailed information about information notices that should be provided prior to or at the time of data collection are described in greater detail in Section 2.10.2 – Information notices.

2.5.2 THE PURPOSE LIMITATION PRINCIPLE

At the time of collecting data, the Humanitarian Organization should determine and set out the specific purpose(s) for which data are processed. The specific purpose(s) should be explicit and legitimate. In particular, the specific purpose(s) that may be of relevance in a humanitarian context may include, for example:
- providing humanitarian assistance and/or services to affected populations to sustain livelihoods;
- restoring family links between people separated due to Humanitarian Emergencies;
- providing protection to affected people and building respect for international human rights law/international humanitarian law (IHL), including documentation of individual violations;
- providing medical assistance;
- ensuring inclusion in national systems (for example for refugees);
- providing documentation or legal status/identity to, for example, displaced or stateless people;
- protecting water and habitat.

Humanitarian Organizations should take care to consider and identify, as far as is possible in emergency circumstances, all possible purposes contemplated and that may be contemplated in any Further Processing prior to the collection of the data, so as to be as transparent as possible.

2.5.2.1 FURTHER PROCESSING

Humanitarian Organizations may process Personal Data for purposes other than those initially specified at the time of collection where the Further Processing is compatible with the initial purposes, including where the Processing is necessary for historical, statistical or scientific purposes.

In order to ascertain whether a purpose of Further Processing is compatible with the purpose for which the data were initially collected, account should be taken of:
- the link between the initial purpose(s) and the purpose(s) of the intended Further Processing;

- the situation in which the data were collected, including the reasonable expectations of the Data Subject as to their further use;
- the nature of the Personal Data;
- the consequences of the intended Further Processing for Data Subjects;
- appropriate safeguards;
- the extent to which such safeguards would protect the confidentiality of Personal Data and the anonymity of the Data Subject.

The situation in which the data were collected, including the reasonable expectations of the Data Subject as to its further use, is a particularly important factor, recognizing that when Data Subjects provide data for one purpose they generally understand that a range of associated humanitarian activities may also be involved and, in fact, may have an expectation that all possible humanitarian protection and assistance may be extended. This is particularly important in humanitarian situations, because an improperly narrow understanding of compatibility could prevent the delivery of humanitarian benefits to Data Subjects.

Consequently, purposes strictly linked to Humanitarian Action, and which do not incur any additional risks unforeseen in the consideration of the initial purpose, are likely to be compatible with each other and, if this is confirmed, Personal Data can legitimately be processed by Humanitarian Organizations beyond the specific purposes for which the Personal Data were originally collected, as long as the Humanitarian Organization does so within the framework of Humanitarian Action. In principle, Further Processing should be permissible if this is necessary and proportionate to safeguard public security and the lives, integrity, health, dignity or security of affected individuals in Humanitarian Action. This requires a case-by-case assessment and cannot be presumed across the board.

Even where the purpose of Further Processing is exclusively related to Humanitarian Action, Processing for a new purpose may not be deemed compatible if the risks for the Data Subject outweigh the benefits of Further Processing, or if the Further Processing entails new risks. This analysis depends on the circumstances of the case. Circumstances leading to this conclusion include risks that Processing may be against the interests of the person to whom the information relates or his/her family, in particular, when there is a risk that the Processing may threaten their life, integrity, dignity, psychological or physical security, liberty or their reputation. This can include consequences such as:
- harassment or persecution by authorities or other Third Parties;
- judicial prosecution;
- social problems;
- serious psychological suffering.

Examples of circumstances in which Further Processing may be considered incompatible include cases where the Personal Data have been collected as part of the information necessary to assist in the tracing of a Sought Person. Processing this information further in order to request that the relevant authorities carry out an investigation into the possible violations of the applicable law (for example, in the context of civilian population protection activities) may not be compatible as Further Processing. This is due to the possible detrimental consequences of the intended Further Processing for Data Subjects and the likely difficulty of providing appropriate safeguards.

Should the intended purpose of Further Processing not be compatible with the purpose for which the data were initially collected, the data should not be further processed, unless it is deemed appropriate to do so under another legal basis. In this case, additional measures may be required depending on the basis that applies.[14]

Further Processing of Personal Data should also not be considered compatible if the Processing conflicts with any legal, professional or other binding obligations of secrecy and confidentiality, or with the principle of "do no harm".

Data aggregation and Anonymization may be used as a method of decreasing the sensitivity of the data to allow data use for ancillary cases, and make the Further Processing compatible.

EXAMPLE:
Data collected to provide food and shelter during a humanitarian operation may also be used to plan the provision of medical services to displaced persons. However, Processing the data collected (if not aggregated/anonymized) to help plan the Humanitarian Organization's budgetary needs for the coming year cannot be deemed to be compatible Further Processing.

2.5.3 THE PRINCIPLE OF PROPORTIONALITY

The principle of proportionality is at the core of data protection law. It is applicable throughout the data Processing cycle and may be invoked at different stages of data Processing operations. It requires consideration of whether a particular action or measure related to the Processing of Personal Data is appropriate to its pursued aim (e.g. is the selected legitimate basis proportionate to the aim pursued? Are technical and organizational measures proportionate to the risks associated with the Processing?).

The data handled by Humanitarian Organizations should be adequate, relevant and not excessive for the purposes for which they are collected and processed. This

---

14   See Chapter 3: Legal bases for Personal Data Processing.

requires, in particular, ensuring that only the Personal Data that are necessary to achieve the purposes (fixed in advance) are collected and further processed and that the period for which the data are stored, before being anonymized or deleted, is limited to the minimum necessary.[15]

The principle of proportionality is particularly important for cross-functional needs assessments conducted by Humanitarian Organizations either internally or between agencies. When carrying out these assessments Humanitarian Organizations are at risk of gathering amounts of data that are excessive to the purpose, for example by conducting surveys with several hundred data fields to be filled, which may or may not be used at a later stage. In these situations, it is important to be able to distinguish between what is "nice to know" and what is "necessary to know" in order to assist affected people. Humanitarian Organizations also need to weigh their need for data against the potential harm to individuals of such data being collected, as well as the risk of "assessment fatigue" and potentially raising unrealistic expectations among the people they seek to help.

Limiting the amount of data collected may not always be possible. For example, when a new Humanitarian Emergency arises, the full extent of humanitarian needs may not be known at the time of data collection. Therefore, the application of this principle may be restricted in exceptional circumstances and for a limited time if necessary for the protection of the Data Subject or of the rights and freedoms of others.

It is also possible that the purpose at the time of collection is particularly broad because of the emergency. In such cases, a large collection of data could be considered necessary. It could then be reduced later depending on circumstances. In considering whether a flexible interpretation of proportionality is acceptable when a new Humanitarian Emergency arises, the following factors should be taken into account:
- the urgency of the action;
- proportionality between the amount of Personal Data collected and the goals of the Humanitarian Action;
- the likely difficulties (due to logistical or security constraints) in reverting to the Data Subject to gather additional data, should additional specified purposes become foreseeable;
- the objectives of the particular Humanitarian Organization's action;
- the nature and scope of the Personal Data that may be needed to fulfil the specified purposes;
- the expectations of Data Subjects;
- the sensitivity of the Personal Data concerned.

---

15   See Section 2.7 – Data retention.

EXAMPLE:
A Humanitarian Organization collects Personal Data to provide humanitarian assistance to a group of vulnerable individuals in a disaster area. At the outset of the action, it was not possible to determine the specific needs of the people affected and what assistance and programmes would be required immediately or further down the line (e.g. the destruction of sanitation facilities could generate the risk of diseases spreading). Accordingly, the Humanitarian Organization in question engages in a broad data collection exercise with the purpose of fully assessing the needs of the people affected and designing response programmes. After the emergency has ended, it turned out that although Humanitarian Action was required, sanitation was restored in time to avoid the spread of diseases. As a result, the Humanitarian Organization may now need to delete the data initially acquired to address this specific concern.

In all cases, the necessity of retaining the data collected should be periodically reviewed to ensure application of the data minimization principle.

2.5.4 THE PRINCIPLE OF DATA MINIMIZATION

The principle of data minimization closely relates to the principle of proportionality. Data minimization seeks to ensure that only the minimum amount of Personal Data is processed to achieve the objective and purposes for which the data were collected. Data minimization requires limiting Personal Data Processing to the minimum amount and extent necessary. Personal Data should be deleted when they are no longer necessary for the purposes of the initial collection or for compatible Further Processing. Data must also be deleted when Data Subjects have withdrawn their Consent for Processing or justifiably object to the Processing. However, even in the above circumstances Personal Data may be retained if they are needed for legitimate historical, statistical or scientific purposes, or if the Humanitarian Organization is under an applicable legal obligation to retain such data, taking into account the associated risks and implementing appropriate safeguards.

To determine whether the data are no longer necessary for the purposes for which they were collected, or for compatible Further Processing, Humanitarian Organizations should consider the following:
- Has the specified purpose been achieved?
- If not, are all data still necessary to achieve it? Is the specified purpose so unlikely to be achieved that retention no longer makes sense?
- Have inaccuracies affected the quality of Personal Data?
- Have any updates and significant changes rendered the original record of Personal Data unnecessary?

- Are the data necessary for legitimate historical, statistical or scientific purposes? Is it proportionate to continue storing them, taking into account the associated risks? Are appropriate data protection safeguards applied to this further storage?
- Have the Data Subject's circumstances changed, and do these new factors render the original record obsolete and irrelevant?

2.5.5 THE PRINCIPLE OF DATA QUALITY

Personal Data should be as accurate and up to date as possible. Every reasonable step should be taken to ensure that inaccurate Personal Data are deleted or corrected without undue delay, taking into account the purposes for which they are processed. The Humanitarian Organization should systematically review the information collected in order to confirm that it is reliable, accurate and up to date, in line with operational guidelines and procedures.

In considering the frequency of review, account should be taken of (i) logistical and security constraints, (ii) the purpose(s) of Processing, and (iii) the potential consequences of data being inaccurate. All reasonable steps should be taken to minimize the possibility of making a decision that could be detrimental to an individual, such as excluding an individual from a humanitarian programme based on potentially incorrect data.

2.6 SPECIAL DATA PROCESSING SITUATIONS

The following are a few common data Processing situations that require more specific explanation.

2.6.1 HEALTH PURPOSES

Improper handling (including disclosure) of Health Data could cause significant harm to the individuals concerned. Accordingly, Health Data should be considered as particularly sensitive and specific guarantees should be implemented when Processing such data. This also applies to other Sensitive Data. Health Data are also increasingly becoming a target for cyber attacks. Humanitarian health-care providers should process data in accordance with the World Medical Association (WMA) International Code of Medical Ethics[16] which includes specific professional obligations of confidentiality.

Humanitarian Organizations may process Health Data for purposes such as the following:
- preventive or occupational medicine, medical diagnosis, provision of care or treatment;

---

16   WMA – The World Medical Association, *International Code of Medical Ethics*, 9 July 2018: www.wma.net/policies-post/wma-international-code-of-medical-ethics.

- management of health-care services;
- reasons of vital interest, including providing essential and life-saving medical assistance to the Data Subject;
- public health, such as protecting against serious threats to health or ensuring high standards of quality and safety, *inter alia* for medicinal products or medical devices;
- historical, statistical or scientific research purposes, such as patient registries set up for improving diagnoses and differentiating between similar types of diseases and preparing studies for therapies, subject to conditions and safeguards.

Health Data should be kept separate from other Personal Data, and should only be accessible by health-care providers or personnel specifically delegated by the humanitarian health-care providers to manage Health Data under confidentiality guarantees ensured by employment, consultant or other contracts and only for such predefined data management purposes, or by personnel carrying out research under confidentiality and other data protection guarantees ensured by employment, consultant or other contracts and only for such predefined research purposes.

Humanitarian Organizations engaged in protection or assistance activities may also process Health Data, for example, when this is necessary to locate persons unaccounted for (where Health Data may be required to identify and trace them) or to advocate for adequate treatment of individuals deprived of their liberty, or for the establishment of livelihood programmes addressing the needs of particularly vulnerable categories of beneficiaries (such as people suffering from malnutrition or particular diseases).[17]

2.6.2 ADMINISTRATIVE ACTIVITIES

Humanitarian Organizations typically process Personal Data for employment purposes, career management, assessments, fundraising, marketing and other administrative requirements. In some instances, this may also include sensitive Processing activities such as, for example, GPS tracking of their vehicles for fleet and security management. In some operational circumstances, the Processing of staff Personal Data may be particularly sensitive due, for example, to the geopolitical conditions in which certain humanitarian assistance is provided. In these cases, additional safeguards will be necessary, to the extent possible, in the Processing of such data.

2.7 DATA RETENTION

Each category of data should be retained for a defined period (e.g. three months, a year, etc.). When it is not possible to determine at the time of collection how long

---

[17] See Subsection 2.5.2.1 – Further Processing.

data should be kept, an initial retention period should be set. Following the initial retention period, an assessment should be made as to whether the data should be deleted, or whether the data are still necessary to fulfil the purpose for which they were initially collected (or for a further legitimate purpose). If so, the initial retention period should be renewed for a limited period of time.

When data have been deleted, all copies of the data should also be deleted. If the data have been shared with Third Parties, the Humanitarian Organization should take reasonable steps to ensure such Third Parties also delete the data. This consideration should be taken into account in initial reflections as to whether to share data with Third Parties and should be expressed in any data sharing agreement.[18]

2.8 DATA SECURITY AND PROCESSING SECURITY

2.8.1 INTRODUCTION

Data security is a crucial component of an effective data protection system. Personal Data should be processed in a manner that ensures appropriate security of the Personal Data, such as preventing unauthorized access to or use of Personal Data and the equipment used for the Processing. This is even more the case for the volatile environments in which Humanitarian Organizations often operate.

Any person acting under the authority of the Data Controller who has access to Personal Data should not process them except in a manner compliant with any applicable policies as explained in the present Handbook.

In order to maintain security, the Data Controller should assess the specific risks inherent in the Processing and implement measures to mitigate those risks. These measures should ensure an appropriate level of security (taking into account available technology, prevailing security and logistical conditions and the costs of implementation) in relation to the nature of the Personal Data to be protected and the related risks. This includes measures involving:
- training of staff and partners;
- management of access rights to databases containing Personal Data;
- physical security of databases (access regulation, water and temperature damage, etc.);
- IT security (including password protection, safe transfer of data, encryption, regular backups, etc.);
- discretion clauses;
- Data Sharing Agreements with partners and Third Parties;

---

18 See Section 2.12 – Data sharing and International Data Sharing, and Chapter 4: International Data Sharing.

- methods of destruction of Personal Data;
- standard operating procedures for data management and retention;
- any other appropriate measures.

These measures are intended to ensure that Personal Data are kept secure, both technically and organizationally, and are protected by reasonable and appropriate measures against misuse, unauthorized modification, copying, tampering, unlawful destruction, accidental loss, improper disclosure or undue transfer (collectively, "Data Breach"). Data security measures should vary depending, *inter alia*, on the:
- type of operation;
- level of assessed data protection risks;
- nature and sensitivity of the Personal Data involved;
- form or format of storage, transfer and sharing of data;
- environment/location of the specific Personal Data;
- prevailing security and logistical conditions.

Data security measures should be routinely reviewed and upgraded to ensure a level of data protection that is appropriate to the degree of sensitivity applied to Personal Data, as well as the possible development of new technologies enabling enhanced security.

The Data Controller is responsible for:
- setting up an information security management system. This includes establishing and regularly updating a data security policy based on internationally accepted standards and on a risk assessment. The policy should consist of, for example, physical security guidelines, IT security policy, email security guidelines, IT equipment usage guidelines, guidelines for information classification (i.e. classifying information as public, internal, confidential or strictly confidential), a contingency plan and document destruction guidelines.
- developing the communication infrastructure and databases in order to preserve the confidentiality, integrity and availability of data, in compliance with the security policy.
- taking all appropriate measures to protect the security of data processed in the Data Controller's information system.
- granting and administering access to databases containing Personal Data, including ensuring access is granted on a need-to-know basis.
- the security of the facilities which enable authorized personnel to access the system.
- ensuring that the personnel given access to data are in a position to fully respect security rules. This includes relevant training, a pledge of discretion and/or duty of confidentiality clause in the employment contract to be signed before access to databases is granted.
- maintaining a register of personnel having access to each database, and updating it when appropriate (e.g. personnel being given different responsibilities who no longer require access).

- if feasible, keeping a historical log and potentially running audits of personnel having had access to a database, for as long as the data processed by such personnel are present in the database.

Personnel should process data within the limits of the Processing rights granted to them. Personnel with higher access rights or responsible for administering access rights may be subject to additional contractual obligations of confidentiality and non-disclosure.

2.8.2 PHYSICAL SECURITY

Each Data Controller is responsible for:
- laying down security rules defining procedural, technical and administrative security controls that ensure appropriate levels of confidentiality, and physical integrity and availability of databases (whether physical or IT-based), based on the prevailing risks identified;
- ensuring that personnel are informed of such security rules and comply with them;
- developing appropriate control mechanisms to ensure that the security of data is maintained;
- ensuring adequate electrical and fire safety standards are applied to storage locations;
- ensuring storage volumes are kept to a strict necessary minimum.

2.8.3 IT SECURITY

The Data Controller should:
- lay down security rules defining procedural, technical and administrative controls that ensure appropriate levels of confidentiality, integrity and availability for the information systems used, based on risk assessment;
- develop appropriate control mechanisms to ensure that data security is maintained;
- introduce specific security rules for a part of the IT communication infrastructure, a database, or a specific department if necessary, for instance where particularly sensitive or critical Personal Data are being processed.

All email correspondence, internal and external, containing Personal Data should be processed on a need-to-know basis. Recipients of email correspondence should be carefully selected to avoid the unnecessary dissemination of Personal Data to individuals who do not need such Data in the context of their role. Private email accounts should not be used to transfer Personal Data.

Remote access to servers and the use of home-based computers should comply with the standards set out in the Data Controller's IT Security Policy. Unless absolutely necessary for operational reasons, the use of Internet outlets and unsecured wireless connections to retrieve, exchange, transmit or transfer Personal Data should be avoided.

Staff members handling Personal Data should take due care when connecting remotely to the Data Controller's servers. Passwords should always be protected, regularly changed and not be automatically entered through "keychain" functions.[19] Staff should check that they have logged off properly from computer systems and that open browsers have been closed.

Special consideration must be given to securing laptops, smartphones and other portable media equipment, especially when working in a difficult environment. Portable media equipment should be stored in safe and secure locations at all times.

Portable or removable devices should not be used to store documents containing Personal Data classified as sensitive. If this is unavoidable, Personal Data should be transferred to appropriate computer systems and database applications as soon as possible. If flash memory such as USB flash drives and memory cards are used to temporarily store Personal Data, they should be kept safe, and the electronic record must be encrypted. Information should be deleted from the portable or removable device once it has been stored properly, if no longer needed on the portable device.

Effective recovery mechanisms and backup procedures should cover all electronic records, and the relevant information and communications technology (ICT) officer should ensure that backup procedures are performed on a regular basis. The frequency of backup procedures should vary according to the sensitivity of the Personal Data and available technical resources. Electronic records should be automated to allow for easy recovery in situations where backup procedures are difficult due to, *inter alia*, regular power outage, system failure or disasters.

When electronic records and database applications are no longer needed, the Data Controller should coordinate with the relevant ICT officer to ensure their permanent deletion.

2.8.4 DUTY OF DISCRETION AND STAFF CONDUCT

The duty of discretion is a key element of Personal Data security. The duty of discretion involves:
- all personnel and external consultants signing discretion and confidentiality agreements or clauses as part of their employment/consulting contract. This

---

19 A keychain or password manager is an application or hardware function that enables users to store and organize several passwords centrally under one master password.

requirement goes together with the requirement that personnel should only process data in accordance with the Data Controller's instructions.
- any external Data Processor being contractually bound by confidentiality clauses. This requirement goes together with the requirement that the Data Processor should only process data in accordance with the Data Controller's instructions.
- the strict application of the guidelines for information classification based on their confidentiality status.
- ensuring that Data Subject requests are properly addressed and accurately recorded in the Data Subject's file in a secure and confidential manner, and that such requests are not shared with Third Parties.
- limiting the risk of leaks by having only authorized personnel in charge of the collection and management of data from confidential sources, and ensuring these personnel access documents according to the applicable guidelines for information classification.

Personnel are responsible for attributing levels of confidentiality to the data they process based on the applicable guidelines for information classification, and for observing the confidentiality of the data they consult, transmit or use for external Processing purposes. Personnel who originally attributed the level of confidentiality may, at any time, modify the level of confidentiality that they have attributed to data, as appropriate.

2.8.5 CONTINGENCY PLANNING

The Data Controller is responsible for devising and implementing a plan for protecting, evacuating or safely destroying records in case of emergency.

2.8.6 DESTRUCTION METHODS

When it is established that retention of Personal Data is no longer necessary, all records and backups should be safely destroyed or rendered anonymous. The method of destruction shall depend, *inter alia*, on the following factors:
- the nature and sensitivity of the Personal Data;
- the format and storage medium;
- the volume of electronic and paper records.

The Controller should conduct a sensitivity assessment prior to destruction to ensure that appropriate methods of destruction are used to eliminate Personal Data. In this regard, the following three paragraphs are based on information taken from the *IOM Data Protection Manual*:[20]

Paper records should be destroyed by using methods such as shredding or burning, in a way that does not allow for future use or reconstruction. If it is decided that

---

20   International Organization for Migration (IOM), *IOM Data Protection Manual*, pp. 83–84.

paper records should be converted into digital records, following accurate conversion of paper records to electronic format, all traces of paper records should be destroyed, unless retention of paper records is required by applicable national law, or unless a paper copy should be kept for archiving purposes. The destruction of large volumes of paper records may be outsourced to specialized companies. In these circumstances the Data Controller should ensure that, throughout the chain of custody, the confidentiality of Personal Data, the submission of disposal records and the certification of destruction form part of the contractual obligations of the Data Processors, and that the Data Processors comply with these obligations.

The destruction of electronic records should be referred to the relevant ICT personnel because the erasure features on computer systems do not necessarily ensure complete elimination. Upon instruction, the relevant ICT personnel should ensure that all traces of Personal Data are completely removed from computer systems and other software. Disk drives and database applications should be purged and all rewritable media such as, *inter alia*, CDs, DVDs, microfiches, videotapes and audio tapes that are used to store Personal Data should be erased before reuse. Physical measures of destroying electronic records such as recycling, pulverizing or burning should be strictly monitored.

The Data Controller should ensure that all relevant contracts of service, memoranda of understanding (MOUs), agreements and written transfer or Processing contracts include a retention period for the destruction of Personal Data after the fulfilment of the specified purpose. Third Parties should return Personal Data to the Data Controller and certify that all copies of the Personal Data have been destroyed, including the Personal Data disclosed to its authorized agents and subcontractors. Disposal records indicating time and method of destruction, as well as the nature of the records destroyed, should be maintained and attached to project or evaluation reports.

2.8.7 OTHER MEASURES

Data security also requires appropriate internal organizational measures, including regular internal dissemination of data security rules and their obligations under data protection law or internal rules for organizations enjoying privileges and immunities to all employees, especially regarding their obligations of confidentiality.

Each Data Controller should attribute the role of data security officer to one or more persons of their staff (possibly Admin/IT) to carry out security operations. The security officer should, in particular:
- ensure compliance with the applicable security procedures and rules;
- update these procedures, as and when required;
- conduct further training on data security for personnel.

2.9 THE PRINCIPLE OF ACCOUNTABILITY

The principle of accountability is premised on the responsibility of Data Controllers to comply with the above principles and the requirement that they be in a position to demonstrate that adequate and proportionate measures have been undertaken within their respective organizations to ensure compliance with them.

This can include measures such as the following, which are all strongly recommended in order to allow Humanitarian Organizations to meet data protection requirements:
- drafting Personal Data Processing policies (including Processing Security policies);
- keeping internal records of data Processing activities;
- creating an independent body to oversee the implementation of the applicable data protection rules, such as a Data Protection Office, and appointing a Data Protection Officer (DPO);
- implementing data protection training programmes for all staff;
- performing Data Protection Impact Assessments (DPIAs);[21]
- registering with the competent authorities (including data protection authorities), if legally required and not incompatible with the independence of an international organization or with the principle of "do no harm".

2.10 INFORMATION

In line with the principle of transparency, some information regarding the Processing of Personal Data should be provided to Data Subjects. As a rule, this information should be provided before Personal Data are processed, although this principle may be limited when it is necessary to provide emergency aid to individuals.

Data Subjects should receive information orally and/or in writing. This should be done as transparently as circumstances allow and, if possible, directly to the individuals concerned. If this is not possible, the Humanitarian Organization should consider providing information by other means, for example, making it available online, or on flyers or posters displayed in a place and form that can easily be accessed (public spaces, markets, places of worship and/or the organizations' offices), radio communication, or discussion with representatives of the community. Data Subjects should be kept informed, insofar as practicable, of the Processing of their Personal Data in relation to the action taken on their behalf, and of the ensuing results.

The information given may vary, depending on whether the data are collected directly from the Data Subject or not.

---

21 See Chapter 5: Data Protection Impact Assessments (DPIAs).

2.10.1 DATA COLLECTED FROM THE DATA SUBJECT

Personal Data may be collected directly from the Data Subject under the following legal bases:[22]

- vital interest of the Data Subject or of another person;
- public interest;
- individual Consent;
- legitimate interest of the Humanitarian Organization;
- legal or contractual obligation.

Some of the information to be provided to Data Subjects in each of the above cases will vary depending on the particular circumstances. A priority in this respect is that the information provided must be sufficient to enable them to exercise their data protection rights effectively.[23]

2.10.2 INFORMATION NOTICES

In the specific cases where Consent may be used as the legal basis,[24] the individual must be put in a position to fully appreciate the risks and benefits of data Processing, otherwise Consent may not be considered valid.

When using Consent or when the Data Subjects are exercising their rights to object to the Processing or to access, rectify and erase the data, detailed information will need to be provided. It is important to note that the Data Subject may object to the Processing or withdraw their Consent at any time. The following are the types of information to be provided when Consent is the legal basis:

- the identity and contact details of the Data Controller;
- the specific purpose for Processing of their Personal Data and an explanation of the potential risks and benefits;
- the fact that the Data Controller may process their Personal Data for purposes other than those initially specified at the time of collection, if compatible with a specific purpose mentioned above and an indication of these further compatible purposes;
- the fact that if they have given Consent, they can withdraw it at any time;
- circumstances in which it might not be possible to treat his/her Personal Data confidentially;
- the Data Subject's rights to object to the Processing and to access, correct and delete their Personal Data; how to exercise such rights and the possible limitations on the exercise of their rights;
- to which third countries or International Organization/s the Data Controller may need to transfer the data in order to achieve the purpose of the initial collection and Further Processing;

---

22 See Chapter 3: Legal bases for Personal Data Processing.
23 See Section 2.11 – Rights of Data Subjects.
24 See Section 3.2 – Consent.

- the period for which the Personal Data will be kept or at least the criteria to determine it and any steps taken to ensure that records are accurate and kept up to date;
- with which other organizations, such as authorities in the country of data collection the Personal Data may be shared;
- in case decisions are taken on the basis of automated Processing, information about the logic involved;
- an indication of the security measures implemented by the Data Controller regarding the data Processing.

Under other legal bases for Processing, the responsibility for conducting a risk analysis rests with the Data Controller, and it is sufficient to provide more basic information. The following is recommended as the minimum information that should be provided in the case of a legal basis other than Consent:
- the identity and contact details of the Data Controller;
- the specific purpose for Processing of their Personal Data;
- whom to contact in case of any questions concerning the Processing of their Personal Data;
- with whom the data will be shared, in particular if they may be shared with authorities (e.g. law enforcement authorities) or entities in another territory or jurisdiction.

Additional information must be provided where necessary to enable individuals to Consent and exercise their rights of access, objection, rectification, erasure and/or if the Data Subject requests more information.[25]

In exceptional circumstances where, due to prevailing security and logistical constraints, including difficulties gaining access to the field, it is not possible to provide this information immediately or at the place where individuals are located, or where the data have not been collected directly from the Data Subject, the information should be made available as soon as possible in a way that is easy for individuals to access and understand.[26] Humanitarian Organizations should also refrain from collecting extensive data sets from affected populations until this information can be adequately provided, unless absolutely necessary for humanitarian purposes.

2.10.3 DATA NOT COLLECTED FROM THE DATA SUBJECT

Where the Personal Data have not been obtained from the Data Subject, the information set out under Section 2.10.2 – Information notices, above, depending on the legal basis used for the collection of data, should be provided to the Data Subject within a reasonable period after obtaining this data, having regard to the specific circumstances in which the data are processed or, if a disclosure to another recipient is envisaged, at the latest when the data are first disclosed, subject to logistical and

---

25 See Section 2.10 – Information, and Section 3.2 – Consent.
26 See Section 2.10 – Information.

security constraints. This requirement will not apply where the Data Subject already has the information or where providing it is impossible or would involve a disproportionate effort, in which case the measures outlined above in Section 2.10 – Information should be considered.

EXAMPLE:
Information may be provided after obtaining the data, for example, where a protection case is documented involving multiple victims and the information is collected from only one of them or from a third source, or where lists of displaced persons are collected from authorities or from other organizations for the distribution of aid.

2.11 RIGHTS OF DATA SUBJECTS

2.11.1 INTRODUCTION

The respect of Data Subjects' rights is a key element of data protection. However, the exercise of these rights is subject to conditions and may be limited as explained below.

An individual should be able to exercise these rights using the internal procedures of the relevant Humanitarian Organization, such as by lodging an inquiry or complaint with the organization's DPO. However, depending on the applicable law, and in cases where the Data Controller is not an International Organization with immunity from jurisdiction, the individual may also have the right to bring a claim in court or with a data protection authority. In the case of International Organizations, claims may be brought before an equivalent body responsible for independent review of cases for the organization.[27]

2.11.2 ACCESS

A Data Subject should be able to make an access request orally or in writing to the Humanitarian Organization. Data Subjects should be given an opportunity to review and verify their Personal Data. The exercise of this right may be restricted if necessary for the protection of the rights and freedoms of others, or if necessary for the documentation of alleged violations of international humanitarian law or human rights law.

---

27 See ICRC, "The ICRC Data Protection Commission", 22 January 2016: www.icrc.org/en/document/icrc-data-protection-independent-control-commission; "Commission for the Control of INTERPOL's Files (CCF)", accessed 17 October 2021: www.interpol.int/en/Who-we-are/Commission-for-the-Control-of-INTERPOL-s-Files-CCF.

With due consideration for the prevailing situation and its security constraints, Data Subjects should be given the opportunity to obtain confirmation from the Humanitarian Organization, at reasonable intervals and free of charge, whether their Personal Data are being processed or not. Where such Personal Data are being processed, Data Subjects should be able to obtain access to them, except as otherwise provided below.

The Humanitarian Organization's staff should not reveal any information relating to Data Subjects, unless they are provided with satisfactory proof of identify from the Data Subjects and/or their authorized representative.

Access to documents does not apply when overriding interests require that access not be given. Thus, compliance by Humanitarian Organizations with a Data Subject's access request may be restricted as a result of the overriding public interests or interests of others. This is particularly the case where access cannot be provided without revealing the Personal Data of others, except where the document or information can be meaningfully redacted to blank out any reference to such other Data Subject/s without disproportionate effort, or where the Consent of such other Data Subject/s to the disclosure has been obtained, again without disproportionate effort.

Access that would jeopardize the ability of a Humanitarian Organization to pursue the objectives of its Humanitarian Action or that creates risks for the security of its staff will always constitute an overriding interest. This may also be the case for internal documents of the Humanitarian Organizations, disclosure of which may have an adverse effect on Humanitarian Action. In such cases, the Humanitarian Organization should make every effort to document the nature of the overriding interests, to the extent possible and subject to prevailing circumstances.

Communication to Data Subjects on the information set out in this section should be given in an intelligible form, which means that the Humanitarian Organization may have to explain the Processing to the Data Subjects in more detail or provide translations. For example, just quoting technical abbreviations or medical terms in response to an access request will usually not suffice, even if only such abbreviations or terms are stored.

It may be appropriate to disclose Personal Data to family members or legal guardians in the case of missing, unconscious or deceased Data Subjects or of Data Subjects' families seeking access for humanitarian or administrative reasons or for family history research. Here too, the staff of Humanitarian Organizations should not reveal any information unless they are provided with satisfactory proof of identity of the requesting person and proof of legal guardianship/family link, as appropriate, and they have made a reasonable effort to establish the validity of the request.

2.11.3 CORRECTION

The Data Subject should also be able to ensure that the Humanitarian Organization corrects any inaccurate Personal Data relating to them. Having regard to the purposes for which data were processed, the Data Subject should be able to correct incomplete Personal Data, for instance by providing supplementary information.

When this involves simply correcting factual data (e.g. requesting the correction of the spelling of a name, change of address or telephone number), proof of inaccuracy may not be crucial. If, however, such requests are linked to a Humanitarian Organization's findings or records (such as the Data Subject's legal identity, or the correct place of residence for the delivery of legal documents, or more sensitive information about the humanitarian status of, or medical information concerning, the Data Subject), the Data Controller may need to demand proof of the alleged inaccuracy and assess the credibility of the assertion. Such demands should not place an unreasonable burden of proof on the Data Subject and thereby preclude Data Subjects from having their data corrected. In addition, Humanitarian Organization staff should require satisfactory proof of identify from the Data Subjects and/or their authorized representative before carrying out any correction.

2.11.4 RIGHT TO ERASURE

A Data Subject should be able to have their own Personal Data erased from the Humanitarian Organization's databases where:
- the data are no longer necessary in relation to the purposes for which they were collected or otherwise processed and/or further processed;
- the Data Subject has withdrawn their Consent for Processing, and there is no other basis for the Processing of the data;[28]
- the Data Subject successfully objects to the Processing of Personal Data concerning them;[29]
- the Processing does not comply with the applicable data protection and privacy laws, regulations and policies.

The exercise of this right may be restricted if necessary for the protection of the Data Subject or the rights and freedoms of others, for the documentation of alleged violations of international humanitarian law or human rights law, for reasons of public interest in the area of public health, for compliance with an applicable legal obligation, for the establishment, exercise or defence of legal claims, or for legitimate historical or research purposes, subject to appropriate safeguards and taking into account the risks for and the interests of the Data Subject. This can include the interest in maintaining archives that represent the common heritage of humanity. In addition, Humanitarian Organization staff should require proof of identify that

---

[28] See Section 3.2 – Consent.
[29] See Section 3.4 – Important grounds of public interest, and Section 3.5 – Legitimate interest.

satisfies them that the Data Subjects are who they say they are before carrying out any erasure.

> **EXAMPLE:**
> A Humanitarian Organization suspects that a request for erasure is being made under pressure from a Third Party, and that erasure would prevent the protection of the Data Subject or documentation of an alleged violation of international humanitarian law or human rights law. In such a case, the Humanitarian Organization would be justified in refusing to erase the data.

2.11.5 RIGHT TO OBJECT

Data Subjects have the right to object, on compelling legitimate grounds relating to their particular situation, at any time, to the Processing of Personal Data concerning them.

The exercise of this right may be restricted if necessary if the Humanitarian Organization has compelling legitimate grounds for the Processing which override the interests, rights and freedoms of the Data Subject. Such grounds may include, for example, the protection of the Data Subject or the rights and freedoms of others, the documentation of alleged violations of international humanitarian law or human rights law, the establishment, exercise or defence of legal claims, or legitimate historical or research purposes, subject to appropriate safeguards and taking into account the risks for and the interests of the Data Subject. In these cases, the Humanitarian Organization should:
- inform the organization's DPO, if there is one
- inform, if possible, the Data Subject of the Humanitarian Organization's intention to continue to process data on this basis
- inform, if possible, the Data Subject of his/her right to seek a review of the Humanitarian Organization's decision by the DPO or the competent state authority, court or equivalent body in the case of International Organizations.

In addition, Humanitarian Organization staff should require proof of identify that satisfies them that the Data Subjects are who they say they are before accepting an objection.

2.12 DATA SHARING AND INTERNATIONAL DATA SHARING

Humanitarian Emergencies routinely require Humanitarian Organizations to share Personal Data with Data Processors and Third Parties, including those based in other countries, or with International Organizations. Data protection laws restrict

International Data Sharing, which means any act of making Personal Data accessible outside the country in which they were originally collected or processed, as well as to a different entity within the same Humanitarian Organization not enjoying the status of International Organization, or to a Third Party, via electronic means, the Internet or others.[30]

Data sharing requires due regard to all the various conditions set out in this Handbook. For example, since data sharing is a form of Processing, there must be a legal basis for it, and it can only take place for the specific purpose for which the data were initially collected or further processed. In addition, Data Subjects have rights in relation to data sharing and must be given information about it. The conditions governing International Data Sharing are given in Chapter 4: International Data Sharing.

---

30 See Chapter 4: International Data Sharing.

CHAPTER 3

LEGAL BASES FOR PERSONAL DATA PROCESSING

3.1 INTRODUCTION

Under the principle of the lawfulness of data Processing outlined in Chapter 2: Basic principles of data protection, a legitimate legal basis is required in order for Personal Data Processing operations to take place.

In their humanitarian work, Humanitarian Organizations may rely on the following legal bases to process Personal Data:
- vital interest of the Data Subject or of another person;
- public interest;
- Consent;
- legitimate interest;
- performance of a contract;
- compliance with a legal obligation.

In the emergency situations in which Humanitarian Organizations usually operate, it can be difficult to fulfil the basic conditions of valid Consent, in particular that it is informed and freely given. For example, this can be the case where consenting to the Processing of Personal Data is a precondition to receive assistance. It could also apply to human resources, for example, if consenting to the Processing is a condition for recruitment.

Processing by Humanitarian Organizations may often be based on vital interest or on important grounds of public interest,[1] for example in the performance of a mandate established under national or international law. This would require that the following conditions be met:
- in the case of vital interest, having sufficient elements to consider that in the absence of Processing the individual could be at risk of physical or moral harm. In the case of important grounds of public interest, being clear that the specific Processing operation is within a mandate established for the Humanitarian Organization under national, regional or international law, or that the Humanitarian Organization is otherwise performing a specific task or function that is in the public interest and is laid down by law.
- providing clear information to the individual as to the proposed Processing operation.
- ensuring the individual has a say and is in a position to exercise the right to object.[2] In any case, the opportunity to object to the Processing should be offered as soon and as clearly as possible, preferably at the moment of data collection. If the Data Subject provides adequate justification for their objection to the

---

1   See Section 3.3 – Vital interest, and Section 3.4 – Important grounds of public interest.
2   See Chapter 2: Basic principles of data protection.

Processing, and if the Processing is not necessary for any other legal basis (e.g. Section 3.3 – Vital interest, or Section 3.4 – Important grounds of public interest), then the Processing of the Data Subject's Personal Data should cease.

Relying on an appropriate legal basis does not discharge a Humanitarian Organization of its responsibility to assess the risk, for an individual, a given group or the Humanitarian Organization itself, of collecting, storing or using Personal Data. In cases involving particularly high risks, Humanitarian Organizations should consider whether it is not more appropriate to refrain from collecting and/or Processing the data in the first place. Such risks may be immediately evident from the Humanitarian Organization's experience or hidden in the complexity of the data flows inherent in a new technological solution. The performance of a Data Protection Impact Assessment (DPIA) therefore remains a key tool to ensure that all relevant risks are identified and mitigated.[3]

3.2 CONSENT

Consent is the most popular and often the preferred legal basis for Personal Data Processing. However, given the vulnerability of most people affected by Humanitarian Emergencies and the nature of Humanitarian Emergencies themselves, many Humanitarian Organizations will not be in a position to rely on Consent for most of their Personal Data Processing. In particular, the choice of another legal basis is appropriate when:
- The Data Subject is not physically in a position to be informed and give free Consent, either because, for example, he/she is a Sought Person, or he/she is unconscious.
- The Humanitarian Organization is not in a position to inform and obtain the Consent of the Data Subject due to the prevailing security or logistical conditions in the area of operations.
- The Humanitarian Organization is not in a position to inform and obtain the Consent of the Data Subjects due to the scale of the operation that needs to be carried out. This can be the case, for example, (i) when preparing lists for distribution of humanitarian assistance to large numbers of displaced people, or (ii) when authorities provide Humanitarian Organizations with lists of protected persons, under a provision deriving from international humanitarian law or human rights law.
- In the organization's assessment, the Consent of the Data Subject cannot be valid due, for example, to the Data Subject being particularly vulnerable (e.g. children, elderly or disabled persons) at the time of giving Consent, or having no real choice to refuse Consent due to a situation of need and vulnerability, including a lack of

---

3   See Chapter 2: Basic principles of data protection.

alternative to the specific assistance being offered and the data Processing involved.
- New technologies are involved, characterized by complex data flows and multiple stakeholders, including Data Processors and sub-Data Processors in multiple jurisdictions. This makes it difficult for an individual to fully appreciate the risks and benefits of a Processing operation and, therefore, take the responsibility for it as entailed by giving Consent. In this case, other legal bases, which require Humanitarian Organizations to take more responsibility for the assessment of risks and benefits of Processing, would be more appropriate.

It should be noted that obtaining Consent is not the same as providing information about data Processing (Section 2.10 – Information). That is, even when Consent cannot be used, informational requirements still apply, including information on the rights to objection, erasure, access and rectification.

The following requirements must be fulfilled in order for Consent to be valid.

3.2.1 UNAMBIGUOUS
Consent should be fully informed and freely given by any appropriate method. This means that the Data Subject signifies their agreement to the Processing of their Personal Data. Consent may be given in writing or, where written Consent is not possible, orally or by another clearly affirmative action by the Data Subject (or by his or her guardian, as applicable).

3.2.2 TIMING
Consent should be obtained at the time of collection or as soon as it is reasonably practical thereafter.

3.2.3 VALIDITY
Consent should not be regarded as freely given if the Data Subject has no genuine and free choice, or is unable to refuse or withdraw Consent without detriment, or has not been informed sufficiently in order to understand the consequences of the Personal Data Processing.

3.2.4 VULNERABILITY
The Data Subject's vulnerability should be taken into account when considering the validity of Consent. Assessing vulnerability involves understanding the social, cultural and religious norms of the group to which Data Subjects belong and ensuring that each Data Subject is treated individually as the owner of his/her Personal Data. Respect for the individual implies that each person is regarded as autonomous, independent and free to make his/her own choices.

Vulnerability varies depending on the circumstances. In this respect, the following factors should be considered:[4]
- the characteristics of the Data Subject, such as illiteracy, disability, age, health status, gender and sexual orientation;
- the location of the Data Subject, such as a detention facility, resettlement camp, remote area;
- environmental and other factors, such as unfamiliar surroundings, foreign language and concepts;
- the Data Subject's position in relation to others, such as belonging to a minority group or ethnicity;
- social, cultural and religious norms of families, communities or other groups to which Data Subjects belong;
- the complexity of the envisaged Processing operation, particularly if complex new technologies are employed.

EXAMPLE:
A Humanitarian Organization carries out an assessment of a Humanitarian Emergency. In doing so, it collects data on possible beneficiaries, including information about household livelihood and specific vulnerabilities with a view to developing a suitable assistance programme, which may include nutrition, health and protection components. This involves collecting and Processing a great deal of Personal Data. The organization should inform the individuals it interviews about the purposes for which the data collection will be used, but it would not be meaningful to base the data collection on their Consent. Such individuals have no meaningful possibility to give Consent to data collection, because they are in an extremely vulnerable position and have no genuine choice but to accept whatever Processing operation may be involved in accepting the aid offered. Another legal basis should be identified, and the relevant information provided, including the option to object to the envisaged Processing.

3.2.5 CHILDREN

Children are a particularly vulnerable category of Data Subjects, and the best interests of the child are paramount in all decisions affecting them. While the views and opinions of children should be respected at all times, particular care should be taken to establish whether the child fully understands the risks and benefits involved in a Processing operation and to exercise his/her right to object and to provide valid Consent where applicable. Assessment of the vulnerability of children will depend on the child's age and maturity.

---

[4] International Organization for Migration (IOM), *IOM Data Protection Manual*, pp. 45–48.

The Consent of the child's parent or legal guardian may be necessary if the child does not have the legal capacity to Consent. The following factors should be taken into account:
- providing full information to the parent or legal guardian and obtaining the signature of the parent or guardian to indicate their Consent;
- ensuring that the Data Subject is clearly informed and his/her views are taken into account.

3.2.6 INFORMED

Consent should be informed if it is to be accepted as the legal basis for Processing. This requires that the Data Subject receive explanations in simple, jargon-free language, which allows for full appreciation and understanding of the circumstances, risks and benefits of Processing.[5]

3.2.7 DOCUMENTED

Where Processing is based on the Data Subject's Consent, it is important to keep a record of it to be able to demonstrate that the Data Subject has consented to the Processing. This may be done by requesting a signature or cross mark witnessed by a Humanitarian Organization or, in case of oral Consent, documentation by a Humanitarian Organization that Consent has been obtained. The practice, not unknown in the humanitarian world, to ask for the impression of a fingerprint solely to confirm Consent is highly problematic since it can amount to the collection of biometric data and should therefore be avoided. For an analysis of the risks involved in the collection of biometric data, see Chapter 8: Biometrics.

When using Consent, it is important to record any limitations/conditions for its use, and the specific purpose for which Consent is obtained. These details should also be recorded in all databases used by Humanitarian Organizations to process the data in question and should accompany the data throughout the Processing.

Where Consent has not been recorded, or no record of Consent can be found, the data should not be processed further (including transferred to a Third Party if there is no record of Consent for the transfer) unless it is possible to do so under a legal basis other than Consent (e.g. vital interest, legitimate interest or public interest).

3.2.8 WITHHOLDING/WITHDRAWING CONSENT

If Data Subjects expressly withhold Consent, they should be advised about the implications, including the effect this may have on assistance that might or might not be rendered by Humanitarian Organizations and/or Third Party organizations. If,

---

5   See Section 2.10 – Information.

however, assistance could not be provided in the absence of Consent, note that Consent could not be considered as a legal basis for the Processing.[6]

Data Subjects have the right to object to the Processing and withdraw any Consent previously given at any stage of data Processing. In cases in which a Humanitarian Organization suspects that Consent is being withdrawn under pressure from Third Parties, it is likely that the Humanitarian Organization may be in a position to continue Processing the Personal Data of the Data Subject on another basis, such as vital interests being at stake (see Section 3.3 below).

3.3 VITAL INTEREST

When Consent cannot be validly obtained, Personal Data may still be processed if the Humanitarian Organization establishes that this is in the vital interest of the Data Subject or of another person, i.e. where data Processing is necessary in order to protect an interest which is essential for the Data Subject's life, integrity, health, dignity or security or that of another person.

Considering the nature of Humanitarian Organizations' work, and the emergency situations in which they operate, Processing of data by Humanitarian Organizations may be based on the vital interest of a Data Subject or another person in the following cases:
- The Humanitarian Organization is dealing with cases of Sought Persons.
- The Humanitarian Organization is assisting authorities with the identification of human remains and/or tracing the family of the deceased. In this case the Personal Data would be processed in the vital interest of the family members.
- The Humanitarian Organization is assisting an individual who is unconscious or otherwise at risk, but unable to communicate Consent.
- The Humanitarian Organization is providing medical care or assistance.
- The Processing, including disclosure, of information is the most appropriate response to an imminent threat against the physical and mental integrity of the Data Subjects or other persons.
- The Processing is necessary to provide for the essential needs of an individual or a community during, or in the aftermath of, a Humanitarian Emergency.

In these cases, however, the Humanitarian Organization should, if possible, ensure that the Data Subjects are aware of the Processing as soon as possible, that they have sufficient knowledge to understand and appreciate the specified purpose(s) for which Personal Data are collected and processed, and are in a position to object to the Processing if they so wish. This can be achieved preferably through direct

---

6   See Section 3.2 – Consent, fourth bullet point.

explanations at the moment of the collection and, for example, during distributions of assistance, using posters, group explanations or by making further information available on leaflets or on websites when affected people are registered or aid is distributed.[7]

EXAMPLE:
A Humanitarian Organization needs to collect Personal Data from vulnerable individuals following a natural disaster in order to provide vital assistance (e.g. food, water, medical assistance, etc.). It may use the vital interests of the individuals as the legal basis for the collection of Personal Data, without the need to obtain their Consent. However, it should (1) ensure that this legal basis is used only to provide such assistance; (2) offer the individuals the right to object; and (3) process the data collected in accordance with its privacy policy, which should be available to Data Subjects upon request. It should provide all relevant information about the data Processing, for example through posters, or group explanations, or by making further information available on leaflets or websites when affected people are registered or aid is distributed.

3.4 IMPORTANT GROUNDS OF PUBLIC INTEREST

Important grounds of public interest are triggered when the activity in question is part of a humanitarian mandate established under national or international law or is otherwise an activity in the public interest laid down by law. This, for example would be the case for the International Committee of the Red Cross (ICRC), National Societies of the Red Cross/Red Crescent, the United Nations High Commissioner for Refugees (UNHCR), the United Nations Children's Fund (UNICEF), the United Nations World Food Programme (WFP), the International Organization for Migration (IOM), and other Humanitarian Organizations performing a specific task or function in the public interest, which is laid down by law, insofar as the Processing of Personal Data is necessary to accomplish those tasks.[8] In this case, the term 'necessary' is to be strictly construed (i.e. the data Processing should be truly necessary, rather than just convenient,[9] to fulfil the relevant purpose).

---

[7] See Section 2.5.1 – The principle of the fairness and lawfulness of Processing, and Section 2.10 – Information.

[8] For example, the ICRC has a mandate under the four Geneva Conventions and Additional Protocol I to act in the event of international armed conflict. The ICRC has a right of humanitarian intervention in non-international armed conflict. See: ICRC, "The ICRC's Mandate and Mission", Page, International Committee of the Red Cross, Geneva, 6 August 2014: www.icrc.org/en/mandate-and-mission.

[9] See example at Section 3.6 – Performance of a contract.

Cases where this legal basis may be relevant include distributions of assistance, where it may not be practicable to obtain the Consent of all the possible beneficiaries, and where it may not be clear whether the life, security, dignity and integrity of the Data Subject or of other people are at stake (in which case 'vital interest' may be the most appropriate legal basis for Processing).

Other scenarios where this legal basis may be relevant include the Processing of Personal Data of persons in detention, where this type of activity is within the mandate of the Humanitarian Organization in question. This may happen, for example, when the Processing of Personal Data relates to persons deprived of their liberty in an armed conflict or other situation of violence, where the Humanitarian Organization has not yet been in a position to visit the Data Subject deprived of liberty and therefore obtain his/her Consent and, subsequently, if Consent is not considered as a valid legal basis due to the vulnerability of the Data Subjects, linked to their deprivation of liberty.

In these cases, too, the Humanitarian Organization should, if possible, ensure that the Data Subjects are aware of the Processing of their Personal Data as soon as possible and that they have sufficient knowledge to understand and appreciate the specified purpose(s) for which Personal Data are collected and processed, and are in a position to object to Processing at any point if they so wish.

3.5 LEGITIMATE INTEREST

Humanitarian Organizations may also process Personal Data where this is in their legitimate interest, in particular, where it is necessary for the purpose of carrying out a specific humanitarian activity listed in their mission, and provided that this interest is not overridden by the fundamental rights and freedoms of the Data Subject. In all of these situations, the term 'necessary' is to be strictly construed (i.e. the data Processing should be truly necessary, rather than just convenient,[10] to fulfil the relevant purpose).

Legitimate interest may include situations such as the following:
- The Processing is necessary for the effective performance of the Humanitarian Organization's mission, in cases where important grounds of public interest are not triggered.
- The Processing is necessary for the purposes of ensuring information systems and information security,[11] and the security of the related services offered by, or

---

10   See example at Section 3.6 – Performance of a contract.
11   Information security may include preservation of confidentiality, integrity and availability of information, as well as other properties such as authenticity, accountability, non-repudiation and

accessible via, these information systems, by public authorities, Computer Emergency Response Teams (CERTs), Computer Security Incident Response Teams (CSIRTs), providers of electronic communications networks and services, and by providers of security technologies and services. This could, for example, include preventing unauthorized access to electronic communications networks and malicious code distribution and stopping 'denial of service' attacks and damage to computer and electronic communication systems.
- The Processing is necessary for the purposes of preventing, evidencing and stopping fraud or theft.
- The Processing of Personal Data is necessary for the purposes of anonymizing or pseudonymizing Personal Data.[12]
- The Processing is necessary for the establishment, exercise or defence of legal claims, regardless of whether in a judicial, administrative or any out-of-court procedure.
- The Processing is necessary to make the work of the organization more effective and efficient.

EXAMPLE:
A Humanitarian Organization processes Personal Data in the course of scanning its IT systems for viruses; verifying the identity of beneficiaries for anti-fraud purposes; and defending itself in a legal proceeding brought by an ex-employee. All these Processing activities are permissible based on the legitimate interest of the organization.

3.6 PERFORMANCE OF A CONTRACT

Under this legal basis Humanitarian Organizations may process Personal Data where it is necessary for the performance of a contract to which the Data Subject is party, or in order to take steps at the request of the Data Subject prior to entering into a contract. Once again, the term 'necessary' is to be strictly construed (i.e. the data Processing should be truly necessary, rather than just convenient, to fulfil the relevant purpose).

---

reliability. See: International Organization for Standardization (ISO), "ISO/IEC 17799:2005 | Information Technology – Security Techniques – Code of Practice for Information Security Management", ISO Geneva, 2005–2006): www.iso.org/cms/render/live/en/sites/isoorg/contents/data/standard/03/96/39612.html.

12 See Section 2.3 – Aggregate, Pseudonymized and Anonymized data sets. Pseudonymization means Processing of Personal Data in such a manner that the Personal Data can no longer be attributed to a specific Data Subject without additional information.

This will generally be the case with regard to data Processing for the following purposes:
- the management of human resources files, including recruitment;
- the management of relations with suppliers of goods/services;
- relationships with donors.

> **EXAMPLE:**
> A Humanitarian Organization keeps personnel files about its staff in order to fulfil its employment obligations to them. This is permissible in order to perform its contractual employment obligations to its staff. On the other hand, if the same organization has outsourced its data Processing to a Third Party in the same country where its headquarters are located, granting access to its databases to the outsourcing firm will not be regarded as necessary for the performance of its contract with the firm, since the choice to outsource data Processing was a choice of convenience rather than a matter of necessity. In this case it should be considered whether the legitimate interest of the organization would be a suitable legal basis.

3.7 COMPLIANCE WITH A LEGAL OBLIGATION

Under this legal basis, Humanitarian Organizations may process Personal Data where it is necessary to comply with a legal obligation to which Humanitarian Organizations are subject, or to which they submit. This may be the case, for example, in the area of employment law, or for organizations not benefiting from privileges and immunities, if this is necessary to comply with an enforceable legal obligation.

> **EXAMPLE:**
> In the country where a Humanitarian Organization operates there is a legal obligation to provide information to the social security and tax authorities about wage payments made to staff. If the organization is subject to domestic law, this is permissible based on the legal obligation to which the organization is subject.

However, given the environment in which Humanitarian Organizations operate, the following factors should be taken into account when considering a legal obligation as a basis for the Processing. These will be relevant in particular when authorities require access to Personal Data for law enforcement, intelligence or other purposes:
- existence of the rule of law and separation of powers in the country requiring access to the data;

- respect for human rights, including the right to effective judicial redress;
- existence of an armed conflict or a situation of violence, where the authority requiring access may represent a party;
- nature of the data, and whether inferences could be made from the data leading to discrimination or persecution (for example, if names or data relating to food needs reveal religious affiliation or ethnicity, if Health Data reveal sexual orientation in a country where homosexuals are persecuted, or if the Data Subject whose data are being requested faces the death penalty);
- whether the Humanitarian Organization enjoys privileges and immunities, and the obligation is not, therefore, enforceable.

In this respect, it is also important to stress that Humanitarian Organizations should consider whether any legal obligation to disclose data applicable to them may put their Data Subjects at risk of discrimination, persecution, marginalization or repression, in which case they should consider not engaging in data collection in the first place.

3.7.1 THE DISCLOSURE OF PERSONAL DATA TO AUTHORITIES

Issues may arise regarding the disclosure and transfer of Personal Data by Humanitarian Organizations to authorities, particularly when they represent a party to a conflict or an actor in other situations of violence. Such disclosure may be problematic for Neutral, Impartial and Independent Humanitarian Action. This is particularly true if disclosure is prejudicial to a Data Subject in view of his/her humanitarian situation, or where such transfers would jeopardize the organization's security or its future access to persons affected by armed conflict or violence, to parties to a conflict, or to information necessary to perform its mandate.

Humanitarian Organizations enjoying privileges and immunities as International Organizations should ensure that their specific status is respected and refuse to accede to such requests unless necessary in the best interest of the Data Subjects and Humanitarian Action. When a Humanitarian Organization enjoying privileges and immunities needs to transfer data to Humanitarian Organizations that do not enjoy such privileges and immunities, the risk that the recipient may not be in a position to resist such requests should be taken into account. This risk is specifically recognized in the International Conference of Privacy and Data Protection Commissioners' Resolution on Privacy and International Humanitarian Action of 2015:[13]

> Humanitarian organizations not benefiting from Privileges and Immunities may come under pressure to provide data collected for humanitarian purposes to authorities wishing to use such data for other purposes (for example control of

---

13   International Conference of Data Protection and Privacy Commissioners, *Resolution on Privacy and International Humanitarian Action*.

migration flows and the fight against terrorism). The risk of misuse of data may have a serious impact on data protection rights of displaced persons and can be a detriment to their safety, as well as to Humanitarian Action more generally.

As a specific measure to address this very concern, the 33rd International Conference of the Red Cross and Red Crescent in 2019, in its Resolution on Restoring Family Links while respecting privacy, including as it relates to Personal Data protection urged:[14]

States and the Movement to cooperate to ensure that personal data is not requested or used for purposes incompatible with the humanitarian nature of the work of the Movement, [. . .], or in a manner that would undermine the trust of the people it serves or the independence, impartiality and neutrality of RFL services.

---

14 International Conference of the Red Cross Red Crescent Movement, *Restoring Family Links While Respecting Privacy, Including as It Relates to Personal Data Protection*, Resolution, International Conference of the Red Cross Red Crescent Movement, December 2019, para. 11: https://rcrcconference.org/app/uploads/2019/12/33IC-R4-RFL-_CLEAN_ADOPTED_en.pdf.

CHAPTER 4

INTERNATIONAL DATA SHARING

4.1 INTRODUCTION

Humanitarian Emergencies know no borders and regularly create the need for Humanitarian Organizations to share data with other entities across borders to provide the necessary humanitarian response. Accordingly, ensuring efficient cross-border flows of Personal Data between different countries is essential to the work of Humanitarian Organizations. In addition, the adoption of new technologies in humanitarian responses requires the involvement of multiple Data Processors and Sub-Processors which are, almost inevitably, established in various jurisdictions other than that where the Humanitarian Emergency takes place. This may be the case, for example, when cloud-based solutions are used by Humanitarian Organizations to process Personal Data, in which case data may be hosted in the territory where the organization is headquartered, and service providers may be acting as Data Processors and Sub-Processors in a number of jurisdictions.[1]

As discussed in Section 2.4 – Applicable law and International Organizations, some Humanitarian Organizations are International Organizations which enjoy privileges and immunities to ensure they can perform the mandate attributed to them by the international community under international law in full independence. Accordingly, they process Personal Data according to their own rules, which apply across their work irrespective of the territory they operate in, and are subject to the control of and enforcement by their own compliance systems.[2] Thus, they constitute their own "jurisdiction", and data flows within them, for example between HQ and field locations or between field locations, and between them and their subordinate bodies, do not fall within the scope of this chapter.[3]

The following are just a few examples of entities with which a Humanitarian Organization may need to share data across national borders:
- offices within the same non-governmental organization (NGO) operating in different countries;
- other NGOs, International Organizations, and United Nations agencies;
- government authorities;
- Data Processors such as service providers, consultants or researchers collecting and/or Processing Personal Data on behalf of the Humanitarian Organization;
- academic institutions and/or individual researchers;
- private companies;
- museums.

---

1   See Chapter 10: Cloud Services.
2   Massimo Marelli, "The law and practice of international organizations' interactions with personal data protection domestic regulation: At the crossroads between the international and domestic legal orders", *Computer Law and Security Review*, Vol. 50, 2023, 105849: https://doi.org/10.1016/j.clsr.2023.105849.
3   See Section 2.4 – Applicable law and International Organizations.

International Data Sharing includes any act of making Personal Data accessible outside the country or International Organization where they were originally collected or processed via electronic means, the Internet or others. Publication of Personal Data in newspapers, the Internet or via radio broadcast usually counts as data sharing if it makes it possible for data to be accessed across borders.

International Data Sharing includes any act that results in Personal Data being transferred, shared or accessed across national borders or with International Organizations. Accordingly, International Data Sharing may involve one of the following situations:
- The Humanitarian Organization transfers data to an organization in another jurisdiction. The receiving entity is a new Data Controller, which determines the means and purposes of Processing.
- The Humanitarian Organization transfers data to an organization in another jurisdiction, but remains the entity which decides on the means and purposes of Processing, and the receiving entity processes Personal Data exclusively according to the instructions of the sharing entity. In this case, the receiving entity is a Data Processor.

Both these scenarios involve a risk that, once Personal Data are shared, they lose some or all of the protection that they enjoyed when they were processed exclusively by the Humanitarian Organization. In both of these scenarios, therefore, it is important to ensure that all reasonable measures are put in place by the sharing organization to avoid unintentional loss of protection.

It should not be forgotten that data sharing is a Processing operation and is therefore subject to all the requirements set out in the previous chapters.[4] This chapter explains the additional precautions Humanitarian Organizations should take whenever carrying out International Data Sharing.

4.2 BASIC RULES FOR INTERNATIONAL DATA SHARING

In order to provide protection for International Data Sharing, all of the following steps should be followed:
- Any data protection rules or privacy requirements applicable to the data sharing[5] (including any data protection or privacy requirements of local law, if applicable) have been satisfied prior to the transfer.
- A legal basis must be provided for the transfer.
- An assessment should be carried out to determine whether the transfer presents any unacceptable risks for the individual (e.g. discrimination or repression).

---

4   See Chapter 2: Basic principles of data protection and Chapter 3: Legal bases for Personal Data Processing.
5   See Chapter 2: Basic principles of data protection.

- The organization that initiates the transfer must be able to demonstrate that adequate measures have been undertaken to ensure compliance with the data protection principles set forth in this Handbook by the recipient entity in order to maintain the level of protection of Personal Data with regard to International Data Sharing (accountability).
- The individual should be informed about the recipient(s) of the transfer. The transfer should not be incompatible with the reasonable expectations of the individuals whose data are transferred.

4.3 PROVIDING A LEGAL BASIS FOR INTERNATIONAL DATA SHARING

4.3.1 INTRODUCTION

As mentioned above, this Handbook is designed to assist in the application and respect of data protection principles and rights in humanitarian situations. It does not, however, replace or provide advice on domestic legislation on data protection, where such applies to a Humanitarian Organization that does not benefit from the privileges and immunities enjoyed by an International Organization. It should therefore be noted that the considerations covered in this chapter are in addition to any requirements of local law that may apply in the country from which the data are to be transferred, insofar as they apply to a particular Humanitarian Organization. Dozens of countries in all regions of the world have enacted data protection laws that regulate International Data Sharing. In order to assess such laws, the Humanitarian Organization should consult with its Data Protection Officer (DPO), legal department and/or local legal adviser.

4.3.2 LEGAL BASES FOR INTERNATIONAL DATA SHARING

International Data Sharing may be carried out:
- when the transfer serves the vital interests of Data Subjects or other persons;
- for important grounds of public interest, based on the Humanitarian Organization's mandate;
- for the legitimate interest of the Humanitarian Organization, based on the organization's declared mission, in cases when this interest is not overridden by the rights and freedoms of the Data Subjects and the Humanitarian Organization has provided suitable safeguards for the Personal Data;
- with the Consent of the Data Subject;
- for the performance of a contract with the Data Subject.

These legal bases are used in similar ways to their application in Personal Data Processing.[6] In addition, as International Data Sharing involves additional risks, the factors listed below in Section 4.4 – Mitigating the risks to the individual should be given due consideration.

---

6   See Chapter 3: Legal bases for Personal Data Processing.

4.4 MITIGATING THE RISKS TO THE INDIVIDUAL

The following factors are important when carrying out International Data Sharing:
- Risks may be lower if the transfer is to an organization that is subject to the jurisdiction of a country or to an International Organization that has been formally assessed as adequate from a data protection point of view. In general terms, this means that the recipient of data is in a country, or is an international organization, that has been formally determined to have a regulatory regime for data protection in line with high international standards, including an independent supervisory authority, freedom from mass surveillance and access to judicial redress for individuals. However, only a small number of countries have been found to offer adequate protection in a formal sense by national or regional governmental authorities. This means that relying on an adequacy finding is unlikely to be of use to Humanitarian Organizations in most circumstances. Adequacy is not a prerequisite for International Data Sharing, but is a factor to be taken into account.
- Appropriate safeguards should be used for International Data Sharing, when this is logistically feasible, such as contractual clauses binding the recipient to provide appropriate data protection or checking whether the recipient is committed to complying with a code of conduct on Personal Data protection.
- The Humanitarian Organization should be accountable for the International Data Sharing it engages in.

These last two factors are considered in more detail below.

EXAMPLE:
A humanitarian NGO has its headquarters in Country X and wants to transfer files containing Personal Data on vulnerable individuals to whom it provides humanitarian services to another NGO in Country Y. The files will be made available by putting them on its secure web-based platform, allowing the organization in Country Y to access them. Country Y has been formally found to provide an adequate level of data protection by the public authorities of Country X. Making the files available on the web-based platform qualifies as International Data Sharing, but the transfer may take place on the basis that there is an adequate level of protection in Country Y, subject to the further considerations set out under Section 4.4.1 – Appropriate safeguards/Contractual clauses, below.

4.4.1 APPROPRIATE SAFEGUARDS/CONTRACTUAL CLAUSES
One of the measures for a Humanitarian Organization to consider when deciding on the mitigation of the risks involved in International Data Sharing is to ensure that the recipient puts appropriate safeguards in place to protect Personal Data.

In practice, such safeguards may be provided by a legally binding contractual agreement, developed by the Humanitarian Organization itself or adapted from other internationally recognized sources, by which the organization and the party to which the data are transferred commit to protect the Personal Data in question on the basis of the data protection standards that apply to the Humanitarian Organization.

The European Commission has issued standard contractual clauses for transfers from Data Controllers to Data Controllers and to Data Processors established outside the European Union/European Economic Area[7] for Humanitarian Organizations subject to EU data protection law or wishing to use these clauses.

Another factor to consider when deciding on risk mitigation is whether the other party involved in data sharing is committed to a code of conduct covering Personal Data Processing[8] and the extent to which such a code of conduct is applied in practice, whether it is binding and enforceable or not.

Even when a legal basis exists for the transfer and mitigating measures are put in place, it may not be appropriate to carry out International Data Sharing, because of factors such as the following:
- The nature of the data could put individuals at risk.
- There are good reasons to believe that the parties receiving the data may not be able to ensure that they receive adequate protection.
- The conditions in the country where the data are to be sent make it unlikely that they will be protected.
- The data are being processed on the basis that they are protected by an International Organization's immunity from jurisdiction and the receiving organization does not enjoy such immunity.

EXAMPLE:
A Humanitarian Organization that is an International Organization with offices in Country X wants to transfer files containing Personal Data on vulnerable individuals to whom it provides humanitarian services to an NGO in the same country. As a transfer from an International Organization to an organization subject to the

---

[7] See European Commission, "Standard Contractual Clauses for Data Transfers between EU and Non-EU Countries", Text, European Commission – European Commission, 4 June 2021: commission.europa.eu/law/law-topic/data-protection/international-dimension-data-protection/standard-contractual-clauses-scc_en.

[8] See for example: International Conference of the Red Cross Red Crescent Movement, "Restoring Family Links Code of Conduct on Data Protection", 18 January 2016: www.icrc.org/en/document/rfl-code-conduct.

jurisdiction of X, the sharing constitutes International Data Sharing. The Humanitarian Organization signs standard contractual clauses with the NGO. However, there is a significant danger that an armed group may attack the facilities of the NGO. The NGO also has a record of losing data that is sent to it. The Humanitarian Organization should seriously consider not transferring the data, irrespective of contractual clauses being signed.

To identify and address or mitigate such risks properly, a DPIA should be carried out.[9] In case of doubt, the Humanitarian Organization's DPO should be consulted.

4.4.2 ACCOUNTABILITY

It is important for the Humanitarian Organization that initiates the transfer to be able to demonstrate that adequate and proportionate measures have been undertaken to ensure compliance with basic data protection principles with regard to International Data Sharing. The Humanitarian Organization is accountable to the Data Subject whose data are being shared. This can include measures such as the following:
- keeping internal records concerning data Processing and, in particular, a log of the transfer and a copy of the data transfer agreement made with the party to which the Personal Data are being transferred, if applicable;
- appointing a DPO;
- drafting Personal Data Processing policies, including a data security policy;
- performing and keeping a record of the DPIA(s) relating to the transfer;
- registering the transfer with the competent authorities (i.e. data protection authorities), if required by applicable law.

For any International Data Sharing, appropriate measures should be used to safeguard the transmission of Personal Data to Third Parties. The level of security[10] adopted and the method of transmission should be proportionate to the nature and sensitivity of Personal Data and to the risks involved. It is also advisable to consider this factor as part of any DPIA to further specify the precautions to be taken.

4.5 DATA CONTROLLER/DATA PROCESSOR RELATIONSHIP

In the event that a Data Processor is employed by a Data Controller, irrespective of whether the Data Processor is located in a country other than that of the establishment of the Data Controller, their relationship should as much as possible be

---

9   See Chapter 5: Data Protection Impact Assessments (DPIAs).
10 See Section 2.8 – Data security and Processing security.

governed by a binding agreement to protect the Processing of the Personal Data that are shared between them.

A number of issues may have to be clarified in the relevant contractual documents, in order to ensure that Personal Data are properly protected, for example:
- whether the retention policies of the Data Processor are acceptable (e.g. mobile phone operators/financial institutions are subject to domestic data retention requirements);
- what additional types of data are collected by the Data Processor as part of the Processing (e.g. for mobile phone operators, geolocation and other phone metadata);
- whether the Processing of Personal Data by the Data Processor follows the instructions provided by the Data Controller;
- how Personal Data are disposed of by the Data Processor after the contracted Processing.

CHAPTER 5

DATA PROTECTION IMPACT ASSESSMENTS (DPIAS)

5.1 INTRODUCTION*

The Processing of Personal Data can increase risks for individuals, groups and organizations, as well as society as a whole. The purpose of a Data Protection Impact Assessment (DPIA) is to identify, evaluate and address the risks to the Data Subject – arising from a project, policy, programme or other initiative. A DPIA should ultimately lead to measures that contribute to the avoidance, minimization, transfer and/or sharing of data protection risks. A DPIA should follow a project or initiative that requires Processing of individuals' data throughout its life cycle. The project should revisit the DPIA as it undergoes changes or as new risks arise and become apparent.

Here are examples of when a DPIA is appropriate:
- The offices of the Humanitarian Organization have been looted once too often. The Humanitarian Organization wants field offices either to dispose of their paper files or send them to headquarters and to rely instead on a cloud-based storage system. Should field offices do away with paper, CDs and flash drives?
- A local NGO or authority approaches a Humanitarian Organization saying it wants to reunite family members separated because of violence in the country. It wants the Humanitarian Organization to supply all the information it has on missing persons in the country. Should the information be shared? If so, how much personal information should be shared in order to trace missing persons? Under what conditions should personal information be disclosed?
- A tsunami sweeps away dozens of coastal villages. Thousands of people are reported missing. How much personal information should the Humanitarian Organization collect from the families of persons unaccounted for? Should it be as much information as is available, or should there be limits? Should it include information on health or genetic data, religious affiliation or political views, or other information which, if disclosed, could potentially give rise to significant harm to the individuals concerned?
- Should Humanitarian Organizations publish pictures of unaccompanied children who are unaccounted for on the Internet? Should the Humanitarian Organization produce posters with these pictures? Under what circumstances?

The DPIA can play a key role in determining who might be adversely affected by privacy or data protection risks, and how they might be harmed.

This chapter is a step-by-step guide for Humanitarian Organizations on how to conduct a DPIA and what should be included in a DPIA report. Appendix 1 contains a template for a DPIA report.[1] Although a DPIA report is not the end of a DPIA

---

*   The author thanks Trilateral Research for permission to use their material on Data Protection Impact Assessments, and Alessandro Mantelero and Nahide Basri for their input and feedback.
1   See Appendix 1 — Template for a DPIA report.

process, it is crucial to its success. The report helps the Humanitarian Organization identify the privacy impacts of a proposed project and what must be done to ensure that the project protects Personal Data. It also helps the Humanitarian Organization reassure stakeholders that it takes their rights to privacy and data protection seriously and that it seeks the views of those who might be affected by or interested in the programme. Humanitarian Organizations should consider making the DPIA report or, at least, a summary of it available to stakeholders.

5.2 THE DPIA PROCESS

This section provides a guide through the steps necessary to undertake a DPIA. There are different approaches to conducting DPIAs. The following guidance draws on best practices from a range of sources.[2]

5.2.1 IS A DPIA NECESSARY?

Any organization that collects, processes, stores and/or transfers Personal Data to other organizations should consider conducting a DPIA, the scale of which will depend on the severity of the risks assessed by the organization. A Humanitarian Organization may not be aware of all relevant data protection risks beforehand, and certain risks may only become apparent during the course of the DPIA. The Humanitarian Organization may view the risks as being so small that they do not justify a DPIA. Some risks may be real, but still relatively small, so the DPIA process and report may be correspondingly short. Other risks may be very serious, and the Humanitarian Organization will want to conduct a thorough DPIA. There is no one-size-fits-all solution.

5.2.2 THE DPIA TEAM

The second step involves identifying the DPIA team and setting the terms of reference. The DPIA team should include or consult the Humanitarian Organization's DPO. Depending on the scale of the DPIA to be undertaken, the DPIA team could include experts from the Humanitarian Organization's IT, legal, operations, protection, policy, strategic planning, archives and information management, and public relations groups. The team undertaking the DPIA should be familiar with data protection requirements as well as the Humanitarian Organization's confidentiality

---

2 David Wright, "Making Privacy Impact Assessment more effective", *The Information Society*, Vol. 29, No. 5, 2013, pp. 307–15: https://doi.org/10.1080/01972243.2013.825687; Information and Privacy Commission New South Wales, *Guide to Privacy Impact Assessments in NSW* Information and Privacy Commission New South Wales, May 2020: www.ipc.nsw.gov.au/guide-privacy-impact-assessments-nsw; International Organization for Standardization (ISO), "ISO/IEC 29134:2017 | Information Technology – Security Techniques – Guidelines for Privacy Impact Assessment", 2016–2017: www.iso.org/cms/render/live/en/sites/isoorg/contents/data/standard/06/22/62289.html.

rules and codes of conduct. Importantly, it should also include staff familiar with the planned project. Setting the terms of reference includes planning the time frame for the DPIA, the scope of the DPIA, the stakeholders to be consulted, the budget for the DPIA, and the steps that will be taken after the DPIA in terms of review and/or audit.

5.2.3 DESCRIBING THE PROCESSING OF PERSONAL DATA

The DPIA team should prepare a description of the programme or activity to be assessed. The description should include:
- the aims of the project;
- the scope of the project;
- linkages with other projects or programmes;
- the team responsible for the programme or activity;
- a brief description of the type of data that will be collected.

Mapping data flows is a key step of any DPIA. In mapping the information flows of a particular programme or activity, the DPIA team should consider the following questions:
- What type of Personal Data is being collected, from whom and why?
- How will that data be used, stored and/or transferred?
- Who will have access to the Personal Data?
- What security measures are in place to protect the Personal Data?
- For how long will those data be retained or when will they be deleted? Have different layers of data retention been identified? This can include steps such as (1) storing data deemed sensitive for up to X days, (2) pseudonymizing data then storing the data for a longer time period, and finally (3) full deletion of the data.
- Will the data undergo any aggregation, Pseudonymization, or Anonymization to protect sensitive information?

5.2.4 CONSULTING STAKEHOLDERS

Identifying stakeholders is an important part of conducting a DPIA. Stakeholders include anyone who is interested in or affected by a data protection risk, possible processors, and Sub-Processors. Stakeholders may be internal and/or external to an organization. The need for and value of consulting external stakeholders will depend on how serious the Humanitarian Organization considers the risk to be. For a Humanitarian Organization, consulting stakeholders is a way to identify risks and/or solutions it may not have considered. It is also a way of raising awareness about data protection and privacy issues. The views of stakeholders should be taken into consideration in the DPIA report and recommendations. In order to ensure that the consultation is effective, stakeholders should be provided with sufficient information about the programme and given the opportunity to express their views. There are different ways to engage stakeholders, so the DPIA team should determine the most appropriate one depending on the programme or activity.

5.2.5 IDENTIFY RISKS

One way to identify risks is to create a spreadsheet listing privacy and data protection principles, threats to those principles, vulnerabilities (susceptibility to the threats), and risks arising from the threats and vulnerabilities. A threat without a vulnerability or vice versa is not a risk. A risk arises when a threat acts to exploit a vulnerability.

5.2.6 ASSESS THE RISKS

A data protection risk assessment addresses the likelihood or probability of a certain event and its consequences (i.e. impact). One can assess the risks by undertaking one or more of the following steps:
- Consult and deliberate with internal and/or external stakeholders to identify risks, threats and vulnerabilities.
- Evaluate the risks against agreed risk criteria.[3]
- Assess the risk in terms of likelihood and severity of impact.
- Assess against the necessity, suitability and proportionality tests.

ASSESSING THE SEVERITY AND LIKELIHOOD OF ANTICIPATED RISKS: PRECAUTIONARY PRINCIPLE

The criterion of **severity of impact** refers to the "magnitude of the risk or its impact if it materializes".[4] The determination thereof involves asking various questions including but not restricted to: how many people will it put at risk? What kinds of risks may it generate (e.g. threat to the life, security, dignity and rights of individuals; discrimination; economic harm; reputational harm; risk that an individual may not be in a position to exercise a data protection right; risk that Third Parties may gain access to data, etc.)? What are the profiles of people to whom such risks might be posed (in particular, whether this would include vulnerable people, i.e. those belonging to groups that are particularly susceptible to harm)?[5]

It should be noted that in certain Humanitarian Emergencies, such as situations of armed conflict or violence, there can be an assumption that risks can have particularly severe impacts if they materialize.

The **likelihood** of potential risks refers to the chances that the risk will materialize, and that it will materialize with the possible severity identified under the above

---

3   For definitions of risk terms, see International Organization for Standardization (ISO), *ISO Guide 73:2009(En), risk management – vocabulary*, 2009: www.iso.org/obp/ui/#iso:std:iso:guide:73:ed-1:v1:en.
4   Centre for Information Policy Leadership, *Risk, High Risk, Risk Assessments and Data Protection Impact Assessments under the GDPR: CIPL GDPR Interpretation and Implementation Project*, 21 December 2016: www.informationpolicycentre.com/uploads/5/7/1/0/57104281/cipl_gdpr_project_risk_white_paper_21_december_2016.pdf.
5   Wright, "Making Privacy Impact Assessment more effective".

analysis. In Humanitarian Emergencies it is often difficult to assess the likelihood of a risk materializing, particularly taking into consideration the limited availability of incident documentation. This will often mean that there will be limited or no documented evidence of a risk materializing. Lack of evidence should not be taken to mean that a risk is unlikely to materialize or to materialize with the possible level of severity identified. On the contrary, the identification of a risk with possible significant impact, combined with the inability to determine the likelihood thereof in the absence of evidence, should itself be an indicator of a high risk that deserves careful mitigation as part of the DPIA. The possible severity of the risk if it materializes, the nature, context and the purposes of the Processing activity in a humanitarian context should therefore inform the way in which the criterion of likelihood is interpreted and applied.

In this regard, it is suggested that the precautionary principle should be taken into account in the framework of a DPIA. The precautionary principle is a principle commonly used in other sectors (such as regulation of the environment, health and pharmaceuticals, etc.), informing decision-making in risk management,[6] which calls for particular caution where "a phenomenon, product or process may have a dangerous effect, identified by scientific and objective evaluation" but the available evidence "does not allow the risk to be determined with sufficient certainty".[7] While this does not involve examining in depth every hypothetical risk, the precautionary principle requires that in the face of situations in which "there is uncertainty with regards to the existence or extent of risks ... protective measures ... [should be taken] ... without having to wait until the reality and seriousness of those risks become fully apparent"[8].

5.2.7 IDENTIFY SOLUTIONS

This step involves developing strategies to eliminate, avoid, reduce or transfer the privacy risks. These strategies could include technical solutions, operational and/or organizational controls and/or communication strategies (e.g. to raise awareness). The following example has been provided by OCHA's Centre for Humanitarian Data, and is based on their work on this subject.[9]

---

6 European Commission, Communication from the Commission on the precautionary principle, available at: op.europa.eu/en/publication-detail/-/publication/21676661-a79f-4153-b984-aeb28f07c80a/language-en.

7 Ibid.

8 The Court of Justice of the European Union, the Judgement of the Court of 5 May 1998. *United Kingdom of Great Britain and Northern Ireland v Commission of the European Communities* Case C-180/96 ECLI: EU:C:1998:192.

9 See OCHA Center for Humanitarian Data, "An Introduction to Disclosure Risk Assessment", The Centre for Humanitarian Data (blog), accessed 23 March 2022: https://centre.humdata.org/learning-path/disclosure-risk-assessment-overview.

EXAMPLE: STATISTICAL DISCLOSURE CONTROL IN HUMANITARIAN DATA MANAGEMENT

Data from household surveys, needs assessments and other forms of microdata are critical to determining the needs and perspectives of people affected by crises. This type of data also presents unique risks that should be identified as part of a DPIA process and mitigated before data sharing. Even after names, phone numbers and other direct identifiers are removed from microdata, it may still be possible, through the combination of key variables such as location or ethnicity, to reidentify individuals in the data set or disclose confidential information.

Statistical Disclosure Control (SDC) refers to a set of statistical methods used to assess and reduce the risk of Reidentification or the disclosure of confidential information in order to facilitate the safe sharing of microdata.

The SDC process includes three steps:

(1) **Assess the risk of disclosure**: Assess the probability that disclosure could occur for individual respondents within a given data set by conducting a disclosure risk assessment.
(2) **Reduce the risk of disclosure**: Lower the disclosure risk by applying one or more Statistical Disclosure Control techniques.
(3) **Quantify information loss**: Quantify the information loss and assess the utility of the treated data in line with the original purpose for which they were collected.

Assess the risk of Reidentification

The first step in the SDC process is to conduct a disclosure risk assessment. This helps determine the likelihood of a disclosure taking place and the type of mitigation measures that might be necessary before sharing the data. Conducting a disclosure risk assessment requires selecting the indirect identifiers that are most likely to lead to Reidentification or the disclosure of confidential information, and using statistical methods to calculate different measures of risk.

Common key variables found in humanitarian microdata include age, gender, ethnicity, marital status, religion, income, location and other forms of geographic information. Depending on the context, almost any variable could be considered an indirect identifier (referred to as key variables). Selecting key variables thus requires an understanding of the context and data environment in which the data were produced.

Common risk measures include k-anonymity, l-diversity and individual and global disclosure risk. The Humanitarian Organization will need to set thresholds to be reached for each of the risk measures in order to share the data.

Reduce the risk of Reidentification

The second step in the SDC process is to reduce the disclosure risk to below the agreed threshold. There are two main strategies for reducing disclosure risk. The first is through non-perturbative methods, which reduce the detail in the data through the suppression or data generalization. For example, continuous key variables such as age or income may be recoded into age or income brackets. This process of replacing a data value with a less precise one can be an effective method for reducing disclosure risk while maintaining the analytical power of the data. The second set of methods, known as perturbative methods, aims to limit disclosure risk by altering data values in order to create uncertainty around the true value. Because these methods deliberately change data values, they should be applied with caution.

Quantifying information loss

The application of SDC will always lead to some information loss. In some cases, the information loss would be so high that the data lose their utility. Information loss must be evaluated with respect to the intended uses of the data. In the final step of the SDC process, the disclosure risk is reassessed to determine whether the application of SDC techniques has reduced the disclosure risk to an acceptable level and to evaluate the information loss. The goal of the SDC process is to find the optimal point at which the utility of the data for the intended users is maximized while the disclosure risk is reduced to an acceptable level.[10]

5.2.8 PROPOSE RECOMMENDATIONS

The DPIA team should produce a set of recommendations based on the outcome of the previous steps. Recommendations may include a set of solutions, changes at the organizational level and potentially changes to the Humanitarian Organization's overall data protection strategy or that of the programme. A set of recommendations should be included in the DPIA report.

5.2.9 IMPLEMENT THE AGREED RECOMMENDATIONS

The DPIA team should prepare a written report on the considerations and findings of the DPIA. As organizations will need to conduct DPIAs regularly, the length and level of detail of a DPIA report will vary greatly. For example, if an organization is considering publication of Personal Data for research purposes, it should produce documentation reflecting the full details of its data protection impact analysis. Conversely, an organization that is deciding whether to switch from using one brand

---

[10] For more information on SDC in the humanitarian sector, consult the following resources: OCHA Center for Humanitarian Data, "An Introduction to Disclosure Risk Assessment"; OCHA Center for Humanitarian Data, "Statistical Disclosure Control", The Centre for Humanitarian Data (blog), accessed 23 March 2022: https://centre.humdata.org/guidance-note-statistical-disclosure-control; "Statistical Disclosure Control for Microdata: A Practice Guide for SdcMicro", SDC Practice Guide documentation, accessed 23 March 2022: https://sdcpractice.readthedocs.io/en/latest.

of word-processing software to another should consider data protection issues, given that the software will be used to process personal information, but a detailed DPIA may not be necessary (unless the software involves new data flows in a cloud environment).

In addition to documenting and implementing data protection decisions, a Humanitarian Organization should consider whether it would be useful for Data Subjects or to the public to understand the considerations underlying its data protection decision-making. Accordingly, the organization might then share the report (in whole or in part) with relevant stakeholders. Sharing the DPIA report may also be a way of raising awareness and inviting further comments or suggestions from stakeholders. However, in some cases, the Humanitarian Organization may decide against sharing the DPIA report if it contains sensitive information (e.g. for reasons of physical security, continuity of operations, access, etc.). In such cases, the Humanitarian Organization could consider sharing a summary of the DPIA report or a redacted version.

5.2.10 PROVIDE EXPERT REVIEW AND/OR AUDIT OF THE DPIA

Humanitarian Organizations should ensure that a data protection expert, such as the organization's Data Protection Officer (DPO) or their staff, reviews or audits the implementation of the DPIA. In the interest of an accurate audit, the DPIA report must contain a methodology section.

5.2.11 UPDATE THE DPIA IF THERE ARE CHANGES IN THE PROJECT

The Humanitarian Organization should update the DPIA if the activity covered by it changes in some significant way or if new data protection risks emerge.

PART II
SPECIFIC PROCESSING SITUATIONS, TECHNOLOGIES AND TECHNOLOGY AREAS

DATA PROTECTION BY DESIGN

these digital systems can help Humanitarian Organizations connect with, assist and deliver services to people

digital systems from external service providers are increasingly embedded in humanitarian programming

these same digital systems can also create risks for the people that Humanitarian Organizations assist

CHALLENGES

Third Party digital systems often fulfill multiple purposes by allowing the collection or processing of unnecessary amounts of data

regulatory compliance alone may not reduce all risks to people in a humanitarian crisis

RISK MITIGATION

identify precisely what a system needs to achieve

require a technical design that only achives this specific purpose

CHAPTER 6

DESIGNING FOR DATA PROTECTION

Carmela Troncoso and Wouter Lueks

6.1 INTRODUCTION

Humanitarian Organizations assist the most vulnerable populations in extremely challenging circumstances. For reasons of efficiency, accountability, and out of a desire to help as many people as possible, Humanitarian Organizations increasingly rely on digital technology in their programmes. The livelihood and safety of vulnerable populations often relies on the assistance provided by these organizations. As a result, individuals have very little agency in whether to accept the assistance and whether to participate in these digital systems if they wish to accept the assistance. Digital systems bring data protection and privacy risks. Especially for vulnerable populations, these risks might be significant. Therefore, humanitarian organizations have an obligation not just to safeguard individuals' livelihood in the short term, but also to uphold data protection as well as privacy rights and the dignity of the people they help.

This relevance of digital systems is not limited to the humanitarian sector. As these systems gained prominence, in the early 2010s policymakers and researchers redoubled their efforts to ensure that the design of these digital systems ensured strong privacy protection. On the policy side, regulatory efforts aimed to set a legal basis for respectful and privacy-preserving digital services.[1] On the research side, a vast number of privacy-enhancing technologies and building blocks have also been produced for privacy-friendly systems, in addition to end-to-end privacy-preserving systems for a wide range of particular use cases such as electronic voting, document Searches for investigative journalists, and gun registration databases. There have also been efforts to articulate specific strategies to design privacy-friendly systems.[2]

Despite these advances, the process of designing and engineering systems with strong privacy and data protection remains a challenge. One of the main reasons is that privacy-preserving properties of technological outputs are often difficult to map onto data protection regulations, policies and principles.

Typically, Humanitarian Organizations do not design their own systems but instead provide requirements to potential service providers. As a result, they need to assess

---

[1] See, for example, efforts such as: EU Regulation 2016/679 of the European Parliament and of the Council of 27 April 2016 on the protection of natural persons with regard to the processing of Personal Data and on the free movement of such data, and repealing Directive 95/46/EC (EU General Data Protection Regulation), [2016] OJ L119/1; California Consumer Privacy Act, 2018 Cal. Legis. Serv. Ch. 55 (A.B. 375) (WEST); and Ann Cavoukian, "Privacy by Design: The 7 Foundational Principles", Information and Privacy Commissioner of Ontario, January 2011: www.ipc.on.ca/wp-content/uploads/resources/7foundationalprinciples.pdf.

[2] Jaap-Henk Hoepman, "Privacy design strategies (Extended abstract)", *IFIP Advances in Information and Communication Technology*, No. 428, 1 January 2014, pp. 446–459.

the solutions provided to them by asking the right questions and requesting better analyses. In this chapter, we aim to provide the reader with means to question about the privacy and data protection provided by digital systems. We do so via a privacy-engineering methodology that can be used to produce designs that provide strong privacy protection. Systems that adhere to the privacy-engineering principles we present will, by design, fulfil data minimization and limit the purpose for which the data that are collected can be used. By providing technical means to enforce these data protection principles, systems engineered according to our methodology provide strong protection of individuals, their dignity and rights.

More concretely, this chapter provides guidance on how to determine the purpose of a system and shows how purpose limitation can guide the system designer into creating systems with strong privacy and data protection by design. Finally, this chapter provides concrete guidance on how to analyse a system to determine whether it implements technical means to enforce purpose limitation and therefore provides strong protection for its users, beyond those that could be achieved via data usage policies.

We finally note that the methods and technologies introduced in this chapter address the need for data minimization, purpose limitation and data security included in data protection. However, it does not address other data protection requirements, e.g. accountability. Yet, the design principles introduced in the chapter will enable Humanitarian Organizations to assess whether the mechanisms to be added to fulfil all data protection requirements are detrimental to the technical protection of individuals and their rights.

6.1.1 WHAT IS A SYSTEM?
This chapter often refers to a "system". We define a system as "a combination of interacting elements organized to achieve one or more stated purposes".[3] That is, the system encompasses all the parts (or elements) that are necessary to achieve a purpose. Following this definition, a system is composed of more parts than just a central server. Typically, a system includes at least user devices.

6.2 CASE STUDY: PRIVACY-PRESERVING CONTACT-TRACING APPS

To illustrate how starting from the purpose of an application and using technology to enforce purpose limitation leads to strong privacy guarantees, this chapter uses the

---

3   Joint Task Force Interagency Working Group, *Security and Privacy Controls for Information Systems and Organizations*, NIST Special Publication 800-53, National Institute of Standards and Technology, September 2020: https://doi.org/10.6028/NIST.SP.800-53r5.

example of a privacy-preserving system that has been successfully deployed at large scale: a privacy-preserving contact-tracing system based on mobile apps.

In the beginning of the COVID-19 pandemic, contact-tracing apps were introduced as a public health intervention to help break infection chains. Contact tracing aims to identify close contacts of people infected with COVID-19 so that these contacts – who are likely to have been exposed to the SARS-CoV-2 virus through their proximity to a COVID-19-positive person – can take action (e.g. quarantine) to avoid spreading the disease in case they contract COVID-19 themselves.

To be effective, contact tracing must be timely and reach as many contacts as possible. Traditionally, tracing is done manually. However, due to its reliance on trained personnel, manual contact tracing cannot scale when diseases, such as COVID-19, spread to many people. Manual contact tracing is time-consuming because contact tracers have to manually interview *index cases*, meaning the people that contracted the disease. The index cases have to identify their contacts, and then the tracers have to reach out to these contacts one by one. Furthermore, when dealing with airborne pathogens, index cases may not be able to identify all contacts because the contacts' identities may in fact be unknown to the index case (e.g. passengers on a bus and people waiting in line at the supermarket).

In the initial months of the COVID-19 pandemic, several digital solutions were proposed to address the limitations of manual contact tracing. In this chapter, the focus is on solutions that use Bluetooth technology to measure proximity between people and then use close-proximity events with index cases (people with COVID-19) to automatically notify users of their risk of having been exposed. Such digital systems scale better, because they do not have to rely on manual interactions with index cases or contacts. They also can have better coverage, as they do not require people to know who they came into contact with, nor to have their contact information. At the same time, these digital solutions are inherently limited to only finding close contacts that also use the contact-tracing app.

Contact-tracing applications have the potential to expose Personal Data, including sensitive Personal Data. This type of information has historically been abused to profile, manipulate and control individuals and populations.[4] Thus, privacy-preserving contact-tracing applications were created in a way that ensures that those Sensitive Data are not available, and therefore cannot be abused for purposes other than notifying users of danger of infection.

---

4   See e.g.: Balthasar Staehelin and Cécile Aptel, "COVID-19 and Contact Tracing: A Call for Digital Diligence", Humanitarian Law & Policy Blog (blog), 13 May 2020: https://blogs.icrc.org/law-and-policy/2020/05/13/covid-19-contact-tracing-digital-diligence.

The next section explains the design of privacy-preserving contact-tracing applications. Readers familiar with these applications may skip to Section 6.3 – Protection of individuals and their dignity and rights through purpose limitation.

6.2.1 DECENTRALIZED PRIVACY-PRESERVING PROXIMITY TRACING

This chapter uses the example of privacy-preserving contact-tracing applications based on the Decentralized Privacy-Preserving Proximity Tracing (DP3T) protocol.[5] This protocol enables the creation of a *decentralized* system with strong protection by design. Sensitive data, such as information about social interactions between users, are stored and processed on users' devices rather than in a central entity. Phones locally compute exposure scores and notify users if their exposure to COVID-positive users is too high. Some data are exchanged via a server, but on their own these contain no sensitive information about users and cannot be abused or misused.

Every user of the digital contact-tracing system installs an app on their phone. At a predetermined interval (around 15 minutes), apps generate a fresh random number. Apps broadcast the random numbers via Bluetooth Low Energy (BLE) beacons. Nearby phones record received numbers in a list of seen numbers. Devices in close proximity receive the transmitted Bluetooth beacon with high signal strength, and those further away either receive it with low signal strength or do not receive the beacon at all. Low-strength beacons are not recorded as they indicate the devices are not close enough to indicate risk of infection.

When a user tests positive, the health authority authorizes this user to upload to a central server the random numbers that their phone transmitted during their contagious period. The central server periodically publishes a list of all random numbers transmitted by COVID-positive users. All devices in the system download this list, and check locally whether any entries on their list of seen random numbers (e.g. corresponding to people that were physically close to them) appears in the list of random numbers that they downloaded (corresponding to people that were contagious). Overlap between these lists indicates proximity of the user to index cases, and potential exposure to the SARS-CoV-2 virus. If this exposure – determined by the length of proximity as well as the relative signal strength – passes the threshold, the phone notifies the user.

In this system, very little information leaves the user device. The central server receives only the random numbers transmitted by COVID-positive users. These numbers are randomly generated by the user device and have no relationship to the user's identity or location. These random numbers are also independent of how

---

5   Carmela Troncoso et al., "Decentralized privacy-preserving proximity tracing", *ArXiv:2005.12273 [Cs]*, 25 May 2020: http://arxiv.org/abs/2005.12273.

many people a user has met or the frequency and duration of those meetings. However, if the random numbers of a positive user are published, this user may become easier to track and identify for attackers that can receive Bluetooth beacons (and thus these random numbers) at many locations.[6] In summary, the server holds very little information that could potentially be used to harm users.

Returning to the definition of a system as a combination of components that are organized to achieve a stated purpose, users' phones in the DP3T system collaborate with a central server to fulfil the purpose of notifying users that have been exposed to the SARS-CoV-2 virus. Therefore, both phones and the central server are part of this system. In fact, because the public health authorities must be able to authorize the upload by users that tested positive in a digital manner, the public health authorities (or at least the servers they operate) are part of the contact-tracing system as well.

6.3 PROTECTION OF INDIVIDUALS AND THEIR DIGNITY AND RIGHTS THROUGH PURPOSE LIMITATION

There exist several methodologies and principles that guide the design and analysis of systems to achieve strong data protection and provide strong privacy. This chapter uses a methodology based on guaranteeing **purpose limitation by design**, through the careful introduction of techniques in the design of digital systems to enforce this data protection principle. This methodology is comparatively easy to use, leads to systems with strong privacy guarantees and automatically shows the limits of privacy-friendly designs.

The reader might be most familiar with *purpose limitation* as a data protection requirement, which requires that data are collected for a specific purpose and it forbids these data to be used for any other purposes. Traditionally, purpose limitation is enforced through processes and procedures. This chapter, however, uses purpose limitation in a *technical* sense:

> A system that implements *technical purpose limitation* ensures, through its technical design, that the system as a whole can only be used for the stated purpose. Such systems make pieces of data accessible to adversarial entities only when doing so is part of the stated purpose.

As a result, systems designed to achieve technical purpose limitation minimize the potential harms stemming from how and which data are collected and processed in these systems. In a system with purpose limitation, data cannot be used for anything

---

6   The DP-3T Project, *Decentralized Privacy-Preserving Proximity Tracing: Overview of Data Protection and Security*, GitHub, 2020: https://github.com/DP-3T/documents/blob/master/DP3T%20-%20Data%20Protection%20and%20Security.pdf.

Traditional Approach

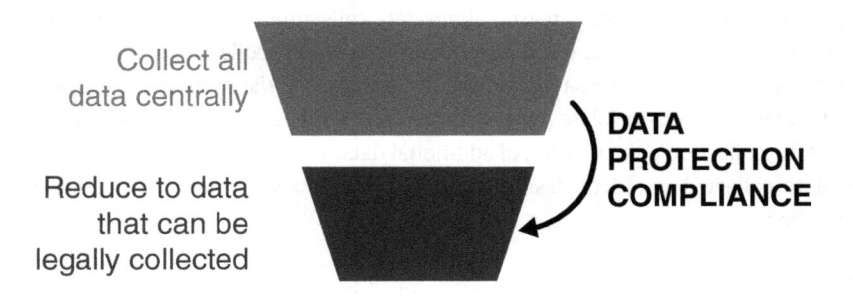

Collect all data centrally

Reduce to data that can be legally collected

DATA PROTECTION COMPLIANCE

Privacy-Friendly Approach

Data centrally available for purpose

Data finally available

OPERATIONAL PURPOSES

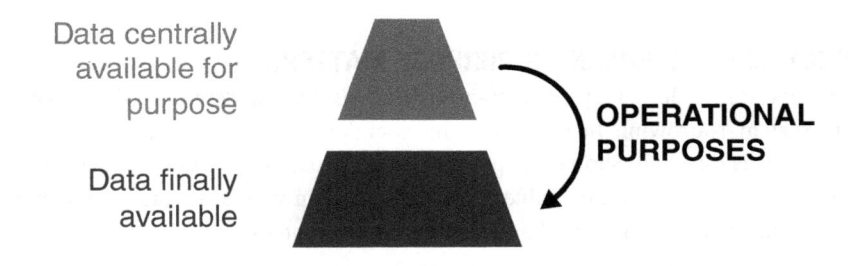

Figure 6.1. Data collected centrally (at entities untrusted by the user) as a result of starting from purpose limitation are strictly less than when minimizing data through compliance mechanisms.

but the purpose of the system. Therefore, users do not need to trust that other actors in the system are going to behave appropriately, or that they will not violate the data protection policy. The protection against abuse holds even if these other actors intentionally try to do harm.

Thinking in terms of technical purpose limitation has strong implications for the amount of data collected by entities that are out of the control of, and therefore not trusted by, the user. The top diagram in Figure 6.1 shows the approach followed most often when deciding what data should be collected when building a digital system. Typically, designers start by creating systems that collect as much data as possible (with the idea that these data will become useful in the future). Then, regulatory compliance – mainly data protection compliance, or operational constraints, such as storage or processing capabilities – limit how much of these data are finally collected (see Figure 6.1 – Data collected centrally).

By contrast, when designers reason about data collection in terms of the purpose of the system, the starting point is a system that, as a whole, collects and processes only those data that are necessary *to fulfil the purpose of the system*. Collecting any additional data would violate purpose limitation. Sometimes, operational constraints force the collection or processing of additional data. However, even then, the amount of data collected is strictly less than would be allowed by looking at regulatory compliance alone.

The remainder of this section will focus on how to evaluate a system using the mechanism of purpose limitation by design. This involves two key steps. First, the evaluator must establish the purpose of the system. Second, the evaluator must assess whether a system implements technical purpose limitation given this specific purpose.

6.3.1 WHY DETERMINING PURPOSE MATTERS

The first step in designing a privacy-preserving system is to determine the purpose of the system. Narrowing the purpose to the essential goal for which the system is to be deployed is essential. Should the purpose be too broad or ill-defined, it may become very difficult, or even impossible, to design a system with strict purpose limitation and hence strong rights and dignity protection guarantees.

Broad purposes are harmful for privacy and limit data protection. To see why broad or ill-defined purposes are harmful, consider contact-tracing apps. Suppose that instead of the narrow purpose "notify contacts of index cases", the much broader purpose had been "perform contact tracing". This latter purpose is so broad that it may be understood as performing all steps associated with the manual contact-tracing process, including epidemiological surveillance, backward tracing (to identify sources of infection rather than potential new cases), monitoring notified patients, and enforcing their quarantine. Satisfying such a broad purpose may require making all kinds of data available to public health authorities, including identities of users, contact information, location, etc. These data could subsequently be abused. None of these data, however, have to be available centrally when the sole and specific purpose of the system is to notify contacts of index cases.

Even narrower purposes can be harmful when they force extra data to be made available. For example, the purpose of the German Luca contact-tracing system was to make available to public health authorities the names and phone numbers of visitors to locations with contagious individuals. By requiring that such information is available, the ability of data protection compliant designs to limit purpose is severely affected, even if data are only available to others under some conditions.

The system has to be trusted, and trust may be violated, e.g. the German police did use the Luca system to access visitor information despite some protections being in place.[7]

Designing privacy-preserving systems for multiple purposes is challenging. Defining multiple purposes can also reduce the privacy guarantees that systems can satisfy, even if they implement purpose limitation. A common example in commercial applications is to include "improving customer experience" among the purposes to motivate central collection of data, regardless of whether the system has a very concrete goal (e.g. a mobile flash light app) or a very broad one (e.g. an app to manage financial assets). When such an "improvement" purpose appears, the amount of data that is collected and made available centrally can increase considerably: from application-related data (e.g. how long the was torch on) to other data that are not strictly about the application but are very related to customer experience (e.g. the battery status of the phone when the app is opened, or the number of apps installed that are running at the same time as the application).

When a purpose makes additional data available centrally, privacy becomes difficult to protect. The relations and correlations among pieces of data, especially when those data are related to humans and their behaviour directly or via their devices, make it extremely difficult to predict the amount of inferences that can be done on these data, the amount of predictions that they can enable, and therefore the amount of uses that they can have in the future. The difficulty in determining the inferences that can be made from different types of data is similar to the problems encountered in the search for robust Anonymization mechanisms:[8] the curse of dimensionality. The fact that there are too many data fields correlated in unpredictable ways prevents the Anonymization algorithm designer from identifying all possible pseudo identifiers. Hence it becomes close to impossible to design robust Anonymization mechanisms without destroying the utility of the data.

Having multiple purposes also constrains the privacy-preserving ways that systems can be designed. For instance, it is the fact that contact-tracing apps are only aimed at notifying that enabled the deployment of a design in which only uninformative random identifiers need to be exchanged through the server. Any extra purpose

---

7   Rachel Pannett, "German police used a tracing app to scout crime witnesses. Some fear that's fuel for covid conspiracists", *Washington Post*, 13 January 2022: www.washingtonpost.com/world/2022/01/13/german-covid-contact-tracing-app-luca.
8   Arvind Narayanan and Vitaly Shmatikov, "Myths and fallacies of 'personally identifiable information'", *Communications of the ACM*, Vol. 53, No. 6, 1 June 2010, pp. 24–26: https://doi.org/10.1145/1743546.1743558; Theresa Stadler and Carmela Troncoso, "Why the search for a privacy-preserving data sharing mechanism is failing", *Nature Computational Science*, Vol. 4, 21 April 2022, pp. 208–210: https://doi.org/10.1038/s43588-022-00236-x.

(e.g. quarantine enforcement or epidemiological surveillance) would probably have forced designers to make more data available centrally. This would then have made it much more difficult to constrain data to be used only for one purpose. For example, enforcement typically requires location information, or at least knowledge of whether a user is home or not; and epidemiological surveillance requires revealing chains of infection, and therefore revealing relationships.

Even when the multiple purposes of a system do not inherently create privacy vulnerabilities, it might be difficult to create practical purpose-limited systems that provide purpose limitation. Building solutions that implement purpose limitation is difficult, especially because these systems must be optimized to be deployable in practice. For example, systems for privacy-preserving medical analysis based on homomorphic encryption require very careful domain-specific optimization to perform well enough.[9] It is difficult to take such systems and use them for different purposes without having to repeat the challenging optimization process to accommodate new constraints.

The temptation of purpose creep. Finally, once a system or infrastructure is built, there is the temptation to add purposes to take advantage of the existing components. For instance, in the contact-tracing applications ecosystem many extensions were suggested, ranging from epidemiological monitoring, to quarantine enforcement, to collecting data on notified users. Ultimately, these were not implemented, but others were. In the second half of 2020, researchers discovered that COVID-19 does not just spread via droplets to close-proximity contacts, but also via aerosols in ill-ventilated rooms. Many countries thereafter adopted check-in solutions applying contact tracing to visitors of shared indoor spaces in addition to the existing proximity-based systems. As soon as this functionality was added, it was immediately suggested that it should also be used to monitor and enforce regulations about maximum capacity in bars and restaurants. However, adding these enforcement mechanisms would mean exchanging more information between users' devices and central servers, making it much harder to implement purpose limitation.

Humanitarian Organizations can expect similar desires and pressures in the humanitarian sector. Systems that are built to prevent double dipping in aid distribution can be seen as opportunities to optimize resource allocation. And systems that are built for authentication of beneficiaries can be seen as opportunities to monitor usage of resources. While these purposes may be perfectly legitimate, and even desirable, it is important to understand that aiming to include all of them simultaneously may make it impossible to design a system that offers strong privacy guarantees, and that

---

9   David Froelicher et al., "Truly privacy-preserving federated analytics for precision medicine with multiparty homomorphic encryption", *Nature Communications*, Vol. 12, No. 1, 11 October 2021, 5910: https://doi.org/10.1038/s41467-021-25972-y.

enforces purpose limitation via technology. The system could still be built, but privacy and data protection may need to solely rely on policy and regulatory protections. Such protections may not be sufficient, depending on the environment where the system is to be deployed.

6.3.2 DETERMINING PURPOSE

Defining the purpose of a system is not an easy task. As a general rule, the narrower the purpose, the easier it is to find technological means to engineer the system in such a way that it ensures purpose limitation and hence provides strong protection for individuals and their dignity and rights. Typically, determining the purpose requires discussions with stakeholders to determine the main goal of the system. In these conversations, many purposes may arise, often as a consequence of the fact that the power of technology as a means to solve problems is often overestimated.

At that point, it is important to isolate these purposes and identify what is the underlying problem that the system should address, and what are additional desirable functionalities that could address other problems or increase the efficiency of the system, or the organization commissioning it. Once purposes are set apart, the designer must decide which of them can be implemented while providing purpose limitation, thereby avoiding information leakage that could lead to abuse. In this step, the designer may discover that the purpose of the system itself induces risks, for example because the purpose requires making Sensitive Data available to untrusted parties.

Risks may also be introduced by design or implementation choices. This is typical for privacy-preserving designs; see Figure 6.2. Designers may aim for designs that only have risks that are inherent to the purpose, but then might end up with a design that has slightly more risks. Often this is because they either do not know how to build a system that fully mitigates these risks, or they know how to but cannot make such a

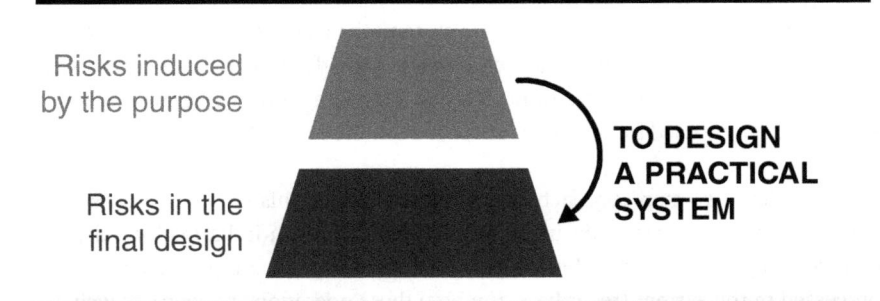

Figure 6.2. Practical and deployable systems might have somewhat higher risks than those induced by the purpose alone.

system efficient enough. At this point, there are two paths forward: decide not to build the system as the risks are too large, or build the system, accepting that the harms to individuals' rights and dignity might be larger than what is induced by the purpose and cannot be controlled other than via policy (see Figure 6.1.)

The example of privacy-preserving apps illustrates both inherent and implementation-specific risks. First, consider a risk that is inherent to the purpose of notifying contacts of index cases. When users receive a notification, they may be able to identify the index case that triggered it (e.g. if they were only with one person on the day when the reported contact took place); and thus learn medical information. This leakage is inherent to the functionality of the system: the system *must* notify the user, so that the user can take appropriate measures. Second, consider an implementation-specific risk. The server only receives uploads from positive users. The server, or any observer of the communication, can thus determine pseudo identifiers (e.g. IP addresses) of users that tested positive for COVID-19. In this case, the processing of pseudo identifiers also means that the system processes more data than would be strictly needed to fulfil its purpose (see Figure 6.1).

Limiting the purpose of the system enables privacy engineering at its best (and not limiting may result in solutions providing no privacy protection and therefore risk harming individuals). However, this decision may have implications on the efficiency and cost incurred by an organization. Adopting purpose limitation by design may require building one or more privacy-preserving system for each desired purpose. It is not the goal of this chapter to determine which option is best, as it may depend on the resources available and the conditions in which systems are to be deployed. Instead, this chapter aims to provide guidance to conduct a risk–benefit analysis that will enable Humanitarian Organizations to make informed decisions about the trade-offs between data protection and other operational constraints.

6.3.3 ANALYSING PURPOSE LIMITATION

After having determined the purpose of a system, the next step is to assess whether a particular technical implementation of a system provides (technical) purpose limitation. This is not a straightforward process, as it may be hard to determine whether a system cannot be used for any other purpose than the one stated by the stakeholders.

The following two-step approach can be used to tackle this complex process. First, identify potential *privacy risks* in the system that can result in harms for individuals and their rights and dignity by analysing *all* the data that are produced, stored or processed in the system (regardless of where these operations happen) as well as an exploration of potential harms that could be caused by the system in general. Second, for each identified risk, determine whether this risk is inherent to the system's purpose (in which case there is nothing to be done; see above) or whether the technical privacy-preserving protections implemented in the system mitigate this risk.

As mentioned in the introduction, this chapter deliberately excludes the design of systems because typically Humanitarian Organizations do not design their own systems.[10]

6.3.3.1 IDENTIFYING POTENTIAL RISKS

Identifying potential risks is a complicated process because risks might not be obvious. Humanitarian Organizations may take a combined bottom-up and top-down approach. For the bottom-up approach, start by looking at all the data that are processed and available in the system. Risks should be derived based on who could be harmed when such data would be made accessible, either directly or indirectly. To identify potential risks, specific implementation details such as whether data are processed on users' devices only, distributed between central servers, or available on a single central server should be ignored.

Because the bottom-up approach might fail to identify some risks, it should be combined with a top-down approach that instead starts by identifying potential harms of deploying the system and derives risks from them. When reasoning about who could be harmed, it is important to remember that the subjects of harms include not only individual users, but also groups or communities. These groups or communities may be significantly affected as a whole even though the harm to individual members may be considered acceptable. In fact, this harm may happen even if they do not actively participate in the system.

From data to risks. The digital contact-tracing system described in this chapter also serves as an example of the data-driven bottom-up approach. The data processed in contact-tracing systems must reflect *social interaction data* (e.g. who meets whom, when and for how long) so as to enable the calculation of exposure risk. Any digital contact-tracing system therefore runs the risk of *leaking social contact information*. Additionally, the system may risk *leaking location data* (and consequently risk becoming a *tracking infrastructure*) and also *leaking users' identities*. Indeed, digital contact-tracing solutions can reveal location data. In Germany, the Luca apps focused on tracing visitors to locations with contagious individuals. The police leveraged contact-tracing information stored in the Luca app to request and obtain contact data of visitors to specific venues.[11] Digital contact-tracing systems also process medical

---

[10] For more details about how to design and implement a privacy-preserving design once purpose has been identified, refer to: Seda Gürses, Carmela Troncoso and Claudia Diaz, "Engineering privacy by design reloaded", in *Amsterdam Privacy Conference*, 2015: http://carmelatroncoso.com/papers/Gurses-APC15.pdf.

[11] Rachel Pannett, "German police used a tracing app to scout crime witnesses. Some fear that's fuel for covid conspiracists", *Washington Post*, 13 January 2022: www.washingtonpost.com/world/2022/01/13/german-covid-contact-tracing-app-luca.

data: who tested positive and who was possibly exposed to this user. Digital contact-tracing systems therefore risk leaking sensitive medical status such as *leaking who tested positive* and *risk leaking who is exposed*.

Risks can also relate to data that do not, in any way, correspond to individuals. For example, contact-tracing solutions such as Luca that focus on tracing visitors to locations with contagious individuals potentially risk *leaking data about locations* because the system must keep track of which locations exist. While this risk is probably low when such a system is only used for bars and restaurants (whose locations are probably already public), this is not necessarily the case for other locations. When such a system is deployed more broadly, the risk of *leaking data about locations* is definitely present. In fact, when the database of a comparable system in Australia leaked, it revealed the location of defence sites and domestic violence shelters.[12]

From harms to risks. The above risks mostly relate to Personal Data (social contacts, location data, medical status). However, risks can also relate to groups of people. To identify these risks, Humanitarian Organizations may apply the top-down approach. In the case of contact-tracing applications, civil society groups identified the harm of stigmatization. Stigmatization can manifest in different risks. First, there is the risk that the system can be used to create *heat maps of medical data*. Such heat maps could then result in stigmatization of particular venues or neighbourhoods, for example, when it turns out that immigrant neighbourhoods have a higher incidence of COVID-19 cases or contacts. Similarly, there is the risk of revealing *demographic information about index cases*. This could result in stigmatization of particular minorities, for example, if it turns out that the prevalence of a certain disease is higher among gay men.

Finally, privacy and other human rights are not always related to keeping data secret or minimizing their disclosure. Instead, they can relate to other rights such as freedom of movement. The way to elicit such risks is to reflect on what the system is or could be used for. For example, the consequence of being notified via a contact-tracing app is that users self-quarantine. This is a serious restriction of movement. Potentially, such a mechanism could be abused, leading to a risk of *population control*.

6.3.3.2 ASSESSING THE PRESENCE OF RISKS
Once risks are identified, Humanitarian Organizations can use them to either drive the design of new systems[13] or to assess the design of existing systems. This chapter

---

12   Jonathan Kearsley and Clair Weaver, "Sensitive business addresses among 500,000 published in COVID data breach", *Sydney Morning Herald*, 14 February 2022: www.smh.com.au/politics/federal/sensitive-business-addresses-among-500-000-published-in-covid-data-breach-20220214-p59wal.html.
13   See for example: Gürses, Troncoso and Diaz, "Engineering privacy by design reloaded"; Hoepman, "Privacy design strategies (Extended abstract)".

6 DESIGNING FOR DATA PROTECTION

describes the latter process, linking the mitigation of risks to the technical enforcement of purpose limitation.

Assessing whether the technological design of a system mitigates all risks is a challenging process which requires specialized technical knowledge. This knowledge might not be available at Humanitarian Organizations. Therefore, Humanitarian Organizations should identify potential risks (see the previous section) and then ask for assistance to determine how and why the proposed system mitigates the identified risks. This can be done by asking the designers of the system to explain how the risks are addressed, or by contacting experts (e.g. academics) that can provide an external assessment of the technology given their knowledge about developing and deploying privacy attacks.

Why the privacy-preserving contact-tracing system implements purpose limitation. Recall the risks that are listed above for the contact-tracing applications. Regarding the risk of leaking social contact information, all information related to social contacts (the lists of received random numbers) is stored only on individual user devices, and never leaves these devices. Therefore, the design mitigates this risk.

Regarding the risk of leaking location data, apps do not collect *any* location data. Thus, there are no location data in the system to be leaked or abused. However, not all data protection risks materialize directly. Recall that devices broadcast random numbers in Bluetooth beacons. These random numbers could, potentially, be used to *track* users if there exists an eavesdropping infrastructure *external* to the system. Because phones rotate their numbers every 15 minutes, users that do not test positive cannot be tracked.

At the same time, the DP3T design cannot fully mitigate the risk of tracking for positive users. Recall that positive users will upload all random numbers that they broadcasted to the server to enable exposure computations at other devices. Because of a performance optimization, all random numbers broadcasted on the same day by the same positive user are linked to each other. This makes it possible to track a positive user, given enough Bluetooth coverage. Notice that here the need to design a deployable system increased the risks (see also: Figure 6.2).

Regarding sensitive medical data, phones determine locally whether a user has been exposed and should be notified. No data about this notification are ever communicated to any other party. This ensures that neither data about individual exposures nor group exposures (heat maps) leak. As discussed above, any contact-tracing system that makes notifications enables the potential identification of users that tested positive. This is also true in this design.

Finally, the decentralized design limits the possibility of population control by making it difficult to falsely trigger a notification. Recall that a phone shows a notification when it (1) received a random number and interpreted it as coming from a close-by device, and (2) this same random number later appears on the list it downloads from the server of numbers transmitted by contagious users. To trigger a false notification, an attacker must be close enough to the target to transmit a random number via Bluetooth, and then trick the server into accepting an upload. Neither of these is strictly speaking impossible, but it seems that performing this attack is difficult at scale.

Even though some residual risks remain, using the data *within* the system none of these risks can be materialized: the system by design ensures that the purpose can only be notification.

A contact-tracing system that does not implement purpose limitation. As a counter-example, consider an alternative contact-tracing system also aimed at notification that does not ensure purpose limitation: the NeedToKnow (NTK) system that was proposed in Germany.[14] Like the decentralized design, in NTK phones exchange numbers and store them locally. But in NTK: (1) these numbers are not random, the server knows which numbers every user transmits, and (2) users that test positive upload the list of numbers *that they received*. Because the server can link numbers to people, such a system could potentially be used to track users. For example, law enforcement could request the list of numbers corresponding to a suspect and then use Bluetooth receivers to track that suspect. Indeed, both in Singapore[15] and Germany,[16] contact-tracing systems have been used to track people.

Additionally, because users that test positive upload the list of numbers that they received to a server and that server can relate numbers to people, the server can learn social interactions of positive users. Finally, the system can also know which users test positive and which have been notified.

Given this analysis, it is clear that data created and collected *within* the system can be used for purposes beyond notifying users. Thus, this system does not technically enforce purpose limitation.

---

14   Pan-European Privacy-Preserving Proximity Tracing (PEPP-PT), *High Level Overview*, 2022: https://github.com/pepp-pt/pepp-pt-documentation/blob/8ba05287c349318a03837fe374fd949e60d4eaf8/PEPP-PT-high-level-overview.pdf.
15   Mia Sato, "Singapore's police now have access to contact tracing data", *MIT Technology Review*, 5 January 2021: www.technologyreview.com/2021/01/05/1015734/singapore-contact-tracing-police-data-covid.
16   Rachel Pannett, "German police used a tracing app to scout crime witnesses. Some fear that's fuel for covid conspiracists", *Washington Post*, 13 January 2022: www.washingtonpost.com/world/2022/01/13/german-covid-contact-tracing-app-luca/.

6.4 THE ROLE OF DATA MINIMIZATION

Regulatory frameworks and researchers have proposed many principles to guide privacy and data protection practices. One of the key principles used to judge the privacy and data protection guarantees of a design is the data minimization principle.[17] It requires that data controllers collect data only when those data are necessary for the stated purpose. These data should be retained only for as long as is necessary to fulfil that purpose. This principle is also reflected in technical literature.[18]

Data minimization is indeed a necessary condition for a privacy-preserving design. Not collecting data that are unnecessary for the operation of the system, and deleting data that are no longer needed, reduces privacy risks for users of the system. Reducing the amount of information stored, for instance via aggregation or using privacy-preserving cryptography, also reduces the likelihood that users' privacy is breached and thus reduces the risk that their rights and dignity are affected.

At the same time, it is not always easy to apply the data minimization principle to assess the level of protection offered by a system. Consider a naive (non-private) contact-tracing system where apps send detailed information about contacts to a central server. The server then uses these data to identify and notify contacts of infected people. In this case, the server stores sensitive social interactions data. To minimize data collection and processing *at the server*, privacy-friendly designs let apps compute a user's exposure to the virus *locally* on the users' devices based on locally stored interaction records.

Here, a data minimization can quickly fall short. Surprisingly, when examining the privacy-friendly system as a whole – including users' devices and server – there is no data minimization. Both centralized and decentralized systems, when seen as a system, collect, process and store contact data. The difference is where these data are stored: centralized systems store most of these data at a central server, whereas the privacy-preserving systems distribute these data across user devices and the server.

As a result, applying the data minimization principle does not let an analyst distinguish between these two designs. Even though they obviously have very different privacy and data protection properties. The purpose limitation by design approach

---

17 See Section 2.5.4 — The principle of data minimization.
18 Hoepman mentions data minimization as one of the key techniques for creating privacy-friendly designs, and Gürses et al. argue that creating privacy-friendly designs requires thinking in terms of data minimization. See: Hoepman, "Privacy design strategies (Extended abstract)"; Gürses, Troncoso and Diaz, "Engineering privacy by design reloaded".

does not suffer from this problem. Moreover, any system that provides purpose limitation by design, also provides data minimization by design. Only data that are explicitly allowed by the purpose can be available at entities that are outside the user's control. If more data are available, purpose limitation is violated because these data could be used for other purposes.

6.5 CHALLENGES TO PURPOSE LIMITATION

The previous sections have shown how the principles of purpose limitation, and data minimization to a certain extent, can be used as guidance to design and evaluate whether a particular system design offers strong privacy protection and therefore can guarantee that rights and dignity are preserved. This section highlights aspects related to the design that may limit the designer's ability to implement purpose limitation, and therefore what an evaluator should look for to understand the level of protection offered by the system.

- **Lack of requirements or evolution of requirements.** In modern software development cycles, the requirements of the system are not fully fleshed out at the beginning of the design process. Instead, the designers augment and modify them in an *agile* manner. While this may be very desirable from a development and deployments perspective, the use of such development techniques greatly limits the privacy guarantees that a system can provide. If requirements are not clear, it is hard to identify the purpose and therefore design for purpose limitation. If the purpose has to remain flexible, then there is little that the designer can do to guarantee strong privacy and ultimately the protection of individuals' rights and dignity.
- **Reliance on Third Party services.** A second characteristic of modern software is that designers and developers do not program all modules in their system. Instead, they rely on tools, libraries or services programmed and executed by others. While this speeds up the development and ensures high-quality dedicated modules that offer very good performance at low cost, the use of these elements hinders the application of the purpose limitation system. These Third Party elements constrain, via their interfaces, what data the application can use, and in which format. This in turn limits the number of privacy-preserving technologies that the designer can use, as most will not be compatible with the requirements of the Third Party service.
- **All system layers play a role in data protection.** Humanitarian Organizations typically reason about privacy protection from the point of view of the application: what its is purpose, what data it requires, where these data are stored and processed, etc. In reality, the data of the application are a small portion of the overall (meta)data existent in the system that can lead to a breach of a Data Subject's rights and freedoms. In this sense, it is important to think about privacy as a *weakest link* property: either protection is ensured at all layers, or the users' protection is limited to the protection provided by the weakest of the layers.

6 DESIGNING FOR DATA PROTECTION

- For example, one of the risks in contact-tracing systems is that attackers learn which users tested positive (see Section 6.2.1 – Decentralized privacy-preserving proximity tracing). The weakest link here is not the application (which hides which users are positive from everyone but the server), but the network layer. Recall that only users that test positive upload data to the central server. Any network observer could thus conclude, based on the existence of this network traffic alone, that the user tested positive. Therefore, deployed systems use countermeasures against such network attackers.[19]
- **What is technologically viable.** Deciding which technologies to use in order to implement the strongest purpose limitation can be challenging. In many cases, the most constrained implementation requires the use of non-mainstream techniques, or the development of new technologies – as in the case of contact-tracing apps. Such knowledge may not be available to Humanitarian Organizations, and in many cases also not to the developers of the products they commission. Similar to the evaluation, Humanitarian Organizations may partner with academic institutions to gain knowledge on the possible technologies and designs. Even when those designs are not economically or operationally viable, knowledge of what would be the ideal situation may help the organization to be able to make better decisions as to whether a system is desirable or not.

---

19 See also: Section 5.2.5 – Identify risks.

DRONES

POSSIBLE USE

- SEARCH AND RESCUE OPERATIONS
- MAPPING EMERGENCY SITUATIONS
- COMPLEMENT TRADITIONAL ASSISTANCE
- MONITORING THE SPREAD OF DISEASE

CHALLENGES

- ISSUES OF TRANSPARENCY
- SENSITIVE INFORMATION
- LEGITIMATE PROCESSING AND EXERCISE OF RIGHTS
- CROWDSOURCING TO PROCESS AND ANALYSE BIG DATA

CHAPTER 7

DRONES/UAVS AND REMOTE SENSING

Massimo Marelli

7.1 INTRODUCTION

Drones are a promising and powerful technology potentially capable of helping Humanitarian Organizations to improve their situational awareness, their response to natural and man-made disasters, and their relief operations. They can complement traditional manned assistance by making operations more efficient, effective, faster and safer. If deployed correctly, Drones could have a significant impact on Humanitarian Action.

Drones are small aerial or non-aerial units that are remotely controlled or operate autonomously. They are also known as Unmanned Aerial Vehicles (UAVs) or Remotely Piloted Aircraft Systems (RPAS). Depending on what they are used for, they are often equipped with cameras, microphones, sensors or GPS devices, all or any of which may make Personal Data Processing possible.

From a data protection perspective various concerns have been raised about the use of Drones. However, it is important to clarify at this early stage that what is of interest in the case of Drones is not their use *per se*, but the different technologies they are equipped with, such as high-resolution cameras and microphones, thermal imaging equipment or devices to intercept wireless communications, because it is these technologies that are used for data collection and Processing. In this respect, the considerations addressed in this chapter could also apply to the use of satellites and, more generally, to remote sensing.

This chapter focuses only on the data protection issues posed by the use of Drones. Other issues and fields of law may be relevant, but will not be dealt with. For instance, guidance will not be provided on air traffic control issues, flight licences, equipment safety certificates or similar matters.

In general terms, the most common humanitarian use of Drones today entails observation and data collection to enhance situational awareness. Below is an indicative list of the applications for which Drones are or could be used in a humanitarian setting:
- search and rescue;
- determining the whereabouts of people unaccounted for;
- collection of aerial imagery/situation awareness/post-crisis assessment (e.g. surveying the condition of power lines and infrastructure, assessing the number of wounded people, destroyed homes, dead cattle, etc.);
- monitoring the spread of a disease through the use of heat sensors;
- mapping emergency housing settlements;
- real-time information and situation monitoring, by providing videos or photos and thus giving an overview;

- locating unexploded ordnance (UXO);
- mapping natural disasters or conflict sites;
- locating and following people displaced by a Humanitarian Emergency;
- delivery of medicines/other rescue equipment in remote areas;
- setting up a mesh network/restoring communication networks by relaying signals.

In disaster situations "drones may be used to provide relief workers with better situational awareness, as they can locate survivors amidst the rubble, perform structural analysis of damaged infrastructure, deliver needed supplies and equipment, evacuate casualties, and help extinguish fires – among many other potential applications".[1] Drones can also supply aerial data from areas which are considered unsafe for Humanitarian Action providers (e.g. sites contaminated by radioactivity or wildfire locations).[2]

Nevertheless, while Drones may be an invaluable source of direct and indirect information when responding to emergencies, a critical assessment has to be made before they are used in any particular case. Their use may include significant risks.[3] Apart from safety issues *per se* (e.g. accidents during their deployment that could result in bodily injury or even death), they may be perceived as spying or intruding in a conflict scenario, something that could severely compromise the safety of their operators and the staff of Humanitarian Organizations, as well jeopardizing local people who may be perceived by the parties in the conflict as having given Consent to the use of Drones on their behalf.

EXAMPLE:

A Humanitarian Organization may have acquired the approval of local community leaders for Drones to be used for the provision of aerial imagery over a large geographical area. However, during its deployment a Drone may accidentally photograph, and consequently provide evidence of, illegal activity taking place in some specific place in the above-mentioned geographical area. The groups carrying out the illegal activity, aware of the Drone flying over them, may seek to find and punish the

---

1 Joint Legislative Committee on Emergency Management and the Senate Committee on Judiciary, *Drones and Emergencies: Are We Putting Public Safety at Risk?*, in Oversight Hearing, Background Paper, California State Senate, 2015, 10: https://sjud.senate.ca.gov/sites/sjud.senate.ca.gov/files/background_paper_-_drones_and_emergencies.pdf.
2 American Red Cross, *Drones for Disaster Response and Relief Operations*, ed. Measure, a 32 Advisors Company, April 2015: www.issuelab.org/resources/21683/21683.pdf.
3 Florian Delafoi, "Le drone, l'allié ambigu des humanitaires", *Le Temps*, 11 April 2016, Online edition: www.letemps.ch/monde/drone-lallie-ambigu-humanitaires; ICTworks, "What Do Tanzanians Think about Drones? Now We Know", ICTworks (blog), 22 February 2016, www.ictworks.org/what-do-tanzanians-think-about-drones-now-we-know.

community leaders who provided their approval and also seek the Humanitarian Organization's operators in order to destroy the evidence collected.

As noted above, concerns about potential violations of Personal Data protection rights are not caused by the use of Drones, but rather by the on-board equipment which can process Personal Data. Information technologies embedded in Drones or connected to them can perform various data Processing activities and operations (e.g. data collection, recording, organization, storage and combination of collected data sets). Data typically collected by Drones include video recordings, "images (e.g. images of individuals, houses, vehicles, driving license plates, etc.), sound, geolocation data or any other electromagnetic signals related to an identified or identifiable natural person".[4] Depending on the quality of the data, it may be possible to identify individuals directly or indirectly. This can be done either by a human operator or automatically, for instance by capturing an image from a facial recognition program/algorithm, scanning to detect a smartphone and using it to identify the person or using radio-frequency identification (RFID) chips in passports.[5]

The following factors may be relevant while assessing Humanitarian Organizations' data protection response to the use of Drones:
- It is technically possible to make aerial Drones flight-specific, on the basis of unique identifiers embedded in their basic equipment.
- Permission to fly Drones and a remote pilot's licence issued by the state authorities are required in many countries.[6]
- Imagery data (of various levels of analysis and quality) are the most common type of data collected by Drones.
- Altitude of flight and angle of capture of the imagery also have a significant impact on the likelihood that the imagery captured may directly or indirectly identify an individual.
- Although technology is advancing rapidly, at present Drones can capture extremely detailed pictures, but most cannot capture individuals' faces. The picture has to be connected to other data sets in order to lead to identification. When facial identification is not possible, identification may be possible through the use of location and other types of data. The use of metadata (data that provide information about other data) is crucial in this context.

---

4 Article 29 Data Protection Working Party, *Opinion 01/2015 on Privacy and Data Protection Issues Relating to the Utilisation of Drones*, European Commission, 23 November 2016, 7: https://ec.europa.eu/newsroom/article29/items/640602.
5 Ibid., 14.
6 Storyhunter, "Storyhunter Guide to Commercial Drone Regulations around the World", Medium (blog), 3 April 2018: https://blog.storyhunter.com/storyhunter-guide-to-commercial-drone-regulations-around-the-world-5795c31165d9.

- It is important to establish where data collected are kept and what types of Processing are performed on them; in this respect there is a correlation between Drones and the use of Data Analytics.[7]
- A number of international initiatives on standards and other Drone-use specifications are currently under way, some looking specifically at the use of Drones for humanitarian purposes. Humanitarian Organizations are advised to follow these initiatives closely and apply their findings in their practices.[8]
- Humanitarian Organizations often outsource their drone operations to professionals, which therefore raises specific data protection issues (e.g. Data Controller/Data Processor relationship, access to data, etc.).
- Drone-related Personal Data Processing often involves cross-border transfers, which require a legal basis under data protection law.

However, it is worth noting that, given the pace of change in these technologies, a number of the above findings may change substantially in the near future.

Humanitarian Organizations should also take into account that, even when identification of individuals is not possible via the use of Drones, their use may still have substantial implications for the life, liberty and dignity of individuals and communities. Humanitarian Organizations should accordingly take precautions to protect Drone-collected data, even if the individuals recorded in them are not immediately identifiable.

EXAMPLE:
If the data from tracking streams of displaced people with Drones are accessed by ill-intentioned Third Parties, vulnerable individuals can be put at risk, even if they cannot be individually identified.

7.2 APPLICATION OF BASIC DATA PROTECTION PRINCIPLES

The data protection discussion in this chapter builds on the principles set out in Part I, which examines them in greater detail.

---

7   See Chapter 17: Artificial Intelligence.
8   See for example: "Guidelines", Humanitarian UAV Code of Conduct (blog), 6 December 2017: https://uavcode.org/further-guidance; "Humanitarian UAV Guidelines on Data Protection", Humanitarian UAV Code of Conduct (blog), 6 December 2017: https://uavcode.org/further-guidance/131-2.

7.2.1 LEGAL BASES FOR PERSONAL DATA PROCESSING

Humanitarian Organizations can process Personal Data collected by Drones using one or more of the following legal bases:[9]
- the vital interest of the Data Subject or of another person;
- the public interest, in particular stemming from an organization's mandate under national or international law;
- Consent;
- a legitimate interest of the organization;
- the performance of a contract;
- compliance with a legal obligation.

Lawfully acquiring Consent will most likely prove unrealistic in practice for work carried out by Humanitarian Organizations using Drones.

For example, Consent would not be "freely given" whenever an individual is not free to enter or leave a surveyed area.

This means that Consent as a lawful basis for Personal Data Processing in the context of Drone operations by Humanitarian Organizations seems to be generally unrealistic. Drones are used in most cases where there is limited or no access to communities. Even if such access was provided, it would still be almost impossible to obtain Consent from all the people who may potentially be affected by the Drone-related Processing. In addition, depending on the circumstances in which Drones might be used, it is questionable whether Consent from people in distress and in need of humanitarian assistance could be considered free.

The idea of acquiring the "Consent of the community" or the "Consent of authorities" has also been suggested for the use of Drones in Humanitarian Action as a plausible alternative to individual Consent. This could involve, for example, obtaining Consent only from representatives of a group of vulnerable individuals and not the individuals themselves. However, under data protection law Consent must be provided by the individual in order to be used as a valid legal basis.

EXAMPLE:
Community leaders or the state authorities concerned could give their Consent to the use of Drones by a Humanitarian Organization in order to map a refugee camp, but the individuals present in the area may not be aware of the Drones, or not wish to be photographed/have their Personal Data collected by Drones.

---

9   See Chapter 3: Legal bases for Personal Data Processing.

Where Consent cannot be obtained from the individual concerned, Personal Data can still be processed by the Humanitarian Organization if it establishes that Processing may be in the vital interest of the Data Subject or of another person, or if another legal basis applies (as noted in Section 7.2.1). In other words, Personal Data can be processed where the Processing is necessary in order to protect an interest which is essential for the Data Subject's life, integrity, health, dignity or security or that of another person.

As has already been mentioned in Chapter 3: Legal bases for Personal Data Processing, given the nature of Humanitarian Organizations' work and the emergency situations in which they operate, in some circumstances there may be a presumption that the Processing of data necessary for humanitarian purposes is in the vital interest of a Data Subject.[10]

The use of Drones by Humanitarian Organizations should be assessed in each particular case to determine whether it is actually necessary for the protection of the vital interests of the Data Subject or another person. The Drones' contribution to the protection of overriding private interests such as life, integrity and security has to be proven or, at least, be probable given the type and scale of the emergency, or concerns about a lack of information relating to the emergency, which could only be remedied by the use of Drones. Strict standards should therefore be applied to determine whether this legal basis is present.

EXAMPLES:
- The use of Drones in search and rescue operations by a Humanitarian Organization would most likely qualify under this legal basis, because it would protect the vital interest of the Data Subject (i.e. the person unaccounted for).
- The use of Drones in mapping operations by a Humanitarian Organization, in the absence of a specific emergency, would most likely not qualify under this legal basis, because there is no direct connection with the vital interests of the Data Subjects living or moving around in the areas being mapped.

It is important for Humanitarian Organizations to make careful assessments when important grounds of public interest are triggered and are to be used as a lawful basis for Processing Personal Data collected by Drones. For example, this will usually be the case when the activity in question is an important part of a humanitarian mandate established under national or international law (e.g. for the ICRC, IFRC, National Red Cross and Red Crescent Societies, UNHCR, UNICEF, WFP or IOM).

---

10 See EU, Regulation 2016/679 of the European Parliament and of the Council of 27 April 2016, Recital 46.

Humanitarian Organizations may also process Personal Data collected by Drones where this is in their legitimate interest, and provided that this interest is not overridden by the Data Subjects' fundamental rights and freedoms. A legitimate interest of an organization can be established when Personal Data Processing is necessary to further or support its mission. It can be argued, however, that where no public or vital interest can be established, it may be difficult to envision circumstances in which the rights and freedoms of the Data Subjects would not override the organization's legitimate interest, particularly in cases where the individuals whose Personal Data are likely to be captured cannot be informed, nor can they effectively exercise their data protection rights.

EXAMPLE:
A Humanitarian Organization may use a Drone to demonstrate successful completion of an action, for instance, to collect footage for a promotional video. This may fall under the legal basis of legitimate interest, although careful consideration of the potential infringement of the rights and freedoms of the individuals appearing in the video would need to be undertaken. In this respect, the extent to which Data Subjects can be informed and effectively exercise their rights (including the right to object) are critical factors.

7.2.2 TRANSPARENCY/INFORMATION

The principle of transparency requires that at least a minimum amount of information concerning the Processing be provided to the Data Subject. In addition, information and communications about the Processing should be easily accessible and easy to understand, expressed in clear and plain language. For obvious practical reasons these requirements can be difficult to satisfy in the case of Drones. Timing of information is also important: in non-emergency situations, this should ideally take place in advance of and during Drone flights. The involvement of community leaders and authorities or media campaigns targeted at the envisaged Data Subjects (e.g. radio, newspapers, and posters in public areas) can help fulfil transparency obligations.

EXAMPLE:
In order to fulfil transparency and information obligations, Humanitarian Organizations using Drones could affix their institutional marks and signs on them; maintain websites or provide relevant information on social media; use available local communication channels (e.g. radio, television, the press); and hold discussions with community leaders.

7.2.3 PURPOSE LIMITATION AND FURTHER PROCESSING

The specific purpose(s) for which Personal Data are collected should be explicit and legitimate. Humanitarian Organizations may use Drones for purposes such as the following:
- search and rescue;
- determining the whereabouts of people unaccounted for;
- collection of aerial imagery, situation awareness, post-crisis assessment (e.g. locating displaced people who need help, surveying the condition of power lines and infrastructure, assessing the number of wounded persons, destroyed homes, dead cattle, etc.);
- monitoring the spread of a disease through the use of heat sensors;
- crowd modelling in protests;
- mapping emergency housing settlements;
- real-time information and situation monitoring, by providing videos or photos and thus giving an overview;
- mapping of natural disasters or conflict sites;
- locating unexploded ordnance (UXO);
- locating and following people displaced by a Humanitarian Emergency;
- delivery of medicines and rescue equipment in remote areas;
- setting up a mesh network or restoring communication networks by relaying signals.

It was also established in Chapter 2: Basic principles of data protection that, irrespective of the legal basis used for the Processing, Humanitarian Organizations may process Personal Data for purposes other than those specified at the time of collection where such Further Processing is compatible with those initial purposes.

7.2.4 DATA MINIMIZATION

Personal Data may only be processed if adequate, relevant and not excessive in relation to the purposes for which they were collected. Therefore, a strict assessment of the necessity and proportionality of the processed data should take place.[11] Moreover, when Drones are used for humanitarian purposes, the principle of data minimization should be respected by choosing proportionate technology and by adopting measures of data protection and privacy by design and by default.

For instance, Humanitarian Organizations could consider the following options:
- Privacy settings on services and products should by default avoid the collection and/or the Further Processing of unnecessary Personal Data.
- Anonymization techniques should be implemented.
- Faces/human beings should be blurred automatically (or only certain particular categories of more vulnerable individuals).

---

11 See Chapter 2: Basic principles of data protection.

- Flight altitude or angle of capture of imagery should be increased to minimize the likelihood of capturing imagery that can directly identify individuals.

7.2.5 DATA RETENTION

Personal Data processed via Drones should not be stored for a period longer than necessary for the purpose of the Processing. In other words, collected data should be deleted or anonymized when the purpose for which they were collected has been served. The adoption of storage and deletion schedules is also advisable. Data collection devices, carried by Drones or connected to them remotely, should be designed in such a way that, should they need to retain data, a defined storage period for the Personal Data collected can be set and, as a result, Personal Data which are no longer necessary can be automatically deleted according to defined schedules.

> **EXAMPLE:**
> Data collected by Drones to help a Humanitarian Organization respond to an incident should, in principle, be deleted when the incident has been dealt with successfully; if the Humanitarian Organization wishes to archive this information (for instance, for historical purposes), it should take adequate measures to protect the integrity and security of the data and to prevent any unauthorized access.

7.2.6 DATA SECURITY

A Humanitarian Organization deploying Drones should implement adequate security measures that are appropriate for the risks involved.[12] For Drones, this could include encryption of databases or temporary storage devices on board, as well as end-to-end encryption of data in transit between the Drone and the base, where applicable.

7.3 RIGHTS OF DATA SUBJECTS

The rights of the Data Subject have already been described in Chapter 2: Basic principles of data protection. The following are some further remarks about Data Subjects' rights with respect to Humanitarian Organizations' use of Drones.[13]

As far as the right to information is concerned, Data Subjects exposed to Drone-related Processing should be provided with the following:
- the identity of the Data Controller of the Drone and of its representative;
- the purposes of the Processing;

---

12 See Chapter 2: Basic principles of data protection.
13 See Section 2.11 – Rights of Data Subjects.

- the categories of Personal Data collected;
- recipients or categories of recipients of the data;
- the existence of the right of access to and the right to specify and correct the data concerning them;
- the existence of the right to object, where this is realistic.

In practice, however, it could prove challenging for Humanitarian Organizations to provide Data Subjects with information along the above lines when using Drones to collect Personal Data. Nonetheless, the various options to be decided on a case-by-case basis could include information campaigns, public notices and other similar measures. Drone operators should publish information on their website or on dedicated platforms to inform individuals about the different operations that have taken place as well as forthcoming ones. In remote areas or where it is unlikely that individuals can access the Internet, information can be published in newspapers, leaflets or posters, or provided by means of a letter or radio broadcast.

As far as drone applications that may cover larger geographical areas are concerned, where the provision of information to Data Subjects proves difficult or impossible, the creation of a national or cross-national information resource (easier to trace than websites of single operators) has been suggested to enable individuals to identify the missions and operators associated with particular Drones.

Data Subjects should also have the right to opt out of the Processing, even though this can be challenging in the case of Drones, as individuals might not be able to avoid the surveyed area, or might not even be aware of the data collection through Drone sensors. Furthermore, Humanitarian Organizations are strongly encouraged to implement complaint procedures in their Personal Data Processing practices and internal data protection policies. These procedures should enable data correction and erasure. However, it should be recognized that there may be legal bases for data Processing that do not allow the exercise of all individual rights (for instance, requests for opt-outs by individuals may not be observed in the event of Processing undertaken under the public interest legal basis described above).

Finally, as far as the right to access information is concerned, access should be limited in order to mitigate the risks that access by one Data Subject could expose the Personal Data of other Data Subjects, or that ill-intentioned Data Subjects may take action detrimental to vulnerable individuals, whether identifiable or not.

Limiting access exclusively to aerial imagery or footage including Personal Data of a Data Subject is particularly challenging, since, by its nature, it may include Personal Data of many other individuals and it is highly unlikely that it may be practicably and meaningfully redacted.

EXAMPLE:
In the case of aerial photography collected by Drones, the exercise of the right to access by Data Subjects may require the blurring of other faces or Personal Data not related to the applicant; in the same cases, the right to object could include de-identification of the applicant's Personal Data on the same photograph, but not the destruction of the photograph itself or the Personal Data of other individuals appearing on it.

7.4 DATA SHARING

The circumstances under which personal information is exchanged between Humanitarian Organizations or between Humanitarian Organizations and Third Parties need to be identified and addressed with respect to data protection. Information collected by Drones may be shared either at the moment of collection or at a later stage. Humanitarian Organizations may outsource drone-related work to Data Processors. In the event that any of the above involves Personal Data being shared across national borders, the relevant issues concerning International Data Sharing also need to be addressed.[14]

In these cases, it is important to consider:
- the data protection roles of the Humanitarian Organizations concerned;[15]
- whether imagery or other information exchanged should include Personal Data or whether it is sufficient to share only the conclusions and findings of the analysis and assessment of the imagery collected (no raw data exchange);
- involuntary or accidental data sharing (e.g. if imagery is saved on the device and the device is captured), or if an aerial imagery feed is transmitted in a non-secure and unencrypted way; the impact of this should also be taken into consideration by the Humanitarian Organizations involved.

Crowdsourcing is a common way of Processing and analysing large data sets collected by Drones. Its importance derives from the fact that aerial imagery or footage is often massive and reviewing all this material is impossible for Humanitarian Organizations themselves. An increasingly common practice is to post the imagery online and invite volunteers to review it in order to spot, for instance, interrupted power lines, destroyed houses, affected people, and cattle, etc. However, this can have severe negative consequences (e.g. enabling access to online material by potentially ill-intentioned Third Parties). It is important, therefore, to ensure that:

---

14 See Chapter 4: International Data Sharing.
15 See Section 7.6 – Data Controller/Data Processor relationship.

- the volunteers accessing the imagery are vetted and trained by the Humanitarian Organization;
- the volunteers commit to a Processing agreement which includes provisions covering discretion and confidentiality;
- the material is not published or otherwise shared beyond the group of vetted volunteers;
- volunteers receive appropriate support to understand the purpose of the data Processing;
- volunteers' Processing is properly logged.

7.5 INTERNATIONAL DATA SHARING

Data protection law restricts International Data Sharing, so Humanitarian Organizations should have mechanisms in place to provide a legal basis for it when Drones are used, as discussed in Chapter 4: International Data Sharing. Humanitarian Organizations should examine whether International Data Sharing has a legal basis under applicable law and in line with their own internal policies before carrying it out. Performing a Data Protection Impact Assessment prior to the International Data Sharing concerned could further strengthen the lawfulness of such Processing.[16]

7.6 DATA CONTROLLER/DATA PROCESSOR RELATIONSHIP

The roles of Data Controller and Data Processor may be unclear when operating Drones or when Processing data collected by them. As noted, outsourcing is also frequent in Drone-related Processing. It is thus crucial to determine which parties actually determine the purposes and means of data Processing (and thus are Data Controllers), and which parties merely take instructions from Data Controllers (and thus are Data Processors). It is also possible that multiple parties might be considered to be joint Data Controllers.

EXAMPLES:
- A Humanitarian Organization whose own staff operate Drones for its own purposes is the (only) Data Controller for such Processing.
- A Humanitarian Organization outsourcing a Drone operation to a specialized corporation, whose sole task is to pilot the Drones, would be the (only) Data Controller for such Processing; the corporation would be the Data Processor for this operation.

---

16   See Section 7.7 – Data Protection Impact Assessments.

- Two Humanitarian Organizations who wish to use Drones and outsource all relevant operational work to a corporation having no access to the data collected will be joint Data Controllers. The corporation would be the Data Processor for the operation.

7.7 DATA PROTECTION IMPACT ASSESSMENTS

As discussed in Chapter 5: Data Protection Impact Assessments (DPIAs), DPIAs are important tools used during project design to ensure that all aspects of data protection regulations and applicable risks are addressed. Apart from clarifying the Processing details and specifications, DPIAs should focus on risks posed by the operation as well as on mitigating measures. In this regard, it is important to note that DPIAs should be drafted prior to any Drone operations.

In order to avoid hindering humanitarian operations, template DPIAs for the use of Drones should be developed beforehand. These templates should cover the specific risks and considerations outlined in the present chapter and be easy and quick to complete and implement.

BIOMETRICS

SENSITIVITY LEVEL

POSSIBLE USE

EFFICIENTLY IDENTIFIES INDIVIDUALS

UNIQUELY IDENTIFIES INDIVIDUALS WITHOUT OTHER MEANS OF PROVING WHO THEY ARE

CHALLENGES

DATA MINIMIZATION

RELIABILITY OF DATA

TECHNICAL DIFFICULTIES

IRREVERSIBLE

DIFFICULTIES WITH CONSENT

HUMANITARIAN PURPOSE ETHICAL ISSUES

CHAPTER 8
BIOMETRICS
Massimo Marelli*

---

* The author thanks Vincent Graf Narbel and Justinas Sukaitis for the input and feedback.

8.1 INTRODUCTION

The International Organization for Standardization defines biometric recognition and Biometrics as the "automated recognition of individuals based on their biological and behavioural characteristics".[1] Biometrics are therefore measurable and unique human signatures that may include fingerprints, iris scans or behavioural characteristics such as the way a person walks.

The data protection implications of the use of biometric data, with particular reference to the use of biometric data in passports, identity cards and travel documents, have been highlighted by the International Conference of Data Protection and Privacy Commissioners in its Resolution on Biometrics, adopted in Montreux, Switzerland, in 2005.[2]

Humanitarian Organizations around the world increasingly deploy biometric recognition as part of their identification systems because of the benefits it can bring in efficiently identifying individuals and preventing fraud and/or misuse of humanitarian aid. Indeed, paper-based identification mechanisms (identity cards, ration cards, wrist bands, etc.) that constitute the non-digital alternative have limitations, as they may easily be lost or counterfeited, require substantial resources to cross-check (thereby giving rise to potential duplication and inefficiency) and in most cases do not allow for automated Processing. In certain situations, it is suggested that these shortcomings may be overcome through the use of biometric identification systems (often as an additional means of verification). Biometric data are more difficult to counterfeit and, being digitally produced and stored, facilitate the efficient management of humanitarian aid in the field and can also be used for Data Analytics or other types of advanced data Processing operations. In addition, by focusing on the individual's unique features, Biometrics can confirm the identity of individuals who have no other means of adequately proving it, which is often the case with displaced people, and therefore put individual identity and dignity at the heart of Humanitarian Action.[3]

---

1 See International Organization for Standardization ISO/IEC 2382-37:2022 Information Technology - Vocabulary. Part 37: Biometrics. March 2022: https://www.iso.org/standard/73514.html.
2 International Conference of Data Protection and Privacy Commissioners, *Resolution on Use of Biometrics in Passports, Identity Cards and Travel Documents*, Resolution, 27th International Conference of Data Protection and Privacy Commissioners, Montreux, 16 September 2005: https://edps.europa.eu/sites/default/files/publication/05-09-16_resolution_biometrics_en.pdf.
3 See for example: Hugo Slim, "Eye Scan Therefore I Am: The Individualization of Humanitarian Aid", European University Institute (blog), 15 March 2015: https://iow.eui.eu/2015/03/15/eye-scan-therefore-i-am-the-individualization-of-humanitarian-aid; Paul Currion, "Eyes wide shut: The challenge of humanitarian biometrics", *The New Humanitarian* (formerly *IRIN News*), 26 August 2015, Online edition, sec. Solutions and Innovations | Opinions: www.thenewhumanitarian.org/opinion/2015/08/26/eyes-wide-shut-challenge-humanitarian-biometrics.

However, these promises have not always been fulfilled in the actual deployment of Biometrics identification systems. Some projects to implement Biometrics have reportedly faced considerable problems with regard to the reliability of the relevant systems.[4] Inherent limitations, such as the fact that individuals' fingerprints are not always readable, provide further difficulties in implementation. Ethical issues also arise, for example, by virtue of the use of biometric data in national identification systems and the problematic legacies of such systems in certain countries.[5] Additionally, due to the interest in biometric data for national law enforcement and national security purposes, Humanitarian Organizations may find themselves under increasing pressure to share data with national and regional authorities for purposes which go beyond humanitarian work. At the same time, Third Parties may be interested in accessing biometric data also through unauthorized means, for example through hacking.

Humanitarian Organizations may use biometric technologies for Processing operations such as the collection and management of data on displaced persons who have to be registered for the purposes of humanitarian aid distribution, including aid delivered through cash and vouchers.[6]

At the current state of technological development technologies used for the above Processing operations involve mainly automatic fingerprint recognition systems (fingerprints being the dominant form of biometric data collected) and iris scans. Other forms of biometric data could, however, be envisaged, including:
- palm vein recognition;
- voice recognition;
- facial recognition;
- behavioural characteristics.

The benefits of the use of biometric technologies by Humanitarian Organizations could include:
- accurate individual identification;
- combatting fraud and corruption;
- increased donor support and credibility of programming (as a consequence of the points above);
- greater efficiency through the digital Processing of identification data;
- greater efficiency in the physical protection of individuals/minimization of the risk of disappearance;
- putting individual identity and dignity at the heart of Humanitarian Action;
- enhancing the right of individuals to move freely;

---

4   Gus Hosein and Carly Nyst, *Aiding Surveillance*, Privacy International, 1 November 2013: http://privacyinternational.org/report/841/aiding-surveillance.
5   Ibid., 19.
6   See Chapter 9: Cash and Voucher Assistance.

- enhancing the resettlement of individuals into third countries;
- enabling bank account acquisition.

However, a number of risks and challenges have equally been raised:
- reliability and accuracy of data (including the risk of false matches) and/or of systems – the quality of the biometric identification system ultimately depends upon the quality of the sensors used and the quality of the Biometrics provided;
- inherent technical difficulties (e.g. the unreadability of fingerprints in the case of certain people with depleted fingerprints);
- biometric information is unique and cannot be modified, consequently resulting in data leaks exposing affected persons to potential identity thefts through the synthetization of the biometric information;
- hardware and software modules of most current biometric systems are incompatible across different solution providers and thus may lock the Humanitarian Organization into a single vendor;
- as biometric data contains inherently more information about the individual than what is strictly necessary for authentication and even identification purposes (e.g. health-related information), Biometrics are excessive by nature;
- ethical issues (cultural sensitivities, affected people's perceptions and/or concerns about surveillance);
- function creep (same systems used for other purposes than the ones originally designated, including non-humanitarian purposes);
- possible pressure by various national or regional authorities (including donors) to acquire the biometric data sets collected by Humanitarian Organizations, with the risk of the data being used for purposes other than strictly humanitarian purposes (e.g. law enforcement, security, border control or monitoring migration flows).

It is very important, therefore, that Humanitarian Organizations carefully analyse and consider the possible need for the use of biometric data, and clearly and transparently set out how they intend to use them in a way that is compatible with Data Protection requirements, ideally through public policies on the use of biometric data.[7]

8.2 APPLICATION OF BASIC DATA PROTECTION PRINCIPLES

The use of biometric technologies raises significant data protection issues. Biometric information is considered to be Personal Data and therefore covered by data

---

7   See for example: Massimo Marelli and Ben Hayes, "Facilitating Innovation, Ensuring Protection: The ICRC Biometrics Policy", Humanitarian Law & Policy Blog (blog), 18 October 2019: https://blogs.icrc.org/law-and-policy/2019/10/18/innovation-protection-icrc-biometrics-policy.

protection legislation. For example, the EU General Data Protection Regulation expressly regulates biometric data, defining them as "Personal Data resulting from specific technical Processing relating to the physical, physiological or behavioural characteristics of a natural person, which allow or confirm the unique identification of that natural person, such as facial images or dactyloscopic data".[8] In many legal systems, biometric information is considered "Sensitive Data".[9] Consequently, special, detailed requirements apply to the Processing of this type of data, directly affecting the lawfulness of the Processing in the event that they are not met.

This higher level of protection is justified due to the following special characteristics of biometric information:
- it is unique and cannot be modified, consequently increasing the risks involved in identity theft; and
- technological developments may affect its Processing in unpredictable ways, because the type of personal biometric data collected today may reveal a great deal more information about an individual in the future (e.g. retina information revealing genetic information, ethnic origin, health conditions and age).

Accordingly, while a basic assumption underlying this Handbook is that it is not possible in Humanitarian Action to establish clear-cut categories of Personal Data requiring special protection (because data that may not be sensitive in one emergency situation may be sensitive in another and vice versa), there is an assumption that biometric data require special protection, irrespective of the situation and the circumstances. It is for this reason that DPIAs should always be carried out before Biometrics are used.

When undertaking DPIAs, Humanitarian Organizations should take into account the fact that different types of biometric data may have different levels of "sensitivity". Some categories of biometric data, while sensitive for the reasons set out above, may be more or less sensitive than others. Fingerprints, for example, may be depleted or erased, whether unintentionally (e.g. through heavy manual work) or intentionally, thus making this type of data less sensitive than others. Iris scans may potentially enable the extraction of very sensitive information beyond the identification of the individual. Furthermore, certain types of biometric data may only be collected and read with the direct participation of a Data Subject, such as palm vein recognition, thus making this type of data less sensitive than others. Other categories of biometric data, such as iris information, can be read from a distance, thus making it particularly sensitive.[10]

---

8   EU Regulation 2016/679 of the European Parliament and of the Council of 27 April 2016, Article 4(14).
9   For example, in the EU, biometric data are considered to be a special category of Personal Data: EU Regulation 2016/679 of the European Parliament and of the Council of 27 April 2016, Article 9.
10   See for example: Patrick Tucker, "How Facial Recognition Might Stop the Next Brussels", Defense One, 22 March 2016: www.defenseone.com/technology/2016/03/how-facial-recognition-might-stop-next-brussels/126883.

Consequently, even when the legislation governing Personal Data Processing mentioned above does not apply, Processing biometric data presents special risks and requires an increased level of care. Processing should therefore be subject to a careful preliminary review, in order to establish whether certain safeguards (for example, increased security measures) need to be in place before, during and after its execution, as discussed further below, or if biometric data should be used at all, considering the potential risks involved.

The data protection discussion in this chapter builds on the principles set out in Part I, which examines them in greater detail.

8.2.1 LEGAL BASES FOR PERSONAL DATA PROCESSING

Humanitarian Organizations may process Personal Data using one or more of the following legal bases:[11]

- the vital interest of the Data Subject or of another person;
- the public interest;
- Consent;
- a legitimate interest of the Organization;
- the performance of a contract;
- compliance with a legal obligation.

As discussed in Chapter 3: Legal bases for Personal Data Processing, it may be difficult to prove validity of Consent in a humanitarian situation. However, biometric data are considered to be Sensitive Data, and therefore Data Controllers should obtain the Data Subjects' Consent. In addition, given that biometric information may only be collected directly from the individuals concerned, and in contrast to some other methods of data collection and Processing, it is generally feasible for Humanitarian Organizations to obtain Consent to use biometric data. However, it will not always be possible for Humanitarian Organizations to collect unambiguous, free, informed and documented Consent for the Processing of biometric data, for reasons also set out in Chapter 3: Legal Bases for Personal Data Processing, such as:

- the individuals' physical inability to provide it, such as in cases of unconscious patients (where, for example, biometric data may be required to unlock a patient medical file, combined with other legitimate authority to unlock);
- the shortage of time and staff to ensure adequate counselling during the first phases of an emergency, when the priority is to provide life-saving assistance;
- the individuals' vulnerability and/or legal inability to provide it;
- the highly technical and irreversible nature of the data potentially exposing individuals to risks that are difficult to understand or contemplate when Consent is given. This refers particularly to the possibility that science and technology may

---

11 See Chapter 3: Legal bases for Personal Data Processing.

develop in ways that pose new risks not foreseen at the time of Consent (e.g. genetic information becoming accessible from a scan of an individual's iris);
- no real choice is provided as to alternative ways of receiving assistance or protection (for example, if you are dependent on humanitarian aid for your survival or that of your family, or if you need to register to remain legally in the country in which you are located, there is very limited opportunity for you to refuse the collection of your biometric data).

When valid Consent cannot be obtained from the individual, i.e. the Data Subject, Personal Data can still be processed by the Humanitarian Organization concerned if it establishes that it is necessary for reasons of substantial public interest or that it is in the vital interest of the Data Subject or of another person, i.e. where data Processing is necessary in order to protect an interest which is essential for the Data Subject's life, integrity, health, dignity or security, or that of another person.

In some cases, the nature of Humanitarian Organizations' work and the emergency conditions in which they operate in armed conflicts and other situations of violence lead to a presumption that their Processing of Personal Data is in the vital interest of a Data Subject or another person (for instance, in cases of imminent threats against the physical and mental integrity of the persons concerned).

It could be argued that in difficult conditions, because of the effectiveness of Biometrics to identify individuals, the vital interests of the Data Subject or another person might constitute a plausible alternative legal basis for the relevant Processing in cases when Humanitarian Organizations are unable to obtain the individuals' Consent. Furthermore, it is possible to imagine a situation in which the use of biometric systems can be arguably be justified by the promotion of the person's vital interests. For example, if only limited resources are available for Humanitarian Action and some potential beneficiaries do not receive essential assistance because aid is fraudulently overprovisioned to another group of individuals, biometric systems can facilitate accurate resource allocation and fraud prevention. On the other hand, it can also be argued that biometric data are not essential for the purposes of distributing aid. The use of biometric data responds more to the Humanitarian Organizations' need to carry out their work in an efficient and effective manner, avoiding the risk of duplication and the waste of financial resources, rather than responding to the vital interests of the individuals concerned.

In addition, it is important to clarify the life cycle of biometric data. If these data are intended to be used for the entire duration of an individual's life, then the legal basis of that person's vital interest will most likely not be applicable, and Consent should be acquired instead.

A final consideration in this area relates to the intrinsic value of biometric data in establishing a clear and univocal identity to persons affected by Humanitarian

Emergencies and the role that this could have in restoring and/or strengthening their dignity and protecting their rights over their data. In this light, the vital interests of the individual as Data Subject may indeed be at stake.

In some cases, important grounds of public interest may be used as the legal basis for Processing biometric data. For example, this will usually be the case when the activity in question is part of a humanitarian mandate established in national or international law. Cases where this may be relevant include distributions of assistance, where it may not be possible to obtain the Consent of the people concerned. It is important to note that if the life, security, dignity, and integrity of the Data Subject or of other people are at stake, then vital interest may be the most appropriate legal basis.

Public interest could constitute the suitable legal basis for Processing biometric data where a mandate to carry out Humanitarian Action is established in national, regional, or international law, and where Consent and or vital interest do not apply, as per the cases discussed above.

Humanitarian Organizations may also process Personal Data where this is in their legitimate interest, provided that this interest is not overridden by the fundamental rights and freedoms of the Data Subject. Such legitimate interests may include Processing necessary to increase the efficiency of the delivery of humanitarian assistance, reduce costs, and risks of duplication and fraud. However, considering that biometric data can be used for potentially intrusive purposes and given the specific features highlighted above, it can be questioned whether the rights and freedoms of a Data Subject do not always override the legitimate interests set out above. Before the legitimate interests of the Data Controller can be used as a legal basis, a careful analysis of the risks and of possible interference with the fundamental rights and freedoms of the Data Subject would have to be included in the relevant DPIA. This is particularly important in cases where there is a credible risk that Third Parties could gain unauthorized access to the data, or put pressure on Humanitarian Organizations to provide such highly Sensitive Data and use them for purposes other than exclusively humanitarian purposes.

8.2.2 FAIR AND LAWFUL PROCESSING

Under data protection law, Personal Data need to be processed lawfully and fairly.[12] Lawfulness of the Processing refers to the identification of an appropriate legal basis. The requirement for fairness is generally connected to the provision of information as well as to the uses of the data. Humanitarian Organizations involved in biometric

---

12 See Section 2.5.1 – The principle of the fairness and lawfulness of Processing, and Section 8.2.2 – Fair and lawful Processing.

8.2.3 PURPOSE LIMITATION AND FURTHER PROCESSING

As discussed in Chapter 2: Basic principles of data protection, at the time of collecting Personal Data the Humanitarian Organization concerned should determine and set out the specific purpose(s) for which data are processed. The specific purpose(s) should be explicit and legitimate and could include humanitarian purposes such as distributing humanitarian assistance, restoring family links, protecting individuals in detention, providing medical assistance or forensic activities.

The purposes of the Processing need to be clearly communicated to individuals at the time of collection. Given that biometric information is used for individual identification, the purposes of the Processing should refer to the initial purposes of the identification (e.g. identification itself or aid disbursement, whether through in-kind items or cash payments).

Personal Data may be processed for purposes other than those initially specified at the time of collection where the Further Processing is compatible with those purposes, including where the Processing is necessary for historical, statistical or scientific purposes. In order to establish whether Further Processing is compatible with the purpose for which the data were initially collected, attention should be paid to the following factors:
- any link between the purposes for which the data were collected and the purposes of the intended Further Processing;
- to what extent the Further Processing is humanitarian in nature;
- the situation in which the Personal Data were collected, in particular regarding the relationship between Data Subjects and the Data Controller;
- the nature of the Personal Data;
- the possible consequences or risks of the intended Further Processing for Data Subjects;
- the existence of appropriate safeguards;
- the reasonable expectation of the Data Subjects as to possible further uses of the data.

EXAMPLE:
If a Biometrics identification system is deployed for aid distribution by a Humanitarian Organization, and the individuals concerned have consented to this, the same system cannot be used to transmit participants' data to donors of the Humanitarian Organization for cross-referencing purposes, unless the participants also consented to this purpose.

In considering the above factors, the humanitarian aspects of the Processing purpose should be given particular consideration.

As explained above,[13] purposes within the wider category of "humanitarian purposes" are likely to be compatible with Further Processing operations. This would, however, not be the case if new risks are involved, or if the risks for the individuals concerned outweigh the benefits of Further Processing. This assessment would depend on the circumstances of the case, and include an analysis of any risks that Processing may be against significant interests of the person to whom the information relates or his/her family, in particular, when there is a risk that the Processing may threaten their life, integrity, dignity, psychological or physical security, liberty or reputation.

In the same vein, Further Processing for non-humanitarian purposes (e.g. for law enforcement or national security, security checks, migration flux management or asylum claims) should be deemed to be incompatible with the initial Processing undertaken by the Humanitarian Organization. Similarly, purposes which could be interpreted as humanitarian purposes, but involving new risks for the individuals, such as migration management and asylum claims, or identification by authorities, cannot be deemed to constitute compatible Further Processing.

8.2.4 DATA MINIMIZATION

The Personal Data processed should be adequate and relevant for the purposes for which they are collected. In particular, this means ensuring that the data collected are not excessive and that the time period for which the data are stored is limited to the minimum necessary. The amount of Personal Data collected and processed should, ideally, be limited to what is necessary to fulfil the specified purpose of data collection and data Processing or compatible Further Processing.

Biometric information collected for identification purposes needs to be proportionate to these purposes. This means that only the amount of biometric information necessary for the identification of individuals needs to be collected and processed; any information not relevant to the identification should be seen as "in excess" and not be collected and, if collected, should be deleted. In particular, once the raw biometric data have been processed and are ready to be stored for further use for authentication or identification purposes, any intermediary or original raw biometric data should be deleted.

Similarly, the range of biometric data sets collected should be limited to what is proportionate (e.g. collecting facial imagery or iris scans may not be considered as

---

13   See Section 8.2.3 – Purpose limitation and Further Processing.

proportionate if photos and fingerprints are already being used for identification purposes).

Compartmentalization of data collected within a Biometrics system (i.e. with access being provided on a need-to-know basis) could provide a meaningful way for Humanitarian Organizations to address data minimization requirements.

Finally, when designing a programme involving biometric data collection, the data minimization principle should guide Humanitarian Organizations to collect as few biometric identifiers as possible in order to achieve the purpose of identification for the specific Humanitarian Action.

> **EXAMPLE:**
> For the purposes of identifying a specific person and avoiding fraud and duplication, collection of one source of biometric data may be sufficient (such as one fingerprint), and collection of a combination of more than one fingerprint and iris may be disproportionate and in breach of the data minimization principle.

8.2.5 DATA RETENTION

Biometric information poses security challenges that may be addressed through either deletion or destruction after completion of their Processing or a carefully structured data retention policy, which would describe the conditions for deletion or destruction or other options to be applied, such as de-identification or access restriction. Retention for Further Processing, therefore, should be avoided, unless such Further Processing is clearly defined and required within the necessary retention period for the purposes for which the data were originally collected. Humanitarian Organizations need to develop their own internal data retention policies, based on the type of data collected and their potential uses in the future.

8.2.6 DATA SECURITY

Given the sensitive nature of biometric information as well as its potential misuse if unauthorized access is granted to it or otherwise obtained,[14] it is imperative that adequate, proportionate security measures are implemented by the Humanitarian Organization determining the purposes and means of the Processing (i.e. by the Data Controller). For example, encryption or compartmentalization of information could constitute viable solutions to this end for Humanitarian Organizations.

---

14 Sarah Soliman, "Tracking Refugees with Biometrics: More Questions than Answers", War on the Rocks (blog), 9 March 2016: https://warontherocks.com/2016/03/tracking-refugees-with-biometrics-more-questions-than-answers.

8.2.7 "EXCESSIVENESS" BY NATURE

Part of the reason behind the sensitivity of biometric information is the fact that it involves excessive Processing by nature. Biometric systems and biometric information involve an intrinsic link between the data and the individual the data originate from. In the current state-of-the-art of biometric technology, Processing biometric data involves, by nature, Processing more information about the individual than is strictly necessary for authentication and, in the vast majority of cases, also for identification purposes. The data may reveal the individual's health, gender, ethnicity and other personal information.[15]

Though the risk may never be fully alleviated, Humanitarian Organizations should reach for a higher level of data security for Biometrics or even re-evaluate whether their needs and identified benefits for affected persons and communities outweigh this intrinsic risk.

8.3 RIGHTS OF DATA SUBJECTS

The rights of the Data Subject as described in Chapter 2: Basic principles of data protection, include the rights to information, access, correction, deletion and objection.

With regard to the right to information, when data are collected directly from the individuals concerned, such as in the case of biometric data, it is often easier for Data Controllers to provide them with adequate information as to the details of Processing. The level of information to be provided if data are processed on the basis of Consent will be high, considering the significant additional risks involved. This should include information as to the possible implications of biometric data being accessed by Third Parties as part of the Processing required to implement the Biometrics project. Additional access by Third Parties may not be contemplated initially, nor the possible consequences known. This may be the case, for example, when sharing biometric data of displaced people with the concerned states to facilitate resettlement. This scenario, not anticipated at the time of collection, would require a separate Consent collection after the initial registration/biometric enrolment.

Adequate infrastructure should be put in place to facilitate the rights to access, objection, deletion and rectification when Biometrics are used. In this regard, it is

---

[15] Daniel Hartung and Christoph Busch, "Why Vein Recognition Needs Privacy Protection", IEEE Press, 2009, pp. 1090–1095: https://doi.org/10.1109/IIH-MSP.2009.132; Justinas Sukaitis, "Building a Path towards Responsible Use of Biometrics", thesis, EPFL, Lausanne, 2021: https://infoscience.epfl.ch/record/285077; Stelvio Cimato et al., "Privacy in biometrics", in Nikolaos V. Boulgouris, Konstantinos N. Plataniotis and Evangelia Micheli-Tzanakou (eds.), *Biometrics: Fundamentals, Theory, and Systems*, Wiley–IEEE Press, Hoboken, NJ, 2010, 633–654.

advisable to define complaint procedures in internal data protection policies and implement them in Personal Data Processing practices.

8.4 DATA SHARING

Biometrics Processing may include data sharing with Third Parties in the following scenarios:
- The Humanitarian Organization hires an external Data Processor to provide the Biometrics technology required to collect and process the data. In this case a Data Controller/Data Processor relationship is established.
- The Humanitarian Organization carries out a transfer of data to a Third Party, which becomes a new Data Controller.
- The authorities of the host country request or require a copy of biometric data collected on their territory, either in bulk or for specific individuals.

It is important to take into consideration data protection requirements before undertaking such sharing, and to note that "sharing" includes not only situations where data are actively transferred to Third Parties, but also those when they are made accessible to others. Because of the sensitivity of Biometrics data, particular caution should be used before any data sharing is carried out.

8.5 INTERNATIONAL DATA SHARING

Biometric information Processing may involve the sharing of Personal Data with various parties located in different countries, such as in the case of International Data Sharing among different Humanitarian Organizations, or International Data Sharing among Humanitarian Organizations and private or public sector Third Parties.

Data protection laws restrict International Data Sharing and Humanitarian Organizations should have mechanisms in place to provide a legal basis for it when Biometrics are used, as discussed above.[16] Humanitarian Organizations should examine whether International Data Sharing has a legal basis under applicable law and their own internal policies before carrying it out. Performing a DPIA[17] prior to the International Data Sharing concerned could further strengthen the lawfulness of such Processing from a data protection perspective.

---

16   See Section 8.2.1 – Legal bases for Personal Data Processing.
17   See Section 8.7 – Data Protection Impact Assessments.

8.6 DATA CONTROLLER/DATA PROCESSOR RELATIONSHIP

The deployment of biometric identification systems by a Humanitarian Organization may involve outsourcing work to local operators for project implementation on-site. These highly sophisticated technologies require the support of specialized technology providers. Humanitarian Organizations may also cooperate among themselves in sharing databases of biometric information (see above). State authorities (for example, law enforcement agencies) may apply pressure on Humanitarian Organizations to access biometric information held by them (for example, when people migrate and/or are forcibly displaced), either in bulk or for specific individuals.

In view of the above, it is crucial to define which parties actually determine the purposes and means of data Processing (and thus are Data Controllers), and which merely take instructions from Data Controllers (and thus are Data Processors). When the roles have been clearly defined and the corresponding tasks assigned, International Data Sharing across Humanitarian Organizations and/or national borders and/or private or public sector Third Parties should only take place if appropriate contractual clauses are concluded, that set forth the responsibilities of the parties. It should also be carefully established whether any Data Processors engaged are in a position to fully comply with security and segregation requirements. This is particularly important for biometric technologies, when some Data Processors may manage work outsourced from multiple Data Controllers and, where such Data Controllers include both Humanitarian Organizations and authorities, the risks that the data sets may not be properly segregated should be carefully assessed. DPIAs, drafted prior to the Processing of Biometrics data, may be a suitable means of clarifying the roles of different parties engaged in the Processing.

8.7 DATA PROTECTION IMPACT ASSESSMENTS

Data Protection Impact Assessments (DPIAs) are important tools during project design to ensure that all aspects of data protection regulations and the specific risks, highlighted above, are addressed.

It is essential to carry out DPIAs whenever biometric information is processed by Humanitarian Organizations. DPIAs should clarify the Processing details and specifications, and highlight the potential risks and possible mitigating measures, so as to determine whether biometric data should be collected and, if so, what kind of safeguards should be put in place. It is important to note that DPIAs should be conducted prior to the Biometrics Processing.

CASH TRANSFER PROGRAMMING
POSSIBLE USE
SUPPORTING LOCAL MARKETS
GIVING PEOPLE CHOICE
TRANSPARENCY AS TO HOW MUCH AID REACHES BENEFICIARIES
CHALLENGES
MORE PERSONAL DATA COMPARED TO AID IN KIND
ACTIVE, INFORMED CONSENT CAN BE DIFFICULT TO OBTAIN
DATA RETENTION
DATA SHARING
INCOMPATIBLE FURTHER USE

CHAPTER 9
CASH AND VOUCHER ASSISTANCE

Massimo Marelli

9.1 INTRODUCTION

Cash and Voucher Assistance[1] are a set of promising tools for supporting processes of survival and recovery from Humanitarian Emergencies. The terms Cash and Voucher Assistance, Cash Transfer Programming, cash-based interventions and cash-based assistance can be used interchangeably and are understood to encapsulate all types of cash transfers, i.e. both vouchers and cash, and all types of physical and digital delivery mechanisms.[2]

Cash transfers maximize the respect for affected people's choices and the trade-offs they face. The world of humanitarian response continues to use several different varieties of Cash and Voucher Assistance, ranging from vouchers that have to be exchanged for specific products or services from specific suppliers, to cash transfers that are made conditional on beneficiaries meeting some kind of requirement, or unrestricted and unconditional cash transfers that can be spent on anything affected people require.[3]

There are different forms of digitally delivered cash assistance, all of which is spent without restrictions, such as electronic cash (e-cash), which is a monetary value sent to people that can be spent digitally, or converted into hard cash (e.g. mobile money, pre-paid cards, bank transfers); and electronic vouchers, which are sent to people (through smart cards or mobile phones) that can be exchanged with approved merchants for approved items, with restrictions on spending possible.[4] Hard cash is sometimes also used, as well as paper vouchers.

It is widely recognized that the effectiveness and appropriateness of humanitarian aid provided through Cash and Voucher Assistance depends on the situation (e.g. can individuals obtain the items they need in a particular situation?).[5] Although some concerns have been raised about Cash and Voucher Assistance (e.g. inflation of the

---

1 Since the second edition of this Handbook, the terminology in the humanitarian sector has evolved: "Cash Transfer Programming" is more commonly referred to as "Cash and Voucher Assistance".
2 See Cash Learning Partnership (CaLP), "Cash Transfers Glossary", accessed 20 January 2022: www.humanitarianresponse.info/sites/www.humanitarianresponse.info/files/documents/files/calp-glossary_of_cash_transfer_programme_terminology.pdf.
3 The High Level Panel on Humanitarian Cash Transfers, "Doing Cash Differently: How Cash Transfers Can Transform Humanitarian Aid", Center For Global Development, London, 14 September 2015, 11: www.cgdev.org/publication/doing-cash-differently-how-cash-transfers-can-transform-humanitarian-aid.
4 European Commission, *10 common principles for multi-purpose cash-based assistance to respond to humanitarian needs*, March 2015: http://ec.europa.eu/echo/files/policies/sectoral/concept_paper_common_top_line_principles_en.pdf; European Commission, *The use of cash and vouchers in humanitarian crises*. DG ECHO Funding Guidelines, 11 March 2013: http://ec.europa.eu/echo/files/policies/sectoral/ECHO_Cash_Vouchers_Guidelines.pdf.
5 Paul Harvey and Sarah Bailey, "Cash Transfer Programming and the Humanitarian System", Background Note for the High Level Panel on Humanitarian Cash Transfers, Overseas Development Institute, London, March 2015: https://odi.org/en/publications/cash-transfer-programming-and-the-humanitarian-system.

local market), there is evidence supporting it as a "good value for money compared to in-kind alternatives".[6]

Research has shown that the greater use of humanitarian cash transfers where appropriate, without restrictions and delivered as electronic payments wherever possible, has benefits such as the following:[7]
- providing crisis-affected people with choice and greater control over their own lives;
- aligning the humanitarian system better with what people actually need;
- increasing the transparency of humanitarian aid and the prevention of fraud, by showing how much aid actually reaches the target population;
- increasing accountability of humanitarian aid, both to affected populations and to the tax-paying public in donor countries;
- potentially reducing the costs of delivering humanitarian aid to make limited budgets go further;
- supporting local markets, jobs and the incomes of local producers;
- increasing support for humanitarian aid from local people;
- increasing the speed and flexibility of humanitarian response;
- increasing financial inclusion by linking people with payment systems.

However, a number of difficulties and challenges also exist. Using Cash and Voucher Assistance in some Humanitarian Emergencies may not be an optimal solution (for example, in cases where the goods and services needed are not available, where local authorities oppose this type of humanitarian aid, or where the relevant market is at a risk of inflation).[8] Cash transfers are simply a tool to reach a programme objective, and so cash transfers are used as part of broader humanitarian assistance programmes, including measures providing protection, sanitation or health services.[9]

For Cash and Voucher Assistance to function, Humanitarian Organizations need to process individuals' Personal Data. This often includes data about an individual's or group's socioeconomic status and vulnerabilities. This poses inherent privacy-related threats and risks associated with the collection and handling of beneficiaries' Personal Data, in particular in light of the complex data flows they involve. Moreover, the use of digital technologies for Cash and Voucher Assistance often requires the involvement of non-humanitarian Third Parties (e.g. domestic and international mobile network providers, financial institutions and financial intelligence units). This means that Humanitarian Organizations lose control over the data collected and the metadata generated by the Cash and Voucher Assistance. These data can then be used for non-humanitarian purposes (e.g. to profile potential

---

6   Ibid.
7   The High Level Panel on Humanitarian Cash Transfers, *Doing Cash Differently*, 8.
8   Ibid., 11.
9   Ibid.

How mobile money data can reach other parties

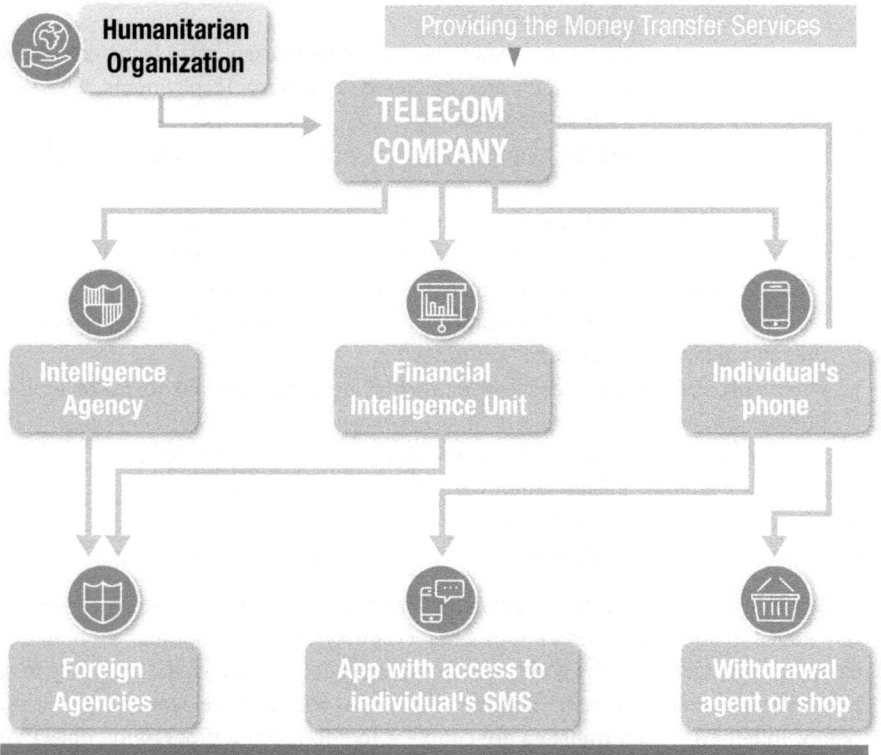

Figure 9.1: ICRC and Privacy International, chapter 6: Cash Transfer Programming, *The Humanitarian Metadata Problem: Doing No Harm in the Digital Era*, October 2018, p. 73.

customers). They can also be shared with external parties in order to comply with a legal obligation or under partnership agreements.[10]

In addition, a joint ICRC and Privacy International study stressed that, beyond knowingly collected and processed data, every single interaction generates what is known as metadata, i.e. data about data. These metadata are the inevitable result of the interaction with the system or service.

Finally, it is important to note that while the growing use of digital technology and connectivity is rendering previously "invisible" people "visible" to financial

---

10   ICRC and Privacy International, *The Humanitarian Metadata Problem: "Doing No Harm" in the Digital Era*, October 2018, chap. 6: www.icrc.org/en/download/file/85089/the_humanitarian_metadata_problem_-_icrc_and_privacy_international.pdf.

Different types of data and metadata

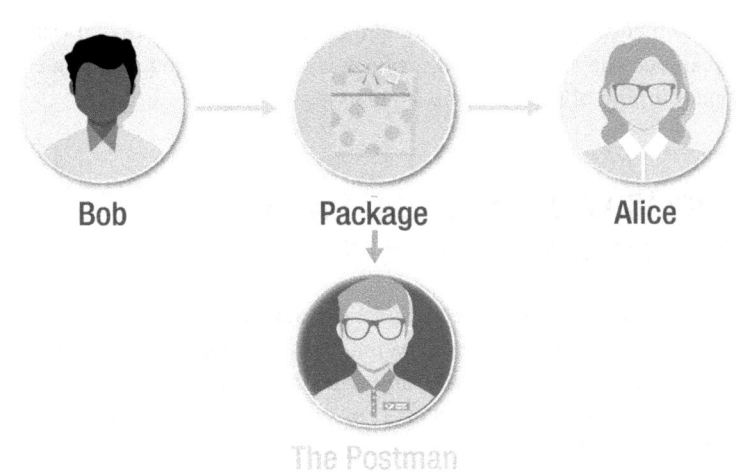

Bob → **Package** → **Alice**

↓

The Postman

The Postman might have an idea of what the package contains based on:

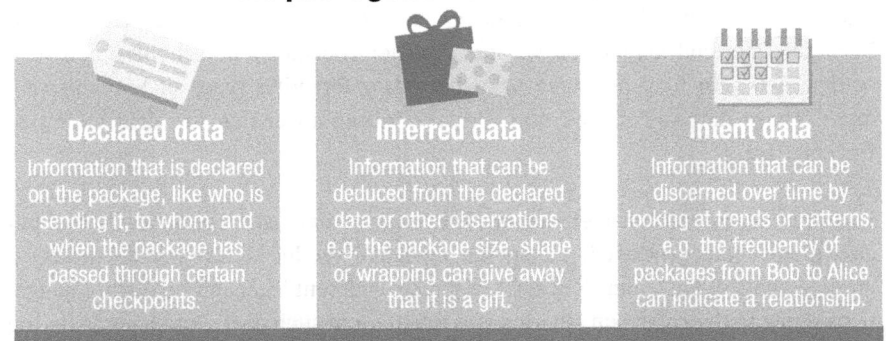

Declared data	Inferred data	Intent data
Information that is declared on the package, like who is sending it, to whom, and when the package has passed through certain checkpoints.	Information that can be deduced from the declared data or other observations, e.g. the package size, shape or wrapping can give away that it is a gift.	Information that can be discerned over time by looking at trends or patterns, e.g. the frequency of packages from Bob to Alice can indicate a relationship.

Figure 9.2. ICRC and Privacy International, chapter 2: Processing Data and Metadata, *The Humanitarian Metadata Problem: Doing No Harm in the Digital Era*, October 2018, p. 33.

institutions, these digital identities and footprints can help to include people who were overlooked under previous programmes. However, this new visibility can also expose affected people to risks.[11] The mere fact that they are seeking assistance from

---

11 For a longer exploration of this, see Jo Burton, "'Doing no harm' in the Digital Age: What the digitalization of cash means for humanitarian action", *International Review of the Red Cross*, Vol. 102, No. 913, April 2020, pp. 43–73: https://doi.org/10.1017/S1816383120000491. The advantages and disadvantages of "making the invisible visible" were discussed during the DigitHarium months on Digitalized Assistance and Digital identities. See: ICRC, "DigitHarium Month #2: Digitalized Assistance, Social Protection and Humanitarian Data Concerns", International Committee of the Red Cross,

a Humanitarian Organization can reveal their affiliation with a particular group and expose them to discrimination. In other words, the inevitable visibility created by digital engagement can pose a threat in humanitarian situations. Digital visibility and profiling can become an instrument for financial discrimination, running counter to the original purpose of the Cash and Voucher Assistance.[12]

9.2 APPLICATION OF BASIC DATA PROTECTION PRINCIPLES

The inherent privacy-related threats and risks associated with the collection and handling of beneficiaries' Personal Data for Cash and Voucher Assistance can arise from inadequate organizational and technical data security measures. Humanitarian Organizations should also consider the long-term impact of the data generated, directly or indirectly, by Cash and Voucher Assistance. As Cash and Voucher Assistance makes use of existing services and systems including banks and telecommunications operators, Humanitarian Organizations may be required to collect data from affected people in order to comply with Know Your Customer,[13] SIM card registration[14] and other obligations to which such bodies are subject. Personal Data collected for Cash and Voucher Assistance can involve a variety of data sets that may not have been necessary for other types of humanitarian aid.[15] These data are shared with private entities to enable the distribution of financial aid.

Furthermore, careful consideration needs to be given not just to the data collected but also to the data generated, i.e. to the metadata produced through the practical arrangements of Cash and Voucher Assistance. Different legal and regulatory obligations apply to the collection, sharing and retention of such data. For example, in the case of mobile money, this includes data such as: the sender's and recipient's phone numbers; the date and time of the financial transaction; the transaction ID; the location and size of the transaction; the store where it was conducted; and any

---

9 March 2021: www.icrc.org/en/digitharium/digitharium-month-2; ICRC, "DigitHarium Month #9: Digital Identities and Humanitarian Operations", International Committee of the Red Cross, 18 February 2022: www.icrc.org/en/digitharium/digitharium-month-9.

12   ICRC and Privacy International, *The Humanitarian Metadata Problem*, 68–69.
13   Know Your Customer (KYC) is a process by which businesses check the identity of their customers in order to comply with anti-money laundering and anti-corruption regulations and legislation.
14   Kevin P. Donovan and Aaron K. Martin, "The rise of African SIM registration: The emerging dynamics of regulatory change", *First Monday*, Vol. 19, No. 2, 26 January 2014, sec. IV: https://doi.org/10.5210/fm.v19i2.4351.
15   Cash Learning Partnership (CaLP), "Protecting Beneficiary Privacy, Principles and Operational Standards for the Secure Use of Personal Data in Cash and e-Transfer Programmes", 2020, 4: www.calpnetwork.org/wp-content/uploads/2020/01/calp-beneficiary-privacy-web.pdf.

agents involved at either end. Such data can be used to infer other information and intelligence, which could be used to profile, target and monitor users.[16] Humanitarian Organizations must therefore be aware of the ways in which data can be used to infer information about their beneficiaries' behaviours, movements, affiliations and other characteristics. The ability to draw inferences about affected people is possible long after the programme ends.

With an increasing number of Humanitarian Organizations opting for Cash and Voucher Assistance to provide aid, there is a pressing need to consider the impact (e.g. will individuals receiving financial aid be subject to discrimination?) and measures mitigating the risks associated with the Personal Data Processing needed to distribute this type of aid.[17]

Data protection issues result from the fact that data are collected, stored and cross-matched by Data Controllers or Data Processors during cash assistance operations. Often, the data collected during Cash and Voucher Assistance relates to socioeconomic factors and vulnerabilities. The data are used to target assistance, either for a subset of the affected people (for needs assessment research), or for a wider group, potentially including people who do not ultimately receive cash transfers. For all recipients, the Personal Data collected during the process typically include the following: name, surname, mobile phone number, "Know Your Customer"[18] data, geolocation/other phone metadata and Biometrics. Humanitarian Organizations may also collect data related to socioeconomic factors or vulnerabilities for the purposes of targeting assistance. These data, once collected and stored, may enable Processing for other purposes and/or other types of data Processing, such as Data Analytics or data mining.[19]

The complexity of the flow of data between Humanitarian Organizations and partner organizations using Cash and Voucher Assistance also gives rise to data protection issues, which are dealt with in Section 9.5 – Data sharing.

9.3 BASIC PRINCIPLES OF DATA PROTECTION

The basic principles of data protection constitute the baseline to be respected while engaging in any type of Personal Data Processing. These include the principle of the

---

16 ICRC and Privacy International, *The Humanitarian Metadata Problem*, 73–75.
17 Ibid., 4.
18 See Glossary.
19 See Chapter 17: Artificial Intelligence, and particularly Section 17.1.2 – Artificial Intelligence in the humanitarian sector.

fairness and lawfulness of the Processing, the principle of transparency, the purpose limitation principle, the data minimization principle and the data quality principle.[20]

The data protection discussion in this chapter builds on the principles set out in Part I, which examines them in greater detail.

9.3.1 LEGAL BASES FOR PERSONAL DATA PROCESSING

Humanitarian Organizations may process Personal Data using one or more of the following legal bases:
- the vital interest of the Data Subject or of another person;
- the public interest, in particular based on an organization's mandate under national or international law;
- Consent;
- a legitimate interest of the organization;
- the performance of a contract;
- compliance with a legal obligation.

Obtaining the valid informed Consent[21] of beneficiaries in programmes using Cash and Voucher Assistance can be challenging, due to the amount and complexity of information that would need to be provided to ensure that the beneficiaries fully appreciate the risks and benefits of Processing. Moreover, merely interacting with the service inevitably generates metadata without the user's say.[22] As with other cases when Personal Data are collected as a prerequisite for assistance to be provided to affected people, unless an alternative method of providing assistance is also made available, it can be argued that an individual in need of assistance has no real choice as to whether to give Consent or not and, accordingly, Consent may not be considered valid. If Consent is not possible, then another legal basis should be used, as set out below.

Regardless of the legal basis selected, and following the principle of transparency, beneficiaries should at least be informed individually or collectively as to the nature of the programme being provided, the legal basis for Processing, what data are being collected, by whom and why, whether providing the data is mandatory or voluntary, the sources of the data, how long it will be stored for, which Data Processors are involved, who else the data will be shared with, and their rights (including the right to redress).

Humanitarian Organizations should:[23]
- aspire to obtain the active and informed Consent of beneficiaries for the use of their Personal Data when using Cash and Voucher Assistance.

---

20 See also Chapter 2: Basic principles of data protection.
21 See Section 3.2 – Consent.
22 ICRC and Privacy International, *The Humanitarian Metadata Problem*. 21.
23 CaLP, "Protecting Beneficiary Privacy", 14.

- only use alternatives to active and informed Consent where obtaining it is impractical or valid Consent cannot be obtained for other reasons set out herein. Legitimate reasons for not seeking active and informed Consent include urgency, or if the circumstances of the distribution make "active and informed Consent" meaningless.
- if possible, ensure that valid Consent can be provided or offer an alternative method of assistance for the individuals who are not comfortable with the data flows and/or stakeholders involved in the use of Cash and Voucher Assistance.
- to the best of their knowledge given publicly available information, inform beneficiaries about the data and metadata which may be generated, collected and processed by Third Parties whose services and systems the Humanitarian Organization is using (including KYC for banks and SIM card registration by telecommunications operators).

In light of the potential effectiveness of cash-based operations in disaster and emergency conditions and the rapidity of deployment if properly prepared in advance (e.g. if compared to in-kind assistance), the vital interests of the Data Subject or another person might constitute a plausible alternative legal basis for the relevant Processing when Humanitarian Organizations are unable to obtain the individuals' Consent. However, as always with this legal basis and as set out elsewhere in this Handbook, its use should be carefully considered.

Public interest could constitute a suitable legal basis for Processing data in the use of Cash and Voucher Assistance where a mandate to carry out Humanitarian Action is established in national, regional or international law and where no Consent is obtained and no vital interests are triggered, as per the cases discussed above.

Humanitarian Organizations may also process Personal Data where this is in their legitimate interest, provided that this interest is not overridden by the fundamental rights and freedoms of the Data Subject. Such legitimate interests may include making humanitarian aid delivery more effective and efficient, preventing fraud and duplication of aid.

9.3.2 PURPOSE LIMITATION AND FURTHER PROCESSING

At the time of data collection, the Humanitarian Organization concerned must determine and set out the specific purpose(s) for which data are processed.[24] The specific purpose(s) should be explicit and legitimate and, in the case of Cash and Voucher Assistance, should involve the provision of assistance to enable affected people to access the goods and services they need.

The purposes of the Processing need to be clarified and communicated to individuals at the time of collection.

---

24 See Section 9.3.1 – Legal bases for Personal Data Processing.

Personal Data may be processed for purposes other than those initially specified at the time of collection where the Further Processing is compatible with those purposes, including where the Processing is necessary for historical, statistical or scientific purposes. In order to establish whether Further Processing is compatible with the purpose for which the data were initially collected, attention should be paid to the following factors:
- any link between the purposes for which the data were initially collected and the purposes of the intended Further Processing;
- the situation in which the Personal Data were collected, in particular, the relationship between Data Subjects and the Data Controller, as well as the relationship with the Data Processor;
- the nature of the Personal Data;
- the possible consequences of the intended Further Processing for Data Subjects;
- the existence of appropriate safeguards;
- the reasonable expectation of the Data Subjects as to possible further uses of the data.

When assessing the above, the humanitarian purposes of the data Processing should be given particular consideration.

Additional purposes that may be involved in the Processing by or of interest to commercial processors (e.g. financial institutions and mobile phone operators) should also be considered. This may potentially include: cross-checking lists of beneficiaries against lists of designated persons; retention of metadata for law enforcement purposes; profiling beneficiaries for creditworthiness, etc.[25] The following consequences could occur should commercial Data Processors be obliged or in a position to process Personal Data for purposes other than the exclusively humanitarian purpose envisaged:
- It would become questionable whether the entities in question are indeed Data Processors, and not new Data Controllers, deciding on the means and purposes of Processing.
- The additional Processing may be incompatible with the initial purpose for collection and require a new legal basis. While a new legal basis may perhaps be found (such as compliance with a legal obligation to report designated persons), Humanitarian Organizations should carefully consider whether this is compatible with the Neutral, Impartial and Independent nature of Humanitarian Action.

Contractual clauses in the Processing agreement should restrict Further Processing by Data Processors as much as possible.

In the case of Cash and Voucher Assistance, Humanitarian Organizations should be aware of the data and metadata processed by Data Processors whose services and

---

25 ICRC and Privacy International, *The Humanitarian Metadata Problem*, chap. 6.

systems they are using. These should be included in the DPIA to identify any areas that need to be regulated through contractual clauses.[26]

EXAMPLE:
In the case of a system set up to disburse cash or voucher assistance by a Humanitarian Organization, to which purpose the individuals concerned have consented, the same system cannot be used to transmit participants' data to donors of the Humanitarian Organization for cross-referencing purposes.

Likewise, any data collected cannot be used by a financial institution to assess a beneficiary's creditworthiness and eligibility for financial services, including after they have received aid from a Humanitarian Organization.

9.3.3 DATA MINIMIZATION

The information collected for the purposes of cash assistance operations needs to be proportionate to these purposes. That is, only the Personal Data necessary for the identification of individuals should be collected and processed and any "excess" information that is not relevant to the Cash and Voucher Assistance purposes should not be collected and, if collected, should be deleted.

Given that many types of data are collected when using Cash and Voucher Assistance, compartmentalization of the data is recommended as a way to meet data minimization requirements, with access being provided on a need-to-know basis. Additionally, contractual provisions could be provided against the Further Processing by commercial entities.

In assessing the application of the data minimization principle, it is also important to take into account the data generated as part of the Cash and Voucher Assistance by Data Processors, such as credit transaction metadata and mobile network metadata.

One possible option in programmes using Cash and Voucher Assistance is for the Humanitarian Organization, once the individual is identified, to only transfer to the commercial service provider (e.g. bank or mobile network operator), when feasible, a unique identifier (from which the receiving entity cannot identify the final beneficiary) and the amount of cash to be distributed, so as to limit the risks to the individuals concerned. However, it is important to consider the limitations of these approaches, since programmes such as these depend on rigid systems provided by financial institutions, telecommunications operators and other relevant organizations. Likewise, it is important to recognize the limitations of current Pseudonymization (or imperfect

---

26　For more consideration about DPIAs, see Section 9.8 – Data Protection Impact Assessments

Anonymization) techniques and the implications for Reidentification, especially when data can be correlated with other sources to enable Reidentification.[27]

9.3.4 DATA RETENTION

Humanitarian Organizations are advised to ensure that beneficiary data are not held (whether by them or by Third Party Data Processors) for longer than is required to fulfil the specific purposes for which they were collected, unless retention is potentially useful for repeat distributions. The Personal Data of beneficiaries who have left the programme should be deleted by the organization, its Data Processors, and any Third Parties that have had access to the data. The Humanitarian Organization should verify data deletion by the commercial service provider, as far as this is possible. Any information that is deemed necessary to keep at the end of a programme should only be kept if it is related to data for which there is a legitimate purpose, such as possible future programmes, auditing or reporting purposes, monitoring and evaluation. Ideally, and to the extent that this is meaningful, data retained for these reasons should be aggregated and/or anonymized.

In considering data retention, Humanitarian Organizations should also consider the retention obligations that may apply by virtue of domestic law to some Data Processors, such as financial institutions, credit card companies and mobile phone network operators. These should be included in programme DPIAs and privacy policies.

9.3.5 DATA SECURITY

In order to avoid potential misuse of the Personal Data collected and processed during Cash and Voucher Assistance, it is essential that adequate and proportionate security measures are implemented. Humanitarian Organizations are advised to implement appropriate technical and operational security standards for each stage of the collection, use and transfer of beneficiary data, and processes should be put in place for the protection of beneficiary Personal Data from loss, theft, damage or destruction; this includes backup systems and effective means to respond to security breaches and prevent unauthorized access, disclosure or loss.[28]

It is also advisable for the Humanitarian Organizations to protect "by design" the Personal Data they obtain from beneficiaries either for their own use or for use by Third Parties for each programme using cash or vouchers that they initiate or implement. This means that they should build privacy protections into the processes

---

[27] Larry Hardesty, "How Hard Is It to 'de-Anonymize' Cellphone Data?". MIT News | Massachusetts Institute of Technology (blog), 27 March 2013: https://news.mit.edu/2013/how-hard-it-de-anonymize-cellphone-data. See also Section 2.3 – Aggregate, Pseudonymized and Anonymized data sets.

[28] See Section 2.8 – Data security and Processing security.

and mechanisms they use to implement Cash and Voucher Assistance. Encryption or compartmentalization of information can be viable solutions to meet this need.

Humanitarian Organizations must take steps to inform themselves about the measures taken by potential Data Processors and other Third Parties on whose systems, services and infrastructure they rely prior to contracting them. Personal Data, at rest and in transit, as well as the infrastructure relied upon for Processing, should be protected by security safeguards against risks such as unlawful or unauthorized access, use and disclosure, as well as loss, destruction or damage of data. As part of their due diligence and DPIAs, Humanitarian Organizations should inform themselves about any publicly known security incidents experienced by Data Processors and other Third Parties on whose systems, services and infrastructure they rely, and what measures they have subsequently put in place to ensure the security and integrity of the data, at rest and in transit, and the infrastructure relied upon.

Data storage and potential International Data Sharing also need to be taken into consideration. For example, for refugees, there may be serious data protection risks associated with using a regional bank that has a branch or storage facility in the country of origin of the refugees, as the data may be requested by national authorities.

When selecting external Data Processors, the security measures they can guarantee should be a key factor.

9.4 RIGHTS OF DATA SUBJECTS

The right to information should be respected by ensuring that beneficiaries are informed individually or collectively as to the nature of the programme being provided, what information is being collected, by whom and why, and which Data Processors are involved. Humanitarian Organizations should be transparent about how they intend to use the Personal Data they collect and process. They should provide privacy notices accounting for the full data flow and data retention envisaged to beneficiaries who want more detailed information.

Adequate infrastructure and resources should be put in place to facilitate the rights to access, objection, deletion and rectification with regard to any programme using Cash and Voucher Assistance. In this respect, it is advisable to incorporate complaint procedures into Personal Data Processing practices and internal data protection policies.

9.5 DATA SHARING

Personal Data Processing for Cash and Voucher Assistance may include data sharing with Data Processors and Third Parties when the datasets have been collected and processed by different Data Controllers or Data Processors (for example, if Humanitarian Organizations implementing a cash assistance programming system outsource individual identification in the field to on-site operators). It is important to take into consideration data protection requirements before sharing data and to note that 'sharing' includes not only situations where data are actively transferred to Third Parties, but also those when they are made accessible to others (e.g. sharing a database which contains beneficiaries' Personal Data).

Humanitarian Organizations may rely on partner organizations to collect data on their behalf, or on commercial organizations (such as financial institutions and mobile operators) involved in carrying out such programmes. These other organizations may be subject to a variety of legal and organizational requirements that lead them to share data with Third Parties (including regulators), which can include the following:
- "Know Your Customer" (KYC) obligations requiring the collection of more Personal Data than is strictly necessary for the purposes of providing assistance.
- obligations to cross-check KYC information against lists of designated persons established by local authorities, including entities potentially involved in a conflict or situation of violence. This process may potentially be monitored by public authorities, and may involve reporting obligations. This in turn gives rise to questions as to inclusion (i.e. can beneficiaries be excluded from an assistance programme on the basis of a match being found) and compromises the neutrality and independence of Humanitarian Action.
- collection of additional data as part of the process, such as geolocation or unique telephone identifiers and other mobile network metadata, when mobile phone operators are involved;
- requirements for SIM card registration;
- retention obligations incompatible with the information provided by Humanitarian Organizations at the time of collection;
- additional commercial purposes, such as profiling individuals for creditworthiness or advertising;
- additional obligations imposed on them by national law.

Privileges and immunities are also of great significance with respect to Cash and Voucher Assistance. In this regard, the provisions of Section 10.9 – Privileges and immunities and the cloud should be considered for Cash and Voucher Assistance.

9.6 INTERNATIONAL DATA SHARING

Data protection law restricts International Data Sharing, so Humanitarian Organizations should have mechanisms in place to provide a legal basis for it in Cash and Voucher Assistance, as discussed in Chapter 4: International Data Sharing.

Humanitarian Organizations should examine whether International Data Sharing has a legal basis under applicable law and their own internal policies before carrying it out.

Financial services are highly interconnected in a way that Humanitarian Organizations cannot control. The way in which data might travel within and outside national borders is affected by this interconnectedness, as well as by national laws, regulations and practices. For this reason, Humanitarian Organizations must discuss, with all institutions involved in the Cash and Voucher Assistance: (i) who their main partners are, nationally and internationally, and (ii) whether Cash and Voucher Assistance data can be kept outside any information exchanges.[29]

9.7 DATA CONTROLLER/DATA PROCESSOR RELATIONSHIP

The use of Cash and Voucher Assistance by a Humanitarian Organization may involve local or international commercial service providers for project implementation. Humanitarian Organizations may also cooperate among themselves in sharing databases of the information collected via these operations. It is thus crucial to determine which parties actually determine the purposes and means of data Processing (and thus are Data Controllers), and which merely take instructions from Data Controllers (and thus are Data Processors). It is also possible that multiple parties might be considered to be joint Data Controllers. When the roles have been clearly defined and the corresponding tasks assigned, data sharing across Humanitarian Organizations and/or national borders and/or third (private or state) bodies should generally be covered by appropriate contractual arrangements.

It should be remembered that although Personal Data may be protected while kept in the systems of Humanitarian Organizations which benefit from privileges and immunities under international law, the same data may lose such protection when transferred to Data Processors not enjoying those privileges and immunities. In addition, Data Processors may be obliged by local legislation to share data with government agencies and may even be obliged not to tell the Humanitarian Organizations from which the data originated about this data sharing.

9.8 DATA PROTECTION IMPACT ASSESSMENTS

Data Protection Impact Assessments (DPIAs) need to be drafted and tailored to each programme utilizing cash and vouchers. Cash and Voucher Assistance may differ not

---

29   ICRC and Privacy International, *The Humanitarian Metadata Problem*, 79.

only from organization to organization, but also within an organization itself. Each programme constitutes a separate data protection activity which should be subject to a DPIA. DPIAs will help the Humanitarian Organization to (a) identify the privacy risks to individuals, in particular, those deriving from the data flow and stakeholders involved; (b) identify the privacy and data protection compliance liabilities for the organization; (c) protect the organization's reputation and instil public confidence in the programme; and (d) ensure that the organization does not compromise on the neutrality of its Humanitarian Action.

It is recommended that Humanitarian Organizations analyse, document and understand the flow of beneficiary data for each programme they initiate or implement internally within their own organization or externally with others, identify the risks involved and develop risk mitigation strategies. Particular issues often associated with commercial service providers and relating to KYC regulations, mandatory reporting to national authorities, International Data Sharing and potential cloud storage, need to be specifically assessed and weighed against the benefits of using Cash and Voucher Assistance.

A template DPIA for Cash and Voucher Assistance has been developed by the Cash Learning Partnership.[30]

---

30   CaLP, "Protecting Beneficiary Privacy", 18.

CLOUD SERVICE

POSSIBLE USE

- STRONG COMPUTING POWER OVER SHORT PERIOD OF TIME
- AGILITY IN SCALING UP
- DATA HOSTED SAFELY AND SECURELY
- FLEXIBILITY IN LOCATION

CHALLENGES

- LIMITED CONTROL OVER THE CLOUD SERVICE
- INTERCEPTION OF SENSITIVE INFORMATION
- ENSURE ALL BACKUPS ARE DELETE ON REQUEST
- POSSIBLE ACCESS BY THE GOVERNMENT
- POSSIBLE ACCESS BY CLOUD SOLUTION PROVIDERS
- CARRY OUT AUDITS

CHAPTER 10

CLOUD SERVICES

Paolo Balboni

10.1 INTRODUCTION

The most widely used definition of "cloud computing" is the one published by the US National Institute of Standards and Technology (NIST),[1] according to which, "cloud computing is a model for enabling ubiquitous, convenient, on-demand network access to a shared pool of configurable computing resources (e.g. networks, servers, storage, applications, and services) that can be rapidly provisioned and released with minimal management effort or service provider interaction". The NIST document defines three service models: Software as a Service (SaaS), Platform as a Service (PaaS) and Infrastructure as a Service (IaaS), and four deployment models: public, private, community and hybrid cloud environments,[2] although it should be borne in mind that new models are being developed all the time.

Cloud computing can facilitate and accelerate the creation and Processing of large collections of data and the production of new services and applications. It also makes deployment more agile. As humanitarian assistance is driven by information, cloud computing services and their related data Processing paradigm have become a helpful tool for Humanitarian Organizations. Their benefits include access to large amounts of computing power over short periods of time, elasticity and flexibility about the location and flow of data, and cost savings.[3]

However, Cloud Services can also bring risks and challenges for privacy and data protection. These can generally be grouped into two main categories: first, the lack of control over the data, and second, the absence of transparency about the Processing operation itself. For Humanitarian Action the following risks are of particular importance:

- the use of services from unprotected locations;
- the interception of sensitive information;
- weak authentication;
- data can be stolen from the Cloud Service provider, for instance by hackers;
- possible access by government and law enforcement authorities;[4]

---

1 Mell and Grance, *The NIST Definition of Cloud Computing*.
2 European Data Protection Supervisor (EDPS), "Opinion of the European Data Protection Supervisor on the Commission's Communication on 'Unleashing the Potential of Cloud Computing in Europe'", Opinion (Brussels, 16 November 2012), 4: https://edps.europa.eu/sites/default/files/publication/12-11-16_cloud_computing_en_0.pdf.
3 See Dara G. Schniederjans, Koray Ozpolat and Yuwen Chen, "Humanitarian supply chain use of cloud computing", *Supply Chain Management: An International Journal*, 8 August 2016: https://doi.org/10.1108/SCM-01-2016-0024.
4 On law enforcement access to the cloud see Chapter 11: Cloud and government access. For further considerations, see also, for example, Paolo Balboni and Enrico Pelino, "Law enforcement agencies' activities in the cloud environment: A European legal perspective", *Information & Communications Technology Law*, Vol. 22, No. 2, 2013, pp. 165–190.

- long data Processing chains of subcontractors out of effective control;
- further Processing, incompatible with the original purpose(s), by the cloud provider and/or its subcontractors;
- extra retention of data by the cloud provider and/or its subcontractors;
- unauthorized (International) Data Sharing.

The data protection implications of cloud computing were highlighted by the International Conference of Privacy and Data Protection Commissioners in its Resolution on Cloud Computing, adopted in Uruguay in 2012.[5]

In addition, those Humanitarian Organizations that enjoy privileges and immunities under international law should be aware that outsourcing Personal Data Processing to a Third Party Cloud Service provider may put their data at risk of loss of such privileges and immunities. More details on the possible implications of privileges and immunities in a cloud environment are set out in Section 10.9 – Privileges and immunities and the cloud, below.

The three main types of Cloud Service models can be described as follows:[6]
- **Infrastructure as a Service (IaaS):** an IaaS cloud offers access to the raw computing resources of a Cloud Service. Rather than purchasing hardware itself, the cloud customer purchases access to the cloud provider's hardware according to the capacity required.
- **Platform as a Service (PaaS):** a PaaS cloud offers access to a computing platform which allows cloud customers to write applications to run on that platform or another instance of it. The platform may in turn be hosted on a cloud IaaS.
- **Software as a Service (SaaS):** a SaaS cloud offers access to a complete software application which the cloud user accesses through a web browser or other software. Accessing the software in this manner eliminates or reduces the need to install software on the client machine and allows the service to support a wider range of devices. The software may in turn be hosted on a cloud platform or infrastructure.

There are also different types of cloud infrastructure. A private cloud is operated solely for a single organization, whether managed internally or by a Third Party, and hosted either internally or externally. In a public cloud, the services are rendered over a network that is open for public use. A community cloud is a cloud service jointly available to a number of organizations that shares common interests, concerns and/or requirements

---

5   See International Conference of Data Protection and Privacy Commissioners, Resolution on Cloud Computing, Resolution (34th International Conference of Data Protection and Privacy Commissioners, Punta del Este / Canelones, Uruguay, 26 October 2012): http://globalprivacyassembly.org/wp-content/uploads/2015/02/Resolution-on-Cloud-Computing.pdf.

6   UK Information Commissioner's Office (ICO), *Guidance on the use of cloud computing*, Version: 1.1, 2 October 2012, 5–6: https://ico.org.uk/your-data-matters/online/cloud-computing.

(e.g. security, compliance requirements, jurisdiction, privileges and immunities, etc.). A hybrid cloud is a composition of two or more clouds that remain distinct entities but are bound together, offering the benefits of multiple deployment models.

Each of these models has advantages and disadvantages. A public cloud is more accessible, as the information is stored offsite and therefore is available from anywhere via the Internet. It offers the ability to scale up server capacity at short notice and can potentially save money. It can also be reviewed regularly with security and performance updates and improvements. On the other hand, as a public cloud is dependent on Internet connectivity there is the risk of losing control over data because of unknown or unauthorized data transfer from one jurisdiction to another, false deletion of data, retention after the termination of services, hacking and security attacks. It is difficult to identify where the data are stored in a public cloud at a particular point in time, and deletion is almost never possible because of the many unmonitored backups. In addition, there are many privacy and confidentiality concerns, such as the fact that the Processing may be subject to a range of different applicable legislation which could mandate compulsory and unauthorized release of data and the potential for authorities to exercise jurisdiction.

In a private/internal cloud, data are kept within the organization's internal network, and therefore are not publicly accessible. It offers a more controlled environment and a limited number of users, so creating less risk of Third Party disclosure. A private cloud can have the same usability, scalability and flexibility as a public cloud. Its disadvantages, though, are the cost and the fact that it may not have the latest performance and security upgrades/improvements.

A community cloud can be managed internally or by a Third Party and hosted internally or externally. So, the advantages and disadvantages of this typology depend on how it is managed. Interestingly, organizations that share common interests, concerns and/or requirements can have together more negotiating power towards the cloud provider and achieve customized service-level agreements (SLAs) which are fit for their similar purposes.[7]

A hybrid cloud allows organizations to determine which option to use, depending on the classification of information to be stored. Less sensitive information is usually sent to a public cloud, whereas more sensitive and confidential information is kept on a private or internal cloud. While this model offers cost savings, scalability, security and performance updates/improvements, it entails the same risks as a public cloud in terms of loss of control over data and unauthorized disclosure.

---

[7] On cloud contracts negotiations, see Paolo Balboni, "Managing legal compliance risk in the cloud and negotiating personal data protection requirements with vendors", in *Cloud Computing Security: Foundations and Challenges*, CRC Press, Abingdon, UK, 2016, 267–276.

10.2 DATA CONTROLLER/DATA PROCESSOR RELATIONSHIP

As discussed in Section 4.5 – Data Controller/Data Processor relationship, the relationship between a Humanitarian Organization that puts Personal Data in the cloud and a cloud provider that it contracts with to do so is, generally speaking, that of a Data Controller and a Data Processor. However, in practice these roles may be more difficult to categorize than is at first apparent, as this will depend on how much discretion the cloud provider has, which should be defined in the agreement between the provider and the client. What is crucial is that these uncertainties should not affect the rights of Data Subjects, meaning that Humanitarian Organizations should be as transparent as possible about their use of Cloud Services and not allow cloud providers to disadvantage Data Subjects.

The use of Cloud Services by a Humanitarian Organization routinely involves the cloud provider hiring Sub-Processors. The contract with the provider should specify that Sub-Processors may only be used on the basis of an authorization given by the Data Controller (i.e. the Humanitarian Organization). The Data Processor (cloud provider) should have a clear duty to inform the Data Controller of any changes in this regard, with the Data Controller retaining the option of objecting to such changes or terminating the contract.

10.3 RESPONSIBILITY AND ACCOUNTABILITY IN THE CLOUD

The cloud client/provider relationship is a Data Controller/Data Processor relationship.[8] However, in exceptional cases the cloud provider may act as a Data Controller as well, in which case it has full (joint) responsibility for the data Processing and must comply with all relevant legal obligations for data protection. As the Data Controller, the cloud client (i.e. the Humanitarian Organization) is responsible for complying with legal obligations stemming from data protection law. Furthermore, the cloud client is responsible for selecting a cloud provider that complies with data protection legislation.

The notion of accountability expresses the direct compliance obligations that Data Controllers and Data Processors have under data protection law. This means that they must be able to ensure and demonstrate that their Processing activities comply with the relevant legal requirements, through the adoption and implementation of appropriate data protection policies and notices.

---

8   See Section 10.2 – Data Controller/Data Processor relationship.

EXAMPLE:
When a Humanitarian Organization contracts with a cloud provider to store Personal Data in the cloud, it will remain liable to the Data Subjects for any breaches of data protection that the provider commits. It is therefore essential for the Humanitarian Organization to take the following steps before Personal Data are stored in a cloud:

- undertake a DPIA on the proposed storage of Personal Data in the cloud, and be prepared to cancel the project if the results show that this would cause undue risk for individuals' data protection;
- perform due diligence on the Cloud Service provider to ensure that the provider will use due care and takes data protection/security seriously;
- discuss data protection openly with the provider and assess whether the provider seems ready and able to fulfil their data protection obligations;
- carefully review the contract with the provider before signature and ensure that it contains adequate data protection language; and
- for Humanitarian Organizations enjoying privileges and immunities, ensure that such privileges and immunities are properly built into the cloud solution design, and are respected.

10.4 APPLICATION OF BASIC DATA PROTECTION PRINCIPLES

All data protection principles apply to Cloud Services; special attention is paid here to a number of issues that are of particular relevance.

The data protection discussion in this chapter builds on the principles set out in Part I, which examines them in greater detail.

10.4.1 LEGAL BASES FOR PERSONAL DATA PROCESSING

Before engaging a cloud provider Humanitarian Organizations need to demonstrate that one of the following legal bases is present:[9]

- the vital interest of the Data Subject or of another person;
- the public interest, in particular based on an organization's mandate under national or international law;
- Consent;
- a legitimate interest of the organization;
- the performance of a contract;
- compliance with a legal obligation.

---

9   See Chapter 3: Legal bases for Personal Data Processing.

It is important in this regard to differentiate between the initial Processing of the Personal Data by the Humanitarian Organization and its Processing in the cloud. The Humanitarian Organization must have a legal basis for collecting and Processing the Personal Data in the first place, which can be any of the legal bases referred to in Chapter 3: Legal bases for Personal Data Processing. If the cloud provider acts as processor, the same legal basis will extend to the Processing in the cloud (which is to be regarded as a means of Processing). However, in the residual instance that the cloud provider acts as controller, a separate legal basis for the sharing of data with the cloud provider should be found. In any case, the Humanitarian Organization should perform a DPIA in order to identify the possible risks for individuals, including possible loss of exclusive "jurisdictional" control over the data by the Humanitarian Organization, and adequately mitigate them.

EXAMPLE:
A Humanitarian Organization collects Personal Data from vulnerable individuals on the basis that it is in their vital interest. In order to provide humanitarian services more efficiently, it then wants to store the data in a private cloud, and to this end engages a Cloud Service provider. The vital interest of the individuals is a sufficient legal basis for collecting the Personal Data and storing them in the cloud (with the provider acting as processor for the Humanitarian Organization), provided that the relevant DPIA has been carried out and the risks for the individuals have been adequately mitigated.

10.4.2 FAIR AND LAWFUL PROCESSING

Personal Data must be processed lawfully and fairly. The lawfulness of the Processing refers to the identification of an appropriate legal basis,[10] while the requirement for fairness is a broad principle that is generally connected to the provision of information as well as to the uses of the data. Humanitarian Organizations using Cloud Services should bear in mind that these Principles apply during all stages of Processing (i.e. collection, Processing and storage). Fundamental actions that Humanitarian Organizations should undertake in order to assure conformity with these fundamental data protection principles are: one, performing a DPIA before using Cloud Services, and two, monitoring ongoing compliance in the cloud environment during the service provisions by way of audits.

10.4.3 PURPOSE LIMITATION AND FURTHER PROCESSING

Humanitarian Organizations must determine and set out the specific purposes of Personal Data Processing. The purposes of the Processing need to be clarified and communicated to individuals at the time of collection.

---

10   See Section 10.4.1 – Legal bases for Personal Data Processing.

Humanitarian purposes offer a wide basis upon which to justify Further Processing operations. Compatibility would, however, not be found if the risks for the individuals concerned outweigh the benefits of Further Processing. This depends on the particular case. For example, circumstances leading to a finding of incompatibility include risks that the Processing may run counter to the significant interests of the person to whom the information relates or of his/her family, in particular when there is a risk that the Processing may threaten their life, integrity, dignity, psychological or physical security, liberty or their reputation.

In cloud computing environments, the cloud client is responsible for determining the purpose(s) of the Processing prior to the collection of Personal Data from the Data Subject and must inform the Data Subject accordingly. Based on the prohibition that the cloud client must not process Personal Data for other purposes that are inconsistent with the original ones, a Cloud Service provider cannot unilaterally decide or arrange for Personal Data (and its Processing) to be transmitted automatically to unknown cloud data centres. Furthermore, the Cloud Service provider cannot use Personal Data for its own purposes (such as, for example, marketing, carrying out research for other purposes or profiling). It is worth pointing out that the same holds true for the Cloud Service provider subcontractors, as a typical cloud scenario may easily involve a larger number of them. In order to mitigate the risk of Further Processing, the contract between cloud provider and cloud client should include technical and organizational measures and provide assurances for the logging and auditing of relevant Processing operations on Personal Data that are performed by employees of the cloud provider or the subcontractors.

10.4.4 TRANSPARENCY

Transparency is an aspect of the fair and legitimate Processing of Personal Data and is also closely related to the provision of information to Data Subjects. The cloud client is obliged to provide Data Subjects, whose Personal Data or data related to them are collected, with detailed information; this includes the cloud client's identity, address and the purposes of the Processing; the recipients or categories of recipients of the data, including Data Processors, insofar as such further information is necessary to guarantee fair Processing; and information about their rights.

Transparency must also be guaranteed in the relationship(s) between cloud client, cloud provider and subcontractors (if any). The cloud client can assess the lawfulness of the Personal Data Processing in the cloud only if the provider informs the client about all relevant issues. A Data Controller contemplating the engagement of a cloud provider should carefully check the provider's terms and conditions of service and assess them from a data protection point of view.

Another aspect of transparency in cloud computing is the fact that the cloud client must be informed about all the subcontractors involved in the provision of the respective Cloud Service, not merely those with which it is in a direct contractual relationship, and the locations of all data centres in which Personal Data are processed, as these elements may trigger International Data Sharing (see Section 10.7 – International Data Sharing).

10.4.5 DATA RETENTION

Humanitarian Organizations are advised to ensure that Personal Data are not held (whether by them or by Data Processors) for longer than is required to achieve the purposes for which they were collected, unless they have clear, justifiable and documented reasons for doing so; otherwise, data held by the organization and any relevant Third Parties should be destroyed. Deletion or destruction after completion of their Processing or a carefully structured data retention policy is recommended. When the purposes for which the Personal Data were collected have been achieved, then the Personal Data should be deleted both by the organization and any Third Parties that have had access to the data, unless they can rely on a relevant legal ground to hold that data. For example, data should only be retained in Cloud Services if they are related to a legitimate Processing purpose. Legitimate purposes in this regard might include possible future programmes, monitoring and evaluation, whereas for research purposes anonymized or aggregated data might be appropriate. Only the minimum amount of data necessary should be retained, in accordance with the data minimization principle.

The responsibility to ensure that Personal Data are erased as soon as they are no longer necessary lies with the cloud client. Erasure of data is a crucial issue not only throughout the duration of a cloud computing contract, but also upon its termination. It is also relevant if a subcontractor is replaced or withdraws. In such a case, the cloud client might either request a certificate of destruction by the Cloud Service provider or adequate evidence confirming that the data were transferred to a new Cloud Service provider.[11]

The principle of data erasure is applicable to Personal Data irrespective of whether they are stored on hard drives or other storage media (e.g. backup tapes). Since

---

11 Examples of measures for data deletion in the cloud include: the initial deletion from databases, storage and backup systems followed by data overwrite (e.g. using zeros and ones to overwrite data) or crypto-shredding (i.e. the practice of encryption of data and the destruction of the encryption keys), in order to ensure the complete deletion of the subject data. After the implementation of such a practice, evidence of deletion can be provided via extensive controls documentation of how the data are handled and deleted, and then the associated logs of the activities. As a caveat, it should be noted that providing 100 per cent assurance that data have been deleted is very difficult to achieve. For instance, to ensure this, a cloud customer would need to encrypt the data with a strong key before they store it in the cloud; never lose the key; and delete the key when they are done. This would bring the likelihood of full deletion close to 100 per cent (depending on the crypto-algorithm) since the CSP has never had access to both the key and the data at once.

Personal Data may be kept at the same time on different servers at different locations, it must be ensured that each instance is erased irretrievably (i.e. previous versions, temporary files and even file fragments should also be deleted).

Secure erasure of Personal Data requires that either the storage media are destroyed or demagnetized, or that the stored Personal Data are deleted effectively. Special software tools that overwrite Personal Data multiple times, in accordance with a recognized specification, should be used. The cloud client should make sure that the cloud provider ensures secure erasure in the above-mentioned sense and that the contract between the provider and the client contains clear provision for Personal Data erasure. The same holds true for contracts between cloud providers and subcontractors.

10.5 DATA SECURITY

Data security measures can be legal, technical and organizational. Legal measures may include not only contractual arrangements, but also Data Protection Impact Assessments (DPIAs). A holistic perspective must be adopted, which takes the following phases of contracting for Cloud Services into account:
- assessing the decision to use cloud computing (via DPIAs and a "go/no go" decision by management);
- the Cloud Service procurement process, including due diligence on prospective Cloud Service providers that takes both legal and technical perspectives into account;
- contracting (i.e. getting the right terms and conditions);
- operating, maintaining and decommissioning the service.[12]

A comprehensive data protection strategy is recommended, and attention should be paid to data protection issues in all phases before, during and after contractual arrangements. This should include an overall assessment of the contractual framework, including service-level agreements (SLAs), general (non-data protection) clauses (e.g. applicable law, variations to the contract, jurisdiction, liability, indemnification, etc.) and the general principle of "parallelism in/outside the cloud" (e.g. having the same data retention period for cloud or non-cloud Processing).

When a Humanitarian Organization decides to contract for cloud computing services, it should choose a cloud provider that can give sufficient guarantees for technical security and organizational measures governing the envisaged Processing, and

---

12 On procuring Cloud Services see, for example, Paolo Balboni et al., *Procure Secure: A Guide to Monitoring of Security Service Levels in Cloud Contracts*, European Union Agency for Cybersecurity, Attiki, Greece, 2012: www.enisa.europa.eu/publications/procure-secure-a-guide-to-monitoring-of-security-service-levels-in-cloud-contracts.

ensure compliance with those measures. Furthermore, a written contract with the Cloud Service provider must be signed, as there must be a binding legal act to govern the relationship between the Data Controller and the Data Processor. The contract must at a minimum establish that the Data Processor is to follow the instructions of the Data Controller and that the Data Processor must implement technical and organizational measures to adequately protect Personal Data, in accordance with the applicable data protection law.

In order to ensure legal certainty, the contract between the Humanitarian Organization and the Data Processor should also contain the following core data protection clauses:
- Provision of information on the location of the data centres, the identity and location of subcontractors and on any subsequent changes to the nature of the Processing. This should include the subject and time frame of the Cloud Service to be provided by the cloud provider; the extent, manner and purpose of the Processing of Personal Data by the cloud provider; and the types of Personal Data processed.
- Details about the cloud client's instructions to be given to the provider, with particular regard to the applicable SLAs and the relevant penalties (financial or otherwise including the ability to sue the provider in case of non-compliance).
- Clarification of the responsibilities of the cloud provider to notify the cloud client in the event of any Data Breach which affects the cloud client's data. Note that a security incident does not necessarily constitute a Data Breach.
- Recognition of the obligation to process Personal Data only for the explicitly mentioned and specified purposes, and to delete data at the end of the contract. There must be specification of the conditions for returning the data or destroying them once the service is concluded. Furthermore, it must be ensured that Personal Data are erased securely at the request of the cloud client.
- Confirmation, in case of a private cloud located outside the cloud client premises, that the data of the Humanitarian Organization are kept in separate servers.
- Specification of security measures that the cloud provider must comply with, depending on the risks represented by the Processing and the nature of the data to be protected.
- A confidentiality clause, binding both upon the cloud provider and any of its employees who may be able to access the data. Only authorized persons can have access to the data.
- An obligation on the provider's part to support the client in facilitating the exercise of Data Subjects' rights, e.g. to access, correct, delete their data, etc.
- An obligation on the provider's part to respect the cloud client's privileges and immunities, if applicable.
- A clause to the effect that Sub-Processors may only be commissioned on the basis of an authorization that can be generally given by the Data Controller (cloud client), in line with a clear duty for the Data Processor to inform the Data

Controller of any intended changes in this regard, with the Data Controller retaining at all times the possibility of objecting to such changes or terminating the contract. There should be a clear obligation for the cloud provider to name all the subcontractors commissioned. It must be established that contracts between the cloud provider and subcontractors reflect the stipulations of the contract between cloud client and cloud provider (i.e. that Sub-Processors are subject to the same contractual duties as the cloud provider). In particular, it must be guaranteed that both the cloud provider and all subcontractors act only on instructions from the cloud client. The chain of liability should be clearly set out in the contract.

- Arrangements for audits to be conducted during and at the end of the contract by the cloud client. The contract should provide for logging and auditing of relevant Processing operations on Personal Data that are performed by the cloud provider or the subcontractors.
- A general obligation on the provider's part to give assurance that its internal organization and data Processing arrangements (and those of its Sub-Processors, if any) are compliant with the applicable national and international legal requirements and standards.

With regard to the technical aspects of data security, the following are some important considerations for Humanitarian Organizations to bear in mind:[13]

- **Availability**: Providing availability means ensuring timely and reliable access to Personal Data. Availability in the cloud can be threatened by accidental loss of network connectivity between the client and the provider or of server performance caused by malicious actions such as (Distributed) Denial of Service (DoS) attacks. Other availability risks include accidental hardware failures both on the network and in the cloud Processing and data storage systems, power failures or other infrastructure problems. Data Controllers should therefore check that the cloud provider has adopted reasonable measures to cope with the risk of interferences such as backup Internet network links, redundant storage and effective data backup mechanisms.
- **Integrity**: Integrity relates to the maintenance of data quality which should not be maliciously or accidentally altered during Processing, storage or transmission. For IT systems, integrity requires that Personal Data undergoing Processing on these systems remain unmodified. Personal Data modifications can be detected by cryptographic authentication mechanisms such as message authentication codes, signatures or cryptographic hash functions. Interference with the integrity of IT systems in the cloud can be prevented or detected by means of Intrusion

---

[13] Adapted from Article 29 Data Protection Working Party, "Opinion 05/2012 on Cloud Computing (WP196)", 1 July 2012, 14–17: https://ec.europa.eu/justice/article-29/documentation/opinion-recommendation/files/2012/wp196_en.pdf.

Detection and Prevention Systems (IDS/IPS). These security tools are particularly important for the open network environments in which clouds usually operate.
- **Confidentiality**: In a cloud environment, encryption can significantly contribute to the confidentiality of Personal Data if applied correctly, although it does not render Personal Data irreversibly anonymous. It is simply a tool for the cloud client to ensure that the Personal Data they are responsible for can only be accessed by authorized persons who have the correct key. Personal Data encryption should be used for all data "in transit" and, when available, to data "at rest". This applies particularly for Data Controllers who plan to transfer Sensitive Data. Communications between cloud provider and client, as well as between data centres, should also be encrypted. When encryption is chosen as a technical measure to secure data, it is also important to guarantee the security of the key. Further technical measures aiming at ensuring confidentiality include authorization mechanisms and strong authentication (e.g. two-factor authentication). Contractual clauses should also impose confidentiality obligations on employees of cloud clients, cloud providers and subcontractors.
- **Isolation (purpose limitation)**: Isolation is an expression of the purpose limitation principle. In cloud infrastructures, resources such as storage, memory and networks are shared among many users. This creates new risks for data disclosure and illegitimate Further Processing. Isolation is meant to address this issue and ensure that data are not used beyond their initial original purpose and to maintain confidentiality and integrity. Isolation is achieved by adequate governance of the rights and roles for accessing Personal Data, and should be reviewed on a regular basis. The implementation of roles with excessive privileges should be avoided (e.g. no user or administrator should be authorized to access the entire cloud). More generally, administrators and users must only be able to access the information that is necessary for legitimate purposes (least privilege principle).
- **Intervenability**: Data Subjects have the rights of access, rectification, erasure, blocking and objection, as discussed below.[14]
- **Portability**: The use of standard data formats and service interfaces by the cloud providers is very important, as it facilitates interoperability and portability between different cloud providers. Therefore, if a cloud client decides to move to another cloud provider, any lack of interoperability may make it difficult or impossible to transfer the client's (Personal) Data to the new cloud provider, which is known as "vendor lock-in". The cloud client should check whether and how the provider guarantees the portability of data and services prior to ordering a Cloud Service. Data portability also refers to the ability of a Data Subject to obtain from the Data Controller a copy of data undergoing Processing in a commonly-used, structured, electronic format. In order to implement this right,

---

14 See Section 10.6 – Rights of Data Subjects.

it is important that, once the data have been transferred, no trace is left in the original system. In technical terms, it should become possible to verify the secure erasure of data.

The following are further IT security principles for Humanitarian Organizations to consider when moving to the cloud.

10.5.1 DATA IN TRANSIT PROTECTION

Data transmissions must be properly secured against eavesdropping and tampering. This is relevant not only for connections between the premises of the organization and the cloud application, but also for data paths inside the service and for connections between the application and other services (API).[15] A common solution is the encryption of network traffic, using network level traffic encryption (VPN),[16] transport layer security (TLS) or application level encryption. Due care must be taken to choose the correct protocols and implementation of encryption, as well as in the management of secret keys for the encryption itself. Dedicated fibre-optic connections can also be used, where they are convenient and the situation allows it.

10.5.2 ASSET PROTECTION

Protecting assets in cloud situations is different from protecting them in on-site arrangements. Consequently, several specific points need to be considered when evaluating a cloud solution.

10.5.2.1 PHYSICAL LOCATION

It is important to know the physical location(s) of data storage in order to understand which legislation applies, but also the likelihood of specific threats, such as power and network outages, actions by hostile groups and organizations and other country-specific threats. It is therefore important to obtain a detailed statement regarding the physical location of data centres and be aware that data exchanges between data centres in different locations can happen without the organization's knowledge.

For Humanitarian Organizations with privileges and immunities, it is also essential that the country in which data centres are stored has a legal obligation to respect privileges and immunities, and is known to respect them in practice.

---

15 API – an application programming interface is a set of subroutine definitions, protocols and tools for building application software: "API", in *Wikipedia*, accessed 13 January 2022: https://en.wikipedia.org/wiki/API.
16 VPN – A virtual private network extends a private network across a public network, such as the Internet. It enables users to send and receive data across shared or public networks as if their computing devices were directly connected to the private network: "Virtual Private Network", in *Wikipedia*, accessed 16 January 2022, https://en.wikipedia.org/w/index.php?title=Virtual_private_network&oldid=1065922505.

10.5.2.2 DATA CENTRE SECURITY

In Cloud Service arrangements, the physical security of data centres is fully controlled by the service provider; it is therefore important to have a clear idea of the security at the premises in which the data and applications are stored. This can be achieved by verifying the certifications (if any) obtained by the data centre and/or the contractual obligations underlying the relationship between the Cloud Service provider and the organization. The level of security guaranteed should match the level of security required by the application to be hosted in the cloud. Physical inspection could give useful information, but is unlikely to be possible in most cloud environments.

10.5.2.3 DATA AT REST SECURITY

The level of security for data at rest depends on the type of service required and other arrangements with the service provider. However, it is reasonable to assume that data will be stored in shared storage media, so a clear statement of the service provider about the protection level and how it is achieved is required, along with any related Third Party certification. However, it is recommended not to rely only on cloud provider security for data at rest, at least for most Sensitive Data, but to add additional layers of protection, such as encryption.

10.5.2.4 DATA SANITIZATION

Cloud environments are characterized by a high frequency of provisioning, deletion and migration of resources; in other words, data and applications can easily be moved around different parts of the shared infrastructure. If not correctly managed, this could lead to data disclosure, as other customers' applications will likely be run on the same hardware previously used by Humanitarian Organizations. Moreover, data could remain indefinitely in the cloud infrastructure. Measures should be taken to control this threat: using dedicated resources and/or verifying with the provider which measures are in place to erase or otherwise sanitize the data. The use of encryption, independently from the service provider, could offer an additional layer of protection.

10.5.2.5 EQUIPMENT DISPOSAL

Equipment disposal is closely related to the previous point and a fair level of confidence should be achieved that no data or information could remain stored or possibly be disclosed when hardware is decommissioned or disposed of. The cloud provider should give some guarantee that this requirement can be met or other measures must be adopted (i.e. encryption).

10.5.2.6 AVAILABILITY

Cloud Services must offer the required level of availability; service-level agreements (SLAs) are of paramount importance in this respect. The agreement should also be examined in terms of liabilities and responsibility. Verification of any publicly available information, which could help in ascertaining the actual reliability of the service offered, is recommended.

10.5.3 SEPARATION BETWEEN USERS

In a cloud environment, the service provider is responsible for guaranteeing user separation. However, it is important when evaluating a cloud provider, and even more so when the provider and the related technology are not widely known, to assess the technology used and gather any information that can help in understanding how the separation is ensured. The separation is affected by several factors, such as the service model, the deployment model (public versus private cloud) and other factors. To assess the effectiveness of separation measures, a penetration test can be useful, but only to a limited extent: it is valid only for the specific time when the test is carried out and it only gives an indication about known issues. A background check of previous incidents and their management by the provider can also be extremely useful.

10.5.4 GOVERNANCE

The service provider should have a proper security governance framework, as this is the basis to control and coordinate all security efforts, and to manage changes in threat and developments in technology. The provider should then demonstrate that it possesses the required elements that are typically associated with a C* level manager (e.g. CSO, CISO, CTO) in charge of cloud security; that it has a properly implemented framework for security governance; that security and security risks are included in general risk and financial management; and that it complies with regulations and legal requirements. Conformance with recognized standards should be assessed.

10.5.5 OPERATIONAL SECURITY

The cloud provision service must be operated in accordance with strict security requirements and security must be embedded in standard operating procedures. The main elements are:
- Configuration and change management, to control what is in the production environment and related changes, to perform the required tests and receive proper authorization before making changes.
- Vulnerability management, to assess, identify and correct security issues that can arise in services and infrastructure.
- Monitoring, to detect anomalies, attacks and unauthorized actions that can undermine the security of the services.
- Incident management: when an incident occurs, the service provider must be able to address it by taking adequate measures in order to mitigate, contain and properly correct the issue. This includes communications and reports to the customers and law enforcement authorities.

10.5.6 PERSONNEL

The Cloud Service provider must have in place measures to assess the trustworthiness of the personnel involved in the service management. Proper background checks and screening should be implemented for any privileged or sensitive role. Operators should be trained and must understand and acknowledge their responsibilities.

10.5.7 DEVELOPMENT

Service providers usually develop large parts of their infrastructure. They should employ best practices and industry standards to ensure that threats are evaluated during development. Guidelines for secure design, coding, testing and deployment should be in place.

10.5.8 SUPPLY CHAIN

Cloud providers often use Third Party products and services to integrate or manage the services they offer. Any weakness along the supply chain can compromise the security of the entire Cloud Service and applications. The provider should describe how the Third Party suppliers are screened; the acceptance process for services and products; how security risks are managed; how the security posture of the service providers is verified; and how spare parts, updates and other changes are verified. This process is made even more important by the fact that Cloud Services can be layered, relying on other service providers lower down the chain. If possible, verification of the suppliers should be performed or agreements should be in place to prevent the cloud provider from using Third Party suppliers not acceptable to the organization.

Additional supply chain concerns relate to how the choice of technology that shares the same supply chain as organizations of a non-humanitarian nature may have a detrimental impact on the capacity of the Humanitarian Organization to rely on its neutral, impartial and independent exclusively humanitarian approach to security.[17]

10.5.9 USER MANAGEMENT

Depending on the service offered, the authorization process may, in part, be managed by the cloud provider. This process should be assessed to verify its compliance with best practices, regulations and the organization's needs, in order to ensure secure access to management interfaces. These interfaces allow the performance of actions that can be considered equivalent, to a certain extent, to physical actions performed inside a traditional data centre. Consequently, such actions need to be

---

17 Massimo Marelli, "The SolarWinds hack: Lessons for international humanitarian organizations", *International Review of the Red Cross*, Vol. 104, No. 919, 28 March 2022, pp. 1267–1284: https://doi.org/10.1017/S1816383122000194.

carefully guarded. Privileges should be fine-grained, so as to ensure the correct management of roles and privileges.

10.5.10 IDENTITY AND AUTHENTICATION

As with user management, access to any service interface should be strictly guarded. Implementation of identification and authorization processes should be assessed to conform to the security needs of the organization. Examples of different approaches are: two-factor authentication, use of TLS client certificates, single sign-on systems, etc. The methods adopted must be kept up to date with developments in security and the growing sophistication of the threats.

10.5.11 EXTERNAL INTERFACES

When management interfaces are exposed, this increases the attack surface available to hostile entities. The security of those interfaces should therefore be assessed against this threat; the availability of solutions such as private networks or equivalent measures to access private interfaces should be assessed.

10.5.12 SERVICE ADMINISTRATION

The architecture and management of administration systems should be carefully designed and implemented, as these systems are highly valuable for attackers. Thus, a description of administration systems management and procedures can be useful to assess the security posture of the service provider.

10.5.13 AUDITS

The service provider should make available the results of independent audits or allow the cloud customer either to directly perform an audit or to ask a trusted Third Party to carry out such an assessment. Audit data regarding the services (performance, downtime, security incidents and so on) should also be available for scrutiny. These audits should be regularly carried out, with a frequency which is adequate to the nature and purpose of the cloud service. The best practice in this regard, which is also the generally recognized rule for certification and attestation audits, is to set at least an annual frequency for these audits, and to carry out additional ad hoc audits in the event of a substantial or relevant change to the target of the audit.

10.5.14 SERVICE USAGE

The organization must have a clear understanding of the interactions with the Cloud Service: interfaces, data exchanges, authorization process for users, administration, workloads and any other aspect that can influence the service considered as the sum of cloud and organization activities. A detailed assessment of data flow, processes and architectures must be conducted prior to implementing a cloud solution. Proper procedures must be designed and implemented, personnel must be trained, and operators should be provided with the requisite knowledge about the cloud solution, the usage, the relationship with the organization and other information related to correct use and management of the cloud solution.

10.6 RIGHTS OF DATA SUBJECTS

Data Subjects' rights (e.g. access, rectification, erasure, objection, etc.) naturally extend to Processing in the cloud.[18] The Humanitarian Organization must verify that the cloud provider does not impose technical and organizational obstacles to these requirements, even in cases when data are further processed by subcontractors. The contract between the client and the provider should require that the cloud provider facilitates the exercise of the Data Subjects' rights, includes specific stipulations on how this collaboration will be provided and ensures that the same exercise of these rights is safeguarded in its relationship with any subcontractor.

10.7 INTERNATIONAL DATA SHARING

By their very nature Cloud Services may involve International Data Sharing of Personal Data with various parties located in different countries. Data protection laws restrict International Data Sharing; Humanitarian Organizations should therefore ensure that the use of Cloud Services is in compliance with any laws to which they are subject, if any, and with their own internal policies. This means, for example, that any contract with a cloud provider should indicate how the provider complies with legal requirements concerning International Data Sharing (e.g. through the use of contractual clauses with its entities and with subcontractors). Performing a DPIA[19] with specific attention to the impact of the International Data Sharing (such as a Data Transfer Impact Assessment) on the right and freedoms of the concerned Data Subjects contributes to further strengthen the lawfulness of such Processing from a data protection perspective and, where relevant, to preserve privileges and immunities for the Humanitarian Organizations which benefit from them.

10.8 DATA PROTECTION IMPACT ASSESSMENTS

Data Protection Impact Assessments (DPIAs) are important tools during project design to ensure that all aspects of data protection regulations and applicable risks are addressed. It is essential to carry out specific DPIAs tailored to cloud computing whenever there is interest in using Cloud Services.[20] DPIAs should clarify the Processing details and specifications, and also focus on the risks posed by them as

---

18   See Section 2.11 – Rights of Data Subjects.
19   See Section 10.8 – Data Protection Impact Assessments.
20   See Chapter 5: Data Protection Impact Assessments (DPIAs).

well as on mitigating measures. In this respect, it is important to note that DPIAs should be undertaken prior to the use of Cloud Services.

10.9 PRIVILEGES AND IMMUNITIES AND THE CLOUD

Beyond the considerations above, Humanitarian Organizations benefiting from privileges and immunities should also consider that data placed in the cloud may jeopardize the protection of such privileges and immunities, unless specific legal, technical and organizational measures are put in place. This consideration is key, particularly given that in Humanitarian Emergencies, the privileges and immunities of a Humanitarian Organization may be the first line of protection for the Personal Data of vulnerable individuals, particularly in conflicts and other situations of violence. This matter is closely connected to the one of "data sovereignty" in the cloud, i.e. the jurisdictional control or legal authority that apply to data being subjected to the country's laws because the cloud and/or the cloud provider are located within the country.[21]

Humanitarian Organizations should consider implementing the legal, organizational and technical measures suggested below, to ensure that their privileges and immunities are adequately protected in a cloud environment and to keep "sovereignty" over their data.[22]

10.9.1 LEGAL MEASURES
- Data should be hosted and processed by external Data Processors exclusively in jurisdictions where the privileges and immunities of the organization are formally recognized by status agreements recognizing the inviolability of files, archives, correspondence and communication wherever and by whomever the organizations' data are held, as well as immunity from every form of legal process. This legal protection should ideally be backed by a track record of such privileges and immunities being consistently respected.
- Data Processors and Sub-Processors should be bound by contractual obligation to notify any requesting authorities who seek to access data, that the data in question are covered by a Humanitarian Organization's privileges and immunities; to decline any requests for access by authorities, whether informal, administrative or through judicial process, and to redirect the authorities' request to the

---

21 See Marelli, "The SolarWinds hack", and particularly the section "'Data sovereignty' and 'digital sovereignty': Tools for protecting humanitarian principles in cyberspace".
22 Massimo Marelli, "Hacking humanitarians: Defining the cyber perimeter and developing a cyber security strategy for international humanitarian organizations in digital transformation", *International Review of the Red Cross*, Vol. 102, No. 913, April 2020, pp. 367–387: https://doi.org/10.1017/S1816383121000151.

Humanitarian Organization; to immediately notify the Humanitarian Organization of any request for access to its data, whether informal, administrative or through judicial process, the identity of the requesting authority and status of the request; and to assist the Humanitarian Organization with the provision of any information and documentation that may be necessary as part of any proceedings, whether informal, administrative or through judicial process, that may be required by the Humanitarian Organization in order to assert its privileges and immunities over the relevant data.

10.9.2 ORGANIZATIONAL MEASURES

- The data of the Humanitarian Organization should be held in segregated servers, and the data should be segregated from the data of other clients of the Data Processors and Sub-Processors.
- The servers hosting the data of the Humanitarian Organizations should be clearly marked with the emblem of the organization, and the indication "Legally Privileged Information" should be marked on the servers.
- Where possible, the servers hosting the data of Humanitarian Organizations should only be accessed with the authorization of both the Data Processors and of the Humanitarian Organization.
- Staff of the Data Processor and Sub-Processors should be properly informed of the privileged status of the data, and trained on the procedure to follow in case of requests for access by Third Parties.

10.9.3 TECHNICAL MEASURES

- Data hosted in a cloud environment should be encrypted and encryption keys held only by the Humanitarian Organization.
- If the cloud solution envisaged is a SaaS, and the Data Processors and Sub-Processors need to manage the service offered, arrangements should be made to ensure that such Data Processors and Sub-Processors may access the system to manage it, run updates, fix bugs and support users, without ever having access to clear (unencrypted) data.

10.10 CODES OF CONDUCT

Finally, it is worth mentioning that in 2021 the European Data Protection Board (EDPB) approved two codes of conduct[23] for the application of the GDPR to Cloud

---

23 See: Opinion 16/2021 on the draft decision of the Belgian Supervisory Authority regarding the "EU Data Protection Code of Conduct for Cloud Service Providers" submitted by Scope Europe (https://edpb.europa.eu/system/files/2021-05/edpb_opinion_202116_eucloudcode_en.pdf) and Opinion 17/2021 on the draft decision of the French Supervisory Authority regarding the European code of conduct submitted by the Cloud Infrastructure Service Providers (CISPE) (https://edpb.europa.eu/system/files/2021-05/edpb_opinion_202117_cispecode_en_0.pdf).

Services pursuant to Article 40, and a third one is currently being evaluated by the European Supervisory Authorities.[24] For Humanitarian Organizations which are subject to the GDPR, it will be recommendable to check whether a specific service is approved under one of the applicable codes of conduct. The adherence to a code of conduct must be seen just as a good starting point. In fact, given their specific issues and requirements, Humanitarian Organizations will still need to specifically and carefully consider all the matters indicated in this chapter.

---

24 Cloud Security Alliance (CSA), "CSA Code of Conduct for GDPR Compliance", CSA, accessed 9 May 2022: https://cloudsecurityalliance.org/privacy/gdpr/code-of-conduct.

GOVERNMENT ACCESS TO DATA PROCESSED IN A PUBLIC CLOUD ENVIRONMENT

increase in legislation allowing disclosure of data

national security

criminal proceedings

CHALLENGES

governments may require disclosure from service providers directly

Humanitarian Organizations may not be aware of a disclosure order

RISK MITIGATION

need to consider which data to process in a cloud environment

the compelled disclosure of humanitarian data can undermine trust in Humanitarian Organizations

ensure the effectiveness of their privileges and immunities

sensitize states to the importance of refraining from using humanitarian data

CHAPTER 11

CLOUD AND GOVERNMENT ACCESS

Andrea Raab-Gray*

---

* Disclaimer: the opinions and views expressed in this contribution are the author's own and do not necessarily represent those of the Federal Ministry of European and International Affairs of the Republic of Austria.

States around the globe have in place domestic laws authorizing governments to require service providers to disclose to them manifold types of data created by or relating to a customer, in the interest of national security and/or for use in criminal proceedings. The often-cited rationale underlying such legislation is a growing use of digital technologies, including cloud computing, for illicit purposes.[1] Yet, even if only as a side effect, many of these legislations also enable governments to compel the disclosure of data pertaining to action of Humanitarian Organizations, processed in a public cloud environment. Such data could encompass data that Humanitarian Organizations generate, collect or exchange with others, including the contents of communications within the organization, with their partners or persons benefiting from their action. Data subject to disclosure also often include meta, location and traffic data, that is, data about the communications other than their contents, such as data about the recipient of a communication, the duration of a call and the like.[2] For purposes of brevity, this chapter will refer to such content, meta, location and traffic data together as "Humanitarian Data".

In terms of relevance of Humanitarian Data to States, it is important to understand that Humanitarian Organizations often fulfil their mandates in a Neutral, Impartial and Independent manner. As such, several such organizations provide assistance to and generally conduct dialogue with all sides to an armed conflict or other crisis. This may include non-State actors and individuals which States might designate as "terrorists" in relevant legislative frameworks. In granting impartial Humanitarian Organizations a right of initiative, international humanitarian law for instance accommodates – and indeed endorses – this. This right entails that impartial Humanitarian Organizations may offer their humanitarian activities to parties to international and non-international armed conflicts, regardless of how a conflict may be characterized under counterterrorism or sanctions regimes.[3] Thus, Humanitarian Data can be of interest to governments for purposes of counterterrorism action and criminal proceedings.

In selecting technology, and particularly Cloud Services, Humanitarian Organizations should therefore consider legal and operational consequences stemming from legislations allowing governments to require disclosure of data from service providers, including those processing Humanitarian Data. This chapter seeks to inform Humanitarian

---

[1] See for example: US Department of Justice, *Promoting Public Safety, Privacy, and the Rule of Law around the World: The Purpose and Impact of the CLOUD Act*, White Paper, US Department of Justice, Washington, DC, April 2019: www.justice.gov/dag/page/file/1153436/download.

[2] For further information on the importance of metadata for Humanitarian Organizations, see ICRC and Privacy International, *The Humanitarian Metadata Problem*.

[3] See Common Article 3 to the 1949 Geneva Conventions, as well as Common Articles 9/9/9/10. For further information on this, see Tristan Ferraro, "International humanitarian law, principled humanitarian action, counterterrorism and sanctions: Some perspectives on selected issues", *International Review of the Red Cross*, Vol. 103, No. 916/917, 2021, pp. 109–155.

Organizations in their reflections: Section 11.1 maps legislations that, even if only as a by-product, allow governments to require service providers to disclose Humanitarian Data for purposes of national security and/or criminal proceedings. Section 11.2 outlines criteria for Humanitarian Organizations to consider when assessing the impacts such disclosure can have on persons benefiting from their action, and organizations' operations. Finally, Section 11.3 provides guidance as to the legal avenues Humanitarian Organizations could take in mitigating the risk of disclosure of Humanitarian Data if they choose to process Humanitarian Data in a public cloud environment.[4]

11.1 MAPPING LEGISLATIONS ALLOWING GOVERNMENTS TO REQUIRE SERVICE PROVIDERS TO DISCLOSE HUMANITARIAN DATA

Humanitarian Organizations should take into account legislations that allow governments to compel service providers to disclose to governments Humanitarian Data for purposes of national security and/or criminal proceedings, in selecting technology, and particularly when:
- considering whether and which data to process in a public cloud environment; and
- selecting cloud service providers.

Propelled by the increasing use of digital technologies, including Cloud Services, for illicit purposes,[5] the legislations discussed in this chapter are not as such intended to target specifically Humanitarian Data. However, these legislations do not exclude

---

[4] This chapter does not address forms of "illegal access", such as hacking without any legal basis. This is because illegal access is not necessarily cloud-specific and raises broader questions both in relation to legal and cyber security responses. See for instance Massimo Marelli, "Hacking humanitarians: Defining the cyber perimeter and developing a cyber security strategy for international humanitarian organizations in digital transformation", *International Review of the Red Cross*, Vol. 102, No. 913, April 2020, pp. 367–387: https://doi.org/10.1017/S1816383121000151. Equally, this chapter does not discuss so-called cloud extraction, a forensic analysis of user data which is stored on Third Party servers, typically used by device and application manufacturers to back up data. Increasingly used by law enforcement, this new trend raises similar concerns for Humanitarian Organizations to the legislations discussed in this chapter. For further information, see Privacy International, "Cloud Extraction", Privacy International, 9 May 2022: https://privacyinternational.org/learn/cloud-extraction; Privacy International, "Are UK Police Accessing Your Cloud Apps?", Privacy International, 1 April 2020: http://privacyinternational.org/report/3551/are-uk-police-accessing-your-cloud-apps; Privacy International, "Secret Tech Lets Governments Collect Masses of Data from Your Apps", Privacy International, 6 January 2020: http://privacyinternational.org/node/3323.

[5] See for instance: European Commission, "Proposal for a Regulation of the European Parliament and of the Council on European Production and Preservation Orders for Electronic Evidence in Criminal Matters", COM/2018/225 final, 17 April 2018: https://eur-lex.europa.eu/legal-content/EN/TXT/?uri=COM:2018:225:FIN.

Humanitarian Data from their scope, either: indeed, these legislations do not generally contain "humanitarian exemption clauses" explicitly excluding Humanitarian Data. On the contrary, oftentimes legal requirements authorizing governments to require disclosure of data from service providers squarely apply to Humanitarian Data, as will be shown below.

Disclosure requests for Humanitarian Data addressed to service providers differ as compared to disclosure requests for such data served on Humanitarian Organizations themselves. Where a Humanitarian Organization receives such a request itself, it is in a position to evaluate how to respond to this request, in light of its mandate and policies. Should it decide not to accede to a disclosure request, it may resort to remedies enshrined in national law to oppose disclosure. In addition, a Humanitarian Organization might be able to invoke privileges and immunities which they may enjoy under national and/or international law (see also Section 11.3 – Mitigating the risk of disclosure of Humanitarian Data processed in a public cloud environment, further below). This is irrespective of where data are hosted, be it in a private or public cloud environment. Yet, when providers receive disclosure requests from State authorities, Humanitarian Organizations are dependent on how the provider will respond to such a request, for instance whether they will inform the Humanitarian Organization of a disclosure request (provided they are legally permitted to do so), and whether they will raise legal defences to oppose the request.[6]

This chapter draws on illustrative examples of relevant legislations in the United States, the United Kingdom and the European Union. It should however be noted that other States too have adopted legislation enabling them to compel service providers to disclose customer data – including potentially data of Humanitarian Organizations – for purposes of national security and/or criminal proceedings.[7]

11.1.1 LEGAL FRAMEWORKS ALLOWING GOVERNMENTS TO COMPEL SERVICE PROVIDERS TO DISCLOSE HUMANITARIAN DATA FOR PURPOSES OF NATIONAL SECURITY

Several States have adopted legislation providing governments with legal avenues to compel service providers under their jurisdiction to disclose data for purposes of

---

[6] See also Section 10.9 – Privileges and immunities and the cloud, on the legal measures to be taken by Humanitarian Organizations to ensure the effectiveness of privileges and immunities in protecting data processed in a cloud environment.

[7] See for instance the Parliament of Australia, Telecommunications Legislation Amendment (International Production Orders) Bill 2020 (2020): https://parlinfo.aph.gov.au/parlInfo/search/display/display.w3p;query=Id%3A%22legislation%2Fbillhome%2Fr6511%22. See also European Data Protection Board (EDPB), "Government Access to Data in Third Countries", EDPS/2019/02-13, November 2021: https://edpb.europa.eu/system/files/2022-01/legalstudy_on_government_access_0.pdf.

national security. Thus, by choosing cloud service providers under those States' jurisdiction, Humanitarian Organizations should be aware that their data might be subject to disclosure for national security purposes.

A well-known example of such legislation is the US PATRIOT Act, enacted in October 2001 in response to the attacks on the World Trade Center.[8] It allows the US government to require service providers under US personal jurisdiction[9] to disclose certain data to them. It follows that, when a Humanitarian Organization onboards services of a US service provider, its data might come within the scope of the PATRIOT Act and might be vulnerable to disclosure requests under that Act.

Of particular interest for Humanitarian Organizations contemplating the use of Cloud Services are the PATRIOT Act's regimes on orders made under the Foreign Intelligence Surveillance Act (FISA), as well as on National Security Letters.[10] Under the FISA, the US government is authorized to:

- obtain a secret court order requiring Third Parties, such as cloud service providers, to hand over any records or other "tangible thing" if deemed "relevant" to an international terrorism, counterespionage, or foreign intelligence investigation;[11] and
- issue orders requiring, for instance, cloud service providers under US personal jurisdiction to disclose communications data of specific non-US persons located outside the United States to obtain specified types of foreign intelligence information, upon authorization by an independent court, the FISA Court.[12]

---

8   Specifically, to facilitate the investigation of terrorism crimes, the Act amended pre-existing laws by extending the application of surveillance tools to terrorism investigations, and expanded their scope. See on this and on the PATRIOT Act more generally: US Department of Justice, "The USA PATRIOT Act: Preserving Life and Liberty", n.d.: www.justice.gov/archive/ll/what_is_the_patriot_act.pdf; American Civil Liberties Union, "Surveillance under the USA/PATRIOT Act", n.d.: www.aclu.org/other/surveillance-under-usapatriot-act; Greenberg Traurig LLP, "Schrems II – U.S. Legislation", Memorandum, 12 February 2022: https://slmmicrosoftrijk.nl/wp-content/uploads/2022/02.
9   See for instance Daniel Levin and Jacqueline L. Chung, "Patriot Act Subpoenas: Reinvigorated and Reaching across Borders", White & Case LLP, n.d.: www.whitecase.com/insight-alert/patriot-act-subpoenas-reinvigorated-and-reaching-across-borders.
10   While the number of requests for FISA orders is relatively low, National Security Letters have been used more frequently. For 2020 statistics, see Joseph Gaeta, "Letter to Nancy Pelosi", 30 April 2021: www.justice.gov/nsd/nsd-foia-library/2020_fisa/download.
11   Brennan Center for Justice, "Are They Allowed to Do That? A Breakdown of Selected Government Surveillance Programs", accessed 27 November 2022: www.brennancenter.org/sites/default/files/analysis/Government%20Surveillance%20Factsheet.pdf. See also: "Uniting and Strengthening America by Providing Appropriate Tools Required to Intercept and Obstruct Terrorism (USA PATRIOT Act) Act of 2001", Pub. L. No. 107-56, § 215 (2001): www.congress.gov/107/plaws/publ56/PLAW-107publ56.pdf; 50 U.S.C. §1804(a)(6)(B).
12   See "An Act to Authorize Electronic Surveillance to Obtain Foreign Intelligence Information", Pub. L. No. 95-511, § 702 (1978), www.congress.gov/bill/95th-congress/senate-bill/1566. According to the Brennan Center for Justice at New York University, this section has also been cited as the legal

The FISA Court has authorized the collection of both metadata and content of communications pursuant to section 702 under at least some circumstances.[13] Section 702 has been applied to both data in transit and data at rest.[14]

By virtue of National Security Letters, the Director of the Federal Bureau of Investigation (FBI) and other high-ranking FBI officials can require, for example, cloud service providers to disclose subscriber information and toll billing records information, or electronic communication transactional records that are relevant to an authorized investigation to protect against international terrorism or clandestine intelligence activities.[15] It follows that National Security Letters cannot be used to obtain any data about the content of communications.

Humanitarian Data might indeed be "relevant" to the purposes outlined above. For instance, to fulfil their mandate in an impartial and neutral manner, some Humanitarian Organizations might conduct dialogue with groups designated as "terrorist", or furnish humanitarian assistance to persons under the control of such groups. If these organizations choose to process data pertaining to this dialogue in a public cloud environment, some of these data might be subject to disclosure under the PATRIOT Act.

In Europe, case law of the European Court of Justice (CJEU) is instructive in delineating the contours of EU Member States' powers to require service providers to retain, in particular, traffic and location data for purposes of government access. While the case law of the CJEU does not specifically concern cloud computing, the author nevertheless considers it relevant for the discussion at hand: it allows conclusions to be drawn about the general approach towards balancing national security considerations and rights in Europe. As such, it cannot be excluded that the said criteria are equally applied in a cloud context.

In the *Watson* and *Privacy International* cases, the CJEU had to consider, amongst other legislations, UK law allowing authorities to require certain service providers to retain and grant access to certain metadata.[16] In both cases, the Court held that

---

justification for PRISM, a computer network facilitating access to data processed by nine leading US Internet companies, including Google, Facebook, Skype and Apple: Brennan Center for Justice, "Are They Allowed to Do That? A Breakdown of Selected Government Surveillance Programs".

13 Stephen I. Vladeck, "Expert opinion on the current state of U.S. surveillance law and authorities", in *Conference of Independent Data Protection Supervisors of the Federal Government and the Länder*, 2021, 2: www.datenschutzkonferenz-online.de/media/weitere_dokumente/Vladek_Rechtsgutachten_DSK_en.pdf.

14 Ibid., 4.

15 18 U.S.C. § 2709.

16 Joined Cases C-203/15 and C-698/15 (*Tele 2 Sverige* and *Watson*), Judgment (Grand Chamber), 21 December 2016; Case C-623/17 (*Privacy International*), Judgment (Grand Chamber), 6 October 2020. In *Privacy International*, for instance, the CJEU was asked to determine which requirements apply to an

national legislation which provides for the general and indiscriminate retention and disclosure to authorities of all traffic and location data of all subscribers relating to all means of electronic communication is incompatible with EU law.[17] Yet, the Court also stated that "in particular situations, where for example vital national security, defence or public security interests are threatened by terrorist activities, access to the data of other persons might also be granted where there is objective evidence from which it can be deduced that that data might, in a specific case, make an effective contribution to combatting such activities".[18] As such, the criteria set out by the Court do not *per se* target Humanitarian Data, but they also do not exclude such data. On the contrary, where a Humanitarian Organization in fulfilling its mandate conducts dialogue with certain non-State actors, location and traffic data pertaining to such dialogue *might* indeed be considered to contribute to combatting "terrorist activities".

Moreover, Humanitarian Organizations might not even be aware that their data are being sought. For instance, under the PATRIOT Act, US government authorities can impose non-disclosure obligations, whereby service providers are prohibited from informing any Third Party – including Humanitarian Organizations as customers – about the National Security Letter or FISA order.[19]

Finally, in choosing to process Humanitarian Data in a public cloud environment, Humanitarian Organizations should also consider potential risks stemming from interception by security authorities. In the seminal *Big Brother Watch* case, the European Court of Human Rights examined, amongst other issues, the compatibility with Article 8 of the European Convention on Human Rights of warrants issued under the UK Regulation for Investigatory Powers Act 2000 (RIPA), allowing for bulk interception by security agencies of both content and communications data for purposes of national security.[20] In so doing, the Court emphasized the need for clarity of such laws in relation to grounds for bulk interception, applicable procedure, limitations and safeguards.[21] The Court also considered that the same safeguards

---

order by authorities to a service provider to disclose to them bulk communications for national security purposes under the UK Regulation for Investigatory Powers Act 2000 (RIPA) and the UK Telecommunications Act 1984. On data retention, see also Joined Cases C-511/18, C-512/18 and C-520/18 (*La Quadrature du Net and ors*), 6 October 2020.

17 *Watson*, para. 112; *Privacy International*, para. 81.
18 *Watson*, para. 119. See also *Privacy International*, para. 78.
19 50 U.S.C 1861(d); 18 U.S.C § 2709(c).
20 *Big Brother Watch and others v. United Kingdom*, Applications nos. 58170/13, 62322/14 and 24960/15, Grand Chamber, Judgment, 25 May 2021. For a similar case, see *Centrum för rättvisa* v. *Sweden*, Application no. 35252/08, Grand Chamber, Judgment, 25 May 2021.
21 *Big Brother Watch*, para. 361. For a summary of other parts of the judgments, see Marko Milanovic, "The Grand Normalization of Mass Surveillance: ECtHR Grand Chamber Judgments in Big Brother Watch and Centrum För Rättvisa", EJIL: Talk! (blog), 26 May 2021: www.ejiltalk.org/the-grand-

should apply to the collection and Processing of communications data and metadata, not just the content of communications.[22] Importantly, the Court did not define any criteria which might exclude Humanitarian Data from the scope of bulk interception.[23] The UK RIPA was replaced by the UK 2016 Investigatory Powers Act. This piece of legislation too allows for a bulk interception warrant for "content" of communications and/or "secondary data", including certain data which may be used to identify any person or the location of any person, event or thing, if this is necessary in the interests of national security, amongst other grounds, without explicitly excluding Humanitarian Data.[24]

While the *Big Brother Watch* case again does not specifically concern cloud computing, the author considers it relevant for the same reasons as set out above in relation to the case law of the CJEU.

11.1.2 LEGAL FRAMEWORKS ALLOWING GOVERNMENTS TO COMPEL SERVICE PROVIDERS TO DISCLOSE DATA FOR PURPOSES OF CRIMINAL PROCEEDINGS

One of the most prominent examples of such legislations is the US CLOUD Act. The first part of the CLOUD Act clarifies that:[25]

---

normalization-of-mass-surveillance-ecthr-grand-chamber-judgments-in-big-brother-watch-and-centrum-for-rattvisa. While the *Big Brother Watch* case in particular did not concern obligations on the service provider to provide data to national authorities, it is crucial in showcasing the extent of deference courts have paid to national security interests.

22 *Big Brother Watch*, paras. 342, 363–364.

23 Ultimately, the Court found that the bulk interception regime of the RIPA breached privacy obligations under the Convention, *Id*, paras. 424–427. While some human rights organizations have hailed the judgment a landmark victory, other commentators have criticized the decision as normalizing mass surveillance and bulk interception, highlighting that the Court considered those mechanisms as "valuable" and of "vital importance" to the security of Member States of the Council of Europe. See Milanovic, "The Grand Normalization of Mass Surveillance", setting out different positions taken.

24 See sections 136 *et seqq.* of the 2016 Investigatory Powers Act. Note in this regard the case of *Privacy International v. Investigatory Powers Tribunal, [2021] EWHC 27 (Admin)*, 8 January 2021. Privacy International explain that, in that case, the UK High Court held that section 5 of the Intelligence Services Act (ISA) 1994 does not permit the security and intelligence services to rely on non-specific warrants – otherwise known as general warrants – to authorize their wide-ranging hacking and property interference powers. Thematic warrants are general warrants covering an entire class of property, persons or conduct, such as "all mobile phones used by a member of a criminal gang", without specifying the names or locations of the members. Privacy International, "Q&A: PI Case – UK High Court Judgment on General Warrants and Government Hacking Explained", Privacy International, 8 January 2021: http://privacyinternational.org/long-read/4361/qa-pi-case-uk-high-court-judgment-general-warrants-and-government-hacking-explained. It remains to be seen if this judgment will have any impact on the interpretation of the IPA.

25 For more information, see also US Department of Justice, *Promoting Public Safety, Privacy, and the Rule of Law around the World*; Vladeck, "Expert opinion on the current state of U.S. surveillance law and authorities", 13; Greenberg Traurig LLP, "Schrems II – U.S. Legislation", 12 February 2022, 9; Swiss

- US authorities may compel the disclosure of content *and* traffic data over which a service provider under US personal jurisdiction has "possession, custody or control":[26]
    - for purposes of certain criminal proceedings;[27]
    - irrespective of where the data are located.[28]

There is nothing in this first part of the CLOUD Act that exempts Humanitarian Data from its scope of application, nor are there any other limitations within the CLOUD Act that would implicitly exempt such data.

It follows that, if Humanitarian Organizations choose a service provider under US personal jurisdiction to process Humanitarian Data, these data might be vulnerable to requests for disclosure by US authorities, to the extent the US service provider has "custody, possession or control" over such data. The Act does not define the notions of "custody, possession or control", and, at the time of writing, it remains to be seen

---

Federal Department of Justice, "Bericht zum US CLOUD Act", 17 September 2021: www.bj.admin.ch/bj/de/home/publiservice/publikationen/berichte-gutachten/2021-09-17.html.

[26] US Department of Justice, *Promoting Public Safety, Privacy, and the Rule of Law around the World*, 8. It is noteworthy that the DoJ advised that CLOUD Act orders should be subsidiary measures, in that "prosecutors should seek data directly from the enterprise, if practical, and if doing so will not compromise the investigation. Therefore, before seeking data from a provider, the prosecutor, working with agents, should determine whether the enterprise or the provider is the better source for the data being sought": 17.

[27] See 18 U.S.C, §2703(b).

[28] Legal discourse focused on the question of whether the CLOUD Act triggered improper extraterritoriality of sovereign acts. See for example: Johannes Thumfart and Paul De Hert, "Both the US's Cloud Act and Europe's GDPR Move Far Beyond Geography, but Will Not Solve Transatlantic Jurisdictional Conflicts", Just Security, 4 June 2018: www.justsecurity.org/57346/uss-cloud-act-europes-gdpr-move-geography-solve-transatlantic-jurisdictional-conflicts. Everything started with the *Microsoft* litigation: In December 2013, federal law enforcement agents were granted a warrant requiring Microsoft to disclose all emails and other information associated with the account of one of its customers. (US Supreme Court, *United States v. Microsoft Corporation*, 584 U. S. (2018), p. 1.) Microsoft moved to quash the warrant, arguing that the account's email contents were stored solely in Microsoft's data centre in Ireland, i.e. outside the reach of US law. (Ibid., p. 2.) The question hence facing US courts was whether the data location outside the United States would pose an obstacle to enforcing the warrant, constituting improper extraterritorial application of US law. Microsoft and the US government litigated this question in various instances, and courts' opinions differed: While the Magistrate Judge denied Microsoft's motion, the Court of Appeals considered that requiring Microsoft to disclose the electronic communications in question would be an unauthorized extraterritorial application of the relevant US Act that served as a legal basis of the warrant. (*In re Warrant To Search a Certain E-Mail Account Controlled and Maintained by Microsoft Corp.*, 829 F. 3d 197, 205, 222 (CA2 2016).) Ultimately, the matter came before the US Supreme Court, which however vacated the review, as the US CLOUD Act had meanwhile entered into force which resolved the matter, by allowing US authorities to require disclosure from US service providers even if data are located abroad. (US Supreme Court, *United States v. Microsoft Corporation*, pp. 2–3.)

how authorities and courts will construe those terms in the context of the CLOUD Act.

Further to this, the US government can impose a non-disclosure obligation on the service provider under certain circumstances.[29] This means that the service provider may be prohibited from notifying the Humanitarian Organization of the existence of a request for its data.

EXAMPLE (SIMPLIFIED):
In fulfilling its mandate in a manner neutral and impartial, and to secure access to affected populations and provide them with humanitarian assistance, the Humanitarian Organization HO maintains dialogue with the group G, and its leader L. Group G is listed as a "terrorist" group under relevant legislation. HO stores the contents of this dialogue in a public cloud environment. The Cloud Services are provided by service provider SP, incorporated in New York (United States). Data are stored in Europe.

Under the US CLOUD Act, US authorities could have the power to legally oblige SP to disclose such data for purposes of certain criminal proceedings against L. SP might be prohibited from informing HO of this request. On blocking statutes and the impact of privileges and immunities, see Section 11.3 – Mitigating the risk of disclosure of Humanitarian Data processed in a public cloud environment, below.

Humanitarian Organizations should also bear in mind that choosing a US service provider might also allow other States to require disclosure of humanitarian content and traffic data from that service provider, for purposes of criminal proceedings.

This is because the second part of the CLOUD Act authorizes the US government to enter into so-called executive agreements with other countries, allowing one State party to require the disclosure of certain content and traffic data from service providers under the other party's jurisdiction, and vice versa, for purposes of preventing, detecting, investigating or prosecuting serious crime, including terrorism.[30] There is nothing in this second part of the CLOUD Act that exempts Humanitarian Data from its scope of application. The prime example for this is the UK/US

---

29   18 U.S.C, §2703(b), §2705.
30   18 U.S.C. §2523(b)(4)(D)(i). Disclosure orders must not intentionally target US persons. This term is defined as "a citizen or national of the United States, an alien lawfully admitted for permanent residence, an unincorporated association a substantial number of members of which are citizens of the United States or aliens lawfully admitted for permanent residence, or a corporation that is incorporated in the United States". 18 U.S.C. §2523(a)(2).

agreement, concluded under the second part of the CLOUD Act, and the UK Crime (Overseas Production Order) Act.[31]

The UK's equivalent to the second part of the CLOUD Act is the Crime (Overseas Production Order) Act, which received royal assent in February 2019. This law:[32]
- enables UK law enforcement agencies[33] to apply for a court order from a judge with extraterritorial effect ("Overseas Production Order");
- to obtain electronic data directly from service providers operating or based outside the UK but "in the possession or control" of the data sought;
- for purposes of criminal investigations and prosecutions of indictable offences or terrorist investigations;
- where a designated international cooperation arrangement with the State in which the service provider operates, is already in place.

There is nothing that explicitly exempts Humanitarian Data from the scope of the Act, although there is one exemption to the data that can be obtained via an Overseas Production Order that might be relevant for some Humanitarian Organizations: electronic data means data stored electronically and thus encompasses content and telecommunications data hosted in a public cloud environment.[34] Yet, information subject to legal privilege, such as certain communications between a client and their legal counsel, as well as personal records which are confidential information cannot be obtained via an Overseas Production Order.[35] Personal records which are confidential information include Health Data as well as data pertaining to counselling or assistance given, or to be given, to an individual for purposes of their personal welfare by any voluntary organization, if that record was created, amongst others, in circumstances giving rise to an obligation of confidence owed to the individual.[36] This latter exemption could in very rare cases encompass some data pertaining to Humanitarian Action undertaken by a Humanitarian Organization. Yet, the Act does not include any explicit exemption from its scope of application for data pertaining to Humanitarian Action.

Only electronic data that are likely to be of substantial value to these proceedings or investigations can be required to be disclosed under an Overseas Production Order.[37]

---

31 Agreement between the Government of the United States of America and the Government of the United Kingdom of Great Britain and Northern Ireland on Access to Electronic Data for the Purpose of Countering Serious Crime, 3 October 2019: www.justice.gov/dag/cloud-act-agreement-between-governments-us-united-kingdom-great-britain-and-northern-ireland.
32 Crime (Overseas Production Order) Act, sections 1, 2 and 4.
33 These include, *inter alia*, constables, prosecutors, and other persons specified in regulations made by the Secretary of State. Crime (Overseas Production Order) Act, section 2.
34 See Crime (Overseas Production Order) Act, section 3(2).
35 Crime (Overseas Production Order) Act, section 3(3).
36 Crime (Overseas Production Order) Act, sections 3(7) and 3(8).
37 Crime (Overseas Production Order) Act, section 4(5).

As noted above, to fulfil their mandate in an impartial and neutral manner, some Humanitarian Organizations might conduct dialogue with groups designated as "terrorist", or furnish humanitarian assistance to persons under the control of such groups. As such, it cannot be excluded that those Organizations may store information about that dialogue in a cloud environment, and that such information might indeed be of "substantial value" in terrorist investigations.

Premised on the second part of the CLOUD Act and the Crime (Overseas Production Order) Act, the US/UK agreement does not contain any express exemptions for Humanitarian Data. Therefore, such data can in principle also be required from service providers, unless one of the limitations contained in the agreement is applicable.

EXAMPLE 1 (SIMPLIFIED):
In fulfilling its mandate in a manner neutral and impartial, and to secure access to affected populations and provide them with humanitarian assistance, a Humanitarian Organization (HO) maintains dialogue with group G, and its leader L. Group G is listed as a "terrorist" group under relevant legislation. HO stores the contents of this dialogue in a public cloud environment. The Cloud Services are provided by Service Provider (SP), incorporated in New York (United States).

Under the US/UK agreement, UK authorities may require SP to disclose HO's data for purposes of "terrorist investigations", by presenting a duly approved court order to SP. Unless excluded from the scope of the agreement, SP must provide the information sought to UK authorities. On access by US authorities, see above, previous example.

EXAMPLE 2 (SIMPLIFIED):
In fulfilling its mandate in a manner neutral and impartial, and to secure access to affected populations and provide them with humanitarian assistance, the Humanitarian Organization HO maintains dialogue with group G, and its leader L. Group G is listed as a "terrorist" group under relevant legislation. HO stores the contents of this dialogue in a public cloud environment. The Cloud Services are provided by Service Provider (SP UK), incorporated in the UK.

Under the US/UK agreement, US authorities may require SP UK to disclose HO's data for purposes of "terrorist investigations", by presenting a duly approved warrant to SP UK. Unless excluded from the scope of the agreement, SP UK must provide the information sought to US authorities.

As far as is public knowledge, the only other agreement concluded at the time of writing which is similar to the UK/US agreement is an agreement between the United States and Australia.[38]

Humanitarian organisations should also be aware that the EU has adopted adopting legislation similar to the CLOUD Act and Crime (Overseas Production Order) Act, namely the e-Evidence Regulation, which will apply in full from 18 August 2026. The Regulation establishes a regime whereby law enforcement authorities ("LEAs") in one EU Member State will be able to issue legally-binding demands for certain data from certain categories of service providers (namely providers of electronic communications services, domain name and IP registration services, and information society services that enable users to communicate or store data) that are established or have a legal representative in a different EU Member State, or demand such service providers to preserve such data.[39]

On a broader European level, Humanitarian Organizations should note that the Committee of Ministers of the Council of Europe has adopted a Second Additional Protocol to the Convention on enhanced cooperation and the disclosure of electronic evidence. The Protocol aims to:

> *further enhance co-operation on cybercrime and the collection of evidence in electronic form of any criminal offence for the purpose of specific criminal investigations or proceedings through additional tools pertaining to more efficient mutual assistance and other forms of co-operation between competent authorities; cooperation in emergencies; and direct co-operation between competent authorities and service providers and other entities in possession or control of pertinent information.*[40]

To this end, the Protocol foresees for instance that a State Party may issue an order directly to a service provider in the territory of another Party, in order to obtain the disclosure of specified, stored subscriber information in that service provider's possession or control, where the subscriber information is needed for the issuing Party's specific criminal investigations or proceedings.[41]

---

38   Agreement between the Government of the United States of America and the Government of Australia on Access to Electronic Data for the Purpose of Countering Serious Crime, 15 December 2021: www.justice.gov/dag/cloud-act-agreement-between-governments-us-and-australia. For more resources, see Department of Justice, Cloud Act Resources, available at: Cloud Act Resources (justice.gov).

39   Lisa Peets, Marty Hansen, and Paul Maynard, "The EU E-Evidence Package Is Published in the Official Journal," Inside Global Tech, August 23, 2023, www.insideglobaltech.com/2023/08/23/the-eu-e-evidence-package-is-published-in-the-official-journal/#:~:text=In%20summary%2C%20the%20Regulation%20establishes,domain%20name%20and%20IP%20registration.

40   Preamble of the Protocol.

41   See Art. 7(1) of the Protocol.

11.2 IMPACTS OF COMPELLED DISCLOSURE ON HUMANITARIAN ACTION AND PERSONS BENEFITING FROM IT

In considering whether the legislations explained in the previous chapter pose any challenges to a Humanitarian Organization, one should take into account the impacts the disclosure of Humanitarian Data can have on:
- persons benefiting from action of a Humanitarian Organization; and
- operations of the Humanitarian Organization.

As regards the impacts on persons benefiting from Humanitarian Action, much depends on the services the Humanitarian Organization provides, and the type of data it collects from individuals.

EXAMPLE:
In fulfilling its mandate, a Humanitarian Organization might provide health services to survivors of sexual violence, and obtain their medical data as well as information about the circumstances of the sexual violence committed against them. The Humanitarian Organization stores this information in a public cloud environment. A State might seek to obtain data about this survivor when investigating sexual violence crimes in a given context, on the basis of territorial, personal or universal jurisdiction.

The compelled disclosure of medical data and data about the circumstances of the sexual violence for purposes of criminal proceedings can cause harm to the survivor themselves. In the first place, it takes away the agency of the survivor to themselves decide whether to provide this information to authorities. Second, in many communities, rape is still stigmatized, and survivors would be ostracized if it were known that sexual violence was committed against them. Thus, the compelled disclosure of a survivor's data and the subsequent use in legal proceedings can compound the harms facing survivors.

The impacts that compelled disclosure can have on the operations of a Humanitarian Organization depend on their mandate and working modalities. Some Humanitarian Organizations interact regularly with governments and pass on information to them in favour of an individual, for instance to facilitate the granting of rights or a legal status to that individual. By contrast, other Humanitarian Organizations act on a strictly confidential basis and would not share with governments the contents of their dialogue with States, individuals or other actors, since this may be an essential working modality required to build trust and access areas affected by armed conflicts and other situations of violence. For some organizations, this working modality has been endorsed and indeed safeguarded by the international community, and considered as a prerequisite for affected persons to have access to essential humanitarian services.[42] Humanitarian Organizations should bear in mind that the difficulty with the legislations examined above is that they allow authorities to require service providers directly to disclose data of Humanitarian Organizations. Thereby, they do not generally leave space to take into account the differing relations Humanitarian Organizations entertain with law enforcement, and the particularities of Humanitarian Organizations' distinct mandates and practices risk being lost in translation, which can lead to harm for the organization itself, and, ultimately, the people it serves.

Moreover, in considering impacts of compelled disclosure on their operations, Humanitarian Organizations should also consider how the fact that Humanitarian Data might be used for purposes other than those for which they were provided might impact on the trust that stakeholders vest in the organization:[43]

- Persons benefiting from Humanitarian Action might not wish to engage with a Humanitarian Organization and thus not receive essential humanitarian services or aid that could improve their lives and livelihoods, if they do not have confidence that their data will be used exclusively for the purposes for which they were provided, and will only be processed in a Neutral, Impartial and Independent manner.
- The same applies to States: if States in which Humanitarian Organizations operate consider that there is a risk that data which these organizations collect in or receive from a State will be transferred to other States, they might become reluctant to engage with the organization, and even refuse to allow it access to the persons an organization seeks to serve. They, too, expect these data to be treated in a Neutral, Impartial and Independent manner.
- Moreover, Humanitarian Organizations that provide aid indiscriminately to persons in need may further engage with non-State armed groups. Sometimes, this may include groups that some States have designated as "terrorist". Without interacting with such groups or individuals, Humanitarian Organizations might not however be in a position to provide essential humanitarian services to affected populations. If those non-State armed groups were to perceive the risk that the Humanitarian Organization might be directly or indirectly compelled to share the contents of their dialogue with governments, this might affect the

---

42 "The ICRC's privilege of non-disclosure of confidential information", *International Review of the Red Cross*, Vol. 97, No. 897–898 (June 2015), pp. 433–444: https://doi.org/10.1017/S1816383115000533.
43 See on this for example: Council of Delegates of the International Red Cross and Red Crescent Movement, Resolution 12: Safeguarding humanitarian data, 23 June 2022, available at: https://rcrcconference.org/app/uploads/2022/06/CD22-R12-Safeguarding-Humanitarian-Data_23-June-2022_FINAL_EN.pdf; 37th International Conference of Data Protection and Privacy Commissioners, Resolution on Privacy and International Humanitarian Action, 27 October 2015, para. 5 of the Explanatory Statement; 33rd International Conference of the Red Cross and Red Crescent, Resolution 4, December 2019, pp 8 and *op* 8.

organization's perception as neutral. Therefore, those groups might not be willing to interact with Humanitarian Organizations and might potentially prevent the administration of essential humanitarian services to persons under their control.

11.3 MITIGATING THE RISK OF DISCLOSURE OF HUMANITARIAN DATA PROCESSED IN A PUBLIC CLOUD ENVIRONMENT

The preceding sections have shown that it is quintessential for Humanitarian Organizations to make an informed decision about whether to process Humanitarian Data in a public cloud environment, in light of potential disclosure under the legislations and agreements surveyed in Section 11.1 – Mapping legislations allowing governments to require service providers to disclose Humanitarian Data, and the possible impacts such disclosure can have, as set out in Section 11.2 – Impacts of compelled disclosure on Humanitarian Action and persons benefiting from it.

If Humanitarian Organizations choose to process Humanitarian Data in a public cloud environment, they should consider taking the following measures to mitigate the risk of disclosure of such data:
- ensuring the effectiveness of privileges and immunities they may enjoy; and/or
- sensitizing States to the importance of not using or requesting Humanitarian Data for purposes incompatible with their work.

These measures are suggested in addition to the technical, legal and organizational measures explained in Chapter 10: Cloud Services. That said, it is emphasized that Humanitarian Organizations should pay particular attention to encryption. While encryption *per se* cannot mitigate the risk of disclosure of data, it can make it more difficult to use the disclosed data, as such data would not be legible.[44] This is of particular relevance in the context of legal frameworks that do not contain any obligations to furnish decrypted data, such as the CLOUD Act.[45]

11.3.1 ENSURING THE EFFECTIVENESS OF PRIVILEGES AND IMMUNITIES

Some Humanitarian Organizations enjoy privileges and immunities under bilateral or multilateral treaties, or domestic legislation. These are tools that allow them to carry

---

[44] On other technical measures, see European Data Protection Board (EDPB), *Recommendations 01/2020 on measures that supplement transfer tools to ensure compliance with the EU level of protection of personal data*, 18 June 2021, Annex 2: https://edpb.europa.eu/system/files/2021-06/edpb_recommendations_202001vo.2.0_supplementarymeasurestransferstools_en.pdf.

[45] US Department of Justice, *Promoting Public Safety, Privacy, and the Rule of Law around the World*, 18.

out their mandate independently and effectively. Privileges and immunities granted to a Humanitarian Organization remain applicable to data processed in a cloud environment and can therefore in principle serve to prevent the compelled disclosure of data.[46]

Inviolability of archives is particularly pertinent. In the context of the UN, archives have been interpreted to encompass data and infrastructure belonging to, held or used by the organization. Inviolability means, *inter alia*, that a State cannot interfere with those archives, including data, for instance by seizing data.[47] Moreover, immunity from jurisdiction of organizations and their staff can lead to requests for compelled disclosure being declined.

However, the functioning of cloud-specific legislations poses practical obstacles to the effective application of privileges and immunities.

First, some Humanitarian Organizations do not enjoy privileges and immunities universally. For those organizations, whether privileges and immunities can prevent compelled disclosure depends on the availability and scope of the privileges and immunities that the requesting State has granted to the organization. Unless such privileges and immunities are part of customary international law, they only ever bind the State that has granted them to a Humanitarian Organization. They do not establish any obligations on third States. As such, the choice of the service provider and data Processing locations in accordance with the geographical scope of their privileges and immunities are of utmost importance for those organizations.

With a view to the selection of service providers specifically, Humanitarian Organizations might wish to only choose service providers under the jurisdiction of States which have granted privileges and immunities to the organization, and/or that have in place effective blocking statutes. Those can be defined as national legal instruments that prohibit compliance by subjects of national law with requirements

---

46 European Data Protection Supervisor (EDPS), *Guidelines on the use of cloud computing services by the European institutions and bodies*, 16 March 2018: https://edps.europa.eu/sites/default/files/publication/18-03-16_cloud_computing_guidelines_en.pdf. Equally, the US State Department's position is that documents may retain protection covered by privileges and immunities even if they are in the hands of Third Parties acting as an agent or contractor to the state: Estonian Ministry of Economic Affairs and Communications and Microsoft Corporation, *Implementation of the Virtual Data Embassy Solution: Summary Report of the Research Project on Public Cloud Usage for Government*, n.d.: https://query.prod.cms.rt.microsoft.com/cms/api/am/binary/REVmcb.

47 See G. L. Burci, "Inviolability of archives", in *The Conventions on the Privileges and Immunities of the United Nations and Its Specialized Agencies: A Commentary*, Oxford University Press, Oxford, 2016, paras. 8–10.

or prohibitions based on certain foreign laws.[48] One example of such a blocking statute is enshrined in Article 271 of the Swiss Criminal Code, which makes it an offence to "carry out (i) an act reserved to a public authority performed in favour of a foreign State, (ii) on Swiss territory, (iii) without legal entitlement and/or ad hoc authorisation from the Federal Department of Justice and Police and (iv) with a wilful intent to act".[49] As such, depending on the circumstances, the Swiss Blocking Statute may prevent Swiss service providers from assisting foreign authorities in accessing data on Swiss territory without authorization.[50]

In choosing service providers, Humanitarian Organizations should also bear in mind bilateral agreements such as the UK/US agreement, as they could allow States, in which the Humanitarian Organization might not enjoy privileges and immunities, to require disclosure from service providers under the jurisdiction of the other State Party to the agreement.

Moreover, a defining characteristic of Cloud Services is the frequent use of Sub-Processors with access to content and/or meta, traffic or location data. Against this backdrop, Humanitarian Organizations should apply the same considerations as outlined above in selecting or accepting Sub-Processors.

Second, requests under the legislations and case law examined in Section 11.1 – Mapping legislations allowing governments to require service providers to disclose Humanitarian Data enable authorities to require service providers directly to disclose information to authorities, and not the Humanitarian Organization. As such, the Humanitarian Organization might not itself have any standing to rely on their privileges and immunities. This is exacerbated by the fact that some legislations permit authorities to impose a non-disclosure order on the service provider, prohibiting the latter from informing the entity whose information is sought about the disclosure request. As a result, organizations might not even be aware that their data are being sought.

Therefore, if Humanitarian Organizations decide to process Humanitarian Data in a public cloud environment, they should take the following steps to ensure the effectiveness of their privileges and immunities:

---

48 See the European Commission's definition of blocking statutes: European Commission, "Extraterritoriality (Blocking Statute)", n.d.: https://finance.ec.europa.eu/eu-and-world/open-strategic-autonomy/extraterritoriality-blocking-statute_en.
49 Valentine Bagnoud, Deborah Hondius and Sandrine Giroud, "Swiss Blocking Statute: Update on Do's and Don'ts under the Threat of Criminal Sanctions", LALIVE (blog), 3 December 2019: www.lalive.law/swiss-blocking-statute-update-on-dos-and-donts-under-the-threat-of-criminal-sanctions.
50 On this, see David Rosenthal, "US CLOUD Act: Why It Should Not Prevent Cloud Projects", VISCHER, 2 August 2020: www.vischer.com/en/knowledge/blog/us-cloud-act-why-it-should-not-prevent-cloud-projects-38580.

- Take into account relevant legislations and inter-State agreements, such as the UK/US agreement, in selecting cloud service providers, Sub-Processors and data locations;
- negotiate in their contracts with service providers and other technology providers offering public cloud-based services that, in case of a request, the service providers should at least inform authorities of the fact that the data sought may be subject to privileges and immunities.[51]

For purposes of comprehensiveness, it is noted that Humanitarian Organizations, particularly where they do not enjoy privileges and immunities, may of course also resort to remedies and challenges enshrined in national law. Since the availability and scope of those means vary from State to State, Humanitarian Organizations should make themselves familiar with relevant legislation.

11.3.2 SENSITIZING STATES TO THE IMPORTANCE OF NOT USING OR REQUESTING HUMANITARIAN DATA FOR PURPOSES INCOMPATIBLE WITH THE WORK OF HUMANITARIAN ORGANIZATIONS

To make humanitarian data less vulnerable to disclosure requests in the first place, Humanitarian Organizations may wish to sensitize States to the importance of refraining from using or requesting humanitarian data for purposes incompatible with their work, subject to their mandates and working modalities. To this end, humanitarian organizations could, for example, advocate to:
- exclude Humanitarian Data from the scope of relevant legislations and international agreements; and/or
- obtain otherwise a legally binding commitment from States to refrain from using or requesting Humanitarian Data in a manner incompatible with the mandate and working modalities of the organization.[52]

---

51 See also Section 10.9 – Privileges and immunities and the cloud.
52 For instance, with a view to the Red Cross and Red Crescent Movement, the 2022 Council of Delegates of the International Red Cross and Red Crescent Movement "emphasizes the fact that the 33rd International Conference urged States and the Movement to cooperate to ensure that humanitarian data are not requested or used for purposes incompatible with the humanitarian nature of the work of the Movement, and in conformity with Article 2 of the Statutes of the Movement, or in a manner that would undermine the trust of the people it serves or the independence, impartiality and neutrality of humanitarian services"; 2022 Council of Delegates, Resolution 12, *supra* fn [45].

MOBILE MESSAGING APPS

POSSIBLE USE

- EFFICIENT COORDINATION
- IMMEDIATE COMMUNICATION WITH PEOPLE IN REMOTE OR INACCESSIBLE LOCATIONS
- BROADCAST CONTENT TO LARGE NUMBERS OF INDIVIDUALS

CHALLENGES

- NEED FOR CLEAR GUIDANCE ON PROCESSING BY HUMANITARIAN ORGANIZATIONS OF INFORMATION GATHERED FROM MESSAGING APPS
- LACK OF AWARENESS ABOUT TYPES OF DATA PROCESSED
- METADATA COULD BE ACCESSED AND ANALYSED BY THIRD PARTIES AND USED BY THEM IN WAYS DETRIMENTAL TO VULNERABLE

CHAPTER 12

MOBILE MESSAGING APPS

Lina Jasmontaite-Zaniewicz*

---

*   This chapter is based on: The Engine Room and Block Party, *Humanitarian Futures for Messaging Apps*, January 2017: https://shop.icrc.org/humanitarian-futures-for-messaging-apps.html.

12.1 INTRODUCTION

In their daily work, Humanitarian Organizations rely on multiple communication channels, including formal (e.g. radio and television), informal, unofficial and direct means of exchanging information. To employ the most appropriate communication channels in a given situation, Humanitarian Organizations have to understand the cultural background and needs of a particular society affected by a crisis and their means of communication.

In this respect, where mobile messaging apps are widely used, their deployment by Humanitarian Organizations is particularly attractive, because it allows immediate communication with people affected by crisis or conflict, and helps to coordinate internal tasks and actions efficiently. This type of technology can enhance the effectiveness and efficiency of Humanitarian Actions and reach populations in remote or inaccessible locations. However, mobile messaging apps are often employed without due consideration of the risks relating to Personal Data protection.

Despite the great functionality offered by mobile messaging apps, their use may entail significant risks ranging from data protection issues to disinformation. It seems that in practice, Humanitarian Organizations sometimes deploy them ad hoc, without following any formal procedures underpinned by risk analysis or considerations of long-term sustainability and management. Rather, the focus is on the Humanitarian Organizations' pressing information and communications needs. Insofar as this approach fails to include a comprehensive risk analysis, it runs counter to the guiding principles of Humanitarian Organizations, such as accountability, appropriateness, "do no harm" and due diligence.[1] As is the case with any other communication channel, the adoption of mobile messaging apps requires careful consideration of their benefits and risks. Questions to be included in such an analysis depend on the specific circumstances of a particular situation. For example, security concerns about Personal Data of individuals in a situation of political violence may differ greatly from security concerns in a natural disaster.

Mobile messaging apps installed on cellular phones or other smart devices may pose risks to individuals' right to Personal Data protection. This is because apps provide not only the possibility to exchange data between users, but also to process, aggregate and generate huge amounts of data (e.g. metadata, location data and contacts). Some data protection regulators consider that risks to Personal Data protection result from a combination of the following factors: (1) users' lack of awareness of the types

---

[1] For an example of the operationalization of these principles, see ICRC, *Accountability to Affected People Institutional Framework*, January 2019: www.icrc.org/en/publication/accountability-affected-people-institutional-framework.

of data they actually process on a smart device; (2) absence of user's Consent; (3) poor security measures; and (4) the possibility of Further Processing.[2]

In line with the "digital proximity" imperative, i.e. Humanitarian Organizations seeking to be digitally where the beneficiaries are (just as they try to be physically), Humanitarian Organizations tend to use mobile messaging apps that are popular in a particular society at the time of a Humanitarian Emergency, such as WhatsApp, Facebook Messenger, Snapchat, Viber, Telegram and LINE. These proprietary cross-platforms are established by service providers which are usually not willing to customize their applications to meet the needs of Humanitarian Organizations. At the same time, deploying a less popular communication platform may exclude the people the organization is seeking to help. Therefore, it is imperative to know not only which communication channels exist in a particular place, but also which ones affected individuals trust and can use.[3]

The adoption of mobile messaging apps may also result in the Further Processing of collected data, including Personal Data. Mobile messaging apps make it possible to collect information online and may also provide new ways of analysing the available data. In other words, data and metadata collected via mobile messaging apps can help to triangulate information in new ways. In light of this and the probability of Further Processing of Personal Data, it is important to consider that in practice it is going to be challenging to limit the purpose for using a messaging application (e.g. affected individuals may decide to use it for providing feedback or reporting sensitive personal information, although the channel is designed for sharing public health information), and the number of entities with whom the collected data will be shared. Humanitarian Organizations may then find they are unable to state confidently that users can destroy or remove data already submitted, because this could entail multiple negotiations with multiple parties.

Mobile messaging apps were primarily designed to allow private communication between individuals or small groups. This type of functionality could be used by Humanitarian Organizations to provide basic counselling or to obtain information from beneficiaries about incidents, ongoing conflicts or particular needs. However, these apps may also be used in Humanitarian Action to "broadcast" content to large numbers of personal contacts or followers. In particular, in situations where the number of users is very large, mobile messaging apps may work as a one-way broadcasting channel (e.g. to announce the time and place for delivery of humanitarian aid, changed opening hours of a local clinic, or secure routes for transfer and evacuation of people). However, it is

---

2   Article 29 Data Protection Working Party, *Opinion 02/2013 on Apps on Smart Devices (WP 202)*, 27 February 2013: https://ec.europa.eu/justice/article-29/documentation/opinion-recommendation/files/2013/wp202_en.pdf.
3   ICRC, *Accountability to Affected People Institutional Framework*, January 2019, 5.

challenging to ensure that messaging apps are used for one-way communication with beneficiaries as these apps are designed with two-way communication features. It should be highlighted that the latter often carry much higher risks for affected individuals (potentially more Personal Data may be transferred) and it also raises issues of long-term management/sustainability against expectation.

12.1.1 MOBILE MESSAGING APPS IN HUMANITARIAN ACTION

A messaging application (or app) is a software program that allows users to send and receive information using their mobile phones or other smart portable devices. The ease with which apps work has had a great impact on their popularity, public acceptance and continuously increasing demand. There are three key differences between communication through mobile messaging apps and communication through mobile phone networks:[4]

- Mobile messaging apps transmit and receive data using a Wi-Fi Internet connection or a mobile data connection (unlike SMS messages, which are transmitted over conventional telephone networks).
- Mobile messaging apps can transmit or receive a much wider range of data types than is possible using SMS or even its multimedia-enabled successor, MMS. Mobile messaging apps have developed more similarities than differences over time and, in addition to voice calls and text, messaging app users can also send and receive the following types of information: files, including photos, images and (in some cases) documents; audio recordings, including voice recordings that act in the same way as a voicemail message; data identifying their current location, based on their phone's GPS sensor; live video calls (in some apps); and emojis (pictographic representations of emotions or specific objects).
- Mobile messaging apps can transmit end-to-end encrypted content. They may, however, also generate and keep large amounts of – unencrypted – metadata.
- Humanitarian Organizations have been adopting mobile messaging apps for reasons such as the following:[5]
  o to target audiences (staff or beneficiaries) already using messaging apps;
  o to reduce communications costs;
  o to maintain reliable contact with people (whether staff or beneficiaries) in transit;
  o to enable communication with people in environments where other communications methods are unavailable;
  o to increase the speed of communications;
  o to improve the security of digital communications as compared with existing methods of communication (where such apps offer end-to-end encryption of content);

---

4   ICRC, The Engine Room and Block Party, *Humanitarian Futures for Messaging Apps*.
5   For a more detailed explanation of the reasons to adopt mobile messaging apps in Humanitarian Action, see ibid.

- to facilitate information collection from or dissemination to hard-to-reach, remote or inaccessible areas;
- to speed up data collection or increase efficiency;
- to improve inter-office coordination.

The use of mobile messaging apps can benefit affected individuals as such communication tools can enhance community engagement and acceptance, and can lead to a more people-centred, coordinated, accountable and effective response.[6] There is, however, little high-quality, disaggregated data available regarding which apps affected individuals are using and how they are being used.[7] The following usages of digital communications technologies have been identified by people migrating to Europe:[8]

- finding data on the intended country of destination (including legal information);
- initiating contact with smugglers or brokers;
- getting updated information on migration routes, particularly attempting to verify rumours; and
- accessing safety and rescue services while in transit.

Certainly, the reasons for individuals to use messaging apps in the humanitarian context may be diverse and range from meeting basic communication needs to the possibility of sharing documented atrocities.

Based on the considerations above, there are two separate areas of analysis to be distinguished from a data protection point of view:

- Personal Data Processing through the mobile messaging apps themselves;
- Personal Data Processing by Humanitarian Organizations, of data collected through mobile messaging apps.

These are addressed, in turn, below.

12.2 APPLICATION OF BASIC DATA PROTECTION PRINCIPLES

The data protection discussion in this chapter builds on the principles set out in Part I, which examines them in greater detail.

---

6 OCHA, "From Digital Promise to Frontline Practice: New and Emerging Technologies in Humanitarian Action – World | ReliefWeb", United Nations Office for the Coordination for Humanitarian Affairs (OCHA), Policy Branch, New York, 19 April 2021: https://reliefweb.int/report/world/digital-promise-frontline-practice-new-and-emerging-technologies-humanitarian-action.

7 ICRC, The Engine Room and Block Party, *Humanitarian Futures for Messaging Apps*, 32.

8 Bram Frouws, Melissa Phillips, Ashraf Hassan and Mirjam Twigt, "Getting to Europe the WhatsApp Way: The use of ICT in contemporary mixed migration flows to Europe", SSRN Scholarly Paper, Social Science Research Network, Rochester, NY, 1 June 2016: https://papers.ssrn.com/abstract=2862592; John Warnes, *Update: 10 CwC Challenges in the New Face of the European Refugee Crisis*, UNHCR, 2016: www.unhcr.org/innovation/update-10-cwc-challenges-new-face-european-refugee-crisis.

12.2.1 PROCESSING OF PERSONAL DATA THROUGH MOBILE MESSAGING APPS

Communicating with individuals affected by Humanitarian Emergencies through mobile apps requires Humanitarian Organizations, in most cases, to install and use applications already used by the majority of the population. Individuals, or in other words, beneficiaries in most cases have already downloaded and installed such applications and consented to their data protection terms.

By communicating with beneficiaries through mobile messaging apps, however, Humanitarian Organizations may suggest, whether directly or indirectly, that such means of communication are secure and that no harm is likely to arise for the beneficiaries in engaging with the Humanitarian Organization. It is important therefore that, irrespective of the initial Consent given by the beneficiaries to the app provider to process their Personal Data, a clear analysis of the implications of such use is made by the Humanitarian Organization to ensure that no unexpected negative consequences are generated by their engagement. It is recommended to do this with a DPIA, which would take into account the considerations set out below. The outcome of the DPIA may be that only certain types of data can be collected or communicated through a particular app, or that a particular app may be used only in certain circumstances and not others. It may also be that the use of a particularly popular app may be inappropriate for the Humanitarian Organization, and that the Humanitarian Organization may want to use such an app only to notify individuals of its intention to communicate through another, more secure, app. In carrying out the assessment it is also important to note that messaging apps develop and change features fast, and there is no guarantee that a feature offered by an app will be available indefinitely, or that users are running up-to-date software, particularly in countries where encryption is restricted by law. Similarly, companies' policies and statements about data usage, security and privacy may be revised at a later stage. Organizations will often be unable to view technical details of the underlying code, so they may be unable to make a comprehensive assessment of how any such changes affect users' security or privacy. Organizations that use Third Party providers to manage or process information should also prepare to engage with these risks. Changes in app features may require revision of the DPIA.

12.2.1.1 POTENTIAL THREATS

Data protection and privacy concerns arise in every area of a Humanitarian Organization's work, therefore organizations should evaluate particular risks when considering whether to deploy a messaging app or not. Of these, the primary concern is the prospect that unintended Third Parties access data collected by Humanitarian Organizations, for purposes that run counter to the Neutral, Impartial and Independent nature of humanitarian work (e.g. access by local authorities, law enforcement authorities, groups driven by various interests or private entities).

These Third Parties could include:
- entities in refugees' countries of origin, including armed groups and authorities, who may wish to identify groups or individuals for the purpose of harming and/or targeting them;
- entities with migration policy or security interests, who wish to understand and predict displacement trends and flows;
- entities with an interest in surveillance for national security purposes;
- hostile parties who wish to target Humanitarian Organizations and the people that they support and carry out violent attacks against them;
- commercial entities that wish to conduct behavioural profiling of particular groups, which can lead to discrimination.[9]

Concerns in this area have been acknowledged and supported by the International Conference of Data Protection and Privacy Commissioners, in its 2015 Resolution on Privacy and International Humanitarian Action:

Humanitarian organizations not benefiting from Privileges and Immunities may come under pressure to provide data collected for humanitarian purposes to authorities wishing to use such data for other purposes (for example control of migration flows and the fight against terrorism). The risk of misuse of data may have a serious impact on data protection rights of displaced persons and can be a detriment to their safety, as well as to Humanitarian Action more generally.[10]

12.2.2 WHAT KIND OF DATA DO MESSAGING APPS COLLECT OR STORE?

There are three main protocols in the mobile messaging and encryption world: the Signal Protocol, MTProto and iMessage:[11]
- The Signal Protocol (previously known as both Axolotl and TextSecure) is used by Open Whisper Systems' Signal Messenger, Meta's WhatsApp, Facebook Messenger (in secret conversations), Google Allo (in incognito mode), Skype (since mid-2018, in private conversations) and Viber (proprietary, modified implementation).
- MTProto was developed and is used by Telegram (in secret chats).
- The iMessage protocol was developed by Apple and is used in iMessage.

These messaging protocols generate and process different kinds of data, and also protect message contents and metadata to various degrees.

---

9 Maria Xynou and Chris Walker, "Why We Still Recommend Signal over WhatsApp ... Even Though They Both Use End-to-End Encryption", Security in a Box, 23 May 2016: https://securityinabox.org/my/blog/why-we-still-recommend-signal-over-whatsapp/.
10 International Conference of Data Protection and Privacy Commissioners, Resolution on Privacy and International Humanitarian Action.
11 ICRC and Privacy International, *The Humanitarian Metadata Problem*, 50.

Message content: although some major messaging app companies state that their apps offer end-to-end encryption, meaning that they are unable to decrypt or read the contents of messages, other widely used apps such as Facebook Messenger store all message content on their servers. Note that some apps offering end-to-end encryption include it only as an opt-in feature (such as Telegram, LINE and Facebook Messenger). This means that unless users are aware of the need to enable this feature in their settings, all message data may still be sent unencrypted. Communication with most bots on services such as Telegram is not end-to-end encrypted. It is important to note that although the content may be protected, metadata may not enjoy the same kinds of safeguards (see "Metadata" below.)[12]

User information: when users sign up for an app, they are asked to submit information about themselves (ranging from a phone number, in the case of most apps, to images, full names and email addresses in the case of apps such as WeChat and Facebook Messenger). Mandatory SIM card registration is enforced in many countries worldwide. In these countries, an app's requirement to submit a phone number may in effect prevent individuals from using messaging apps anonymously. In parts of Latin America, users may also be required to register their handset number.[13] Many apps automatically access a user's list of phone number contacts during sign-up to find other contacts that already have the app. In some cases, apps may store these data separately (WhatsApp, for example, confirmed in June 2016 that it stores contact list information).[14] Details of any groups to which the user belongs may also be stored in some cases.

Metadata: according to their terms of service, apps collect varying quantities of metadata, including sites and information accessed from within the app. Examples of metadata that could be obtained from a message include IMEI/IMSI (device and SIM identifiers), sender phone number, recipient phone number, message size, location data, time data, IP addresses, hardware model and web browser information.[15] Many app companies state that such data are retained on their servers, although they rarely clarify the length of time that data are retained, or if and how metadata are encrypted (even among apps that claim to have implemented end-to-end encryption). Although some messaging applications on personal computers offer to obscure users' metadata using Tor hidden services (software that enables

---

12 Lucy Handley, "Sheryl Sandberg: WhatsApp Metadata Informs Governments about Terrorism in Spite of Encryption", Yahoo! Finance, 31 July 2017: https://finance.yahoo.com/news/sheryl-sandberg-whatsapp-metadata-informs-112540721.html.
13 GSMA, *Mandatory registration of prepaid SIM cards: Addressing challenges through best practice*, April 2016: www.gsma.com/publicpolicy/wp-content/uploads/2016/04/Mandatory-SIM-Registration.pdf.
14 Micah Lee, "Battle of the Secure Messaging Apps: How Signal Beats WhatsApp", The Intercept, 22 June 2016: https://theintercept.com/2016/06/22/battle-of-the-secure-messaging-apps-how-signal-beats-whatsapp.
15 ICRC and Privacy International, *The Humanitarian Metadata Problem*, 60.

anonymous browsing),[16] this is not an option on the major messaging apps currently available. Instead, even the most privacy-conscious apps, such as Signal,[17] simply aim to collect as little metadata as possible.

Inferred data: even with end-to-end encryption of content, a lot can be inferred from the metadata around messaging.

> **EXAMPLE:**
> *Researchers at MIT and the Université Catholique de Louvain, in Belgium, analyzed data on 1.5 million cellphone users in a small European country over a span of 15 months and found that just four points of reference, with fairly low spatial and temporal resolution, was enough to uniquely identify 95 percent of them.*
>
> *In other words, to extract the complete location information for a single person from an "anonymized" data set of more than a million people, all you would need to do is place him or her within a couple of hundred yards of a cellphone transmitter, sometime over the course of an hour, four times in one year. A few Twitter posts would probably provide all the information you needed, if they contained specific information about the person's whereabouts.[18]*

Data shared with Third Party providers: messaging app companies frequently state that they share users' Personal Data with other companies which provide services to enable the app to operate. However, they rarely state which companies they work with, what services they provide, what data they have access to, or how the data are processed and stored.[19] Twilio, a Third Party provider that works with some messaging app companies, provides limited transparency reports which indicate that it received 376 requests for data from international agencies in the first half of 2016 compared with 46 over the same period in 2015.[20]

---

16   For example, Orbot uses Tor hidden services: "Orbot: Proxy with Tor", Guardian Project, accessed 20 January 2022: https://guardianproject.info/apps/org.torproject.android; Joseph Cox, "'Ricochet', the Messenger That Beats Metadata, Passes Security Audit", Vice, 17 February 2016: www.vice.com/en/article/mg7v3a/ricochet-encrypted-messenger-tackles-metadata-problem-head-on.
17   Signal Messenger, "Grand Jury Subpoena for Signal User Data, Eastern District of Virginia", Signal Messenger, 4 October 2016: https://signal.org/bigbrother/eastern-virginia-grand-jury.
18   Hardesty, "How Hard Is It to 'de-Anonymize' Cellphone Data?"
19   For example, the EDPB's Binding decision 1/2021 on the dispute arisen on the draft decision of the Irish Supervisory Authority regarding WhatsApp Ireland under Article 65(1)(a) GDPR noted that the reference to "other business services" by WhatsApp in its Legal Basis notice is unclear as it neither provides a relation to the specific legitimate interest nor specifies businesses or partners WhatsApp IE refers to, paragraph 63. See: European Data Protection Board (EDPB), Binding Decision 1/2021 on the Dispute Arisen on the Draft Decision of the Irish Supervisory Authority Regarding WhatsApp Ireland under Article 65(1)(a) GDPR, 28 July 2021: https://edpb.europa.eu/system/files/2021-09/edpb_bindingdecision_202101_ie_sa_whatsapp_redacted_en.pdf.
20   See Twilio, "Transparency Reporting", Twilio, accessed 20 January 2022: www.twilio.com/legal/transparency.

Evidence that a user has installed an app on their phone: by accessing an individual's physical device, authorities could find physical evidence that a user has installed a particular messaging app. This could also potentially be accessed through other means – for example, in most cases users must associate an email address with their smartphone to download an app, creating a potentially traceable link between the app and other online activity.

12.2.3 HOW COULD OTHER PARTIES ACCESS DATA SHARED ON MESSAGING APPS?

Other parties may be able to access data transmitted through messaging apps in a number of ways, including:

- A messaging app company (or a Third Party provider that accesses app users' personal information) discloses message content or metadata that it stores on its servers, in response to a disclosure request from an authority in the jurisdiction where such data are stored.
- Another party gains unlawful or covert access to message content or metadata stored on a messaging app company's servers (through hacking) or accesses that information while it is travelling between the two actors (known as a "man-in-the-middle" attack). For example, tests by the University of Toronto's Citizen Lab in late 2013 indicated that the messaging app LINE was not encrypting content sent over 3G connections despite the fact that content sent over Wi-Fi was encrypted.[21]
- When a device (e.g. a mobile phone or computer) is seized, forensic tools can be used to access its metadata, including content and data that the user believed to be deleted.[22] Extraction tools can be used to download data from mobile phones, including:
  - contacts;
  - call data (who we call, when and for how long);
  - text messages;
  - stored files (photos, videos, audio files, documents, etc.);
  - app data (what apps we use and the data stored on them);
  - location information;
  - Wi-Fi network connections (which can reveal the locations of any place where the users connected to Wi-Fi, such as workplace and properties they have visited).

---

21 3G networks are encrypted by default, but only at the level of the network provider, meaning that Internet service providers (ISPs) and telecommunications companies can decrypt information sent over them. Masashi Crete-Nishihata et al., "Asia Chats: Analyzing Information Controls and Privacy in Asian Messaging Applications", The Citizen Lab, 14 November 2013, https://citizenlab.ca/2013/11/asia-chats-analyzing-information-controls-privacy-asian-messaging-applications; Jon Russell, "Thailand's Government Claims It Can Monitor The Country's 30M Line Users", TechCrunch (blog), 23 December 2014: https://social.techcrunch.com/2014/12/23/thailand-line-monitoring-claim.

22 ICRC and Privacy International, *The Humanitarian Metadata Problem*, sec. 5.3.

Some mobile phone extraction tools may also access data stored in the cloud instead of directly on phones, or data that cannot be confirmed to exist or be accessed, i.e. deleted data.[23]

- **Parties access messaging app content through other covert methods.** These include accessing the SMS login codes sent to users when they sign up for an app by redirecting traffic on conventional mobile phone networks,[24] or inducing users to install "malware" (short for malicious software) onto their phone which enables others to remotely gain access to that phone and data stored on it.[25]
- **An individual is forced to hand over their physical device.** End-to-end encryption only encrypts data in transit, not on the user's device. If a party gains physical access to a phone or computer with access to a user's messaging apps account (such as by compelling the user to unlock it), they may be able to access message content as well as details of apps that are installed on the device. In some countries, authorities consider merely installing apps such as WhatsApp as an indicator of subversive behaviour.[26] In view of this, messaging apps allowing "self-destructing" or "disappearing" messages, which can automatically be destructed after a short or predefined period of time and in this way make messages sent untraceable, offer more secure options for affected individuals.
- **A messaging app company allows an authority to directly access content or data transmitted over the app by building a secret feature into its code (known as a "backdoor").** For example, certain countries have reportedly threatened to fine messaging app companies that did not introduce backdoors into their code, specifically citing WhatsApp, Telegram and Viber.[27] Other companies have publicly stated that they have refused requests from government agencies to create backdoors.[28] There have also

---

23 Mobile Phone Extraction, explainer produced by Privacy International and Liberty as part of the joint campaign "Neighbourhood Watched: How policing surveillance technology impacts your rights", available at: Privacy International, "Mobile Phone Extraction" (Neighbourhood Watched: How policing surveillance technology impacts your rights), February 2019: https://privacyinternational.org/sites/default/files/2019-02/Explainers-MPE.pdf.

24 Frederic Jacobs, "How Russia Works on Intercepting Messaging Apps", bellingcat, 30 April 2016: www.bellingcat.com/news/2016/04/30/russia-telegram-hack; thaddeus t grugq, "Operational Telegram", Medium, 5 July 2016: https://medium.com/@thegrugq/operational-telegram-cbbaadb9013a.

25 See for example: "Malware Posing As Human Rights Organizations and Commercial Software Targeting Iranians, Foreign Policy Institutions and Middle Eastern Countries", Iran Threats: Documenting Iranian State Sponsored Hacking, 1 September 2016: https://iranthreats.github.io/resources/human-rights-impersonation-malware; Amnesty International, *Forensic Methodology Report: How to Catch NSO Group's Pegasus*, Amnesty International, 18 July 2021: www.amnesty.org/en/latest/research/2021/07/forensic-methodology-report-how-to-catch-nso-groups-pegasus.

26 Danny O'Brien, "Your Apps, Please? China Shows How Surveillance Leads to Intimidation and Software Censorship", Electronic Frontier Foundation, 8 January 2016: www.eff.org/deeplinks/2016/01/china-shows-how-backdoors-lead-software-censorship; Xynou and Walker, "Why We Still Recommend Signal over WhatsApp ... Even Though They Both Use End-to-End Encryption".

27 Patrick Howell O'Neill, "Russian Bill Requires Encryption Backdoors in All Messenger Apps", Daily Dot, 20 June 2016: www.dailydot.com/debug/encryption-backdoor-russia-fsb.

28 Jon Russell, "Apple Won't Create Universal IPhone 'Back Door' to Aid FBI", TechCrunch (blog), 17 February 2016: https://social.techcrunch.com/2016/02/17/tim-cook-apple-wont-create-backdoor-

been ongoing attempts by intelligence agencies to enable them to access encrypted content.[29]
- **If the group is set as "public"** (i.e. anyone can join without being invited), these data could be accessed. Also, in a messaging group such as on WhatsApp, every member of the group can extract the declared names of other members, their phone numbers and the messages they have sent.[30]
- **The protections used in messaging apps have also been compromised by flaws in SS7, the underlying telecoms protocols.**[31] These flaws allow individuals to impersonate a phone number, create a duplicate account on a messaging app, and send and receive all messages destined for this number without the user's knowledge.[32]

12.2.4 MESSAGING APP FEATURES RELATED TO PRIVACY AND SECURITY

The following are relevant features to look for when choosing a messaging app to exchange information in humanitarian situations.

12.2.4.1 ANONYMITY PERMITTED/NO REQUIREMENT FOR AUTHENTICATED IDENTITY

Enabling users to communicate anonymously via a messaging app enhances their privacy, whereas requiring the use of real names, email addresses and authenticated identities increases the risk that individuals will be monitored or targeted. The less information a user is required to provide in order to use an app, the less information about them other parties may be able to access.

---

to-unlock-san-bernardino-attackers-iphone; Max Eddy, "What It's Like When the FBI Asks You to Backdoor Your Software", PCMag UK, 8 January2014: https://uk.pcmag.com/opinion/11141/what-its-like-when-the-fbi-asks-you-to-backdoor-your-software.

29 For reference see: Privacy International, "Ghosts in Your Machine: Spooks Want Secret Access to Encrypted Messages", 29 May 2019: http://privacyinternational.org/news-analysis/3002/ghosts-your-machine-spooks-want-secret-access-encrypted-messages.

30 Vivek Wadhwa, "WhatsApp Public Groups Can Leave User Data Vulnerable to Scraping", VentureBeat (blog), 3 April 2018: https://venturebeat.com/2018/04/03/whatsapp-public-groups-can-leave-user-data-vulnerable-to-scraping.

31 Today's public switched telephone network (PSTN, i.e. the sum of all nationally, regionally or locally operated circuit-switched telephone networks) uses a signalling system called Signalling System No. 7 ("SS7"). SS7 is also the foundation of mobile telephony, used to route calls, SMS and other mobile services. For more details see: ICRC and Privacy International, *The Humanitarian Metadata Problem*" sec. 5.

32 vijay, "How to Hack Facebook Using SS7 Flaw", TechWorm (blog), 16 June 2016: www.techworm.net/2016/06/hack-facebook-using-ss7-flaw.html; John Leyden, "SS7 Spookery on the Cheap Allows Hackers to Impersonate Mobile Chat Subscribers", The Register, 10 May 2016: www.theregister.com/2016/05/10/ss7_mobile_chat_hack.

12.2.4.2 NO RETENTION OF MESSAGE CONTENT

User privacy is better served when the contents of messages are delivered to a user's device and deleted from the app company's servers after they are read. Apps such as Telegram, WhatsApp, Viber and Signal state that they do not routinely store messages and that they delete messages from their servers immediately after they have been delivered to their intended recipient(s). However, companies such as Skype retain message content on their servers after the user has read the message, without stating a maximum time limit after which they will delete the data.

12.2.4.3 END-TO-END ENCRYPTION

End-to-end encryption restricts the ability of Third Parties such as governments or adversaries to intercept communications between Humanitarian Organizations and their beneficiaries in a way that allows the message contents to be viewed. In this case, even if a company does retain content data, this will be in an encrypted form and thus not legible to the company or to any Third Party seeking access to the data. Encryption thus restricts the type and amount of legible data that messaging-app companies can be compelled to disclose. Ideally, it should be deployed by default in both one-to-one and group chats. There are online resources which assess the levels of security offered by specific apps.[33]

12.2.4.4 USER OWNERSHIP OF DATA

It is essential that messaging-app users be regarded as the lawful owners of their personally identifiable data as well as the contents of their messages. This prevents messaging-app companies from using such data for commercial or other purposes without the explicit Consent of the user. This issue is addressed by national law in some countries and the topic may also be included in the messaging apps' terms-of-service agreements.

12.2.4.5 NO OR MINIMAL RETENTION OF METADATA

The less metadata messaging apps retain on their servers, the less data they can be compelled to disclose to governments or sell to commercial interests. Messaging apps such as Signal and Telegram claim not to retain any metadata on their users, although Telegram's claim is contested,[34] whereas most major apps under consideration state that they collect contact numbers, logs of activity on the app and location information.

---

[33] "Secure Messaging Apps Comparison | Privacy Matters", accessed 8 April 2022: www.securemessagingapps.com.

[34] Jeremy Seth Davis, "Telegram Metadata Allows for 'Stalking Anyone'", SC Media, 30 November 2015, Online edition, sec. Security News, www.scmagazine.com/news/security-news/telegram-metadata-allows-for-stalking-anyone.

12.2.4.6 MESSAGING-APP CODE IS OPEN SOURCE

When the code which underpins a messaging app is open source, the app can be independently scrutinized to verify that it has no vulnerabilities to security threats or hidden surveillance functions such as backdoors. Ideally, an app will publish its entire codebase openly: messaging apps such Signal and Wire are entirely open source, while apps such as Telegram and Threema publish only part of their code.[35]

12.2.4.7 COMPANY VETS DISCLOSURE REQUESTS FROM LAW ENFORCEMENT

It is critical that the company producing the messaging app rigorously vets and responds in a restrained manner to law-enforcement requests for user data. Ideally, they will provide information on their own behaviour in this regard, publishing regularly updated transparency reports that provide details about what requests they have received from which jurisdictions, and what types of information they have provided. At the time of writing, Microsoft[36] and Meta[37] publish regular transparency reports that detail how many requests they receive and how much data they hand over to law-enforcement agencies, while Signal provides more detailed descriptions of the small number of requests they receive.[38]

Additionally, it is important to consider whether an entity providing a messaging app is located in a country where the government has broad surveillance powers or a record of regularly flouting legal restraints on surveillance.[39]

12.2.4.8 LIMITED PERSONAL DATA SHARING WITH THIRD PARTIES

Although messaging apps will need to share some data with Third Parties (typically those playing some technical role in the data Processing) in order to facilitate the delivery of their services, it is critical that companies do not share Personal Data, and only share minimal, de-identified data when this is strictly necessary. Organizations should choose a messaging app that does not share any data with Third Parties other

---

35 For more on this topic, see Lorenzo Franceschi-Bicchierai, "Wickr: Can the Snapchat for Grown-Ups Save You From Spies?", Mashable, 4 March 2013: https://mashable.com/archive/wickr.
36 Microsoft, *Law Enforcement Request Report*, Microsoft Corporate Social Responsibility, accessed 21 February 2022: www.microsoft.com/en-us/corporate-responsibility/lerr.
37 Meta, "Government Requests for User Data | Transparency Center", Meta, accessed 15 February 2022: https://transparency.facebook.com/government-data-requests.
38 Signal Messenger, "Government Requests", Signal Messenger, accessed 21 February 2022: https://signal.org/bigbrother.
39 Useful sources for further research include: Electronic Frontier Foundation, "Digital Citizen", Electronic Frontier Foundation, 4 November 2019: www.eff.org/digital-citizen; Privacy International, "We Demand Change and Litigate | Advocacy", Privacy International, accessed 21 February 2022: https://privacyinternational.org/advocacy; Global Voices Advox, *Defending Free Speech Online*, Global Voices Advox, accessed 21 February 2022: https://advox.globalvoices.org; Electronic Frontier Foundation, "Deeplinks Blog", Electronic Frontier Foundation, accessed 21 February 2022, www.eff.org/deeplinks.

than those which are strictly necessary for the technical operation of the service – and seek to confirm this explicitly with companies before proceeding.

12.2.4.9 RESTRICTING ACCESS THROUGH THE DEVICE'S OPERATING SYSTEM, SOFTWARE OR SPECIFIC SECURITY PATCHES

Newer versions of mobile phone operating systems also include additional security features that, for instance, prevent apps from accessing data elsewhere on the device. Users can also choose to grant individual permissions or enable full-device encryption. However, these newer devices and operating systems are unlikely to be found in the areas in which Humanitarian Organizations operate. This means that unauthorized Third Parties may be able to access the data shared, as well as the metadata generated through the use of messaging apps, using the various means outlined above (Section 12.2.3 – How could other parties access data shared on messaging apps?).[40]

12.2.5 PROCESSING OF PERSONAL DATA COLLECTED THROUGH MOBILE MESSAGING APPS

Once the beneficiaries engage in communications with Humanitarian Organizations through mobile messaging apps, Humanitarian Organizations will need to collect, most likely store on other platforms, aggregate and analyse the information provided.

It is key that this Processing also takes place in line with the data protection principles set out in Part I of this Handbook. A few selected principles, specific to the collection of data through mobile messaging apps, are considered below.

Communicating with communities in humanitarian situations always involves negotiating a range of complex questions, including:
- Do individuals need to give a Humanitarian Organization "permission" to add their details to a group or channel?
- How can an individual opt out of receiving the content? Is this made clear to them at the outset?
- How can people be made aware of who their Personal Data are shared with?
- If requests for support that fall outside the Humanitarian Organization's mandate are shared with another humanitarian agency, are there clear data-sharing protocols to cover this?
- How do people know how long their data will be kept, and for what purposes?
- How can all these issues be communicated in a way that is easy to understand, including for people with limited experience of technology?

---

40 ICRC and Privacy International, *The Humanitarian Metadata Problem*, October 2018, 61–62.

Working with messaging apps adds a new layer of complexity to all these issues.

In their DPIAs, Humanitarian Organizations should include details of the various protocols and the degree to which each protocol protects content and metadata. Doing so will allow them to assess which option is best for a given purpose (i.e. sharing sensitive information), and also the context in which it will be used (i.e. legal and political), as well as the profile of beneficiaries.

12.3 LEGAL BASES FOR PERSONAL DATA PROCESSING

Humanitarian Organizations may process Personal Data collected through mobile messaging apps using one or more of the following legal bases:[41]
- the vital interest of the Data Subject or of another person;
- the public interest, in particular based on an organization's mandate under national or international law;
- Consent;
- a legitimate interest of the organization;
- the performance of a contract;
- compliance with a legal obligation.

In most cases, the Processing of Personal Data collected through mobile messaging apps may be based on Consent, vital interest or the public interest. If individuals have already communicated with a Humanitarian Organization by messaging app, or have given their telephone numbers to them, it can be assumed individuals consented to the privacy policy of the messaging application they use. This Consent, however, should not be confused with the legal ground for Processing Personal Data by Humanitarian Organizations. Consent obtained by Humanitarian Organizations must be informed, and it is key that Humanitarian Organizations provide relevant, clear, transparent and intelligible information concerning the purpose, retention or further sharing of collected data, as discussed in this Handbook.[42]

Otherwise, messages concerning Humanitarian Emergencies can be assumed to fall within the vital interest of Data Subjects or to be in the public interest. These legal bases also require that information be given to individuals, which can be done by sending them a link to the relevant information notice in a message via the mobile messaging application used. The quality, accessibility and comprehensibility of the information is as important as the actual content of the notice concerning the Processing.[43]

---

41   See Chapter 3: Legal bases for Personal Data Processing.
42   See Chapter 2: Basic principles of data protection.
43   Article 29 Data Protection Working Party, *Guidelines on transparency under Regulation 2016/679 (WP260 Rev.01)*, 11 April 2018, para. 4: https://ec.europa.eu/newsroom/article29/redirection/

12.4 DATA RETENTION

Humanitarian Organizations need to set out in their information notices and data protection policies how long they envisage holding the data collected.

Some of the data entered into most messaging apps are retained and stored by Third Parties (messaging-app companies), which in turn share some of those data with other parties – whether service providers that enable an app to function, or parent companies (as with Meta and WhatsApp). It is therefore also worth pointing out in the Humanitarian Organization's information notice that the data provided through the app will also be retained by the app provider and any Third Parties involved, under the responsibility of the app provider and governed by their data protection policies.

Humanitarian Organizations should also consider having a retention policy concerning the exchanges of information or "chats" themselves and delete the chat history at regular intervals to ensure data minimization.

12.5 DATA SUBJECT'S RIGHTS TO RECTIFICATION AND DELETION

As per Part I of this Handbook, Humanitarian Organizations should provide for mechanisms to facilitate the effective exercise of Data Subjects' rights, and inform Data Subjects thereof, in their data protection policies. Such policies should be concise, transparent, intelligible and easily accessible, and written in clear and plain language.[44]

Individuals should be informed that these policies differ from the data protection policy of a particular app, in order to be able to approach the relevant Data Controller. Individuals that seek to exercise their Data Subjects' rights will have to follow different procedures depending on whether they seek to exercise their rights within the communication channel of a Humanitarian Organization or within the scope of an app.

While it may not be problematic to erase or rectify Personal Data extracted from the messaging apps by the Humanitarian Organizations, it may be difficult to state

---

document/51025; European Data Protection Board (EDPB), Binding Decision 1/2021 on the Dispute Arisen on the Draft Decision of the Irish Supervisory Authority Regarding WhatsApp Ireland under Article 65(1)(a) GDPR, para. 51.

44　Article 29 Data Protection Working Party, *Guidelines on transparency under Regulation 2016/679 (WP260 Rev.01)*, 11 April 2018, para. 7.

confidently that messaging apps allow users to destroy or remove data that they have already submitted, because this could entail negotiations with multiple parties (not all of whom are transparent about the data that they hold). It is recommended that this factor also be specified in the data protection policies of Humanitarian Organizations.

12.6 DATA MINIMIZATION

Considering the limited control Humanitarian Organizations have with regard to data collection by mobile messaging apps, organizations seeking to use messaging apps should aim to minimize the amount of information submitted to them. Academic research focused on the United States has also found that users of messaging apps are usually unaware of the privacy implications of installing and sharing data on messaging apps.[45] Therefore, it is suggested that Humanitarian Organizations should provide incentives for crisis-affected individuals to share only Personal Data that are strictly necessary to provide humanitarian aid.

EXAMPLE:
Ahead of South Africa's municipal elections in August 2016, the non-profit Africa's Voices Foundation partnered with Livity Africa to evaluate the impact of Voting is Power, a campaign to encourage young people to vote and highlight issues that mattered to them.[46]

To do so, they used online surveys of young people (conducted via email and through WhatsApp and Facebook Messenger) and posts published on social media. WhatsApp and Messenger were selected as channels because of their popularity with young people (476 people were engaged through Facebook Messenger and 46 through WhatsApp). Africa's Voices Foundation felt that their use of WhatsApp groups encouraged conversations that would yield particularly useful feedback. Impact and Communications Officer Rainbow Wilcox said: "the data that can be gathered [through WhatsApp] is rich, authentic, and provides insights into sociocultural beliefs and behaviours."

However, Africa's Voices had concerns about privacy when using both Facebook Messenger and WhatsApp. "We sought informed consent and stored the data securely, but we cannot control how the data will be used in these platforms," Claudia Abreu Lopes, Head of Research and Innovation, said. "It was problematic

---

[45] Patrick Gage Kelley et al., "A conundrum of permissions: Installing applications on an Android smartphone", in *Financial Cryptography and Data Security*, Lecture Notes in Computer Science, Springer, Berlin/Heidelberg, 2012, 68–79: https://link.springer.com/chapter/10.1007/978-3-642-34638-5_6.

[46] Africa's Voices Foundation, "Youth Priorities for 2016 Municipal Elections in South Africa (Livity Africa)", Africa's Voices Foundation (blog), 2016: www.africasvoices.org/case-studies/youth-priorities-for-2016-municipal-elections-in-south-africa-livity-africa.

because we asked for personal information such as voting and demographics. We have decided not to embark on a [similar] project again if the privacy risks are not well understood before it starts."

As suggested above, it is recommended that Humanitarian Organizations also consider having clear policies on deleting chats at regular intervals, for example, once the necessary data have been extracted.

12.7 PURPOSE LIMITATION AND FURTHER PROCESSING

In most cases data collected through mobile messaging apps will be extracted and analysed by Humanitarian Organizations on other platforms. As part of the Humanitarian Organizations' data protection policies to be communicated to the Data Subjects, Humanitarian Organizations should also clearly specify the purpose of Processing.

This can be particularly challenging considering the flexibility of use and immediacy of communication offered by such solutions, as it is likely that in any one chat numerous issues will be raised by a Data Subject, with each issue requiring one or more follow-up actions. With this in mind, and considering the compatibility of humanitarian purposes, it is suggested that a general humanitarian assistance and protection purpose specification should suffice.

Again, as Processing by mobile messaging applications is beyond the control of Humanitarian Organizations, the fact that such applications may process data for different purposes, according to their own data protection policies, should also be clarified in the Humanitarian Organization's data protection policy.

12.8 MANAGING, ANALYSING AND VERIFYING DATA

Making use of data processed through messaging apps in Humanitarian Action is a challenge. Greater numbers of people can now collect and share larger volumes of data with organizations, but this means the organizations need to ensure they have the capacity to manage, analyse and verify collected data.

Difficulties can arise in creating an effective workflow to manage and analyse the information received. The systems used by messaging apps are not always interoperable with existing information-management systems or databases used by

Humanitarian Organizations. Manual transcription of individual messages into spreadsheets is often used by Humanitarian Organizations to analyse data in a way that would allow for effective decision making.

Challenges also arise with regard to verifying information received through messaging apps. While this is an issue in many online channels,[47] verifying content from messaging apps is made more challenging by the speed at which information can be sent, as well as by message volume and the range of data types that can be sent. News media and human-rights defenders have attempted to respond to these challenges through collaboration and efforts to produce resources and guidance on the issue. Some messaging apps (e.g. WhatsApp) have developed features aiding the verification and fact-checking process.[48] Some of these resources may also be useful to Humanitarian Organizations.[49]

Humanitarian Organizations engage in Further Processing in cases where the Personal Data collected via apps are managed, analysed or verified. Consequently, Humanitarian Organizations have to ensure that Further Processing of Personal Data operations is compatible with the initial purpose for which data were collected.

12.9 DATA PROTECTION BY DESIGN

Prior to launching a communication channel through a messaging app, Humanitarian Organizations, in addition to the guiding principles of humanitarian work,[50] should consider whether the app implements appropriate technical and organizational measures and whether it is designed in such a way that it implements the core data protection principles (e.g. lawfulness, fairness and transparency, purpose limitation and data minimization).

---

[47] The Engine Room, "Verification of Social Media: The Case of UNHCR on Twitter", Responsible Data (blog), 2016: https://responsibledata.io/rd-reflection-stories/social-media-verification.

[48] Mark Sweney, "WhatsApp launches factcheck feature aimed at viral messages", *The Guardian*, 4 August 2020, Online edition, sec. Digital Media: www.theguardian.com/technology/2020/aug/04/whatsapp-launches-factcheck-feature-aimed-at-viral-messages.

[49] See for example: Craig Silverman, ed., *Verification Handbook: An Ultimate Guideline on Digital Age Sourcing for Emergency Coverage*, 1. ed., European Journalism Centre, Maastricht, 2014: http://verificationhandbook.com; AAVV, *DatNav: New Guide to Navigate and Integrate Digital Data in Human Rights Research*, Guide, The Engine Room; Benetech; Amnesty International, June 2016: www.theengineroom.org/datnav-digital-data-in-human-rights-research; First Draft News Partner Network, "Mission Statement", First Draft, accessed 22 February 2022: https://firstdraftnews.org/about.

[50] ICRC, *Accountability to Affected People Institutional Framework*, January 2019.

If Humanitarian Organizations intend to develop a messaging app, they should consider implementing the principle of data protection by design and by default, which requires the development of privacy-friendly systems and services through a set of both technical solutions and organizational measures. The client-server architecture used to store data should give effect to the principle of data protection by design. For more guidance on the topic of data protection by design and by default, see Chapter 6: Designing for Data Protection.

When deciding to develop its own app or platform, there are a few practical considerations for a Humanitarian Organization to keep in mind. First, the organization needs to understand the context, needs and local community communication channels (e.g. what messaging apps are popular in a particular society and how a new app would complement or replace it).[51] Second, promoting the use of a new app among the organization's beneficiaries may prove challenging. It is likely that the local community is going to prefer the established communication platform (i.e. messaging app) over a new app. And finally, app maintenance and security involves ongoing costs. All software, once it has been developed, requires regular updates as new vulnerabilities emerge. A Humanitarian Organization will need to consider whether it has the in-house skills and expertise to develop and maintain such an app or platform.[52]

12.10 INTERNATIONAL DATA SHARING

It is also important to be aware that some services intersect, and they may overlap in terms of the entities and operating methods involved. In practice, this means that the Data Processing activities of social media networks and messaging apps must not, and cannot, be viewed as separate. Often, messaging apps are linked to social media networks directly (e.g. Facebook Messenger), or indirectly because they are owned by the same business group (e.g. WhatsApp is owned by Meta, which also owns Facebook). Here, services may share data for a variety of purposes.[53]

---

51 Ibid.
52 ICRC and Privacy International, *The Humanitarian Metadata Problem*, October 2018, sec. 5.4.
53 Ibid., sec. 4.1.

DIGITAL IDENTITY

COLLECTION OF ELECTRONICALLY CAPTURED IDENTITY ATTRIBUTES

DIFFERENT DIGITAL IDENTITY SOLUTIONS

POSSIBLE USE

USE ACROSS SECTORS

FACILITATE AID DISTRIBUTION

CONTINUUM OF CARE

CHALLENGES

RISK OF HARM

LEGAL BASIS

DATA PROTECTION

DEFINING OBJECTIVES, PURPOSES AND STAKEHOLDERS

CHAPTER 13
DIGITAL IDENTITY
Vincent Graf Narbel*

---

*   The author would like to thank Aiden Slavin (ID2020), Giulio Coppi (Norwegian Refugee Council), Dr Tom Fisher (Privacy International) and Robert Riemann (European Data Protection Supervisor) for their contributions to this chapter.

13.1 INTRODUCTION

Every human being has an identity. The right to identity is undisputed and recognized in international declarations and conventions.[1] But not all human beings have a way to prove their identity. In this regard, everyone should have a means to prove who they are through an identity tool.[2] The form such a tool should take remains a matter of dispute. Yet no matter what its form – document, card, token, mobile app or something else – it needs to be produced and managed. The mandates of Humanitarian Organizations frame their action, and this is particularly acute with Digital Identity as we will see in this chapter.

In most cases, Humanitarian Organizations need to use identity management systems to facilitate programmatic goals (e.g. a beneficiary management system set up to ensure aid is provided to the intended individual(s)).[3] Some organizations have been involved in initiatives that aim to develop identity management systems that go beyond simply supporting a programmatic goal and, in practice, provide a legal identity[4] (sometimes in a digital form) to those who lack identification documents and who, because of that, can be made "invisible, discounted, and left behind".[5]

Sometimes, however, an identity tool that was initially designed and deployed to support programmatic goals shifts with time towards a broader use (such as to prove someone's legal identity). This shift introduces a significant function creep of the identity tool, necessitating a complete reevaluation of the data protection and privacy risks.

Against this background, this chapter analyses the data protection implications of setting up a Digital Identity management system for beneficiaries. The discussion covers, among other issues, the way in which Humanitarian Organizations collect and store data in such a system and how they manage information about participants, users and/or beneficiaries.

---

1   See for example: Universal Declaration of Human Rights, Article 6, and UN Convention on the Rights of the Child, Article 7.
2   See SDG target 16.9: "By 2030, provide legal identity for all, including birth registration": https://sustainabledevelopment.un.org/sdg16.
3   Strategy & Research team, "Identity in a Digital Age: Infrastructure for Inclusive Development", USAID, 2017, 1: www.usaid.gov/sites/default/files/documents/15396/IDENTITY_IN_A_DIGITAL_AGE.pdf.
4   Throughout this chapter, the expression "legal identity" follows the UN operational definition of the term: "Legal identity is defined as the basic characteristics of an individual's identity, e.g. name, sex, place and date of birth conferred through registration and the issuance of a certificate by an authorized civil registration authority following the occurrence of birth. In the absence of birth registration, legal identity may be conferred by a legally-recognized identification authority. This system should be linked to the civil registration system to ensure a holistic approach to legal identity from birth to death. Legal identity is retired by the issuance of a death certificate by the civil registration authority upon registration of death. In the case of refugees, Member States are primarily responsible for issuing proof of legal identity. The issuance of proof of legal identity to refugees may also be administered by an internationally recognized and mandated authority." "UN Legal Identity Agenda", UN Stats, accessed 10 March 2022: https://unstats.un.org/legal-identity-agenda.
5   Strategy & Research team, "Identity in a Digital Age", 1.

To start the discussion, it should be noted that there is no universally accepted definition of the term "Digital Identity", although it can generally be agreed that Digital Identities consist of "a collection of electronically captured and stored identity attributes that uniquely describe a person within a given context and are used for electronic transactions".[6] As a multifaceted concept, however, Digital Identity can relate to a number of other important concepts, such as identification, functional identity, foundational identity and personal identity.[7] Since these terms are used throughout this chapter, a simplified explanation of each of them is given in the Table 13.1.

Table 13.1

Term	Objectives	Typical characteristics	Examples
Functional identity	Enables a specific service (function) to authenticate participants.	Contextual, duplication of information.	Every individual can have multiple functional identities and these can be transnational, such as a student ID, a voter ID or a food distribution programme ID.
Foundational identity (legal identity)	Provides a legal identity to a broad population as a public good without specifying a specific service. It allows individuals to prove who they are. The issuer of such an identity is considered a trusted source of identity – sometimes referred to as an authoritative source of identity.	Generates a legal identity that can be referenced by others. Within its given scope, every person can have only one such identity. However, the same person may have several legal identities (e.g. passports issued by different countries).	Typically, legal identities which are government-based and covering the whole population of a country,[8] such as social security number, a birth certificate or an Aadhaar number (a 12-digit number that, in India, uniquely identifies people based on their biometric and demographic data).
Conceptual identity (personal identity)[9]	Defines an individual's identity in relation to others within a given societal structure, determining how they view themselves and how they are perceived by the society around them.	Intangible, variable and heavily defined by personal and societal perception.	Defining attributes (such as ethnicity, sexuality, religion, or political orientation), according to which individuals define themselves and are defined by others within their society.

---

6   World Bank Group, GSMA and Secure Identity Alliance, "Digital Identity: Towards Shared Principles for Public and Private Sector Cooperation", Mobile for Development, GSMA, Washington, DC, 26 July 2016, 11: www.gsma.com/mobilefordevelopment/resources/digital-identity-towards-shared-principles-public-private-sector-cooperation.
7   Jonathan Donner, "The Difference between Digital Identity, Identification, and ID", Medium (blog), 19 December 2018: https://medium.com/caribou-digital/the-difference-between-digital-identity-identification-and-id-41580bbb7563.
8   Strategy & Research team, "Identity in a Digital Age", 12.
9   This chapter will not address conceptual identity as this cannot be encompassed by an identity system.

In view of these different types of identity, it is important for Humanitarian Organizations to clarify from the outset whether they require a functional or a foundational identity for beneficiaries, since this choice affects the design of the identity system and the associated management processes (e.g. collaboration with a Third Party, links to other existing systems, etc.). On many occasions, various legal frameworks will impose significant constraints and requirements on the design of the identity system. It is crucial to comply with these requirements while upholding data protection principles.

13.1.1 AUTHENTICATION, IDENTIFICATION AND VERIFICATION: WHO ARE YOU AND HOW CAN YOU PROVE IT?

Humanitarian Organizations do not always need to know someone's legal identity. This is true, for example, when the purpose of the interaction is to provide aid. Consequently, before developing a Digital Identity system, Humanitarian Organizations need to identify what information they need from beneficiaries for a specific humanitarian programme. Here, there is an important distinction to be made between authentication, identification and verification.

Identification answers the question: "Who are you?" But when setting up an identity management system, organizations should start by asking a different question, namely: "What do I need to know from that person to provide aid or protection?" Knowing who the person is can be important in some cases. For instance, when reuniting unaccompanied minors with their parents, it is critical to ascertain that the alleged parents are indeed who they purport to be. But quite often – possibly in most cases – it is enough to know that the person is entitled to access a service because they meet a certain criterion or have a particular set of attributes (e.g. they can prove they are under 12 in order to receive a particular vaccine). This is also known as authentication – or being able to prove a claim of who you are.

Even when Humanitarian Organizations only need authentication, they should carry out a verification process when registering beneficiaries in the identity management system. Verification, therefore, is the act of checking someone's identification (such as confirming a person's name on their identity document) or some of their identity attributes (such as confirming that a person is a member of the community that will receive aid by checking with the community leader). When a simple authentication system is used to ensure aid is delivered to affected individuals, verification at the time of enrolment can help to ensure that the people who were entitled to receive it were the ones registered. However, it should be noted, that some aid services may not need verification at all. This is true, for instance, when a Humanitarian Organization makes information available on an online platform where anyone can register.

When Humanitarian Organizations enrol and register beneficiaries, some data about them will need to be collected and stored in the identity management system. As will become clear below, deciding what attributes need to be recorded, and for what purpose(s), is a key decision from a data protection perspective. In particular, only attributes that are necessary to achieve the activity's purpose (e.g. supporting the delivery of aid) should be collected. For example, in most cases, an organization would probably not need to store a copy of an identity document to record the fact that a registered person was verified to be a minor. Once enrolled, the beneficiary may receive some record of their identity, such as an attestation, a card, a pin code, or a digital certificate they can access and manage on a mobile device. There is no need for further verification at the point of delivery, since the beneficiary already has proof that they are entitled to access the service in question.

13.1.2 DIGITAL IDENTITY

Digital Identity is a set of attributes stored digitally that uniquely describe a person in a given context (see the types of identity described previously: functional, foundational and conceptual). In some cases, individuals could have more than one, and potentially hundreds of Digital Identities, each serving as a functional identity. This type of system would allow beneficiaries to access services, assistance or protection in a similar way to a username and password access model or a token system, without having to prove their legal identity.

In other cases, however, organizations may need to distinguish one individual from another with a high degree of certainty, and perhaps have only one Digital Identity for each person. In these scenarios, the identity system should allow a Digital Identity to be linked to a physical person. The aim here is to make it easier to distinguish between individuals, for instance when the organization is providing personalized aid (e.g. health care). Yet even when such a link is necessary, the organization might not need to obtain legal identity documents from beneficiaries. For instance, people might be able to register with their name only, without needing to confirm that the name they have given matches their legal identity (e.g. by checking it against their birth certificate or other identity documents).

Lastly, there may be cases where the Humanitarian Organization needs a system that also allows it to ascertain and verify the individual's legal identity. This is very similar to the previous case, except that a legal identity document (or a foundational entity) will be required in order to formally identify the person in question.

In summary, these are the main steps that a Humanitarian Organization should follow when setting up a Digital Identity management system:

First, the organization decides what it needs to know about the affected people so it can implement a specific humanitarian programme. This will determine whether identification is required or whether authentication alone is sufficient. From a data protection standpoint, the latter option should be preferred wherever possible.

Second, the organization determines, based on programme needs, whether it requires a functional or foundational identity, bearing in mind that only a handful of Humanitarian Organizations have a mandate to establish and/or manage foundational identities, and only for specific purposes.

Third, the organization designs a verification process to cross-check the information provided at the enrolment stage. Depending on the chosen identity system, it can involve no particular formality, some due diligence or an authoritative legal document. The organization should also determine whether or not it needs to retain the information assessed in the verification phase.

13.1.3 SYSTEM DESIGN AND GOVERNANCE

Once the Humanitarian Organization understands its objectives (authentication, identification and verification), it needs to decide how the Digital Identity system will be designed to achieve its intended purposes, and how it will be governed. The Humanitarian Organization (or other body) can control the system centrally, or control can be shared across multiple parties in a decentralized way.[10] Some current initiatives aim to give individuals control over their own identity systems by deciding who can access their identity credentials and when. In this sense, the governance structure is sometimes influenced by where the data will be hosted. When multiple parties access the same system, for instance, there needs to be a shared platform. Likewise, when efforts are made to shift control to individuals, it may be possible to allow them to store their credentials on their own devices or to use a service provider of their choosing.

The following decision tree summarizes both the questions that Humanitarian Organizations should answer, and the factors they should consider, when deciding whether to implement an identity system:

1/ Identity system type:
- Can you rely on authentication only, or do you really need to identify the beneficiaries?
- Are you aiming to generate functional or foundational identity? (Remember: only some organizations have the mandate to generate foundational identity.)

---

10 The difference between decentralized and distributed architecture and a federated identity system is described in detail in the literature. While this is an important point, it is beyond the scope of this chapter and will therefore not be discussed here. For a more detailed description of decentralized identity, refer to the following sources: "DIF – Decentralized Identity Foundation", accessed 22 February 2022: https://identity.foundation; "Decentralized Identifiers (DIDs) v1.0", World Wide Web Consortium, accessed 22 February 2022: https://w3c.github.io/did-core; World Economic Forum, *Trustworthy Verification of Digital Identities*, White Paper, Inclusive Deployment of Blockchain for Supply Chains (World Economic Forum (WEF), April 2019: www3.weforum.org/docs/WEF_Trustworthy_Verification_of_Digital_Identities_2019.pdf.

- Do you need to verify the information at enrolment? If not, is a system without verification acceptable? If so, does verification require a formal, legal identity document (or is a simpler form of verification acceptable)? Do you need to retain the information assessed during the verification process?

2/ Design choices:
- What information should be stored? By whom? And where?
- Note that verifying a particular attribute (such as nationality, to determine whether the person is eligible for inclusion in a humanitarian programme) does not mean that this information has to be stored in the identity system. The system can simply confirm that a person has the necessary attribute without further details.
- In some cases, there may be no need for verification in the first place. This applies, for example, to a generally accessible digital service, where an account can be created freely without disclosing any personal information, or to cases where an individual's mere presence in a place where people are displaced entitles them to access aid (when cards are distributed without collecting information, for instance).
- How will the data be controlled and governed? Who needs to access what information, at what point and for what purposes?

Importantly, Digital Identity programmes are not limited to specific technologies or systems. Such programmes can be designed using one of many technologies or a combination of solutions. Technologies frequently associated with Digital Identity include:
- **Biometrics:**[11] Enrolling beneficiaries in Digital Identity schemes in the humanitarian sector may include the use of Biometrics such as fingerprints or iris scans.
- **Blockchain:**[12] Blockchain is one possible way for individuals with limited access to digital technology and infrastructure to prove their identity.[13] Despite its promise, however, the challenges that come with Blockchain technology demand serious consideration.
- **Data Analytics:**[14] Digital Identities can be created from digital behavioural attributes (also called algorithmic ID) without using official credentials. Here, a person's online activity (social media use, browsing history, online purchases, call history, etc.) could be used to verify their identity.[15] Although the potential of

---

11   See Chapter 8: Biometrics.
12   See Chapter 15: Blockchain.
13   Ana Beduschi et al., *Building Digital Identities: The Challenges, Risks and Opportunities of Collecting Behavioural Attributes for New Digital Identity Systems*, Open Research Exeter, University of Exeter & Coelition, 2017, 15-16, 26: https://socialsciences.exeter.ac.uk/media/universityofexeter/collegeofsocialsciencesandinternationalstudies/lawimages/research/Buiding_Digital_Identities_with_Behavioural_Attributes.pdf.
14   See Chapter 17: Artificial Intelligence for issues related to the use of Data Analytics.
15   Beduschi et al., *Building Digital Identities*, 8.

profile-based identity systems is not yet fully realized, this approach does raise data protection concerns.[16]

13.1.4 DIGITAL IDENTITY IN THE HUMANITARIAN SECTOR: POSSIBLE SCENARIOS

The following four scenarios shed light on the interplay between various Digital Identity systems in the humanitarian sector.

Scenario 1: A Humanitarian Organization issues an identity credential (for example, a registration card or document) to a registered beneficiary of aid. In this scenario, the beneficiary – a Data Subject – would use a functional identity, which enables them to receive aid. In some situations, however, such an identification system could be accepted as proof of the identity of the beneficiary – in other words, as a foundational identity (see scenario 4). Yet under some humanitarian programmes, individuals only have to authenticate to prove that they are legitimately entitled to access certain aid services, without the need for identification.

Scenario 2: A Humanitarian Organization offers multiple services to beneficiaries. In order to provide these services, each unit of the organization needs to have access to a certain part of the data collected from beneficiaries. For example, to provide in-kind aid, the unit may need to access aid distribution records linked to the beneficiary. Another unit, meanwhile, may need to access medical records to provide a follow-up treatment, while a third unit may need information about the individual to restore family links.

Scenario 3: Several Humanitarian Organizations provide multiple services to beneficiaries through a unified identity system. Under this type of shared identity solution, each organization can access the data that are necessary and relevant for the provision of its services. This scenario would entail both authentication and identification. Interoperability between the various bodies and organizations involved could prove beneficial, with the system acting as a single gateway for humanitarian assistance. This would entail applying the "once-only" principle[17] in Humanitarian Action to facilitate the provision of physical or digital services directly to beneficiaries through online platforms and/or the exchange of information or documents (automatically or on request) between various Humanitarian Organizations.[18] Yet organizations will

---

16   For example, Facebook shadow accounts. See: Russell Brandom, "Shadow Profiles Are the Biggest Flaw in Facebook's Privacy Defense", The Verge, 11 April 2018: www.theverge.com/2018/4/11/17225482/facebook-shadow-profiles-zuckerberg-congress-data-privacy.
17   The once-only principle implies that individuals provide their personal information to the authorities only once and that afterwards, at their request or with their Consent, government departments may exchange the information for the fulfilment of their public duties instead of collecting it again.
18   See: European Data Protection Supervisor (EDPS), *Opinion 8/2017: EDPS Opinion on the Proposal for a Regulation Establishing a Single Digital Gateway and the 'Once-Only' Principle*, Opinion, EDPS, Brussels, 1 August 2017: https://edps.europa.eu/sites/edp/files/publication/17-08-01_sdg_opinion_en.pdf.

need to consider a range of factors when opting for such solutions. For example, they should identify the applicable governance framework and ensure that the roles played by those involved in the system (Data Controllers and Data Processors) are clear. Since appropriately segregating access to data can be technically difficult, it is not uncommon for Data Breaches to occur in unified commercial solutions. Likewise, in a unified system, the complex relationships between organizations can make it hard to ensure that data are only used for the purposes for which they were collected. In addition, complex systems such as these can lead to the *de facto* exclusion of certain groups who may lack the requisite digital literacy skills.

Scenario 4: In some contexts, Humanitarian Organizations may issue functional identity documents to beneficiaries, such as registration cards allowing affected people to access their services. These may end up serving as foundational identity documents for authorities or financial institutions that accept them as proof of ID.

EXAMPLE:
In Jordan and Egypt, two countries that receive a large influx of refugees, local authorities require a valid passport or government-issued identification, such as a Jordanian Ministry of Interior service card for refugees and asylum seekers, to meet mobile SIM registration and Know Your Customer (KYC) requirements. UNHCR argues that its own identification documents should also be accepted, as these may be the only forms of ID that asylum seekers and refugees have.

13.1.5 DIGITAL IDENTITY AS FOUNDATIONAL IDENTITY
Various ongoing initiatives are aiming to develop Digital Identity systems that serve as a form of foundational identity for people without ID documents.

These initiatives are inspired by the fact that people who cannot prove who they are find it harder to assert their rights, access public services, and claim benefits and entitlements based upon their age, nationality, circumstances or any other identity and status attributes.[19] Since proof of ID has become a prerequisite for accessing many services, the identity gap is a major barrier to participation in political, social and economic life. For example, private service providers often require a proof of ID to comply with legal requirements or as part of their due diligence processes (such as KYC, prevention of fraud and impersonation, and transaction risk and cost reduction). Digital Identity systems could be one way to help people in need but who lack

---

19 Guglielmo Verdirame and Barbara E. Harrell-Bond, *Rights in Exile: Janus-Faced Humanitarianism*, Berghahn Books, New York, 2005, 59–63.

identity documents. As mentioned above, however, very few Humanitarian Organizations have the mandate – and therefore the legitimate basis – to develop and deploy foundational systems of this type.

13.2 DATA PROTECTION IMPACT ASSESSMENTS

A Data Protection Impact Assessment (DPIA) involves identifying, evaluating and addressing the impacts on Data Subjects and their Personal Data of a project, policy, programme or other initiative that entails the Processing of such data. It should ultimately lead to measures that minimize the risks to the rights and freedoms of individuals and should follow a project or initiative throughout its life cycle. In light of the large-scale Processing that Digital Identity systems involve, and of other potential risks and harm to Data Subjects arising from their use, Humanitarian Organizations should carry out a DPIA both before and during system and programme implementation. In addition, the DPIA process should analyse not just compliance with data protection requirements, but also the potential adverse impacts of the system on a variety of fundamental rights, as well as the ethical and social consequences of the data Processing.[20]

The use of identity systems for multiple humanitarian purposes – some of which are not always identified from the outset – poses the risk of so-called function creep. This occurs when Humanitarian Organizations – intentionally or otherwise – misuse beneficiaries' data by using the identity system for purposes that were not originally foreseen. Moreover, governments and non-State armed groups that do not respect human rights could access identification and other systems to identify enemies or opponents, or to target and profile certain groups based on their ethnicity, political opinion, nationality or other characteristics. This information can then be used to control, discriminate against and harm these individuals or groups in different ways, for instance by excluding them from essential services and aid, depriving them of their liberty and their right to a fair trial, or even committing atrocities (such as the Rwandan genocide or the persecution in Nazi Germany, where identification and profiling played an essential role).

13.3 DATA PROTECTION BY DESIGN AND BY DEFAULT

Data protection by design and by default is a practice that should feature throughout the life cycle of applications that process Personal Data.[21] It involves designing a

---

20   Alessandro Mantelero, "AI and Big Data: A blueprint for a human rights, social and ethical impact assessment", *Computer Law & Security Review*, Vol. 34, No. 4, August 2018, 755: www.sciencedirect.com/science/article/pii/S0267364918302012?via%3Dihub.
21   Lina Jasmontaite et al., "Data protection by design and by default: Framing guiding principles into legal obligations in the GDPR", *European Data Protection Law Review*, Vol. 4, No. 2, 2018, 168–189: https://doi.org/10.21552/edpl/2018/2/7.

Processing operation, program or solution in a way that implements key data protection principles from the outset, and that provides the Data Subject with the greatest possible data protections (see Chapter 6: Designing for Data Protection). The key data protection principles in this sense are:
- lawfulness, fairness and transparency;
- purpose limitation;
- data minimization;
- accuracy;
- storage limitation (limited retention);
- integrity and confidentiality (security);
- accountability.

When designing an identity system, Humanitarian Organizations should therefore start by considering their needs, and then examining whether an identity system is necessary and proportionate to solve the identified problem. If an organization determines that it does require an identity system, it should think carefully about which type of system best fits its needs and is appropriate in the particular circumstances. Following this process will help the organization apply the principles of data minimization and proportionality, as explained in Section 13.6 – Application of basic data protection principles, below.

Data protection by design also requires an organization to conceive systems in a way that makes it possible, and easier, for a Data Subject to exercise their rights (see Section 13.5 – Rights of Data Subjects, below). For example, in a Digital Identity system, Data Subjects should, by default, have access to information notices, to all information linked to their identity, and to logs detailing who has accessed their data and for what purposes.

13.4 DATA CONTROLLER/DATA PROCESSOR RELATIONSHIP

Digital Identity systems can involve a wide range of bodies and entities, including Humanitarian Organizations, governments, and commercial entities such as banks, payment system providers, IT network providers and Biometrics companies. Consequently, it can be difficult to ascertain which parties should be treated as Data Controllers and Data Processors. Likewise, it can be hard to determine where the boundaries of responsibility and liability lie among the parties. To counter this problem, a Digital Identity system must be designed in a way that clarifies who the stakeholders are, what responsibilities and obligations they have, and what data categories and flows each one uses and for what purposes. When a Humanitarian Organization determines the means and purposes of the identification programme, it will act as the Data Controller and, therefore, will be potentially liable for breaches, misuse and other types of harm that may arise from the programme. In situations where joint controllership is established, or where a Data Processor processes Personal Data only on behalf of the Data Controller, it is best practice to allocate responsibilities among the parties in a written agreement.

13.5 RIGHTS OF DATA SUBJECTS

The possibility of developing Digital Identity systems that are controlled by the Data Subject is currently being explored through various initiatives. Such systems aim to shift control to individuals by allowing them to store identity data on their own devices without relying on a central repository and, when necessary, providing credentials to those who need to verify them.[22] As discussed above, this could be achieved, for example, by building a system in which beneficiaries store their personal information on their own devices or in another storage medium of their choosing, and are able to decide when to share it with bodies and organizations involved in the humanitarian response. Some functional or foundational identity initiatives also aim to shift control to individuals, again by allowing them to store their Personal Data on their own devices and sharing them with others if and when they wish. However, whether a control shift would actually happen in practice is still matter of dispute. When pursuing such initiatives, it is important to ensure that individuals are aware of their rights and the risks of having this information stored on their personal devices, and that they are sufficiently equipped to be able to use such tools safely.

EXAMPLE:
The ID2020 Alliance was set up to influence the development of so-called "good" Digital Identities, under which individuals have full control of their identity and can determine which data are shared and with whom. According to the Alliance, "Today, most personal data is stored in silos. The more siloed and numerous your data becomes the less control you have over it." To solve this, the Alliance proposes that individuals "must have control over their own digital identities, including how personal data is collected, used, and shared".[23]

While such initiatives are not yet commonplace, Humanitarian Organizations can give beneficiaries more control over and access to their data by providing them with a login to access all information relating to their identity credentials and, if applicable, a personal profile created by the organization in question. The potential benefits and risks associated with this solution still need to be fully explored, so as to determine

---

22   Michael Pisa and Matt Juden, *Blockchain and Economic Development: Hype vs. Reality*, CGD Policy Paper, Center for Global Development, Washington, DC, July 2017, 25: www.cgdev.org/sites/default/files/blockchain-and-economic-development-hype-vs-reality_0.pdf.

23   All quotes from the ID2020 website: https://id2020.org.

whether it works in practice and whether it genuinely shifts control to individuals. In theory, however, such a system could automatically inform beneficiaries of any Third Parties that have accessed their data, and whenever a Processing activity starts. It could also allow beneficiaries to update their Consent, when this is the legal basis for Processing, and to receive updated information about the Processing. With more control, beneficiaries could directly exercise their rights as Data Subjects through an online profile or platform. In cases where beneficiaries are not digitally literate, or do not have access to the necessary technology, Humanitarian Organizations must provide alternative ways for them to exercise their rights in respect of their Personal Data.

13.5.1 RIGHT OF ACCESS

Beneficiaries have the right to request access to information about the Processing of their data, and to the data that are being processed.[24] While this right can be limited in certain circumstances, Humanitarian Organizations, as Data Controllers, should reply to such requests by informing beneficiaries if their Personal Data are being processed and, if so, granting them access to the data in question. In practice, however, this right may be hard to implement in Digital Identity programmes as it can be difficult to verify that the person requesting access to information is the individual entitled to receive it (verification), particularly if the request is made by digital means (which is the most likely scenario in the case of Digital Identity). While this is an issue that applies to a wide range of digital systems, it must be given equal consideration in the case of Digital Identity. Humanitarian Organizations should therefore take steps to ensure that the rights of Data Subjects can be respected, both before deciding on the design of a Digital Identity system, and when deciding whether or not to implement it.

Another challenge to respecting the rights of Data Subjects in Digital Identity programmes stems from the fact that different units within the same organization might hold different pieces of information about the same Data Subject. Consequently, compiling all this information in order to respond to a request may prove challenging. It could even involve unnecessary effort, since beneficiaries often only request access to a specific category of data, or to data relating to a particular programme, as opposed to all the data about them that the organization holds. Organizations should therefore discuss this with the Data Subject, so as to understand the specifics of the request and avoid any superfluous effort. Humanitarian Organizations should factor this challenge into their thinking at the Digital Identity system design stage, so they can anticipate issues of this type and devise ways to prevent them. A login-based access system, such as the one envisaged above, could allow beneficiaries to access their profile at any time, check what information is held about them, and the purposes for which it is being used.

---

24 See Section 2.11.2 – Access.

13.5.2 RIGHTS TO RECTIFICATION AND ERASURE

Beneficiaries should be able to rectify incorrect data about themselves and, in certain circumstances, to have their data deleted. They could do this directly, for instance by logging into their account (as envisaged above). When beneficiaries do not have control over their data, exercising their rights can again prove challenging, not least when it comes to assessing and confirming the identity of someone requesting to have their data rectified or deleted. To address this problem, Humanitarian Organizations will need to implement a verification system that complies with the minimization principle and does not collect unnecessary Personal Data. Here again, having beneficiaries log into their account would be one way to achieve this aim.

13.6 APPLICATION OF BASIC DATA PROTECTION PRINCIPLES

While this section provides an overview of data protection concerns that may arise when dealing with Digital Identity systems, every case should be examined in detail and on its merits, taking into account the technology used and the type of identification needed to achieve the envisioned programme's objectives. Different programmes will have different requirements. Likewise, different technologies may have different data protection implications.

13.6.1 LEGAL BASES FOR PERSONAL DATA PROCESSING

Humanitarian Organizations need to process Personal Data in order to establish or verify the identity of a beneficiary. These Processing operations may be carried out on one or more legal bases. Under scenarios 2 and 3, for instance, a Humanitarian Organization will have to identify a separate legal basis for each Processing activity, e.g. vital interest for the Processing of medical records, and Consent for the Processing of Personal Data for restoring family links.

On the issue of Consent, it is important to recognize that beneficiaries receiving aid may not be in a position to give it validly.[25] Consent is a freely given, specific and informed indication that a Data Subject agrees to the Processing of their Personal Data. Similarly, while Humanitarian Organizations may use public interest as the legal basis for a programme that provides official identity credentials, failing to obtain Consent could lead to distrust among beneficiaries. They may feel that, because they have no say in the Processing of their Personal Data, their rights are being restricted. This is especially true when the data in question relate to their identity, which is an intrinsic part of a person's life.

---

25 See Section 3.2 – Consent.

13.6.2 PURPOSE LIMITATION AND FURTHER PROCESSING

Personal Data should be collected for specified, explicit and legitimate purposes, and Further Processing should only be undertaken when compatible with the initial purposes.[26] In this regard, it is important to consider whether Personal Data collected from a Data Subject in order to provide them with Digital Identity credentials under a specific humanitarian programme (e.g. with the aim of establishing beneficiaries' identity) could be further processed under a different programme (e.g. to provide assistance or services). Humanitarian Organizations should consider the following factors when applying the purpose limitation principle:[27]

- compatibility between the initial and further purposes;
- the context in which the data are collected, including the relationship between the individual and the controller;
- the nature of the data;
- potential consequences for beneficiaries;
- relevant safeguards (including data security safeguards, such as encryption or Pseudonymization).

As Digital Identity systems can have multiple uses, each with its own purpose, organizations must clearly specify all the purposes of a given Processing operation. If these purposes change or are subsequently clarified, the organization will need to give further notice to the Data Subjects.

13.6.3 PROPORTIONALITY

The principle of proportionality calls for the least intrusive means of Processing to be used in achieving the specified Processing aims. It is worth recalling that some humanitarian activities, such as the provision of aid, may require beneficiaries to prove only that they are entitled to receive the benefit (i.e. authentication), while others will demand a foundational (or "official") identity (i.e. verification). For this reason, Humanitarian Organizations, as Data Controllers, should consider which activities require identification and which ones do not. By limiting the Processing to authenticating the entitlement of beneficiaries to access services, organizations could avoid accidentally or unintentionally repurposing data or gathering unnecessary information, since beneficiaries' legal identities would not be collected or stored by the organization in the first place. In cases where authentication or identification is needed, organizations should also consider how much data they require, and of what type. For example, when using biometric data, organizations should process the least data points possible (e.g. one fingerprint instead of ten).

---

26 See Chapter 2: Basic principles of data protection.
27 EDPS, *Opinion on the Proposal for a Regulation Establishing a Single Digital Gateway and the 'Once-Only' Principle*, 9–10.

13.6.4 DATA MINIMIZATION

Humanitarian Organizations should only collect and process the minimum amount of data they need to fulfil the purpose of the Processing. For that reason, they must fully understand what information they need from beneficiaries before implementing any identification system that processes Personal Data. If an organization establishes that proving entitlement only is sufficient (i.e. authentication), it should not collect or process identity information in any way.

13.6.5 DATA SECURITY

Digital Identity systems such as the one envisaged in scenario 3 could allow beneficiaries to store their Personal Data on their own devices. The same applies to initiatives designed to provide an identity to those who lack identity documents. In such cases, malicious individuals or organizations would, in theory, only be able to access this information if they were able to breach device security. Yet beneficiaries could also be physically coerced into handing over their devices.

In other cases, such as the ones mentioned in scenarios 1 and 2, Humanitarian Organizations may store Personal Data in their own databases as part of a Digital Identity programme. These databases could become a target for malicious individuals or organizations. Consequently, Humanitarian Organizations must ensure that their Digital Identity systems preserve the confidentiality, availability and integrity of data in their systems and, in doing so, adequately protect the data from misuse, Data Breaches and liabilities.[28] Furthermore, the sensitive nature of certain types of Personal Data will generally require a very high level of security. Encryption techniques such as secret sharing (also known as secret splitting) systems can help increase security. In such systems, data are encrypted and the key is fragmented between multiple parties, which then need to work together to decrypt the data (e.g. different Humanitarian Organizations, as envisaged in scenario 3), thereby avoiding a single point of failure. Under this arrangement, the key can easily be destroyed if needed, since deleting a certain number of fragments (the number varies from system to system) would mean the data could no longer be used.

When implementing identity programmes, Humanitarian Organizations should also consider the security measures adopted by any partners. For instance, if beneficiaries' information is shared with other bodies or organizations, they must have appropriate security measures in place to protect the data and avoid the harmful consequences of a Data Breach.

---

28 Strategy & Research team, "Identity in a Digital Age", 25.

13.6.6 DATA RETENTION

Personal Data should be retained for a defined period, which should be no longer than is necessary for the purpose of the Processing. Where the main purpose of the Processing is to provide basic humanitarian assistance in the form of food, shelter and medical care, Personal Data should only be retained for as long as is needed to provide that assistance. Yet the situation is more complicated for Digital Identity programmes that seek to provide a form of identity credentials for beneficiaries who lack identity documents, since beneficiaries may wish to continue using their identity – which replaces or serves as an identity document – throughout their entire lives, as well as updating their status or situation as time passes. Here, determining an appropriate data retention period can prove challenging. Humanitarian Organizations should, however, provide an initial indication of the retention period that is consistent with the initial purpose for which the data are being collected. Once this period ends, organizations involved in programmes of this type should conduct periodic assessments to determine whether they still need to retain the data. Another option would be to allow beneficiaries to decide whether their data can be retained.

13.7 INTERNATIONAL DATA SHARING

Depending on the technical solution and the design chosen, data processed in Digital Identity systems may routinely flow across national borders. In scenario 3 above, for instance, multiple organizations may share information with each other, or beneficiaries may share their data with multiple organizations simultaneously. International Data Sharing raises data protection concerns.[29] Although some jurisdictions have recognized protection arrangements (such as the use of contractual clauses), Humanitarian Organizations operating Digital Identity programmes may struggle to implement these arrangements in practice because the system may involve multiple parties in different locations. As a general rule, Humanitarian Organizations are advised to take whatever steps they can to ensure that any transfer of Personal Data to a Third Party (and any subsequent onward transfer) does not lower the level of protection of individuals' rights. Because organizations are liable for all data transfers they conduct, they are responsible if data are unlawfully shared with other organizations in the envisaged scenario. Beneficiaries' Consent, however, could be an appropriate legal basis for organizations to transfer data in some situations. As mentioned above, however, it is questionable whether beneficiaries receiving aid can always give valid Consent.[30] In such cases, a different legal basis will have to be identified.

---

29 See Chapter 4: International Data Sharing.
30 See Section 3.2 – Consent.

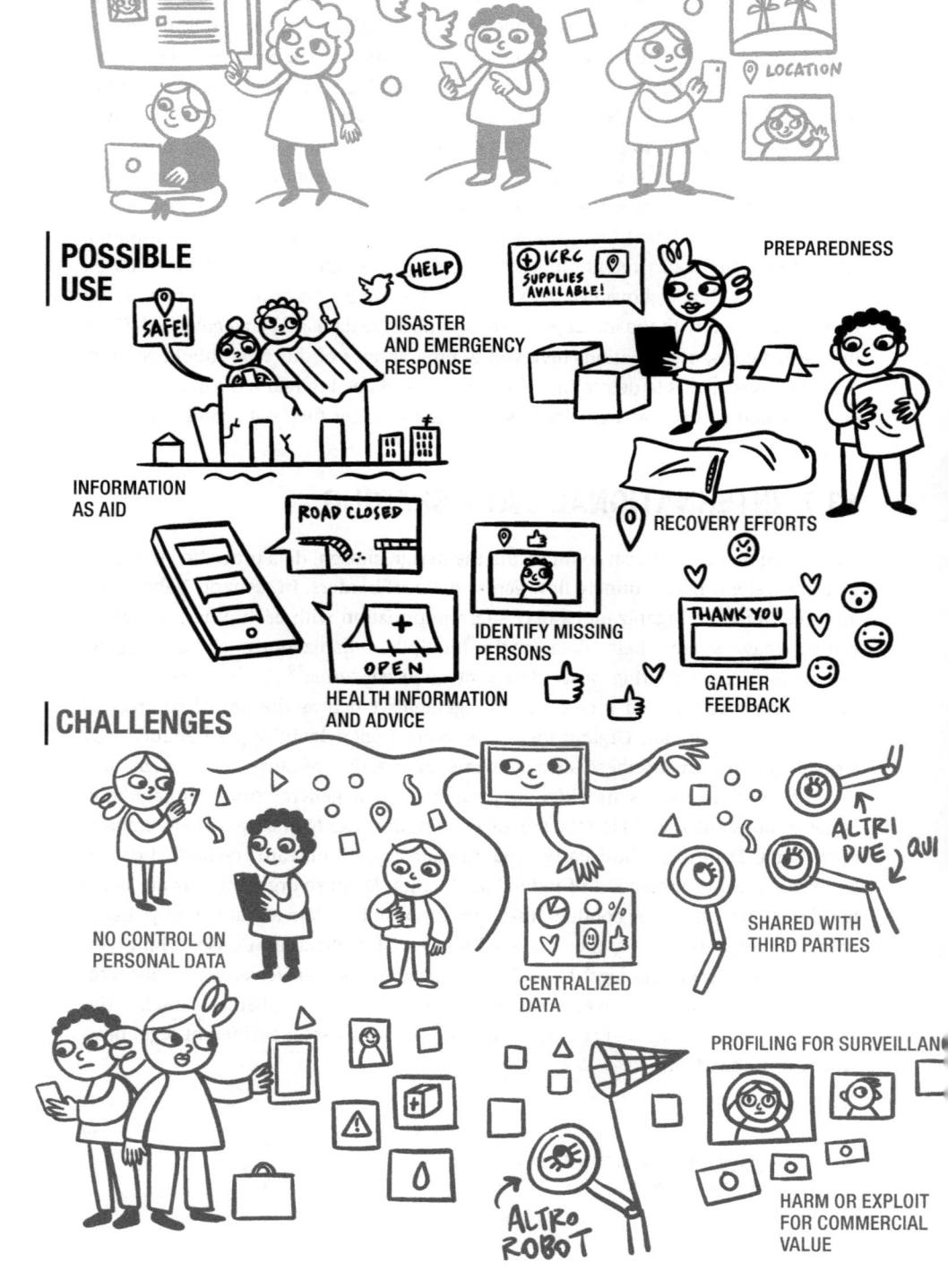

SOCIAL MEDIA

POSSIBLE USE

- DISASTER AND EMERGENCY RESPONSE
- PREPAREDNESS
- INFORMATION AS AID
- RECOVERY EFFORTS
- IDENTIFY MISSING PERSONS
- HEALTH INFORMATION AND ADVICE
- GATHER FEEDBACK

CHALLENGES

- NO CONTROL ON PERSONAL DATA
- CENTRALIZED DATA
- SHARED WITH THIRD PARTIES
- PROFILING FOR SURVEILLANCE
- HARM OR EXPLOIT FOR COMMERCIAL VALUE

CHAPTER 14
SOCIAL MEDIA
Júlia Zomignani Barboza and Lina Jasmontaite-Zaniewicz*

---

* The authors would like to thank Nicolas de Bouville (Facebook), John Warnes (UNHCR), and Camila Graham Wood, Antonella Napolitano and Ed Geraghty (Privacy International) for their contributions to this chapter.

14.1 INTRODUCTION[1]

14.1.1 SOCIAL MEDIA IN THE HUMANITARIAN SECTOR

Humanitarian Organizations often use social media in their work both to engage with those in need and for campaigning and fundraising purposes. While this chapter focuses on the former use case, it will sometimes refer to the latter, as usually the social media "profile" used is the same for both purposes and thus a completely separate analysis is not possible.

Humanitarian Organizations interact with beneficiaries via social media in a variety of ways. In emergencies, for instance, they may use social media to inform people about safe places and the delivery of aid. They may also use social media to raise awareness (such as addressing humanitarian needs arising in the framework of migration), to encourage beneficiaries to share information with each other in an emergency or to provide information about health and medical care.

Engaging with beneficiaries in this way carries a number of risks. When individuals view or reply to public or private social media posts by Humanitarian Organizations, or when they join public or private groups hosted by such organizations, they share a rich variety of data with the platform in question. Both Humanitarian Organizations and beneficiaries may engage with each other on social media without necessarily being fully aware that they are generating both data and metadata (a set of data that describes and gives information about other data)[2] that can be collected by social media platforms, then used to profile an individual to determine characteristics such as key aspects of their identity, their networks, views and opinions, preferences and affiliations. Likewise, organizations and beneficiaries may be unaware of the consequences and risks of such Processing.

Although individuals may engage with Humanitarian Organizations informally, in a manner akin to a private conversation, the way social media platforms are designed and operate means that Third Parties may be able to monitor, collect, retain and analyse their exchanges. These Third Parties include not only social media providers, but also corporate entities, law enforcement agencies, immigration and border authorities,[3] and governments, who use open-source intelligence techniques and

---

1 This chapter focuses on the use of social media by Humanitarian Organizations to communicate and engage with affected communities. For information related to the use of social media to identify crises and improve the humanitarian response, please refer to Chapter 17: Artificial Intelligence. For messaging apps, please refer to Chapter 12: Mobile messaging apps.
2 For more on metadata, see: ICRC and Privacy International, *The Humanitarian Metadata Problem*, October 2018.
3 See for example: Lina Jasmontaite-Zaniewicz and Júlia Zomignani Barboza, "Disproportionate surveillance: Technology-assisted and automated decisions in asylum applications in the EU?",

sophisticated social media monitoring tools. Data, including images shared on social media, can be analysed in a range of ways – from image and facial recognition, to sentiment and emotion recognition[4] – often using opaque algorithms and Machine Learning.[5] This type of profiling adds to the opacity of how individuals can be exposed through their interactions with, and use of, social media. When decisions are made based on such profiling, it can have serious consequences for an individual, because this opacity brings added risks that come from unequal access to data and to justice, such as the inability to challenge incorrect assumptions that influence or determine decision-making processes and outcomes.

While social media can help Humanitarian Organizations provide services, using these platforms can cause organizations to lose control of the data generated and shared, and pose medium- or longer-term risks. These must be assessed through clear procedures and risk assessments (see Section 15.2 – Data Protection Impact Assessments, below).

Below are some examples of cases where Humanitarian Organizations have used social media to engage with beneficiaries:[6]

- **Facilitating emergency management by contributing to the mitigation, preparedness, response, and recovery of disasters and emergency situations.** In Bangladesh, the creation of a national coordination platform allowed Humanitarian Organizations, in coordination with the government, to broadcast easily understandable disaster-preparedness messages through social media during emergencies to facilitate the disaster-preparedness stage of emergencies.
- **Improving the quality of aid delivery.** In 2016, the ICRC doubled the amount of food contained in food parcels delivered in Syria, as the security situation led to longer periods between food distribution. Beneficiaries were informed of this change in a short video shared on ICRC's institutional Facebook page. Through the comments feature, beneficiaries also had the opportunity to reply to the video and explain their needs (e.g. requesting better cardboard boxes so the food inside would not be damaged in transit). The ICRC then replied to the comments, explaining what it was doing to fulfil the requests or why it could not do so.
- **Improving the efficiency of services.** The Kenyan Red Cross Society (KRCS) actively monitors social media platforms to find out about road accidents and

---

International Journal of Refugee Law, Vol. 33, No. 1, 27 October 2021, pp. 89–110: www.icrc.org/en/document/social-media-to-engage-with-affected-people.

4   See for example: Flor Miriam Plaza-del-Arco et al., "Improved emotion recognition in Spanish social media through incorporation of lexical knowledge", *Future Generation Computer Systems*, No. 110, 1 September 2020, pp. 1000–1008: https://doi.org/10.1016/j.future.2019.09.034.

5   See Chapter 17: Artificial Intelligence.

6   The first four examples were taken from: Timo Lüge, "How to Use Social Media to Engage with People Affected by Crisis", News release, ICRC, IFRC, UN OCHA, September 2017: www.icrc.org/en/document/social-media-to-engage-with-affected-people.

dispatch ambulances to those locations. Knowing this, Kenyans frequently flag road-traffic accidents to the KRCS through social media.
- **"Information as aid" and health promotion.** MSF and other NGOs use social media to provide health information and advice to beneficiaries.
- **Combatting misinformation.** In the early days of the COVID-19 pandemic, the International Organization for Migration (IOM) noted that TikTok was a powerful tool to combat misinformation about the pandemic, including falsehoods that migrants were responsible for the crisis, which could lead to xenophobia, stigma and discrimination.[7]

Although social media platforms offer a wide range of opportunities, using them can also pose risks to beneficiaries and raise important responsibility questions for Humanitarian Organizations. This chapter will discuss how data are generated on social media before addressing core data protection concerns.

14.1.2 SOCIAL MEDIA AND DATA

14.1.2.1 WHAT DATA ARE GENERATED ON SOCIAL MEDIA AND HOW?

Social media platforms receive, capture, generate and process large amounts of data from users, including metadata, user location, images, contacts, "likes", and attention and interest indicators, using them for various purposes. Despite this large-scale Processing, there may often be little transparency as to what specific data are being created, and how the platform and other Third Parties are accessing and using these data for profiling and other purposes.

Some of the data collected by social media platforms come directly from the individual (this is known as "declared data"), such as when they sign up for an account (a name or username, sometimes a copy of an identity document, a phone number, an email address and a physical address), or when they post photographs or comments on their profile.[8]

Furthermore, the declared data may include not only data provided directly by the user, but also data about the user coming from other apps or platforms,[9] which sometimes automatically transfer Personal Data to social media platforms when a user opens the app or accesses its services, even before obtaining Consent.[10] This

---

7   IOM-UN Migration, "Humanitarians on TikTok", Medium, 15 May 2020: https://medium.com/digital-diplomacy/humanitarians-on-tiktok-246651af74d.
8   ICRC and Privacy International, *The Humanitarian Metadata Problem*, October 2018, 34.
9   In its guidelines on targeting of social media users, the European Data Protection Board called this type of data "observed data". See: European Data Protection Board (EDPB), *Guidelines 8/2020 on the targeting of social media users*, 13 April 2021, 13: https://edpb.europa.eu/system/files/2021-04/edpb_guidelines_082020_on_the_targeting_of_social_media_users_en.pdf.
10 Privacy International, "Investigating Apps Interactions with Facebook on Android", March 2019: https://privacyinternational.org/appdata.

happens, for example, when an online store notifies a social media platform that a user has accessed its website so that the platform can use their shopping preferences to offer them targeted advertisements.

Social media platforms also process so-called "inferred data" – additional data not provided directly by users themselves but inferred from their declared data. In this regard, social media platforms usually combine data obtained from different sources and, applying Data Analytics,[11] create a user profile that monitors the user's activities and behaviour.[12] For example, providers can infer who someone's close friends are from how often they communicate and interact on social media.[13] Similarly, social media platforms "might infer that an individual is likely to be interested in a certain activity or product on the basis of his or her web browsing behaviour and/or network connections".[14] Understanding someone's routine and behaviour allows platforms to offer targeted services and individualized content to their users.[15]

Evidence shows that it is possible to build a profile-type identity from someone's digital behavioural attributes, i.e. their online activity.[16] Consequently, a person's digital traces can be used to create a digital profile even without their knowledge[17] and infer information about them including their gender, sexual orientation, religion, location, interpersonal relationships and anticipated behaviour.[18] This type of profile is then used for targeted advertising, but has also been used in the past for political campaigning, as well as predictive policing.[19] This means that if Humanitarian Organizations encourage beneficiaries to engage with them on social media, they may be facilitating this kind of targeting. Furthermore, Humanitarian Organizations frequently use the same social media page or profile both for their humanitarian work and for campaigning and fundraising and thus may also benefit from such targeting in other activities, while at the same time contributing to generation of data and user profiles.

---

11 See Chapter 17: Artificial Intelligence.
12 Article 29 Data Protection Working Party, *Guidelines on automated individual decision-making and profiling for the purposes of Regulation 2016/679 (WP251 Rev.01)*, Guideline (Working Party on the Protection of Individuals with regard to the Processing of Personal Data, 22 August 2018), 12: https://ec.europa.eu/newsroom/article29/items/612053.
13 ICRC and Privacy International, *The Humanitarian Metadata Problem*, October 2018, 35.
14 European Data Protection Board (EDPB), *Guidelines 8/2020*, 14.
15 For more on target advertising, see Privacy International, "AdTech", accessed 15 February 2022: https://privacyinternational.org/learn/adtech.
16 Beduschi et al., "Building Digital Identities", 8.
17 For example, Facebook shadow accounts. See: Brandom, "Facebook Has a Shadow Profile for You".
18 ICRC and Privacy International, *The Humanitarian Metadata Problem*, October 2018, 90.
19 See for example: Albert Meijer and Martijn Wessels, "Predictive policing: Review of benefits and drawbacks", *International Journal of Public Administration*, Vol. 42, No. 12, 10 September 2019, pp. 1031–1039: https://doi.org/10.1080/01900692.2019.1575664. Predictive policing is considered to be part of law enforcement practices.

EXAMPLES OF DATA THAT MAY BE COLLECTED:
Facebook divides the data it collects into three categories: things that users do and provide, device information and information from partners.[20] Under each category, there is a long list of data that the platform collects, including:

> communications and other information you provide when you use our Products, including when you sign up for an account, create or share content, and message or communicate with others. This can include information in or about the content you provide (like metadata), such as the location of a photo or the date a file was created.[21]

The list also includes "information about operations and behaviours performed on the device, such as whether a window is in the foreground or background, or mouse movements"[22] as well as Bluetooth signals, and information about nearby Wi-Fi access points, beacons and cell towers.

Similarly, TikTok also divides the data it collects into three categories: information users provide, automatically collected information and information from other sources.[23] The automatically collected information includes inferred information, explained by the platform as follows:

> We infer your attributes (such as age-range and gender) and interests based on the information we have about you. We use inferences to, for example, keep our Platform safe, content moderation, and, where permitted, to serve you personalised ads based on your interests.

X (former Twitter), in turn, collects data related to a user's basic information (such as declared name, username and email address), profile information, contact information and public information (tweets as well as metadata generated by tweets such as time and location).[24]

14.1.2.2 WHAT DATA CAN BE SHARED WITH THIRD PARTIES?

Some social media platforms may share the information they collect with other service providers for purposes such as targeted advertising of individuals with specific profiles. Given the exponential growth of social media platforms, the number of people and advertising companies that have access to personal information has vastly increased in recent years, thereby increasing the possibility that individuals could be tracked through different methods. Moreover, social media platforms receive data from other parties and organizations through partnership arrangements,

---

20   Facebook, "Data Policy", Facebook, accessed 15 February 2022: www.facebook.com/about/privacy.
21   Ibid.
22   Ibid.
23   TikTok, "Privacy Policy", TikTok, accessed 15 February 2022: www.tiktok.com/legal/privacy-policy-eea?lang=en.
24   ICRC and Privacy International, *The Humanitarian Metadata Problem*, October 2018, 96.

and these additional data are used to further develop a user's profile for various purposes, including advertising.

EXAMPLES OF HOW SOCIAL MEDIA DATA MAY BE SHARED:
Facebook shares aggregated information it collects from users and non-users of the network with other Meta companies (including Instagram, WhatsApp and Messenger) and Third Party partners. It also allows users to share data they store on Facebook with Third Party apps, websites or other services that use or are integrated with Facebook.[25] This means that users may (knowingly or otherwise) share data that are not related solely to them, such as their friends list. Consequently, "even when a user 'locks down' their profile, their data could still be collected by a third-party app being used by one of their friends".[26]

Facebook also offers a variety of options for advertisers to benefit from users' profiles. For instance, advertisers may upload an email or phone list of registered customers and ask Facebook to find their social media profiles in order to target them for marketing purposes (known as a "custom audience").[27] This way, advertisers benefit from aggregated information provided by Facebook, while the social media platform also gathers data from the advertiser. Companies may also ask Facebook to find profiles that are similar to existing customers in order to increase their range of advertising, to focus on specific locations, demographics or genders, or even to install pixels[28] on their websites, so that when a Facebook user visits their website, they receive ads from the company on their Facebook page.[29] Since December 2019, however, Facebook no longer allows phone numbers provided by users when signing up for two-factor authentication to be used to make friend suggestions.[30] This change in company practice reflects increased recognition of the implications of data-sharing between platforms and Third Parties.[31] This is further demonstrated by the new

---

25 Facebook, "Data Policy".
26 ICRC and Privacy International, *The Humanitarian Metadata Problem*, October 2018, 96.
27 Facebook, "About Customer List Custom Audiences", Facebook Business Help Center, accessed 15 February 2022: www.facebook.com/business/help/341425252616329.
28 Facebook pixel is a Facebook analytics tool that allows businesses to better target their advertisements by measuring their effectiveness and understanding the actions people take when visiting the business' website. See: Facebook, "About MetaPixel", Facebook Business Help Center, accessed 15 February 2022: www.facebook.com/business/help/742478679120153.
29 Brendan Van Alsenoy et al., *From Social Media Service to Advertising Network: A Critical Analysis of Facebook's Revised Policies and Terms*, Belgian Privacy Commission, 2015, 55–64.
30 Katie Paul, "Facebook Separates Security Tool from Friend Suggestions, Citing Privacy Overhaul", Reuters, 19 December 2019, sec. Internet News: www.reuters.com/article/us-facebook-privacyidUSKBN1YN26Q.
31 In 2020, the platform also removed some of its target audience categories related to race and ethnicity to prevent misuse; however, some have questioned the fact that the platform still uses categories that could be considered as racial proxy categories. See: Meta, "Simplifying Targeting Categories", Meta for Business, 11 August 2020: www.facebook.com/business/news/update-to-facebook-ads-targeting-categories; see

Off-Facebook Activity tool,[32] which allows users to segregate information obtained by Third Parties from their Facebook profile. In the same manner, in recent versions of its mobile operational system, Apple limited the tracking options between mobile applications, including social media applications, with the goal of increasing transparency and control of such activities by mobile users.[33]

With regard to advertising, TikTok shares and receives data from partners in a similar way to Facebook. According to the platform's privacy policy

> *Advertisers and measurement and data partners share information with us such as mobile identifiers for advertising, hashed email addresses, and event information about the actions you've taken on a website or app. Some of our advertisers and other partners enable us to collect similar information directly from their website or app by integrating our TikTok Advertiser Tools (such as TikTok Pixel).*

X (former Twitter), in turn, allows users to opt out of much of its Processing activities. By default, however, everything shared and published on the platform is public unless the user specifies otherwise. In practice, this means X (former Twitter):

> *is allowed to share or disclose a user's public information (such as profile information, public tweets, or followers) to a wide range of users, services and organizations. Twitter further maintains the right to infer, from these data, which topics might be of interest to the user.*[34]

14.1.2.3 WHAT DATA CAN LAW ENFORCEMENT AND GOVERNMENT AUTHORITIES OBTAIN?

National law may require social media platforms to store users' Personal Data so that public authorities can access them to identify an individual or obtain information about their online activity for law enforcement purposes.[35] In some – but not all – jurisdictions, a warrant may be needed to access such information. In this regard, a

---

also: Jon Keegan, "Facebook Got Rid of Racial Ad Categories. Or Did It?", The Markup, 9 July 2021: https://themarkup.org/citizen-browser/2021/07/09/facebook-got-rid-of-racial-ad-categories-or-did-it.

32 Erin Egan and David Baser, "Now You Can See and Control the Data That Apps and Websites Share With Facebook", Meta (blog), 20 August 2019: about.fb.com/news/2019/08/off-facebook-activity/.

33 Apple Inc, "User Privacy and Data Use – App Store", Apple Developer, accessed 15 February 2022: https://developer.apple.com/app-store/user-privacy-and-data-use; see also: "How the Apple IOS 14 Release May Affect Your Ads and Reporting", Facebook Business Help Center, accessed 15 February 2022: www.facebook.com/business/help/331612538028890.

34 ICRC and Privacy International, *The Humanitarian Metadata Problem*, October 2018, 97.

35 Ibid., 34.

few social media companies publish transparency reports containing information on government access requests.[36]

Using various tools, including those provided by the platforms themselves (the so-called "firehose"), law enforcement agencies and other Third Parties can directly access social media through what is known as open-source intelligence (OSINT), i.e. intelligence gathered from publicly available data. They can also use social media intelligence (SOCMINT), which involves monitoring and gathering both publicly available and private information on social media platforms.[37] These practices are unregulated in many jurisdictions, and the law is often unclear as to whether such monitoring is legal. Further invasive techniques also enable data and information physically stored on a device[38] or in cloud-based applications[39] to be extracted. As with SOCMINT, mobile phone and cloud extraction technologies are used with little transparency and remain unregulated in a number of jurisdictions. In practice, as social media storage is often cloud-based, the volume of Personal Data that can be obtained through these methods is very large.

14.2 DATA PROTECTION IMPACT ASSESSMENTS

Humanitarian Organizations cannot fully control how social media platforms operate, or how they generate and process data. But they can – and should – conduct risk assessments to understand the consequences of using social media to interact with beneficiaries before deciding whether to use such platforms, how to use them and for what purpose.

Humanitarian Organizations use social media with the expectation that beneficiaries have already signed up and consented or otherwise agreed to the platform's terms and conditions. This expectation does not relieve organizations of their duty to carry out a Data Protection Impact Assessment (DPIA).[40] The purpose of a DPIA is to identify how

---

36 Meta, "Government Requests for User Data | Transparency Center"; Twitter, "Twitter Transparency Center", Twitter, accessed 15 February 2022: https://transparency.twitter.com/en.html; TikTok; "Reports", TikTok, accessed 15 February 2022: www.tiktok.com/transparency/en-us/reports.
37 Privacy International, "Social Media Intelligence", Privacy International, 23 October 2017: http://privacyinternational.org/explainer/55/social-media-intelligence.
38 See, for example: Privacy International, "Push This Button For Evidence: Digital Forensics", Privacy International, 24 June 2019: http://privacyinternational.org/explainer/3022/push-button-evidence-digital-forensics; Privacy International, "Can the Police Limit What They Extract from Your Phone?", Privacy International, 14 November 2019: http://privacyinternational.org/node/3281.
39 Privacy International, "Cloud Extraction Technology: The Secret Tech That Lets Government Agencies Collect Masses of Data from Your Apps", Privacy International, 7 January 2020: http://privacyinternational.org/long-read/3300/cloud-extraction-technology-secret-tech-lets-government-agencies-collect-masses-data.
40 See Chapter 5: Data Protection Impact Assessments (DPIAs).

social media use will affect beneficiaries and which measures the organization can take to mitigate potential risks. In particular, a DPIA should not only look at data protection risks, but also evaluate whether social media use in a particular context could lead to human rights violations or otherwise harm the individuals in question. These risks should then be weighed against the potential benefits.

It is worth stressing again that, aside from the content users generate and provide when they sign up for their account(s), the use of social media also generates a large amount of data and metadata that platforms do not proactively declare. Consequently, users may not even be aware these data are being generated and processed.[41] For example, merely clicking "like" buttons or links that redirect the user to other websites generates metadata.

In recent years, many governments have gained access to, and made use of, large amounts of social media data and metadata, as well as powerful analysis tools that help them identify patterns in such data and profile individuals and groups.[42] The DPIA must therefore go beyond merely analysing compliance with data protection requirements. It should also address how the use of a certain application or platform could positively or negatively impact a variety of fundamental rights, as well as the ethical and social implications of Processing by Humanitarian Organizations.[43] This does not mean that the DPIA should replace other forms of impact assessment that may take place within a Humanitarian Organization before implementing their programmes, but it should consider the implications that come from the Processing of Personal Data in a holistic way, which may involve including stakeholders from fields other than data protection.

This is because the Processing of Personal Data and especially metadata can carry significant risks. In 2014, for instance, a former director of the US National Security Agency (NSA) said that they would take the decision to kill people based on information acquired via metadata.[44] Fintech and advertising companies are also employing numerous techniques to make use of such data.[45] That is why it is important for Humanitarian Organizations to take the non-humanitarian purposes and consequences of using social media into account when conducting a DPIA and developing their social media use strategy.

Likewise, the DPIA should consider the fact that social media providers' business models rely on monetizing user data (e.g. for ad targeting). This means that data

---

41 ICRC and Privacy International, *The Humanitarian Metadata Problem*, October 2018, 17.
42 Ibid., 29.
43 Alessandro Mantelero, "AI and Big Data: A blueprint for a human rights, social and ethical impact assessment", *Computer Law & Security Review*, Vol. 34, Issue 4, 2018, pp. 754–772: https://doi.org/10.1016/j.clsr.2018.05.017.
44 ICRC and Privacy International, *The Humanitarian Metadata Problem*, October 2018, 22.
45 Ibid., 23–24.

gathered for humanitarian purposes through such platforms might be vulnerable to commercial exploitation and surveillance.

Humanitarian Organizations should also assess whether social media platforms are the safest and most reliable way to communicate with beneficiaries. In places where physical access to Humanitarian Organizations is difficult, for example, social media may provide an effective means of communication between organizations and beneficiaries who cannot reach them in person.[46] In emergencies, however, governments can shut down social media to avoid the spread of fear or false information,[47] meaning Humanitarian Organizations will need to consider alternative means of communication.

14.3 ETHICAL ISSUES AND OTHER CHALLENGES

For Humanitarian Organizations, involving social media platforms in their work inevitably raises ethical issues because the organization does not have control over Third Parties' privacy and data protection policies. Many of these platforms rely on exploiting and monetizing users' data[48] – both declared data and inferred data, which can reveal sensitive information such as a person's sexual orientation, religion, political opinion and ethnicity.[49] Indeed, not only social media platforms but also other entities can make such inferences based on publicly available information from these platforms. An example of this is a 2022 case in which the Belgian and French data protection authorities sanctioned an NGO for publishing a study in which it created a political profile of over 3,300 Twitter accounts without anonymizing the Personal Data of account holders.[50] By engaging with beneficiaries on social media, Humanitarian Organizations contribute to the generation of the data and metadata

---

46 Adapting to current technological changes affecting the humanitarian landscape, social media and other connected means have been suggested as a possible alternative to physical contact by the ICRC. The ICRC's guidelines on how to organize such communication and other actions responsibly are summarized in: ICRC, *Accountability to Affected People Institutional Framework*, Publication, ICRC, Geneva, 15 February 2019: www.icrc.org/en/publication/accountability-affected-people-institutional-framework.

47 See for example: Jane Wakefield, "Sri Lanka Attacks: The Ban on Social Media", *BBC News*, 23 April 2019, Online edition, sec. Technology: www.bbc.com/news/technology-48022530.

48 See for example: Privacy International, "Guess What? Facebook Still Tracks You on Android Apps (Even If You Don't Have a Facebook Account)", Privacy International, 7 October 2020: https://privacyinternational.org/report/2647/how-apps-android-share-data-facebook-report; Privacy International, "How Apps on Android Share Data with Facebook – Report", Privacy International, 29 December 2018: http://privacyinternational.org/report/2647.

49 ICRC and Privacy International, *The Humanitarian Metadata Problem*, October 2018, 89–90.

50 Autorité belge de Protection des Données, *Décision quand au fond 13/2022 du 27 janvier 2022*, 27 January 2022.

from which these inferences are made.[51] Furthermore, it should be noted that not only can these inferences be used to target and even discriminate against social media users, but may also be used to manipulate them. In this regard,

> Targeting mechanisms are, by definition, used in order to influence the behaviour and choices of individuals, whether it be in terms of their purchasing decisions as consumers or in terms of their political decisions as citizens engaged in civic life. Certain targeting approaches may however go so far as to undermine individual autonomy and freedom (e.g. by delivering individualized messages designed to exploit or even accentuate certain vulnerabilities, personal values, or concerns).[52]

It is also important to consider that social media platforms change their terms and conditions, privacy policies and Processing activities very frequently, without always requesting users' Consent. In addition, although users may understand that the platform processes declared data, platforms may not be transparent about what they infer from such data – and, more importantly, from information obtained from other sources (such as online activity, other users and Third Parties), as well as from data generated by design and default because of the way the platform is designed and operates.[53] The information gathered – and, ultimately, the decisions made on the basis of these data – can severely and adversely affect a user's life, as the example below shows:

> Social media data are being increasingly used to assess the credibility of users requesting loans and to monitor those who have already been given a loan. These assessments are based on a selection of indicators that categorize people as either a "reliable, trustworthy borrower" or an "unreliable, risky borrower".[54]

Aside from the risks associated with the sharing of data by beneficiaries on social media platforms, Humanitarian Organizations must also be mindful about the content they themselves share. Some content, such as public photographs or videos including beneficiaries, can have negative consequences for the individuals in question, from profiling and targeting by companies, to persecution, intimidation and blackmail, discrimination, identity theft and loss of control over their data.

Organizations should also remember that social media may not always be the most useful or effective way to reach a given audience. Social media use is often limited in rural and remote areas, and not all members of a target population may have equal access to technology. Likewise, in some contexts, most social media users will be male, so using platforms for women's health initiatives is unlikely to be effective.

---

51 ICRC and Privacy International, *The Humanitarian Metadata Problem*, October 2018, 91.
52 European Data Protection Board (EDPB), *Guidelines 8/2020*, 7.
53 ICRC and Privacy International, *The Humanitarian Metadata Problem*, October 2018, 102.
54 Ibid., 106. See also: Privacy International, "Fintech", Privacy International, accessed 21 February 2022, https://privacyinternational.org/learn/fintech.

14.4 DATA CONTROLLER/DATA PROCESSOR RELATIONSHIP

When Humanitarian Organizations use social media for communication purposes, their role in relation to the Processing of beneficiaries' Personal Data is often not entirely clear. When organizations set up an institutional page or profile on a social media platform, for instance, the platform's terms and conditions might allow the provider to process more data through that page, or to profile users for advertising purposes. Here, the organization could arguably be considered a joint controller with the platform, and therefore bears part of the responsibility for the Processing. However, when an organization simply uses the platform to interact with beneficiaries through a page, profile or group created by beneficiaries themselves, it is harder to establish the organization's role and the extent of its responsibility.

EXAMPLE OF JOINT CONTROLLERSHIP:
In 2018, the Court of Justice of the European Union (CJEU) ruled, in case C-210/16, that administrators of Facebook pages are Data Controllers in relation to the Personal Data collected and processed by Facebook through their fan pages (a fan page is an institutional page, created by the company or organization on the Facebook platform, to communicate with Facebook users and share content about their work).[55] As fan pages are hosted on the Facebook platform, Facebook gathers information about those who access or interact with them, regardless of whether they have a Facebook account. Facebook uses this information to produce statistics about fan page visitors, which are shared with the page's administrator.

According to the Court, the administrators of such pages (i.e. the organizations that create and manage them) are Data Controllers because creating the fan page "gives Facebook the opportunity to place cookies on the computer or other device of a person visiting its fan page, whether or not that person has a Facebook account" (para. 35). Furthermore, where administrators define specific parameters to be collected by Facebook to benefit from statistics about the page's visitors, they are considered to be taking part in the determination of the means and purposes of the Processing.

Although this ruling relates to the European Union regulatory context and only concerns Facebook,[56] the influence of EU data protection law means that this broad

---

55 Court of Justice of the European Union (CJEU), Case 210/16, Unabhängiges Landeszentrum für Datenschutz Schleswig-Holstein v Wirtschaftsakademie Schleswig-Holstein GmbH, Judgement ECLI: EU:C:2018:3885, June 2018.
56 The European Data Protection Board interpreted that joint controllership in activities involving targeting social media users would apply to all social media platforms offering such services. See their analysis of the roles and responsibilities of joint controllers in multiple targeting activities in: European Data Protection Board (EDPB), *Guidelines 8/2020*.

(albeit controversial) definition of controllership may also be adopted in other regions. Should that be the case, Humanitarian Organizations might be considered Data Controllers in relation to the Processing of Personal Data by the social media platforms they use in relation to their page. In practice, this means that, where the platform processes Personal Data collected through the organization's page for non-humanitarian purposes, the organization in question could be responsible for such Processing.

Humanitarian Organizations must therefore do everything they can to fully understand the business models, privacy policies and security protocols of the social media platforms they use, since they could be held liable for misuses by the platform and other Third Parties. If there are any doubts regarding compliance with data protection, human rights and humanitarian principles, organizations should always choose a safer communication option. It is important to note, however, that in some cases Humanitarian Organizations may have no other alternative to reach certain populations, due to their predominant use of a specific social media platform and possible reluctance to use other means of communication. Regardless of choice limitations, however, Humanitarian Organizations should do everything in their capacity to mitigate possible risks arising from their use of such tools.

14.5 BASIC DATA PROTECTION PRINCIPLES

14.5.1 LEGAL BASES FOR PERSONAL DATA PROCESSING

While Humanitarian Organizations cannot control how social media platforms operate and process data, they should still determine the legal basis for Processing data that they may request and/or receive through social media.

Consequently, Humanitarian Organizations must identify a legal basis for each Processing activity.[57] As mentioned above, organizations frequently use the same social media page or profile both for their humanitarian work, and for campaigning[58] and fundraising, which may make it difficult to differentiate each purpose in practice. For instance, Humanitarian Organizations may sometimes use images of beneficiaries in public relations campaigns. Where Consent is relied upon, an individual must be able to withdraw Consent. Yet once an image or video is published online, the

---

57 See Chapter 3: Legal bases for Personal Data Processing.
58 For example, in 2019, the IFRC chose to use its institutional TikTok account as the main tool to promote a global flagship campaign to foster climate action. See: Dante Licona and Melis M. Figanmeşe, "We Were the First Global Humanitarian Organization to Partner with TikTok", Medium, 22 October 2019: https://medium.com/digital-diplomacy/we-were-the-first-global-humanitarian-organization-to-partner-with-tiktok-ea16b280d51.

organization may lose control of its copies and reproductions and, should a beneficiary withdraw Consent, the organization may not be able to remove the content entirely. In such cases, it is important to consider the purpose of each element of a Processing activity and to document it accordingly.[59]

14.5.2 INFORMATION

Individuals should be given clear and timely information regarding the Processing of their data by the Data Controller,[60] explaining what data are collected (in order to provide a service, for instance), what data are generated by the use of the service, what the purposes of the collection are and who can access, share and/or use the individual's Personal Data. This information allows Data Subjects to make informed decisions about whether to use a specific service, and to understand how to exercise their rights. Yet when Humanitarian Organizations interact with beneficiaries through social media, the data are primarily generated and processed directly through the platforms themselves, leaving Humanitarian Organizations with little control over the actions mentioned above. Organizations should nevertheless take responsibility for providing relevant information as far as possible.

Again, it should be stressed that platforms regularly change and update their privacy and data protection policies, which can make it very difficult for users to understand what data are being generated and processed (i.e. how they are used and with whom they are shared).[61] It is therefore challenging for Humanitarian Organizations to understand the risks that using social media platforms presents, and it is unclear what information organizations should provide to Data Subjects. Humanitarian Organizations are advised, at the very least, to inform beneficiaries about the Processing activities for which they are responsible – for instance, explaining why they are communicating through social media, and how the information beneficiaries share with the organization will be used and for what purposes.

Although Humanitarian Organizations have no control over what social media platforms do with the data they collect, some organizations have carried out online awareness-raising campaigns to explain the risks associated with social media and what actions beneficiaries should take to protect their data. In Mexico, for instance, UNHCR uses the El Jaguar page to communicate with beneficiaries. The organization produced a video, shared via the page, warning beneficiaries about the risks associated with using Facebook and how to minimize them.[62]

---

[59] See Chapter 3: Legal bases for Personal Data Processing.
[60] See Section 2.10 – Information.
[61] ICRC and Privacy International, *The Humanitarian Metadata Problem*, October 2018, 17.
[62] See the campaign video (in Spanish) at: El Jaguar, "Privacidad En Facebook", Facebook, 27 October 2018: www.facebook.com/ConfiaEnElJaguar/videos/874221649451680.

Campaigns like these help beneficiaries understand the chain of parties and organizations that may have access to the data they produce on social media, and the risk of harm that might come from these platforms. Yet informing beneficiaries about social media data and privacy policies may not prove helpful if they cannot find an alternative to their current platform. Instead, Humanitarian Organizations should focus on informing beneficiaries about the potential and most likely risks they will encounter when, for instance, they join their groups or follow their pages on social media, and on explaining whether membership of such communities may be visible to others or may be used against them in any way. This is particularly important since, data protection concerns aside, social media use poses other risks such as surveillance and consequent identification (and potential location) of vulnerable people and groups by ill-intentioned parties.

14.5.3 DATA RETENTION

According to the data retention principle, data should be retained for a defined period necessary for the purposes for which they were processed. This period can be three months, a year, the duration of a crisis or some other time frame.[63] When it is not possible to determine the retention period at the time of collection, a review should be conducted at the end of an initial predefined period.

When Humanitarian Organizations interact with beneficiaries through social media, the platforms themselves collect and retain their data. The retention period will therefore vary from one platform to the next.

EXAMPLE OF FACEBOOK'S DATA RETENTION POLICY:

Facebook's data policy stipulates that data are retained until they are no longer necessary to provide the services or until the account is deleted, although there is evidence that the platform keeps some data even after deletion of the account.[64] The policy explains further:

> This is a case-by-case determination that depends on things like the nature of the data, why it is collected and processed, and relevant legal or operational retention needs. For example, when you search for something on Facebook, you can access and delete that query from within your search history at any time, but the log of that search is deleted after 6 months. If you submit a copy of your government-issued ID for account verification purposes, we delete that copy 30 days after review, unless otherwise stated.[65]

---

[63] See Section 2.7 – Data retention.
[64] Aimee Picchi, "OK, You've Deleted Facebook, but Is Your Data Still out There?", *CBS News*, 23 March 2018, Online edition, sec. Moneywatch: www.cbsnews.com/news/ok-youve-deleted-facebook-but-is-your-data-still-out-there.
[65] Facebook, "Data Policy".

Some social media platforms may share data or information with Third Parties. These parties may also have different data retention rules in place. The fact that social media users have to agree to the terms and conditions in order to use these services raises questions about accepting Third Parties' retention policies. Humanitarian Organizations should therefore analyse these policies, assess whether they pose risks to beneficiaries or to the organization itself, and make an informed decision as to whether it is appropriate for the organization to use the platform for its intended objective.

Humanitarian Organizations are also responsible for setting retention periods and/or policies for the data they collect from beneficiaries through social media interactions, groups and pages. They should explain these periods and/or policies to both their staff and beneficiaries.

14.5.4 DATA SECURITY

Humanitarian Organizations should carry out a DPIA (see Section 14.2 – Data Protection Impact Assessment, above), taking into account the platform's business model, policies, and terms and conditions, the wider ecosystem, and whatever security measures the platform takes to protect the data it processes. While the platform may not share this information openly, analysing previous Data Breaches, the platform's response and other known vulnerabilities may be a useful starting point. It is also important to understand how the platform processes users' data and what measures it has in place to guarantee those data are kept safe.

Internally, Humanitarian Organizations are advised to ensure they take appropriate measures to protect the data they collect from beneficiaries, such as protecting data with login and a strong password, granting access on a need-only basis, and training their staff to handle data correctly.

14.6 INTERNATIONAL DATA SHARING

Data processed through social media platforms routinely flow and are accessed across national borders, which raises Personal Data protection concerns. Although recognized contractual mechanisms exist, it can be difficult for Humanitarian Organizations to implement them effectively, especially since social media platforms are often outside their control. That said, organizations must do whatever they can to ensure that the provider has implemented the necessary data transfer arrangements.[66] Determining applicable law and jurisdiction can also present challenges, since a proper and targeted risk analysis is impossible unless choice of jurisdiction and choice of law are clearly embedded in social media governance.

---

66 See Chapter 4: International Data Sharing.

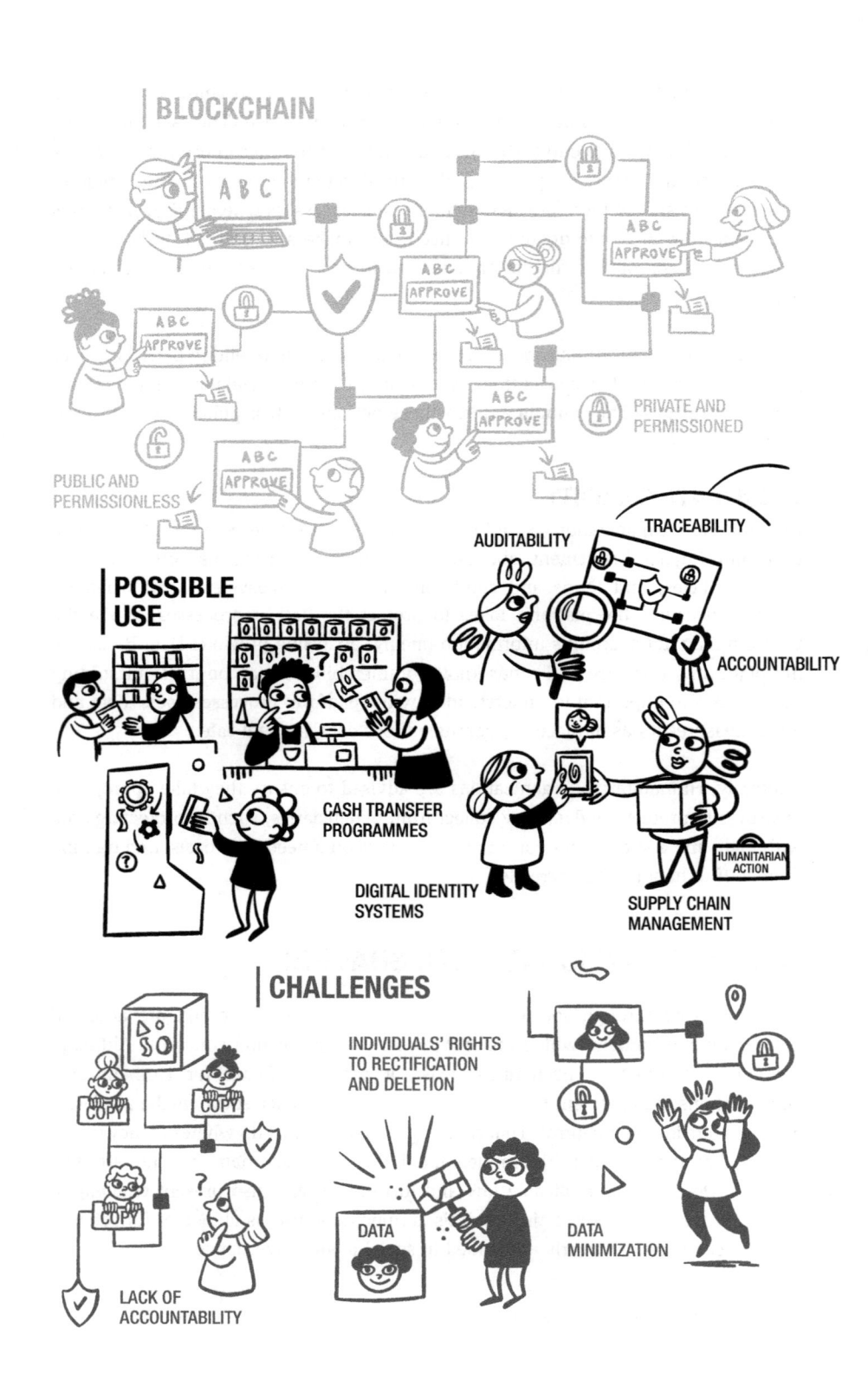

BLOCKCHAIN

PUBLIC AND PERMISSIONLESS

PRIVATE AND PERMISSIONED

POSSIBLE USE

AUDITABILITY

TRACEABILITY

ACCOUNTABILITY

CASH TRANSFER PROGRAMMES

DIGITAL IDENTITY SYSTEMS

SUPPLY CHAIN MANAGEMENT

HUMANITARIAN ACTION

CHALLENGES

INDIVIDUALS' RIGHTS TO RECTIFICATION AND DELETION

DATA MINIMIZATION

LACK OF ACCOUNTABILITY

CHAPTER 15
BLOCKCHAIN
Vincent Graf Narbel*

---

* The author would like to thank Robert Riemann (European Data Protection Supervisor), Giulio Coppi (Norwegian Refugee Council) and Bryan Ford (Swiss Federal Institute of Technology in Lausanne) for their contributions to this chapter.

15.1 INTRODUCTION

In recent years, "Blockchain" has become a buzzword and various organizations, including in the humanitarian sector, are trying to find a use for this technology. It has been argued that Blockchain could improve efficiency in humanitarian programmes involving, for example, financial transactions and supply tracing.[1] It has also been suggested that Blockchain could enhance transparency and trust in information integrity.[2] However, achieving such improvements could be offset by a number of practical and data protection challenges. These are discussed below, along with any anticipated benefits and risks.

This chapter presents a simplified and easy-to-understand explanation of Blockchain technology, the main parties involved and its various architectures (Sections 15.1.1 to 15.1.3). Since Blockchain is a complex technology, this discussion is by no means exhaustive. It merely supports the data protection analysis that follows in Sections 15.2 to 15.7.[3]

15.1.1 WHAT IS BLOCKCHAIN?

A Blockchain is "in essence an append-only decentralized database that is maintained by a consensus algorithm and stored on multiple nodes (computers)".[4] This definition includes a number of complex technical elements that are addressed in more detail below. Essentially, Blockchain technology is a special way to store data in a database. As such, any type of data can be stored on a Blockchain, including Personal Data. On a Blockchain, each piece of data is stored one after the other in a chain (which is why it is called "append-only").[5] This is done by grouping data in blocks and by adding, to each new block, a cryptographic pointer (a reference or link) to the previous block.

The design of Blockchains is guided by a desire to increase security (in the broad sense of the term). In particular, and as mentioned above, Blockchain technology aims to enhance transparency and trust in the integrity of the database. Blockchains are "distributed" and often "decentralized". While these are two different concepts,

---

1 Vanessa Ko and Andrej Verity, *BlockChain for the Humanitarian Sector – Future Opportunities*, DH Network, UN OCHA, November 2016, 12–14: https://reliefweb.int/sites/reliefweb.int/files/resources/BlockChain%20for%20the%20Humanitarian%20Sector%20-%20Future%20Opportunities%20-%20November%202016.pdf.
2 Ibid., 8.
3 For more detailed definitions and explanations of Blockchain technology, please refer to: Jean Bacon et al., "Blockchain Demystified: A Technical and Legal Introduction to Distributed and Centralised Ledgers", *Richmond Journal of Law and Technology* (blog), 6 November 2018: https://jolt.richmond.edu/blockchain-demystified-a-technical-and-legal-introduction-to-distributed-and-centralised-ledgers.
4 Finck, "Blockchains and data protection in the European Union".
5 Note that this property is the reason why they are also called ledgers: a ledger is a book that stores (traditionally monetary) transactions in append-only mode.

they bear a common feature – namely, they indicate that the data being processed are not managed and stored centrally. Here, "distributed" means that there are multiple copies of the database stored on different computers, while "decentralized" means that the power and authority to decide what data are added to the ledger is not held by a single entity or individual, but is instead shared between many entities or individuals that have to work together. In this chapter, these entities or individuals are referred to as "validators" (since they, together, validate the data to be stored on the Blockchain). Usually, the higher the number of validators, the more complex the rules they have to follow to reach an agreement. These rules are reflected in a "consensus protocol" (see Section 15.1.2 – Types of Blockchain, below for further details).

The computers that hold a copy of the Blockchain are called "nodes" (since they represent nodes in a vast network). Nodes can be passive (only storing an up-to-date copy of the Blockchain) or active. Active nodes are also validators, and are said to be "mining" the data (i.e. participating in the consensus protocol to validate new insertions). Sometimes validators are called "miners" by analogy.

"Users" are the parties who wish to add information to the Blockchain (hence creating data that need to be validated and recorded on the Blockchain).

A piece of information will only be inserted into the Blockchain once it has been validated. This makes it extremely difficult for a malicious party to add data to the Blockchain, since any addition has to be accepted by the validators first.

Moreover, the blocks of information on a Blockchain are time-stamped and, as mentioned above, contain a cryptographic link (pointer or reference) to the previous block. This means that, even if a malicious party succeeds in changing data contained in a particular block, it also has to modify the following block (as the cryptographic pointer it contains will have changed), as well as all subsequent blocks through to the end of the chain. These changes would unlikely go unnoticed because of a Blockchain's decentralized design, which means that every validator would have to agree to them. Since, in practice, it is very difficult (though not totally impossible) to change information on Blockchains, they are often referred to as immutable ledgers.[6]

When information is added on the Blockchain, a mechanism involving public and private keys is used to secure the transactions. Blockchain users own one or more such key pairs. The public key, or a value derived from it, serves as the user's address on the Blockchain. It is publicly known and used to verify the origin and destination of added information.[7] Even though Blockchain addresses do not by themselves reveal the

---

6   Finck, "Blockchains and data protection in the European Union", p. 19.
7   Ibid.

identity of the person they relate to, they are still considered to be pseudonymized Personal Data as they are linked to one specified individual (the user who adds or receives information). They could be traced back to the individual's IP address, for instance, which could lead to identification.[8] As Blockchains are near-immutable, public keys could potentially remain on the Blockchain for as long as the ledger exists.

Several companies provide Blockchain analytics services that specialize in providing platforms for investigative and compliance needs in Blockchain-based transactions. They offer Blockchain intelligence to gather, analyse and interpret data from various Blockchain networks. Their platforms enable the identification and monitoring of transactions, addresses and entities involved in Blockchain activities. These investigations help businesses and regulatory agencies to comply with Anti-Money Laundering (AML) requirements. Another use case is to support law enforcement agencies in combating illicit activities using cryptocurrencies. These investigations are possible because the Blockchain public addresses can be used to reidentify users. Several new designs have been proposed to guarantee a higher level of anonymity, for instance Monero or the ZCash protocol. They come with their own limitations and Humanitarian Organizations have to balance those limitations carefully. However, Humanitarian Organizations should also be mindful of the need for more privacy when deploying off-the-shelf Blockchain-based solutions.

Some of the above characteristics of Blockchain technology can be advantageous for Humanitarian Organizations. For example, the decentralized architecture can potentially increase security, since there is no single point of failure or compromise in such systems. This means that potential attackers need to compromise several links in order to compromise the Blockchain as a whole. This set-up increases system integrity because it is claimed to almost always guarantee data immutability.

In light of the fact that information is time-stamped and close to immutable, and the fact that responsibility is shared, it has been argued[9] that Blockchains can be most valuable when:
- they are used to track ownership of complex things over time;
- there are multiple groups or parties involved;
- there is no well-established or effective central authority (also known as a trusted Third Party) in place;
- groups or parties involved need to work collaboratively;
- a record or proof of transactions is required.

These examples show that the one of the main benefits of Blockchain technology is its resistance to a single point of failure or compromise. This is due to the ledger's distributed design, which ensures that multiple nodes have to work together to add

---

8   Ibid., pp. 24–25.
9   Ko and Verity, *BlockChain for the Humanitarian Sector*, 9.

new data to the Blockchain. Moreover, because the whole ledger is copied to multiple nodes, it becomes difficult to change information on the ledger and data remain available even if one node is compromised, thereby increasing their integrity.

It is important to note that Blockchain technology will most likely not be needed when there is no issue with the level of integrity (i.e. there is enough trust between the parties involved in a specific programme and there are sufficient levels of auditability), or simply if other current technology offers a sufficient degree of integrity and availability. In such cases, a more traditional solution with a central database, for instance, may prove more efficient, faster, and cheaper to implement, and, overall more proportionate from a data protection perspective.

Another element to take into account is the exit criteria. Humanitarian Actions are often designed to be temporary. If a Blockchain is used in a CVA program, for example, the process to shut down the program, discard Personal Data and close the beneficiary's account may be complicated by the distributed and immutable nature of the Blockchain.

15.1.2 TYPES OF BLOCKCHAIN

Blockchains can be built in different ways, according to system design choices. One key decision, for instance, is whether or not the Blockchain will be public. Although there is no universally agreed definition of each type of Blockchain, the following definitions are more commonly used:

Table 15.1

Blockchain	Permissionless: Anyone can become a validator (node or miner).	Permissioned: Validators (nodes or miners) are pre-defined and authorized by a governing body.
Public: Everyone can access ("see" or "read") the data stored on the Blockchain and add transactions.	Everyone can read the transactions on the Blockchain (which are public) and participate in the consensus protocol as a validator for new transactions. It is worth noting, however, that data added to the ledger may be encrypted and, therefore, those without the decryption key will not be able to decipher and read their contents. The public keys and time-stamps, however, remain visible to all. This type of Blockchain (public permissionless) is used by Bitcoin.	Everyone can read the transactions on the Blockchain (which are public) but only predefined parties can become validators and participate in the consensus protocol to validate new insertions. Such Blockchains could, for instance, help to improve supply-chain transparency, since only those parties involved in the handling of goods would be authorized to alter the ledger (as validators), whereas any member of the public could check the transactions.

Table 15.1 (*cont.*)

Blockchain	Permissionless: Anyone can become a validator (node or miner).	Permissioned: Validators (nodes or miners) are pre-defined and authorized by a governing body.
Private: Only authorized users can access the data on the Blockchain.	In theory, this type of Blockchain allows only predefined parties to access the data stored on the Blockchain, but anyone to participate in the validation of new insertions. In practice, however, this would be hard to implement because validators are able to store a full copy of the ledger. Consequently, it would be difficult to conceive a platform in which validators are not allowed to access the information on the ledger.	Only predefined users can access ("read") the data stored on the Blockchain and only predefined validators (not necessarily the same users) can participate in the validation of new insertions.

Besides choosing who can "read" or "write" on the Blockchain, system designers must also decide how validation will take place. Blockchain validation processes are regulated by consensus mechanisms (or consensus protocols), which consist of a set of predefined rules that divides trust among the parties. These rules allow them to store data immutably without a central authority (or trusted Third Party), thereby preserving the integrity of the ledger.[10] In other words, consensus mechanisms define how new information is validated by the parties in the Blockchain and, if deemed valid, added to the ledger.

There are different types of consensus protocol. For example, in Blockchains that use proof-of-work protocols, validators need to earn the right to validate a transaction by solving complex mathematical problems using brute computational force, which requires considerable processing power and electricity.[11] In proof-of-stake protocols, meanwhile, the parties have simple voting rights, and the weight of their vote may vary according to their stake in the Blockchain.

To illustrate some of the different choices that have to be made when developing a Blockchain, it is useful to think of the system like a corporation. Corporations

---

[10] Walid Al-Saqaf and Nicolas Seidler, "Blockchain technology for social impact: Opportunities and challenges ahead", *Journal of Cyber Policy*, Vol. 2, No. 3, 2 September 2017, pp. 338–354: https://doi.org/10.1080/23738871.2017.1400084.

[11] Pisa and Juden, *Blockchain and Economic Development: Hype vs. Reality*, 8.

typically hold board meetings. There need to be rules governing how board members are chosen and who has the right to vote and make decisions. One option is to have a closed group decide who joins and leaves the board (akin to a permissioned Blockchain). Another possibility is to allow anyone to sit on the board as long as they buy enough "stock" in the company to give them voting shares (a proof-of-stake Blockchain). A third option is to decide that anyone can sit on the board as long as they can prove they devoted enough energy to a task in the past 10 minutes – an artificial barrier to entry (a proof-of-work Blockchain).

15.1.3 BLOCKCHAIN IN PRACTICE

Scholars and practitioners propose the following advantages and challenges of using Blockchain technology:[12]

Advantages:
- There is no need for a trusted Third Party (a central authority) to maintain the integrity of a shared record: transactions inserted on a Blockchain are verified by participants through a consensus mechanism. The breadth of this benefit, however, varies depending on how the Blockchain is used.
- Eliminating a trusted Third Party reduces costs. For instance, Blockchain could support cross-border cash transfers directly between the parties to a transaction, removing the need for a bank or another financial institution, which often charges fees.
- A Blockchain acts as an audit trail, since the way data are stored and connected can make it easier to track the origin and movement of physical assets tied to a digital token.[13]
- Transparency is increased, especially in public Blockchains, because more parties can access the ledger. In private Blockchains, however, this benefit may be reduced or in some cases non-existent.
- Blockchains improve integrity and availability, since they provide operational resilience and entail no single point of failure or compromise.[14]

Challenges:
- An appropriate governance structure needs to be determined for each Blockchain solution.
- Although Blockchains are considered "trustless", there are parties involved in the system who nevertheless have to be trusted. These include the developers behind the code, as well as designers who create applications that interact with the Blockchain or Cloud Services where data may be stored.

---

[12] For more details, see: Finck, "Blockchains and data protection in the European Union"; Bacon et al., "Blockchain Demystified".

[13] Pisa and Juden, *Blockchain and Economic Development*, 9.

[14] Other characteristics of the technology, however, may make it more vulnerable to attacks (see challenges below, as well as Section 15.5.4 – Data security).

- Blockchain increases the number of access points for possible attacks by malicious parties, thereby posing security risks. Moreover, some consensus mechanisms – albeit not frequently used – accept a transaction as valid when 51 per cent of the validators approve it. So, if a consortium of validators gains control of 51 per cent of the nodes, they could jointly take control over the ledger.
- The technology is dependent on Internet connectivity.
- Some Blockchains, such as those that use proof-of-work protocols, consume much more electricity than alternative technologies.[15]
- Individuals must be informed, through information notices, about the Processing of Personal Data, and must be able to exercise their rights (such as erasure, rectification, and withdrawal of Consent) in respect of their Personal Data.
- Private permissioned Blockchains may be more appropriate for certain types of humanitarian programme (such as Cash and Voucher Assistance), since these architectures involve a limited number of participants. In some cases, however, this may lead to the reintroduction of trusted parties and to a decrease in transparency.
- Compatibility with data protection requirements in different jurisdictions is a concern (see below).

While Blockchain technology can help improve transparency in many situations, it does not solve the underlying problems that create so-called bad data. In other words, if someone stores unreliable records on a Blockchain, they will remain unreliable and the system will not achieve its potential benefits.[16]

These advantages and challenges of Blockchain have significantly influenced their use. Blockchains are frequently used to manage transaction histories recording the ownership or custody of, or responsibility for, assets such as cryptocurrencies. They are also used to notarize or assign time-stamps to supply-chain, digital-credential and other documents, as well as to enforce the terms of a contract (through the use of smart contracts).[17]

15.1.4 HUMANITARIAN USE CASES

Humanitarian Organizations have begun exploring possible applications of Blockchain and have launched pilot projects using the technology.[18] While there is little information available about the benefits and risks that Blockchain technologies

---

15 Bacon et al., "Blockchain Demystified", 15.
16 Pisa and Juden, *Blockchain and Economic Development*, 49.
17 Smart contracts are a feature of Blockchain that will not be addressed in this chapter. For information on smart contracts, see: Michèle Finck, *Smart Contracts as a Form of Solely Automated Processing under the GDPR*, SSRN Scholarly Paper, Social Science Research Network, Rochester, NY, 8 January 2019: https://papers.ssrn.com/abstract=3311370.
18 For more information on the use of Blockchain in the humanitarian sector, see: Larissa Fast and Giulio Coppi, *Blockchain and Distributed Ledger Technologies in the Humanitarian Sector*, Humanitarian

bring in such cases, some of the following uses among Humanitarian Organizations have been proposed:[19]

Cash and Voucher Assistance (CVA).[20] Blockchain could improve the efficiency of CVA through a secure and well-structured transaction record-keeping system, which in turn increases transparency and provides added assurance that data stored in the system have not been tampered with. The application of Blockchain technology to CVA could allow Humanitarian Organizations to make digital cash payments cheaper, more efficient and traceable, as well as interoperable across multiple organizations. In addition, because Blockchain technology is said to provide operational resilience and to entail no single point of failure or compromise, it could make transactions more secure (See Section 15.5.4 – Data security, below for more information on Blockchain and security).

Optimizing and tracking logistics. Humanitarian supply chains are extremely complex and dynamic, which makes it difficult to monitor them properly. Blockchain technology may offer a way to introduce transparency into these operations. In the case of provision of medical supplies, for instance, a Blockchain may contain a near-immutable, time-stamped record of when the supplies left the warehouse, when they were transported out of the country of origin, when they arrived at the country of destination, when they were received by the local branch of the Humanitarian Organization and when they reached the destination hospital. Because a public Blockchain provides a publicly visible ledger, it can serve as a transparent data platform that traces the origins, use and destination of humanitarian supplies.

Tracking donor financing. Peer-to-peer tracking and monitoring of donations may make it possible to scale up finance models that cut out the traditional "middleman"[21] (or trusted Third Party).[22] Such models could reduce transaction costs associated with international humanitarian financing and improve the tracking of donations, including from the general public. However, Blockchain technology could be used to make anonymous donations. This could pose a challenge for Humanitarian Organizations with stricter funding policies that require the donating party to be identified.

Enhancing shared situational awareness in conflicts. The Whiteflag Protocol[23] (in which the ICRC is collaborating) aims to provide a neutral means of communication

---

Policy Group Report, ODI, London, , February 2019: https://odi.org/en/publications/blockchain-and-distributed-ledger-technologies-in-the-humanitarian-sector.

19 Examples taken from Ko and Verity, *BlockChain for the Humanitarian Sector*.
20 See for example: IFRC, *Blockchain Open Loop Cash Transfer Pilot Project*, ALNAP,
    1 September 2018: www.alnap.org/help-library/blockchain-open-loop-cash-transfer-pilot-project.
21 Ko and Verity, *BlockChain for the Humanitarian Sector*, 13.
22 Finck, "Blockchains and data protection in the European Union", p. 18.
23 "WhiteflagProtocol", accessed 16 March 2022: www.whiteflagprotocol.org.

for all parties involved in a conflict. Whiteflag is designed to deliver a messaging system in which real-time information on emergencies, local dangers, landmines, population displacement and other issues can be shared in the knowledge that it has not been altered by a malicious party. In this arrangement, none of the participants need to trust one other. Although having this information publicly available could help to locate civilians and assess distinction and proportionality in attacks, it could also be used to target identified groups.

EXAMPLE:
In the Blockchain Open Loop Cash Transfer Pilot Project,[24] the IFRC and the Kenyan Red Cross Society used Blockchain to record cash-based transfers made to beneficiaries from households affected by drought. The idea behind the pilot was to explore the use and added value of Blockchain in CVA. The transfers themselves were made independently of the Blockchain, through a conventional partnership with a local mobile provider and an information management company. Using a private permissioned Blockchain, however, allowed transactions to be recorded almost immutably and in a distributed manner, thereby increasing transparency between the parties (the only ones allowed to access the Blockchain), creating an audit trail (as records were tamper-proof) and increasing record security (as there was no single point of failure or compromise).

Two notable challenges arose during the project. First, it proved difficult to change records when, for example, a disbursement was requested by mistake and a transaction needed to be reversed. Second, because beneficiaries could not receive assistance without Consent, it was questionable whether such Consent was freely given and informed.[25]

15.2 DATA PROTECTION IMPACT ASSESSMENTS

The use of Blockchain in humanitarian programmes may pose many data protection challenges that do not always occur in other contexts. This is one of the main reasons why it is important to carry out a Data Protection Impact Assessment (DPIA) before deciding to implement Blockchain systems. A DPIA can help identify whether it is necessary and proportionate to deploy such a system. If the organization does decide to proceed, the DPIA can also help to identify, address and mitigate the risks and challenges associated with the use of Blockchain. There are many templates and materials for conducting a DPIA,[26] but none of them have thus far been designed

---

24   IFRC, *Blockchain Open Loop Cash Transfer Pilot Project*.
25   See Section 3.2 – Consent.
26   See for example: French Data Protection Authority (CNIL), *Guidelines on DPIA*, 18 October 2017: www
     .cnil.fr/en/guidelines-dpia; UK Information Commissioner's Office (ICO), *Sample DPIA template*,

specifically for Blockchain in humanitarian contexts. Organizations therefore need to adapt existing DPIA models, or design Blockchain-specific ones.[27]

A DPIA is a systematic and adaptive process that covers both general questions relating to the Processing of Personal Data, and questions about the use of a specific type of technology (in this case, Blockchain). As discussed elsewhere in this chapter, Blockchain presents both advantages and challenges for Humanitarian Organizations. Despite the purported benefits, in most cases no effective improvements have been recorded. During the DPIA process, Humanitarian Organizations should therefore clearly identify the benefits, challenges and risks associated with using Blockchain, comparing them against other technologies. This approach is not new, but it is especially important for an emerging technology like Blockchain.

Since Blockchains can take many different forms, the DPIA must also cover the governance and design of each individual application. Because of the diversity of likely applications and the technical complexity of Blockchain, Humanitarian Organizations may also develop a decision-making framework to help them determine whether to implement Blockchain technologies, and if so, what protections they should implement. Some authors have suggested general decision-making frameworks for implementing Blockchain.[28] Yet these generic templates do not take into account the particular data protection concerns raised by Blockchain in the humanitarian sector. For this reason, an alternative Blockchain-specific decision-making framework is given in the annex to this chapter.

Conducting a DPIA can also be vital in identifying an appropriate legal basis for the use of Blockchain. The DPIA process should take into account the impact that a specific type of Blockchain (i.e. the one envisaged in a given situation) may have on Data Subjects' rights and the application of data protection principles. Based on this assessment, Humanitarian Organizations can choose the best solution to minimize potential risks.

The DPIA should give Humanitarian Organizations a clear picture of the impact Blockchain would have in terms of the proportionality of data Processing. Based on this assessment, an organization will be in a position to judge whether there are less intrusive means, such as traditional databases, that could fulfil its needs with less risk to beneficiaries.

Template, 22 June 2018: https://ico.org.uk/media/for-organizations/documents/2553993/dpia-template.docx?mc_phishing_protection_id=28047-br1tehqdu81eaoar3q10.

[27] More information about DPIA models and their design can be found in Chapter 5: Data Protection Impact Assessments (DPIAs).

[28] Karl Wust and Arthur Gervais, "Do you need a Blockchain?", IEEE, 2018, 45–54: ieeexplore.ieee.org/document/8525392.

As well as assessing the technical design of the system, the DPIA process should also consider the issues and principles detailed in Sections 15.3 to 15.7 below.

15.3 DATA PROTECTION BY DESIGN AND BY DEFAULT

Data protection by design and by default involves designing a Processing operation, programme or solution in a way that implements key data protection principles from the outset, and that provides the Data Subject with the greatest possible data protections (see Chapter 6: Designing for data protection). The key data protection principles in this sense are:
- lawfulness, fairness, and transparency;
- purpose limitation;
- data minimization;
- accuracy;
- storage limitation (limited retention);
- integrity and confidentiality (security);
- accountability;
- support for Data Subjects' rights by design.

Refer to Chapter 2: Basic principles of data protection, for a general description of these principles, some of which are contextualized in the sections below.

At this stage, it is important to take into account the different types of Blockchain, as all options must be considered when designing a model that is compliant with data protection principles.

Private permissioned Blockchains (see Section 15.1.2 – Types of Blockchain, for definitions) are the most restrictive, since one or more parties define(s) who has the right to validate information on the Blockchain and who can access data on the ledger. It may therefore be easier to design private permissioned Blockchains in a way that is compatible with data protection principles.[29] Yet restricting the rights of participants might, in some cases, defeat the very purpose of Blockchain technology by reintroducing a trusted party and, potentially, a single point of failure or compromise.

Public Blockchains, in turn, should always be designed in ways that do not store Personal Data (this is always a preferred option, even for private ledgers). Personal Data could instead be stored "off-chain" (i.e. outside the ledger). Here, the public ledger merely contains a cryptographic pointer confirming that a specific document

---

[29] Michèle Finck, *Blockchain and the General Data Protection Regulation: Can distributed ledgers be squared with European data protection law?*, STUDY: Panel for the Future of Science and Technology, European Parliamentary Research Service (EPRS), 2019: www.europarl.europa.eu/RegData/etudes/STUD/2019/634445/EPRS_STU(2019)634445_EN.pdf.

or piece of information has been stored in a different location (such as on a Humanitarian Organization's server).[30] The data themselves are not kept on the Blockchain. Yet even with this design, it is important to remember that public keys belonging to individuals included on the Blockchain will remain Personal Data. Whether or not cryptographic pointers also qualify as Personal Data is a matter of debate.[31]

15.4 DATA CONTROLLER/DATA PROCESSOR RELATIONSHIP

Blockchains, as distributed ledgers, can involve a wide range of bodies and entities. Consequently, it can be difficult to ascertain which parties should be treated as Data Controllers and Data Processors. For clarification, the respective roles of each are detailed below:

Data Controllers determine the means and purposes of Processing. They are accountable for the Processing of Personal Data and are responsible for implementing Data Subjects' rights. They must comply with data protection principles and respond to individuals' requests to exercise their rights to access, rectification and erasure. If there are multiple Data Controllers in the Blockchain, or if new users considered Data Controllers join the Blockchain, their respective responsibilities for the Processing should be set out in a written agreement.

Data Processors follow the instructions of Data Controllers and are responsible for ensuring data security. They should also inform Data Controllers about which means are being used to process data, and about any problems or complaints that may arise with regard to data integrity, confidentiality and availability.

Each Blockchain architecture (as presented in Section 15.1.2 – Types of Blockchain) may have different implications when determining the roles played by different parties operating on the ledger. Importantly, when identifying the Data Controller, determining the purposes of the Processing is a more important factor than choosing

---

30 A cryptographic pointer (also known as a hash pointer) is the one-way mathematical transformation of any given input (a message or a document) into a fixed-length combination of letters and numbers (output). Every time a specific input is hashed, the output is the same, but any slight change to the input (e.g. adding or removing a comma) will produce a completely different hash (Pisa and Juden, *Blockchain and Economic Development*). Adding a hash pointer to the Blockchain, therefore, allows a person to verify that a document has been stored, since hashing that document again would produce the same pointer as the one contained in the ledger.
31 Finck, *Blockchain and the General Data Protection Regulation*, 30.

the means. With this in mind, and looking at the key parties in Blockchains, one could consider the following arrangements:
- In a permissioned Blockchain, it may be possible to identify a central party (or intermediary) that qualifies as the Data Controller (e.g. system operator that grants "writing" rights), and nodes would qualify as Data Processors.
- In a permissionless Blockchain, there will be no central intermediary, as the network is operated by all nodes in a decentralized manner. Here, every node could potentially qualify as a Data Controller, since they autonomously decide whether to join the chain and pursue their objectives.[32] However, there is no unanimity about this conclusion.

Some argue that nodes are Data Controllers because the fact that they join a Blockchain network can be considered tantamount to determining the purposes of the Processing.[33] Others argue that nodes are not Data Controllers.[34] It is also worth noting that nodes sometimes only see the encrypted version of the data and run a software program that does not allow them to alter the ledger. Consequently, they will be unable to "see" what data, including Personal Data, are being processed or make changes to the data and, therefore, cannot comply with data protection obligations of Data Controllers.

Users (organizations or private individuals deciding to use the Blockchain), in turn, can in some situations qualify as Data Controllers, since they clearly determine the purposes of the Processing (i.e. recording a specific piece of information onto the Blockchain).[35] Furthermore, users choose the means of Processing when selecting a specific version of Blockchain. This interpretation, however, will not apply to every type of Blockchain. This could be the case in a public permissionless Blockchain, but private permissioned Blockchains are more likely to be set up by a consortium of organizations, in which case the consortium will qualify as joint Data Controllers.

The French Data Protection Authority (CNIL) has sought to provide guidance on this matter. According to the CNIL:[36]
- Blockchain participants with "writing" rights will be considered Data Controllers when the data they enter are connected to a professional activity.
- Legal persons who "write" data on a Blockchain are considered Data Controllers.
- Miners (or nodes) who do not add data to the Blockchain, but only verify the authenticity of the data (by participating in the consensus protocol), are not Data Controllers because they do not define the means and purposes of the Processing;

---

32 Finck, "Blockchains and data protection in the European Union", pp. 26–27.
33 Ibid., p. 26.
34 Bacon et al., "Blockchain Demystified", 64–65.
35 Ibid., 64.
36 French Data Protection Authority (CNIL), *BLOCKCHAIN: Solutions for a Responsible Use of the Blockchain in the Context of Personal Data*, September 2018: www.cnil.fr/sites/default/files/atoms/files/blockchain_en.pdf.

instead, they can be considered Data Processors, working under the instructions of the Data Controller.

Blockchain users, meanwhile, can be divided into two types:
- users who use Blockchain for commercial or professional purposes will qualify as Data Controllers;
- users who use the ledger for private purposes will not qualify as Data Controllers, since this would be considered a purely personal activity falling outside the scope of most data protection laws.

Considering the various interpretations and guidance on this matter, Humanitarian Organizations intending to use Blockchain technology must ensure that the governance of the chosen solution incorporates the concepts of Data Controller and Data Processor. They must also determine, as clearly as possible, the responsibilities of each party within a given Processing activity. If it becomes clear that, in a certain situation, it may be impossible for Data Controllers to fulfil their obligations (especially enabling Data Subjects to exercise their rights), an alternative solution should be sought, since the use of Blockchain will most likely be incompatible with data protection principles.

15.5 BASIC DATA PROTECTION PRINCIPLES

As explained above, reconciling the use of Blockchains with basic data protection principles can be challenging. In practice, compatibility between the two will depend on the architecture and design of each Blockchain solution. While this section provides general guidance, organizations must consider the specific features of each application when assessing its compatibility with data protection principles.

15.5.1 DATA MINIMIZATION

By their very nature, distributed ledgers would appear to run counter to the principle of data minimization, which states that the minimum amount of Personal Data should be processed in order to attain the objective and purposes of the Processing.[37] This is mainly because data in Blockchains can potentially be stored perpetually, and because a copy of the full ledger is stored in multiple nodes on numerous devices. However, there may be workaround solutions. Personal Data could be stored off the Blockchain while the ledger only keeps a cryptographic pointer to the data that are stored in a different location. In this case, the data will not be stored perpetually on the ledger or shared with all the nodes. The individual or organization that stores the data will retain full control over them and, therefore, will

---

37 For example, according to the General Data Protection Regulation (GDPR), Article 5(1)(c) and (e), Personal Data must be "adequate, relevant and limited to what is necessary in relation to the purposes for which they are processed", and "kept in a form which permits identification of Data Subjects for no longer than is necessary for the purposes for which the Personal Data are processed".

be able to apply the data minimization principle to the off-chain Processing of data without altering the ledger itself. Whether cryptographic pointers also qualify as Personal Data remains a matter of debate.[38]

15.5.2 DATA RETENTION

The fact that Blockchains are claimed to be immutable distributed ledgers also poses a challenge for the data retention principle.[39] Data stored on a Blockchain will be retained indeterminately on multiple computers. The best solution, therefore, would be not to store Personal Data on Blockchains. Personal Data should not, for instance, be stored in public ledgers, since this type of Blockchain can be accessed (or read) by anyone. In particular, Personal Data that are particularly sensitive – such as ethnicity and health records – should never be stored on Blockchains.

15.5.3 PROPORTIONALITY

Proportionality is a core principle of data protection. It generally requires consideration of whether a particular action or measure related to the Processing of Personal Data is appropriate to its pursued aim. Proportionality involves setting out the options and choosing the one that is the least intrusive with regard to the rights of Data Subjects. The complexity of Blockchains can make it difficult to determine whether a particular implementation is proportionate.

As with the data minimization and data retention principles, one way to address proportionality concerns in a public permissionless Blockchain could be to store Personal Data off-chain. Yet adding an off-chain database can mean reintroducing a trusted Third Party, such as a Cloud Service provider with whom the data will be stored. This, in turn, may negate the supposed benefits of using Blockchain in the first place. The proportionality requirement could, however, be satisfied if the characteristics of Blockchain are essential to achieve the envisaged objective (such as when there is an important need to improve the integrity, transparency and availability of an existing solution), and if that objective could not be achieved with a centralized database model (for instance, because the parties do not trust one another). The risks to Data Subjects, however, cannot be disproportionately high in comparison to the aim pursued.

15.5.4 DATA SECURITY

Data security is a key aspect of an effective data protection system.[40] Security is often related to three key principles:
- **confidentiality**: the data must only be accessible to authorized parties;
- **integrity**: unauthorized parties must not be able to modify the data, and the data must not be lost, destroyed or damaged;
- **availability**: the data must be available (to authorized parties) when needed.

---

[38] Finck, *Blockchain and the General Data Protection Regulation*, 30.
[39] See Section 2.7 – Data retention.
[40] See Section 2.8 – Data security and Processing security.

Blockchains present both strengths and weaknesses when it comes to security across these three aspects. These are detailed, in turn, below.

On the issue of confidentiality, the distributed nature of Blockchains means that the same data are potentially replicated and distributed widely. This leads to increased access points and vulnerabilities. Moreover, even if a Blockchain system uses complex encryption and hashing techniques, advances in quantum computing mean that information could even be decrypted without the decryption key. If, in the future, encryption no longer guarantees the safety and anonymity of the data, all Personal Data stored on a public Blockchain could be exposed. And because, in most situations, data stored on a Blockchain cannot be deleted, the damage can be irreversible. This is yet another reason why it is not recommended to store Personal Data on the Blockchain itself.

With regard to integrity, the immutable character of Blockchain technology and the use of consensus protocols provide a security benefit over centralized databases, not least because "storing sensitive data on centralized servers creates a 'honeypot' for would-be hackers and a single point of failure".[41] In Blockchains, however, there is no single point of failure or compromise and, unless an attacker is able to gain control of enough nodes to control the consensus protocol, the system would most likely not be compromised.

On the question of availability, Blockchain is again beneficial because it consists of a distributed ledger stored simultaneously in multiple computers.

Resistance to a single point of failure or compromise is frequently said to be Blockchain's main added value in relation to security. If that is not an imperative for the organization, then traditional, non-Blockchain technology may be more efficient, faster and cheaper. Secret sharing techniques that are said to enhance the protection of encrypted data in distributed ledgers, for example, can also be used in traditional databases, i.e. they are not exclusive to Blockchain. The technology adds value when integrity and availability are important and when participants do not trust one another.

15.6 RIGHTS OF DATA SUBJECTS

Data Subjects are entitled to certain rights, which allow them to exercise control over their Personal Data. As explained below, however, it can be technically very difficult or impossible to implement these rights on Blockchains.

---

41 Pisa and Juden, *Blockchain and Economic Development*", 6.

15.6.1 RIGHT OF ACCESS

Individuals have a right to know whether their Personal Data are being processed by the Data Controller, and to obtain a copy of the Personal Data in question.[42] In the humanitarian sector, therefore, when Personal Data are stored on the Blockchain, Humanitarian Organizations should always participate as nodes that hold a full copy of the ledger. That way, they can ensure that the entire database is available at all times, and can inform beneficiaries which data are stored on the Blockchain.

When Personal Data are stored off-chain, meanwhile, the ledger only contains a pointer to the off-chain data. In such cases, the most likely scenario is that Humanitarian Organizations will store the data themselves and should be able to reply to Data Subjects' requests in line with the legal requirements.

15.6.2 RIGHT TO RECTIFICATION

Data Subjects have a right to have incorrect data about them rectified.[43] In a Blockchain, however, this can be problematic as it is technically very difficult, albeit not impossible, to change data once they are added to the ledger[44] (hence the term "immutable").

If Personal Data are stored on-chain, one way to uphold this right is to add the new, rectified data to the chain – by way of a supplementary statement – while making the previous data inaccessible (for instance by deleting the decryption key needed to access the incorrect data). However, there is no consensus over this solution among practitioners and academics. In some cases, it is also possible to insert a new transaction indicating that the old data need to be corrected. The problem with these options, however, is that instead of correcting the original data, they merely add more data to the chain. It is unclear whether this would be accepted as rectification.

In view of these limitations, the best way to deal with these challenges is to store Personal Data off-chain, where it can be rectified without altering the ledger itself. Note that this option would to a large extent reduce the integrity and availability advantages of the Blockchain described above. In other words, if integrity and availability are also important for Personal Data, then a Blockchain-based solution is not recommended.

---

42 See Section 2.11 – Rights of Data Subjects.
43 See ibid.
44 Daniel Conte de Leon et al., "Blockchain: Properties and misconceptions", *Asia Pacific Journal of Innovation and Entrepreneurship*, Vol. 11, No. 3, 4 December 2017, pp. 286–300: www.emerald.com/insight/content/doi/10.1108/APJIE-12-2017-034/full/html. And the example of the Ethereum hard fork to correct the DAO hack: https://blog.ethereum.org/2016/07/20/hard-fork-completed.

15.6.3 RIGHT TO ERASURE

The nearly immutable nature of Blockchain stands conceptually in conflict with the right to erasure.[45] Various options have been suggested to address this issue. One option, as mentioned above, is to make the data on the chain inaccessible, albeit still present on the chain. This can be achieved, for example, by deleting the decryption key needed to decipher encrypted data. Yet some scholars and practitioners argue that this approach is unsatisfactory because the Personal Data in question, although encrypted, are not deleted (as the right to erasure implies) but merely made inaccessible. This could prove problematic in light of advances in decryption technology (see Section 15.5.4 – Data security, above).

Since Personal Data stored off-chain can be rectified and deleted in line with data protection requirements without altering the distributed ledger itself, this is again the preferred option.

EXAMPLE:
If a Humanitarian Organization uses Blockchain for Cash and Voucher Assistance (CVA), it is likely to ask beneficiaries to have a "wallet" on the Blockchain. The wallet works in almost the same way as a public key, i.e. it can be compared against a username that does not, by itself, identify the beneficiary. The organization will, however, probably maintain an off-chain database or beneficiary management system that links every wallet to a unique beneficiary.

Every time cash is transferred to a beneficiary, a transaction will be added to the Blockchain specifying how much was sent, to which wallet and when. Once the transaction is validated by the consensus protocol, it is immutably stored in the Blockchain. If beneficiaries request that their data to be erased, it is technically impossible to delete their wallet (which, like a public key, constitutes Personal Data) from the chain. One option in this case would be to remove the person from the off-chain database or management system, since this is the only place where the wallet is associated with an individual. Once the personal profile is removed, immediate Reidentification should no longer be possible.

15.6.4 RESTRICTIONS OF DATA SUBJECTS' RIGHTS

The above discussion on access, erasure and rectification shows how difficult it can be to exercise data protection rights when using Blockchain technology. Since public permissionless Blockchains are mostly incompatible with Data Subjects' rights, it would seem that the only solution is to store Personal Data off-chain. Yet these rights are not absolute and can, therefore, be restricted. The Data Controller is allowed to take into account

---

45   Finck, "Blockchains and data protection in the European Union", p. 30.

available technology and the cost of implementation when Data Subjects request to exercise their rights. Importantly, however, these restrictions may be acceptable only in exceptional cases.[46] Chapter 2: Basic principles of data protection, explains and exemplifies the situations in which Data Subjects' rights can be restricted. Questions remain as to whether it is possible to have a "data-protection-compliant" Blockchain in specific use cases where the Processing legitimately involves derogation from Data Subjects' rights. Even if it is judged legitimate to restrict certain rights, all other data protection principles (data minimization, necessity, proportionality, security, etc.) still apply.

15.7 INTERNATIONAL DATA SHARING

Data processed in Blockchain applications will routinely flow across national borders – especially in public permissionless architectures, which anyone anywhere could potentially join. This raises questions about data protection in Blockchain applications when data are shared internationally.[47] Although contractual clauses and other recognized mechanisms exist, such measures may be all but impracticable in a Blockchain.

Determining applicable law and jurisdiction can also present challenges. The proper and targeted risk analysis as foreseen in Chapter 4: International Data Sharing, is impossible unless choice of jurisdiction and choice of law are clearly embedded in Blockchain governance (e.g. in private permissioned Blockchains that limit the geographical location of those who can join the chain).

International transfers can be problematic in certain types of Blockchain, such as unlimited public permissionless Blockchains like the one used by the cryptocurrency Bitcoin. Here, there is no central party with control over who joins the system and stores a copy of the ledger. Private permissioned and other architectures can, however, provide more control and therefore help to mitigate such risks. It is therefore possible to attempt to address the transfers issue through Blockchain governance, for instance by embedding data protection guarantees (including by hard-coding them in the Blockchain architecture).

Data Controllers also need to inform Data Subjects if their data have been shared with other parties or transferred to a third country. This is generally not possible – albeit with limited exceptions – in public permissionless Blockchains, since anyone in the world could potentially join the system and store a copy of the ledger. In permissioned Blockchains, however, Data Controllers have more control and should therefore be able to comply with this requirement.

---

46   See Section 2.11 – Rights of Data Subjects.
47   See Chapter 4: International Data Sharing.

15.8 ANNEX: DECISION-MAKING FRAMEWORK FOR BLOCKCHAIN IN HUMANITARIAN ACTION

The following decision-making framework is intended to guide Humanitarian Organizations through the process of implementing Blockchain in Humanitarian Action:

STEP 1:
This step is common to the deployment of any new technology and does not apply exclusively to Blockchain. It consists of an initial information-gathering and scoping exercise that should answer the following questions:
- What problem might a Blockchain solution address?
- To which programme will it apply, and what are the programme's needs?
- Is a Blockchain system the least invasive, most risk-averse and most controllable technology available to address the problem at hand?
- In what context will the Blockchain function?
- Where will it function (in one country or region, worldwide)?
- Who are the stakeholders (beneficiaries, local authorities, financial partners, mobile operators, other Humanitarian Organizations, etc.)?
- What are the objectives of the technology (increase internal efficiency, improve positioning, expand existing programmes, meet donor requirements, manage risks, etc.)?
- What are your existing governance arrangements and IT capacity? Can the technology be implemented, and can the associated risks be managed, under current arrangements and capacity?
- Is it clear how the technology will contribute to the local information ecosystem?

STEP 2:
Determine if a Blockchain-based system is necessary to attain the objective(s) of a humanitarian programme or other initiative, taking into consideration the advantages and challenges related to the technology, as identified above, in the particular context in which it will be implemented. Your organization should seek to understand what its needs are, whether or not Blockchain will fulfil those needs, how Data Subjects will experience the system, how their rights will be respected, and whether the same needs could be fulfilled by another system that better protects Data Subjects and their rights. You should ask the following questions:
- Does the order of (trans)actions matter?
- Is there a central authority you can trust?
- Do you need to store data?
- Is there buy-in from your governance/IT support team?
- Do you understand how your system will contribute to the local information ecosystem?

STEP 3:

If your organization decides that its objective can only be achieved with a Blockchain solution, you need to determine what type of Blockchain is most appropriate or necessary. Ask the following questions:
- Do you need to store state? This means whether or not your system needs to store the status and conditions of the system and not only to perform the action.
- Are there multiple contributors? This means contributors that can directly write data to the system. In a classical ecommerce use case where all users access the database through the merchant's website, the merchant is the single contributor as users cannot access the database without the merchant's control. Note that in the case of Blockchain, there are several roles to take into account.
- Can you use an "always-online" trusted Third Party (TTP)? A TTP is the entity that executes certain functions centrally, typically to validate the transactions.
- Are all contributors known?
- Are all contributors trusted?
- Is public verifiability required? It is important not to conflate public verifiability with the publication of audit or transparency report. It is meant here to have a provable verifiablity (in the mathematical sense) of the data.[48]

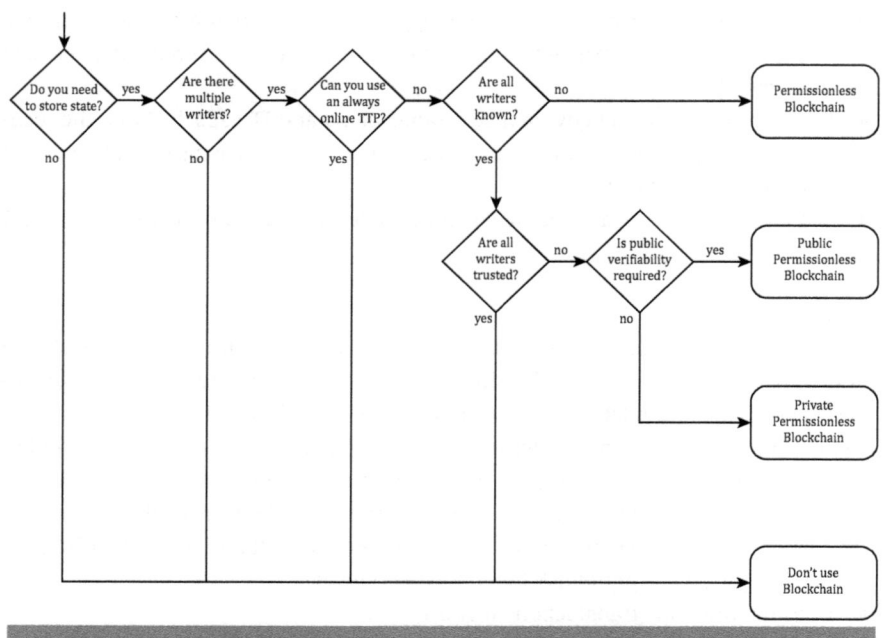

Figure 15.1 Decision tree.
Adapted from Wüst and Gervais, "Do you need a Blockchain?", IEEE, 2018.

---

48   Wust and Gervais, "Do you need a Blockchain?", IEEE, 2018.

STEP 4:
Consult your DPO, IT support and peers:
- Ask for guidance.
- Make use of the experience of others. For example, consult peers that have developed a similar system or used the off-the-shelf solution you intend to use, and seek advice from Blockchain experts.

STEP 5:
Conduct a DPIA to identify and assess Personal Data Processing impacts. A DPIA should include questions such as the following:
- What is the applicable law? Is it applicable to all stakeholders?
- What types of Personal Data are processed? Which of these are necessary for the transaction that will be stored on the Blockchain?
- Is the Processing fair, lawful and transparent?
- What are the alternatives to storing Personal Data on the Blockchain itself? Is off-chain storage possible?
- Are the Data Subjects able to fully exercise their rights? If not, are the restrictions lawful and proportionate?
- Who has the power to determine the governance of the Blockchain?
- How does the platform operate?
- Who can alter the platform and under what circumstances could entries on the ledger be updated?
- What are the risks posed by the chosen technology? How will each risk be treated and mitigated?
- How can individuals exercise their rights?

STEP 6:
Implement the principles of data protection by design and by default:
- Both principles require continuous monitoring and revision of technical and organizational measures, taking into account the following: available technology; the cost of implementation; the nature, scope and context of the Processing; the purposes of the Processing; and the risks (of varying likelihood and severity) to the rights and freedoms of natural persons posed by the Processing. A new DPIA should be conducted whenever there is a relevant change in the technology used or the type of data collected.
- Data protection by design involves considering factors such as:
    o compliance with data protection principles (lawfulness, fairness and transparency, purpose limitation, data minimization, accuracy, storage limitation, integrity, and confidentiality);
    o the rights of the Data Subject (e.g. notification, access, erasure, rectification);
    o other data protection obligations (e.g. accountability and security).

- Data protection by default involves considering factors such as:
  - what types and categories of Personal Data are processed;
  - the amount of Personal Data processed;
  - the purpose for which they are processed;
  - the storage period;
  - accessibility.

The above framework is summarized in the chart below. If, at the information-gathering stage, your organization concludes that other systems may be more appropriate than Blockchain, then you should not proceed past step 1.

Step 1
Determine if a Blockchain-based solution is necessary
What is the context in which the application will function? Does the order of (trans)actions matter? Is there no central authority you can trust? Do you need to store data? Is there buy-in by the IHO governance/IT support team? Do you understand how your system will contribute to local information ecosystem?

Step 2
Determine type of a Blockchain-based solution
Are there multiple contributors? Can you use an "always"-online TTP? Are all contributors known? Are all contributors trusted? Is public verifiability required?

Step 3
Identify if any personal data are processed on a Blockchain-based system:
What type of personal data are processed?

Step 4
Consult your DPO and your IT support and peers:
Ask for guidance
Build on expertise of others

Step 5
Conduct a DPIA allowing identification and evaluation of risks concerning personal data processing

Step 6
Implement data protection by design and data protection by default principles

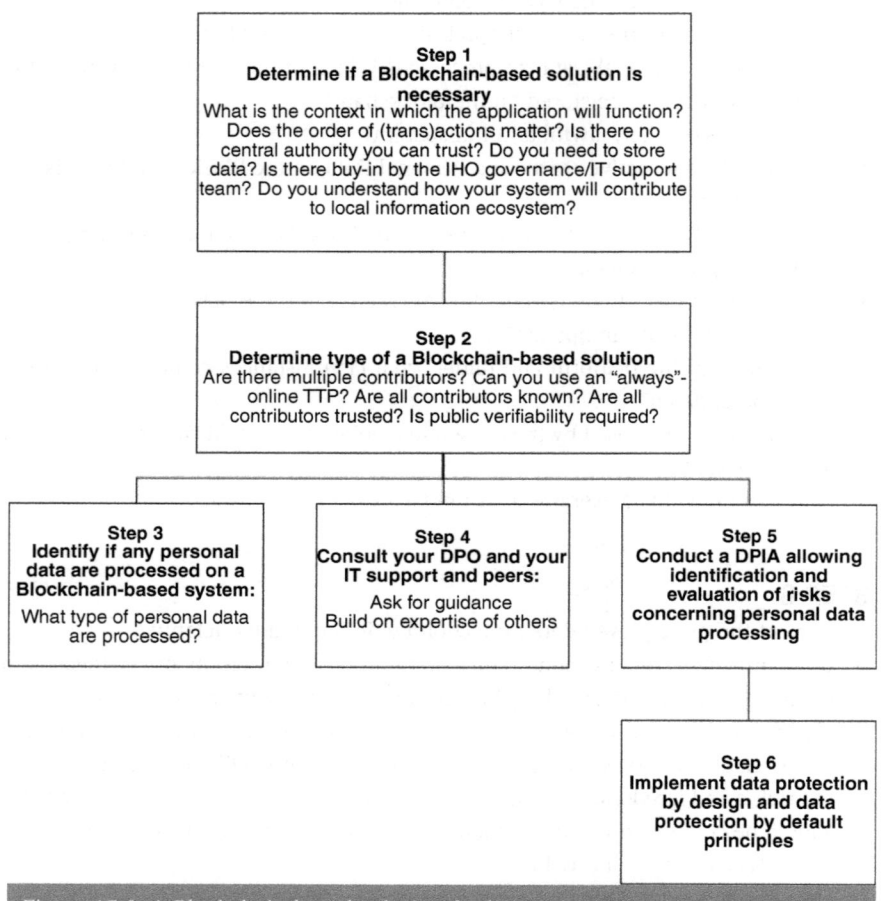

Figure 15.2 A Blockchain-based solution for humanitarian assistance. Adapted from Wüst and Gervais, "Do you need a Blockchain?", IEEE, 2018.

CONNECTIVITY AS AID
POSSIBLE USE
KEEP IN TOUCH WITH FAMILY MEMBERS
SAFE ROUTES
FIND SHELTER
HUMANITARIAN SERVICES
CHALLENGES
DATA CONTROLLER AND PROCESSORS
SURVEILLANCE
ADS
BUY NOW
COMMERCIAL PROFILING AND EXPLOITATION
LENTE
LACK OF TRANSPARENCY

CHAPTER 16
CONNECTIVITY AS AID
Aaron Martin and John Warnes*

---

* The authors would like to thank Robert Riemann (European Data Protection Supervisor), Antonella Napolitano and Ed Geraghty (Privacy International) for their input and feedback on this chapter.

16.1 INTRODUCTION

In emergencies, staying connected can help affected persons get in touch with separated family members, plan safe routes, find shelter, engage with Humanitarian Organizations, and access humanitarian and other services. Yet after disasters, the telecommunications networks on which connectivity[1] relies frequently stop working, depriving affected people of the communication channels on which they increasingly rely. Similar situations arise in conflict settings where networks can become compromised or in other humanitarian situations where perhaps connectivity levels were low even prior to an emergency.

However, affected communities attach considerable importance to connectivity. In 2016, for instance, aid workers assisting migrants in Greece reported that they often asked for Internet access before food and water.[2] Humanitarian Organizations have recognized the importance of connectivity and developed a range of programmes accordingly.

It is important to differentiate between connectivity *as* aid and connectivity *for* aid. The latter refers to providing connectivity to aid workers so they can carry out their work, while the former relates to providing connectivity to affected people and offering related services as a form of aid in times of emergency or in protracted crises.[3]

This chapter focuses on data protection issues arising from connectivity *as* aid, and at two different levels: community and individual. At the community level, Humanitarian Organizations typically set up hot spots or provide connectivity at community centres. In such cases, organizations usually manage the "pipe" (that is, the physical infrastructure such as cables and fibre bundles needed to provide connectivity), which is shared among users. At the individual level, Humanitarian Organizations may support people in their dealings with connectivity providers, but individuals will have greater responsibility for their own access to connectivity.[4] The distinction between these two levels also has implications for the data protection responsibilities of Humanitarian Organizations.

---

1   For the purposes of this chapter, "connectivity" refers to access to mobile and Internet connections.
2   Lin Taylor, "Internet Is As Important As Food And Water To Refugees In Greece", Huffington Post, 22 July 2016: www.huffpost.com/entry/internet-is-as-important-as-food-and-water-to-refugees-in-greece_n_57928a22e4b02d5d5ed1ac5b.
3   For a longer discussion on the distinction and its implications, see: ICRC, "DigitHarium | Month #5: Connectivity as Aid, for Aid, Denial", International Committee of the Red Cross, Geneva, 9 July 2021: www.icrc.org/en/digitharium/digitharium-month-5.
4   See for example: UNHCR Innovation, "Connectivity for Refugees", UNHCR Innovation (blog), 2019: www.unhcr.org/innovation/connectivity-for-refugees.

16.1.1 OVERVIEW OF CONNECTIVITY AS AID INTERVENTIONS

Various initiatives and organizations are working to provide connectivity in emergencies and address connectivity black spots. Most recently, within the United Nations system specific efforts have been made to strengthen and systematize coordination and delivery of connectivity as aid interventions, notably the **UN Secretary General's Roadmap for Digital Cooperation,** an initiative aimed at mobilizing all stakeholders to play a role in advancing a safer, more equitable digital world. One of the key pillars of this initiative is the "Global Connectivity" pillar, with the objective of achieving universal connectivity by 2030, and action 5 within this pillar focusing on humanitarian situations.[5]

Operational initiatives to provide connectivity as aid include but are not limited to:
- The **Emergency Telecommunications Cluster (ETC)** is a global network of organizations that work together to provide shared communications services in humanitarian emergencies. The ETC is one of the 11 clusters designated by the Inter-Agency Standing Committee (IASC).[6]
- The UNHCR **Innovation Service's Digital Innovation programme** undertakes activities that innovate around connectivity solutions for forcibly displaced people and host communities, taking a rights-based approach that emphasizes inclusion in national systems. UNHCR's mandated role in coordinating refugee responses may also include coordination of refugee-facing connectivity interventions.
- A newly formed multi-stakeholder initiative on **Connectivity for Refugees**, supported by UNHCR, the ITU, GSMA and Government of Luxembourg seeks to advance connectivity for 20m forcibly displaced people and their hosts by 2030 by fostering deeper cooperation between states and private enterprise.
- **GIGA** is a programme set up by the International Telecommunication Union and UNICEF to "connect every school to the internet and every young person to information, opportunity and choice".[7]
- **NGOs such as NetHope,**[8] **its members,**[9] **Télécoms Sans Frontières**[10] **and many others** provide connectivity solutions in various emergency preparedness and response settings.

---

5   United Nations, "Secretary-General's Roadmap for Digital Cooperation", United Nations, June 2020: www.un.org/en/content/digital-cooperation-roadmap.
6   "Emergency Telecommunications Cluster (ETC)", accessed 1 April 2022: www.etcluster.org.
7   UNICEF and ITU, "Giga – Connect Every School to the Internet", Giga Initiative, accessed 1 April 2022: https://gigaconnect.org.
8   NetHope, Inc, "Homepage", NetHope, 18 October 2021: https://nethope.org.
9   NetHope, Inc, "Our Members", NetHope, 2 November 2021: nethope.org/who-we-are/our-members.
10   Télécoms Sans Frontières (TSF), "Home", Télécoms Sans Frontières – ONG téléphonie humanitaire | Telecoms Sans Frontieres – NGO in Humanitarian calling, accessed 1 April 2022: www.tsfi.org/en.

Certain private-sector initiatives, beyond commercial connectivity services (cellular or otherwise) provided to the affected population, are also worth noting:
- **CISCO Crisis Response** (TacOps)[11] deploys a range of technologies and network equipment to provide free communication networks to both Humanitarian Organizations and beneficiaries after disasters. After the 8.1-magnitude earthquake in Nepal in 2015, for instance, Cisco Crisis Response was on the ground within 72 hours to restore communications.
- In many contexts, satellite companies[12] operate Corporate Social Responsibility (CSR) programmes that leverage their technology to facilitate connectivity for affected communities in humanitarian contexts, often in partnership with Humanitarian Organizations.
- **Before it was closed in December 2022, Meta Connectivity**[13] was also involved in a number of initiatives, including Free Basics, which aimed to provide free Internet access worldwide, and High Altitude Connectivity, which involved advancing the use of high-altitude platform station (HAPS) connectivity systems and satellite technology to bring connectivity to remote areas at lower costs.
- **Loon**[14] (now defunct) was an initiative initially led by Alphabet Inc. to connect people by deploying balloons containing the essential components of cell towers to bring Internet access to areas not covered by existing networks.

16.1.2 OPERATIONAL CONTEXT

When starting a connectivity as aid programme, it is important to remember that crises are complex situations, and that the circumstances and people affected will differ from one crisis to the next. Likewise, connectivity programmes will vary according to the context. For some, the emphasis will be on building existing network resilience to future natural disasters or emergencies. For others, the focus will be on establishing connectivity in areas where it has never existed. Although practical arrangements will inevitably differ, organizations will need to consider some common factors no matter what type of programme they are implementing. The first is the regulatory landscape, which will determine what the organization and potential service users (such as affected communities) can and cannot do. The second is the commercial and non-commercial organizations currently providing connectivity in the area. Indeed, Humanitarian Organizations often engage with private-sector

---

11 Cisco, "Incident Response – Connecting Communities in Crisis", Cisco, accessed 1 April 2022: www.cisco.com/c/en/us/about/csr/impact/cisco-crisis-response/incident-response.html.
12 Michael Oduor, "Boosting Self Reliance among Refugees through Satellite Connectivity", Africanews, 28 May 2021: www.africanews.com/2021/05/28/boosting-self-reliance-among-refugees-through-satellite-connectivity; SES, "SES Is Enabling Disaster Response and Connecting Affected Communities", Bloomberg.Com, 22 March 2017: www.bloomberg.com/press-releases/2017-03-22/ses-is-enabling-disaster-response-and-connecting-affected-communities; "Intelsat Customer UNHCR Wins Changing Lives Award at AfricaCom 2017", Intelsat (blog), 16 November 2017: www.intelsat.com/newsroom/intelsat-customer-unhcr-wins-changing-lives-award-at-africacom-2017.
13 Meta, "Meta Connectivity", accessed 1 April 2022: www.facebook.com/connectivity.
14 "Loon", X, the moonshot factory, accessed 1 April 2022: https://x.company/projects/loon.

entities throughout part or all of the connectivity chain and, as these partnerships have become increasingly common, organizations in both sectors have developed guidelines on how to cooperate with one another.[15]

When considering partnering with other entities (see Section 16.1.3 – Multiple stakeholders and partnerships, below), Humanitarian Organizations are always advised to assess the risks of such partnerships. One way to do so, at least in part, is through a Data Protection Impact Assessment (DPIA) – an exercise that can be designed to look beyond core data protection issues (see Section 16.2 – Data Protection Impact Assessments, below) and seeks to ensure that the partnership will follow "do no harm" principles and minimize and mitigate risks as far as reasonably possible.

16.1.3 MULTIPLE STAKEHOLDERS AND PARTNERSHIPS

Humanitarian Organizations may not have the necessary expertise, technology or equipment to implement a connectivity programme alone. This means that they may have to partner with one or more connectivity or technology providers in order to achieve their objectives. These can include non-profit organizations, private enterprises (such as telecommunications providers and technology companies), and NGOs providing connectivity solutions in emergencies.

Aside from considering the other parties involved, it is also important to understand that providing connectivity may be a layered process. As mentioned above, there are two different levels: community and individual. At the individual level, beneficiaries bear a greater responsibility for their own connectivity, since connectivity operators may collect data directly from them.

Once connectivity is established, there are additional (so-called "over-the-top") services, such as social media services running on top of a mobile service contract, mobile wallets or mobile money. Some providers of these services may offer their products directly to affected persons receiving aid. Here, although affected persons are technically acting as consumers, they are in fact more vulnerable than the average consumer. There are also less visible parties involved in connectivity programmes, such as infrastructure providers and those working on the backhaul to bring connectivity to Humanitarian Organizations or service providers (such as bandwidth providers). Providers can also add deep package inspection (DPI)[16] to the network as an added layer of protection. DPI involves filtering unwanted packets (units of data sent from an origin to a destination over the Internet) such as viruses or

---

15 See for example: GSMA, "Humanitarian Connectivity Charter", Mobile for Development (blog), accessed 1 April 2022: www.gsma.com/mobilefordevelopment/mobile-for-humanitarian-innovation/humanitarian-connectivity-charter.

16 For more on deep package inspection, see: Rahul Awati and Jessica Scarpati, "What Is Deep Packet Inspection (DPI)?", Tech Target – Search Networking (blog), September 2021: www.techtarget.com/searchnetworking/definition/deep-packet-inspection-DPI.

malware. Importantly, however, DPI makes it possible to identify the originator or recipient of content containing specific packets, meaning it can also be used for monitoring and surveillance purposes.

All these organizations and entities operating at different layers of the connectivity programme – backhaul, pipe, over-the-top and last-mile access – may collect or have access to users' data. This is because additional data and metadata are generated and processed at every layer of connectivity. This Processing by different entities is technically necessary, since sending a message from one location to another usually requires multiple entities knowing its source and destination.[17] These metadata (such as connection end points, "likes" and visits) may be accessible to some or all entities in the connectivity chain, which may be able to extract knowledge about humanitarian emergencies and the individuals involved in ways that are difficult for both beneficiaries and Humanitarian Organizations to anticipate.[18]

EXAMPLE OF CONNECTIVITY OPERATORS COLLECTING DATA DIRECTLY FROM AFFECTED PERSONS:
A domestic mobile network operator usually has access to the following information for billing purposes: unique identifiers for the SIM card and device (IMSI and IMEI numbers); time and location of transactions, such as calls and messages; and data obtained during SIM card registration.[19] The data obtained during SIM card registration may vary considerably from one country to another and according to the type of SIM card purchased (pre-paid or post-paid). Nevertheless, there has been a general tendency towards mandatory registration for all types of card, requiring users to provide Personal Data[20] such as a copy of their ID, their national identification number and their date of birth. In some cases, the individual is also cross-checked against a national ID database (India and Pakistan) or has their fingerprints and photograph taken (Nigeria, for instance).[21] Research[22] has found that, in most cases, refugees and other forcibly displaced people struggle to obtain SIM cards through standard legal channels and resort instead to both formal and informal workarounds that both introduce additional risks to affected people and present challenges for Humanitarian Organizations in terms of mapping relevant data flows.

---

17 ICRC and Privacy International, *The Humanitarian Metadata Problem*, October 2018, 22–23.
18 Ibid., 23.
19 Ibid., 71.
20 Donovan and Martin, "The rise of African SIM registration". See also the European Court of Human Rights (ECHR) judgment in the case of *Breyer v. Germany* (application no. 50001/12), 30 January 2020.
21 GSMA, "Mandatory Registration of Prepaid SIM Cards".
22 UNHCR Innovation, "Displaced and Disconnected", UNHCR Innovation (blog), 2019: www.unhcr.org/innovation/displaced-and-disconnected.

In this context, Humanitarian Organizations will not have control over the whole connectivity chain and, therefore, cannot guarantee to protect individuals against having their data and metadata misused. The risks that may arise from this lack of control should be evaluated through Data Protection Impact Assessments (see Section 16.2 – Data Protection Impact Assessments, below) whenever Humanitarian Organizations and their partners play an active role in improving connectivity for affected communities. As a mitigating measure, some Humanitarian Organizations provide affected people with information and guidance on digital security.[23] While Humanitarian Organizations may opt to not provide connectivity when the risks prove high through a Data Protection Impact Assessment, the alternative options that might be pursued by communities through the open and black market could present even greater risk. Humanitarian Organizations should consider these risks holistically and take appropriate action that minimizes risk in the connectivity ecosystem.

16.2 DATA PROTECTION IMPACT ASSESSMENTS

A Data Protection Impact Assessment (DPIA)[24] is carried out to identify, evaluate and address the risks posed to Data Subjects by the Processing of their Personal Data in connection with a project, policy, programme or other initiative. It should ultimately lead to measures promoting the avoidance, minimization, transfer or sharing of data protection risks. Before launching technology programmes that involve the Processing of Personal Data, Humanitarian Organizations should conduct a DPIA to assess the possible consequences, which could include unlawful use of beneficiaries' data by partners and government interference with the network.

Before entering into a partnership for a connectivity programme, a Humanitarian Organization should assess potential partners and their data protection policies, as well as the legal obligations to which they are subject or any Privileges and Immunities they may hold, in order to fully understand how they process people's data. In some cases, in the absence of ownership of the specific infrastructure needed or local assets required to provide connectivity, it may be very difficult to fully understand and control data flows. Where the organization is able to glean a clear picture of the connectivity landscape, the parties involved and the services they provide, it may be in a position to draft standard guidelines or requirements explaining the services it needs, including technical specifications and data protection requirements. This could help organizations engage with partners and shorten the time between engagement and agreement in times of emergency.

---

23 For more on data security, see Section 2.8 – Data security and Processing security.
24 See Chapter 5: Data Protection Impact Assessments (DPIAs).

It is also important to remember that, in the humanitarian sector, affected persons are especially vulnerable and the risk of harm is high. For these reasons, the DPIA should give due consideration to Data Subjects' other fundamental rights.[25] Since Humanitarian Organizations operate in accordance with humanitarian principles, it may also be appropriate to consider the rights and freedoms of all members of a given group or community when setting up connectivity programmes, including non-data related rights. In parallel to application of other appropriate risk assessment frameworks, a DPIA could, for instance, be designed to also identify issues around unequal access to the network[26] and the potential exclusion of certain groups that are not digitally literate. It is also important to consider that some of the partners with which Humanitarian Organizations work have business models that are based on the monetization of data, which may be incompatible with humanitarian principles. Organizations may also be unwilling to engage with some private-sector partners because of inadequate findings of human rights due diligence processes and the reputational risk that doing so can carry. If the DPIA indicates that a connectivity programme could create more problems than can be adequately mitigated, it may be appropriate to decide not to move forward with the programme.

16.3 DATA CONTROLLER/DATA PROCESSOR RELATIONSHIP

A Data Controller is the person or organization who, alone or jointly with others, determines the purposes and means of the Processing of Personal Data. A Data Processor, meanwhile, is the person or organization who processes Personal Data on behalf of the Data Controller. These concepts are defined and discussed at greater length in Chapter 2: Basic principles of data protection.

---

25 See: EU Article 29 Working Party, Article 29 Working Party, *Guidelines on Data Protection Impact Assessment (DPIA) and determining whether processing is "likely to result in a high risk" for the purposes of Regulation 2016/679*, October, 2017; Raphaël Gellert, "Understanding the notion of risk in the General Data Protection Regulation", *Computer Law & Security Review*, Vol. 34, No. 2, 1 April 2018, pp. 279–288: https://doi.org/10.1016/J.CLSR.2017.12.003.

26 For example, young children and elderly people might not be able to benefit from connectivity programmes or access services that require connectivity as they may lack computer literacy. In addition, "[w]omen in low- and middle-income countries are 10% less likely to own a mobile phone, and are considerably less likely than men to use more transformative services. For example, women in low- and middle- income countries are 26% less likely than men to use mobile internet, and 33% less likely to use mobile money." Source: GSMA, *Connected Women: The Gender Analysis & Identification Toolkit. Estimating subscriber gender using machine learning*, GSMA, 2018, p. 6: www.gsma.com/mobilefordevelopment/wp-content/uploads/2018/08/GSMA-Gender-Analysis-and-Identification-Report-August-2018.pdf.

When Humanitarian Organizations set up and operate connectivity programmes, they can act as either Data Controllers or Data Processors, depending on the role that they and other partners play in a programme. This distinction is important when attributing responsibilities for data Processing.

Since data are collected at different layers of a connectivity programme, it is important to map, as much as possible and based on information that can be made available or acquired from the providers, data flows at each layer, identifying who is collecting them, what the purposes are, how long the data are retained and with whom they are shared. This mapping exercise will help to identify what role each party, including the Humanitarian Organization, plays in deciding how data are processed – and, therefore, whether each one is acting as a Data Controller or a Data Processor.

If a Humanitarian Organization determines the final objective (purpose) of the programme (such as establishing connectivity) and chooses a specific partner to implement it (means), it qualifies as a Data Controller. This means that the organization has a range of obligations, including responding to requests from Data Subjects wishing to exercise their rights.[27] In some cases, Humanitarian Organizations and partners from other sectors will determine the purpose and means of the programme together and, therefore, act as joint controllers. In such situations, the joint controllers must set out their respective responsibilities, including the handling of Data Subjects' requests, in a written agreement.

16.4 BASIC DATA PROTECTION PRINCIPLES

16.4.1 LEGAL BASES FOR PERSONAL DATA PROCESSING

When Personal Data are required to access connectivity services, or generated in the process, an appropriate legal basis for the Processing of these data is necessary. Such legal bases are listed in Chapter 3: Legal bases for Personal Data Processing, which also explains the challenges associated with using Consent as a legal basis in humanitarian settings. Consent in humanitarian contexts may not always be considered freely given, since beneficiaries may feel compelled to Consent when that is the only way to receive a specific service (in this case, connectivity). Moreover, the complexity surrounding connectivity as aid might make it difficult to rely on a properly informed Consent, since Data Subjects with lower levels of digital literacy might not be able to understand all aspects of the Processing. Here, Humanitarian Organizations and service providers should seek a different legal basis for data collection and Processing, such as those listed below:

---

27 See Section 2.11 – Rights of Data Subjects.

- **Public interest**: This may be an option for an organization that has a specific mandate to facilitate access to connectivity, or for a Data Processor operating under instruction of an organization with such a mandate.[28]
- **Legitimate interest of the Humanitarian Organization**: This basis could also be considered where establishing or re-establishing connectivity is in line with the organization's mission, and where doing so could help beneficiaries access other essential services and improve coordination of the humanitarian response. This basis would only apply, however, if the interest(s) pursued by the organization and the anticipated benefits of the Processing are not outweighed by the rights and freedoms of the individuals in question.[29]
- **Performance of a contract**: Private companies providing connectivity services to affected communities on a commercial basis under applicable contract law may utilize performance of a contract as the legal basis for data Processing.[30]
- **Legal obligation**: Some jurisdictions may require connectivity service users to be registered. Here, the legal basis for Processing users' data for registration would be compliance with a legal obligation.[31]

16.4.2 DATA SECURITY

Mobile network operators play an important role as providers of critical connectivity infrastructure. In emergencies, for instance, being able to communicate with ambulances and other health-care providers is vital to effective incident response. These operators are required, depending on the specific telecommunications regulations in a country of operation, to implement technical and organizational security measures in order to protect communication networks and keep the data they carry secure. These measures, which will depend on the degree of risk, include encryption and other technical ways of ensuring the confidentiality, integrity and availability of collected data, as well as the overall resilience of Processing systems and services.[32]

Some metadata stored on individual devices, however, may not be encrypted and may require alternative security measures.[33] Wherever possible, Humanitarian Organizations and individuals should routinely review and update the measures they take, in order to account for the development of new security technologies, and to ensure a level of data protection and security that is appropriate to the degree of risk involved in the Processing of Personal Data. It is important to remain mindful that some entities or organizations may have an interest in accessing the data and

---

28 See Chapter 3: Legal bases for Personal Data Processing.
29 See Section 3.5 – Legitimate interest.
30 See Section 3.6 – Performance of a contract.
31 See Section 3.7 – Compliance with a legal obligation.
32 For more on data security, see Section 2.8 – Data security and Processing security.
33 ICRC and Privacy International, *The Humanitarian Metadata Problem*, October 2018, 25.

metadata generated in connectivity programmes for non-humanitarian purposes, such as commercial targeting and exploitation, or surveillance.

EXAMPLE:
Germany and Denmark have passed laws that allow the authorities to carry out a detailed forensic analysis of asylum seekers' smartphones. The data and metadata extracted from their devices can be used "to verify claims made in their asylum applications or to obtain new information about their identity, their story, the route they took, etc.".[34] Similar legislation has been passed in Belgium, Switzerland[35] and Austria.[36] In practice, such laws could mean that data generated through connectivity programmes end up being used for purposes that, even if legitimate, may not be compatible with the principles by which Humanitarian Organizations abide.

Current surveillance methods can be quite sophisticated and obtain substantial amounts of data and metadata about users of a given network.[37] This is particularly concerning, since metadata can be used to infer information that an individual has not agreed to share, and make predictions about their behaviour, which would mean that data generated in the process of humanitarian services could end up being used as highly valuable information in conflict.

In some cases, a Humanitarian Organization – depending on its mandate and status – may need to cooperate with national or foreign government authorities on a given connectivity programme. This type of cooperation can be in the interest of affected persons, such as when medical data are shared with health authorities to facilitate the provision of medical aid and public health. Humanitarian Organizations should be transparent with affected persons about any such cooperation arrangements, and make clear that their data may be shared with national or foreign authorities.

Where possible, Humanitarian Organizations should negotiate security measures with their partners to ensure the highest level of security throughout the entire connectivity chain – including those parts of the chain outside the organization's control.

---

[34] Ibid., 62.
[35] See Secrétariat d'État aux migrations, "Mise en œuvre de la révision de la loi sur l'asile (LAsi): accélération des procédures d'asile", Governmental website, Confédération Suisse, 12 May 2018: www.sem.admin.ch/sem/fr/home/sem/rechtsetzung/archiv/aend-asylg-neustruktur.html.
[36] ICRC and Privacy International, *The Humanitarian Metadata Problem*, October 2018. See also Parlament Österreich. "Fremdenrechtsänderungsgesetz 2018 – FrÄG 2018", Governmental website, 13 June 2018: www.parlament.gv.at/gegenstand/XXVI/I/189.
[37] See for example: Bruce Schneier, "China Isn't the Only Problem with 5G", Foreign Policy (blog), 10 January 2020, https://foreignpolicy.com/2020/01/10/5g-china-backdoor-security-problems-united-states-surveillance.

16.4.3 DATA RETENTION

Personal Data must not be kept for longer than is necessary to fulfil the purposes for which they were collected or to comply with applicable legal obligations.[38] This means that Personal Data should always be deleted or anonymized as soon as they are no longer needed. In connectivity programmes, however, the various partners may have different roles, policies and needs that could impact how they Process data, including how long they retain them for. Again, it is important at the outset to establish a written agreement setting out each party's responsibilities and data retention policies. This will ensure that Humanitarian Organizations fully understand what data are being held by each partner at a certain point in time, and where they are being stored.

Beyond retention required for fulfilment of a contract for connectivity services with the Data Subject, mobile network operators are also required to retain data about users for periods specified in national law. Requirements such as these are intended, for instance, to give law enforcement authorities access to data in case a crime is committed. Humanitarian Organizations should therefore analyse which data are actually needed to deploy the programme and, as far as they can, avoid the collection of any unnecessary data. If only a minimum amount of data is collected, then only a minimum amount can be retained.

16.4.4 INFORMATION

In connectivity programmes, Data Subjects should be informed in clear and plain language about what data relating to them are being collected, for what purpose and through which means. This is especially important in situations where it may not be obvious to Data Subjects that their data are being collected, such as when metadata are generated or when the data collected are inferred data (information that can be deduced from data explicitly given by the Data Subject or from other observations). Individuals should also be told whom they can contact to exercise their rights. This information will enable them to make informed decisions about whether or not to use a specific service, and to understand how to proceed when they wish to exercise their rights.

In the interest of transparency and full disclosure, Humanitarian Organizations are advised to inform Data Subjects about the Third Parties involved in the programme, which activities they are responsible for and how to contact them. They should also be informed about the actual and potential negative consequences and risks associated with receiving and using connectivity services, and with connectivity programmes in general. The example set by UNHCR, which informs individuals of the privacy risks associated with the El Jaguar campaign, is a helpful model to follow.[39]

---

38 See Section 2.7 – Data retention.
39 See El Jaguar, "Privacidad En Facebook". This campaign video provides tips on privacy and profile safety on social media.

16.5 INTERNATIONAL DATA SHARING

Data processed online routinely flow across national borders. This raises Personal Data protection concerns in relation to connectivity programmes. Although recognized legal mechanisms exist, such as the use of contractual clauses, it can be difficult for Humanitarian Organizations to implement them effectively, especially since connectivity solutions are often outside their control. That said, organizations should undertake due diligence to ensure that the provider has implemented the necessary data transfer arrangements.[40]

---

40 See Chapter 4: International Data Sharing.

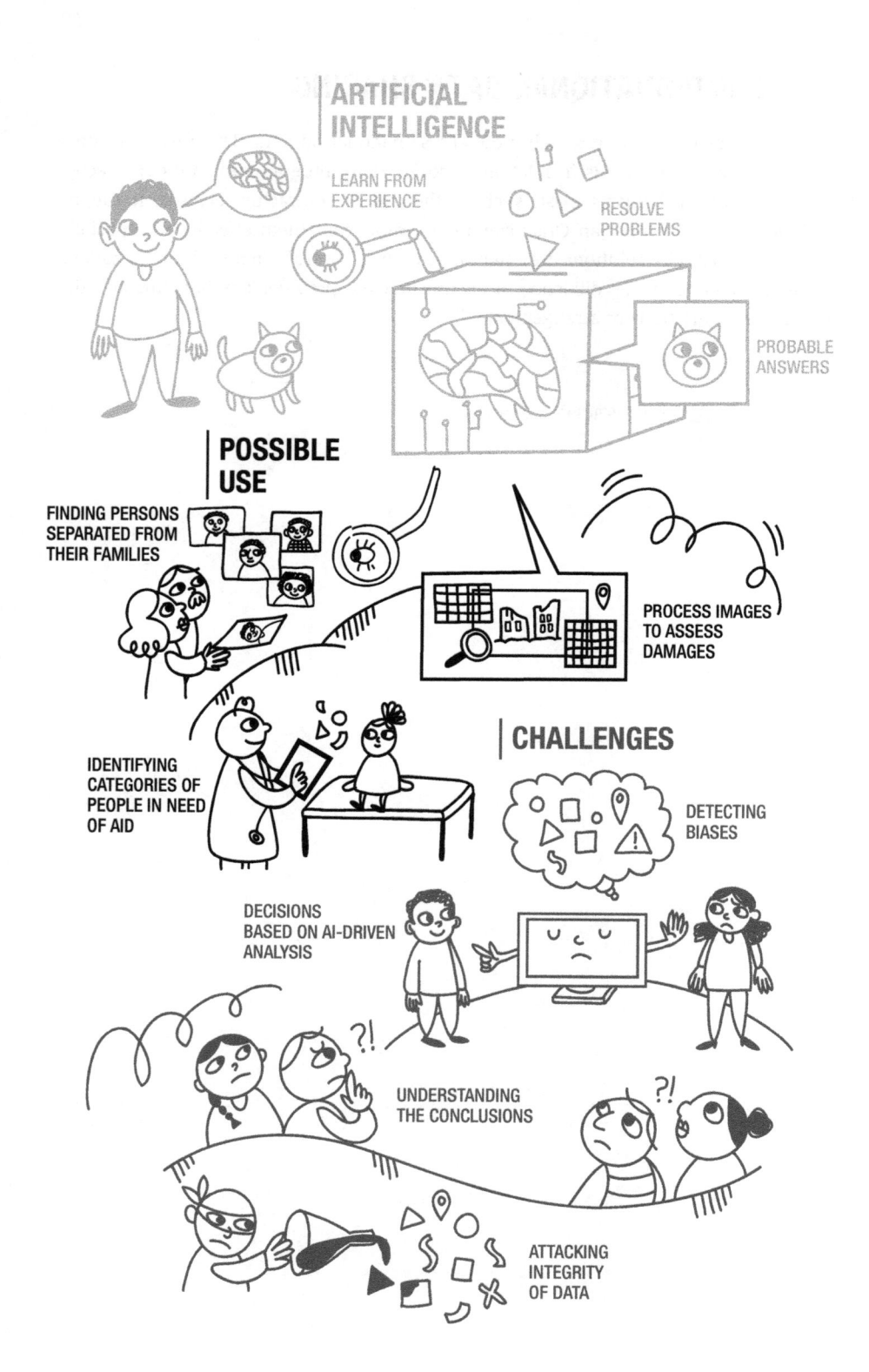

ARTIFICIAL INTELLIGENCE

- LEARN FROM EXPERIENCE
- RESOLVE PROBLEMS
- PROBABLE ANSWERS

POSSIBLE USE

- FINDING PERSONS SEPARATED FROM THEIR FAMILIES
- PROCESS IMAGES TO ASSESS DAMAGES
- IDENTIFYING CATEGORIES OF PEOPLE IN NEED OF AID

CHALLENGES

- DETECTING BIASES
- DECISIONS BASED ON AI-DRIVEN ANALYSIS
- UNDERSTANDING THE CONCLUSIONS
- ATTACKING INTEGRITY OF DATA

CHAPTER 17
ARTIFICIAL INTELLIGENCE
Alessandro Mantelero

17.1 INTRODUCTION[1]

This chapter explores the data protection challenges associated with the use of Artificial Intelligence systems in the humanitarian sector. The most relevant are some key elements of data Processing (such as the use of large data sets) and the purpose of such Processing, particularly as it concerns decision-making processes. The sections that follow first give a basic explanation of the technology in question, then identify the related data protection challenges and provide guidance for Humanitarian Organizations on how to address some of them.

17.1.1 WHAT ARTIFICIAL INTELLIGENCE IS AND HOW IT WORKS

While there is no single, universally accepted definition of the term, Artificial Intelligence is generally understood as "[a] set of sciences, theories, and techniques whose purpose is to reproduce by a machine the cognitive abilities of a human being".[2] In its current form, it aims to allow technology developers "to entrust a machine with complex tasks previously delegated to a human".[3]

Within the context of Artificial Intelligence, Machine Learning (ML) is one of the most relevant processes concerning the use of Personal Data in decision-making processes. This is a specific form of Artificial Intelligence defined as a set of algorithms that get better at completing a certain task over time, with input in the form of machine-readable data.[4] An ML algorithm receives more and more data representing the problem it is trying to solve and "learns" from such data. There are, however, other Artificial Intelligence techniques that are less reliant on data because they "learn" in different ways,[5] but, in recent years, Machine Learning has attracted the vast majority of Artificial Intelligence investment and is therefore the main reference for the considerations expressed in this chapter.

All forms of Artificial Intelligence share a common feature: they are not a set of instructions for a machine to complete a particular task, but rather a set of instructions for the machine to generate strategies or solutions to complete that task. There are different Artificial Intelligence techniques in existence, but for those relying on ML, it is possible to outline some common key elements as follows:

---

1   This chapter builds on and revises two previous chapters of the second edition of this Handbook, on Big Data and AI respectively. The substance of these chapters was developed from a seminar developed with the contribution of the author during the Workshop on Artificial Intelligence/Machine Learning and Data Protection in Humanitarian Action, organised by VUB-Brussels Privacy Hub and the International Committee of the Red Cross in 2019.
2   Council of Europe (CoE), "Glossary on Artificial Intelligence".
3   Ibid.
4   Tom M. Mitchell, *Machine Learning*, McGraw-Hill Series in Computer Science, McGraw-Hill, New York, 1997, 2.
5   Examples of these methods include Bayesian networks and rule-based engines. These methods, however, are not addressed in this chapter.

1. Selected data sets relating to a certain field of investigation (e.g. human images for recognition or classification of persons) are presented to the system expecting that they contain specific patterns or similarities (training data).
2. Artificial Intelligence identifies these patterns by classifying/aggregating data according to relevant features present in the training data set.
3. This process generates a model that is able to recognize a pattern when new data are processed by it; these patterns support predictions or classifications related to the used data (e.g. mobile geolocated data to detect groups' mobility patterns).[6]

To understand the use cases of Artificial Intelligence, it is important to distinguish between three possible approaches to ML:

- **Supervised learning**: Training data are labelled by assigning a "class" to each piece of training data. For instance, images of animals are tagged with labels such as "dog", "cat" or "parrot" and fed into the system. Typically, the ultimate objective will be for the algorithm to be able to classify new (previously unseen) images into one of the learned classes. This type of learning can also be used, for example, to predict a value based on different parameters (or features), such as valuing a house based on the number of rooms, size and/or year of construction. In both cases, the objective is for the model to properly separate the data into their correct classes or evaluate correct values. In this process, data labelling is a crucial stage and requires field experts to identify key relevant elements, based on the data set and purpose of the analysis.
- **Unsupervised learning:** No labels are fed into the system, and Artificial Intelligence groups data based on similarities or patterns that it detects autonomously in the training data set. In this case, the classification is made by Artificial Intelligence during the learning process and no additional classes than those created by the ML process are possible.
- **Reinforcement learning:** This approach requires little training data. Instead, it relies on a method of reward and punishment, whereby "the system is given a 'reward' signal for when it accomplishes what the designer wants, or a step that advances the process toward the outcome the designer described. When the system does something wrong (fails to efficiently advance toward the desired outcome), it is simply not rewarded."[7]

Based on one of the methods described above,[8] it is possible to create static and dynamic models. Static models do not change over time and continue to apply the

---

6 The Norwegian Data Protection Authority, *Artificial Intelligence and Privacy*, The Norwegian Data Protection Authority, Oslo, January 2018, 7: www.datatilsynet.no/globalassets/global/english/ai-and-privacy.pdf.
7 Ibid., 18.
8 This chapter does not address all possible Artificial Intelligence learning methods. For more information on methods not mentioned here (such as neural networks), see e.g.: Larry Hardesty, "Explained: Neural Networks", MIT News | Massachusetts Institute of Technology (blog), 14 April 2017: https://news.mit.edu/2017/explained-neural-networks-deep-learning-0414; Future of Privacy Forum, *The Privacy Expert's Guide to Artificial Intelligence and Machine Learning*, Future of Privacy Forum, Washington, DC, October 2018: https://fpf.org/wp-content/uploads/2018/10/FPF_Artificial-Intelligence_Digital.pdf.

model developed using the training data set. They give the developer better control over the model but prevent the adopted solution from improving over time. Dynamic models, on the other hand, are characterized by a kind of continuous learning, as they can use fresh data for improvements and changes (e.g. spam filter systems). This reduces control over the model development and may lead to unforeseen critical consequences in its outputs and expected behaviour.[9]

By nature, most of these Artificial Intelligence techniques rely on large-scale data sets, which are the main reason for their application and an inherent component of their functioning. Finding common patterns in a large amount of data – such as, for example, those produced at the national level on migration – might be hard for human experts. At the same time, the computer, statistical and mathematical tools used by Artificial Intelligence systems only work properly when applied to large data set minimizing outliers and other "noise" or disturbances.

Against this technology background, the progressive datafication of our society, due to the increasing availability of data produced by a variety of sources and the decreasing of the costs of sensors, IT devices/services and computing power, has made it possible to use Artificial Intelligence and to analyse large-scale data sets in all the fields of human activity, including Humanitarian Action.[10] A shift in the approach to social analysis followed the advent of so-called big data and Artificial Intelligence-based Data Analytics at the beginning of the new millennium. For the first time it was possible to combine very large volumes of diversely sourced information and analyse them, using mathematical algorithms at large scale or sophisticated computer-based tools (e.g. neural networks) to extract further information and make informed decisions.

However, this use of Artificial Intelligence for social analysis raises several questions and the risk of "algorithmic illusions".[11] Likewise, the way data collection is carried out, the design of the Artificial Intelligence model, the training data set used, and all potential errors or biases in this process, have an influence on the representation of human activities, relationships and profiles we use in Artificial Intelligence-supported Humanitarian Action tools.

---

9   See e.g. the Microsoft Tay chatbot case: James Vincent, "Twitter Taught Microsoft's AI Chatbot to Be a Racist Asshole in Less than a Day", The Verge, 24 March 2016: www.theverge.com/2016/3/24/11297050/tay-microsoft-chatbot-racist.
10 See also United Nations Office for the Coordination of Humanitarian Affairs (OCHA), *Humanitarianism in the Age of Cyber-Warfare*. OCHA Policy and Studies series, 2014: www.unocha.org/publications/report/world/humanitarianism-age-cyber-warfare-towards-principled-and-secure-use-information.
11 See also, on the use of Data Analytics in society, Alessandro Mantelero, "Personal data for decisional purposes in the age of analytics: From an individual to a collective dimension of data protection", *Computer Law & Security Review*, Vol. 32, No. 2, 1 April 2016, pp. 238–255: www.sciencedirect.com/science/article/abs/pii/S0267364916300280?via%3Dihub.

Although the term "Artificial Intelligence" suggests that natural intelligence and artificial intelligence are similar, this is not the case. Artificial Intelligence is nothing more than a data-driven and mathematical form of information Processing; it is not able to think, elaborate concepts or develop theories of causality. Artificial Intelligence merely takes a path recognition approach to sort through very large amounts of data and infer new information and correlations. Data dependence and path dependence are therefore both the strength and the weakness of these systems, as well as the fact that AI-based solutions are designed to be applied serially and poor design therefore affects numerous people in the same or similar circumstances.

Finally, given the use of incredibly large data sets and complex Artificial Intelligence systems, the safeguarding role over decision making provided by human supervision may be very challenging and time-consuming, if not impossible in some cases.

In terms of its field-specific application, Artificial Intelligence and large data sets may be used for objectives such as identifying potential threats relevant to Humanitarian Action, enhancing preparedness, identifying individuals or categories of individuals in need, or predicting possible patterns of evolution of contagious diseases, conflicts, tensions and natural disasters. Data-driven technologies can significantly enhance the effectiveness of work carried out by Humanitarian Organizations, including mapping or identification of:
- patterns of events in Humanitarian Emergencies involving protected people in conflicts or other situations of violence;
- the spread of diseases or natural disasters, thus predicting possible developments and preparing to prevent damage;
- the epicentre of a crisis;
- safe routes;
- individual humanitarian incidents;
- vulnerable individuals or communities who are likely to require humanitarian response;
- matches in case of separated families in Humanitarian Emergencies.

Two broad categories of applications for the use of Artificial Intelligence-based solutions in Humanitarian Action can be identified:
(i) applications that recognize general patterns and predict trends;
(ii) applications aimed at identifying individuals or groups of individuals of relevance for Humanitarian Action.

In this context, the massive collection of data and the use of data-intensive applications based on personal information entails several risks. Not only might it lead to misleading and inaccurate results or decisions, but moreover the lack of accurate data protection-oriented design could lead to the development of invasive or disproportionate Artificial Intelligence systems, as well as the adoption of solutions affected by significant weaknesses that make it possible to reidentify individuals in poorly anonymized data sets, Data Breaches and other cybersecurity attacks.[12]

17.1.2 ARTIFICIAL INTELLIGENCE IN THE HUMANITARIAN SECTOR

Recent growth in available data and Processing power has greatly increased the number of Artificial Intelligence applications in everyday life: from virtual digital assistants to biometric recognition systems to unlock devices or allow access to buildings, from traffic management in smart cities to content moderation for online platforms, and in many other functionalities of online and offline products and services. Artificial Intelligence can also be applied to a wide variety of tasks traditionally performed by humans, such as medical diagnosis, image recognition and stock market prediction.

Regarding the application of Artificial Intelligence in the humanitarian sector, its ability to collect, process and analyse large data sets and to extract inferences and predictions to inform decision-making processes turns Artificial Intelligence into a valuable option to increase the efficiency and effectiveness of humanitarian work. This is evident, for example, in the use cases detailed below:
- **Reading public opinion.** In Uganda, the UN Global Pulse programme piloted "a toolkit that makes public radio broadcasts machine-readable through the use of speech recognition technology and translation tools that transform radio content into text".[13] This tool, developed by the Pulse Lab Kampala, aims to identify trends among different population groups, particularly those in rural areas. The rationale behind the initiative is that these trends could then provide government and development partners with a better understanding of public opinion on the country's development needs, which could then be taken into consideration when implementing development programmes.
- **Identifying and locating missing children.** It has been reported[14] that India's National Tracking System for Missing & Vulnerable Children identified nearly 3,000 missing children within four days of launching a trial of a new facial recognition system that matches the faces of missing individuals with photographs of children living in children's homes and orphanages.

---

12   Marelli, "Defining the Cyber Perimeter", April 2020, 367.
13   Pulse Lab Kampala, "Making Ugandan Community Radio Machine-Readable Using Speech Recognition Technology", UN Global Pulse (blog), 2016: www.unglobalpulse.org/project/making-ugandan-community-radio-machine-readable-using-speech-recognition-technology/.
14   Anthony Cuthbertson, "Indian police trace 3,000 missing children in just four days using facial recognition technology", The Independent, 24 April 2018: www.independent.co.uk/tech/india-police-missing-children-facial-recognition-tech-trace-find-reunite-a8320406.html; see also: PTI, "Delhi: facial recognition system helps trace 3,000 missing children in 4 days", The Times of India, 22 April 2018: https://timesofindia.indiatimes.com/city/delhi/delhi-facial-recognition-system-helps-trace-3000-missing-children-in-4-days/articleshow/63870129.cms. For the system's official website, see: https://trackthemissingchild.gov.in/trackchild/index.php/index.php.

- **Tracking attacks on civilians and human rights violations.** Amnesty International's Decode the Difference project[15] recruited volunteers to compare images of the same location at different time periods to identify damaged buildings, which could potentially demonstrate systematic attacks against civilians. In the future, the data could be used to train Machine Learning tools to analyse the images, thereby speeding up the process and increasing capacity.
- **Preventing and diagnosing disease.** "Since the 1990s, AI has been used to diagnose various types of diseases, such as cancer, multiple sclerosis, pancreatic disease and diabetes."[16] More recently, Microsoft's Project Premonition was developed to detect pathogens before they cause outbreaks. The project deploys robots that aim to monitor the presence of mosquitoes in an area, make predictions about their distribution and capture targeted species. Through Machine Learning techniques, the captured mosquitoes are searched for pathogens they may carry from animals they have bitten.[17]

When dealing with Artificial Intelligence-based projects, concerns may also be raised when applying basic data protection principles[18] in this context. Artificial Intelligence-based profiling and hidden nudging practices challenge the idea of freedom of choice based on the notion of Data Subjects' control over their information, and the widespread complexity and obscurity of Artificial Intelligence algorithms hamper the chances of obtaining real informed Consent and transparency requirements. Similar challenges relate to another key principle, data minimization, as big data and Machine Learning Artificial Intelligence algorithms rely on large amounts of data to produce useful results.[19]

---

15   Amnesty International, "Amnesty Decoders | Join Decode Surveillance NYC", Amnesty International, accessed 17 March 2022: https://decoders.amnesty.org.
16   Heather M. Roff, "Advancing Human Security through Artificial Intelligence", Chatham House – International Affairs Think Tank, 11 May 2017, 5: www.chathamhouse.org/2017/05/advancing-human-security-through-artificial-intelligence.
17   Microsoft, "Microsoft Premonition", Microsoft Research (blog), accessed 21 March 2022: www.microsoft.com/en-us/research/product/microsoft-premonition/.
18   See Chapter 2: Basic principles of data protection.
19   See Council of Europe (CoE), *Guidelines on Artificial Intelligence and data protection | T-PD(2019)01*, Guideline (Strasbourg: Consultative Committee of the Convention for the Protection of Individuals with regard to Automatic Processing of Personal Data (Convention 108), 25 January 2019): rm.coe.int/guidelines-on-artificial-intelligence-and-data-protection/168091f9d8; Council of Europe (CoE), *Guidelines on the protection of individuals with regard to the processing of personal data in a world of Big Data | T-PD(2017)01* (Strasbourg: Consultative Committee of the Convention for the Protection of Individuals with regard to Automatic Processing of Personal Data (Convention 108), 23 January 2017): rm.coe.int/CoERMPublicCommonSearchServices/DisplayDCTMContent?documentId = 09000016806ebe7a. See also Alessandro Mantelero, *Beyond Data Human Rights, Ethical and Social Impact Assessment in AI*, 1st ed., Information Technology and Law Series, Springer, The Hague, 2022), chap. 1.

Before considering the specific issues related to Artificial Intelligence and large-scale data Processing, several specificities relating to data protection should be highlighted at the outset of this analysis:
- **Data sources.** First of all, it is important to identify the source of data. Much Artificial Intelligence-based data Processing undertaken by Humanitarian Organizations is based on publicly available data, such as information from government agencies or public records, social media networks, census data and other publicly available demographic and population surveys. In other cases, Humanitarian Organizations may partner with private enterprises such as telecommunications or infrastructure companies, Internet services, health-care providers or other commercial organizations to improve the humanitarian and disaster response.
- **Emergency response.** The outputs from Artificial Intelligence-ased data Processing can provide important benefits to Humanitarian Organizations. However, they may not always be used for an ongoing emergency or to address the vital interests of the people concerned: the exceptional, "outlier" circumstances where Humanitarian Organizations operate may become a limitation in predictive Machine Learning algorithms. Historical data sets and models in data-driven analyses, developed outside emergencies might find themselves scarcely able to cope due to outliers created in the extremely changeable circumstances of emergencies. Thus, it is important to consider Artificial Intelligence derived uniquely from Humanitarian Data since these models would integrate information learned during an emergency to support administrative work or to contribute to strategies to improve the response to future emergencies.
- **Accuracy.** Given the data-driven nature of Artificial Intelligence, the quality of the data used to train it significantly impacts both the development of the models and their performance. Here it is therefore crucial to verify that data used for training and running the Artificial Intelligence models are representative and accurate and do not contain any bias.[20]
- **Automated decisions.** Although in emergency situations automation can facilitate timely responses, it is important to be aware of the risks associated with a lack of human intervention and oversight, including in terms of ability to fully understand the complexity of the contextual background to prevent incorrect insights and decisions.
- **Reuse of data for other purposes.** The availability of large data sets often raises questions about the use of collected data for purposes other than those for which they were collected. This poses questions under Data Protection laws, which

---

[20] UN Global Pulse and Leiden University, "Big Data for Development and Humanitarian Action: Towards Responsible Governance", Global Pulse Privacy Advisory Group Meetings 2015–2016, December 2016: www.unglobalpulse.org/document/big-data-for-development-and-humanitarian-action-towards-responsible-governance. See also Mireille Hildebrandt, "The issue of bias: The framing powers of machine learning", in *Machine We Trust: Perspectives on Dependable AI*, ed. Marcello Pelillo and Teresa Scantamburlo, The MIT Press, Cambridge, MA, 2021, 44–59: https://dx.doi.org/10.2139/ssrn.3497597.

generally require that personal data be collected for specific purposes and processed for such purposes or for compatible purposes only, and not reused for other purposes without the Consent of the person concerned or another legal basis (see Section 17.2.1 – Legal bases for Personal Data Processing).

- **The sensitivity of data output created by Personal Data Processing in humanitarian situations.** It is important to understand that publicly available data, such as data on social media networks, mobility data or data generated by mobile phone connections, may generally be considered non-Sensitive Data but may generate Sensitive Data in different contests and mainly in a humanitarian situation. This can occur when the Processing of non-Sensitive Data enables the profiling of individuals that could be subjected to discrimination or repression, such as, for example, potential victims, people affiliated with a particular group in a situation of violence, or persons suffering from a particular illness. In these cases, specific computing techniques, such as *differential privacy*,[21] can be a valuable way to protect individual and group privacy while allowing access to data.[22]
- **Anonymization.** There may be doubts about the effectiveness of Anonymization of Personal Data and the possibility of Reidentification in Artificial Intelligence-based operations, regardless of whether for humanitarian or other purposes. Again, privacy-enhancing technologies, such as *synthetic data*,[23] can complement Anonymization attempts to provide higher protection and prevent Reidentification.[24]
- **Regulatory fragmentation.** While many states have enacted data protection laws and many Humanitarian Organizations have already implemented data protection policies and guidelines, the question of how specifically data and Artificial Intelligence-based data Processing are regulated across borders in times of humanitarian crises remains open.[25]

It is important to stress that when Artificial Intelligence is used for Humanitarian Action, the implications for individuals may be much more serious than in other

---

21 Cynthia Dwork, "Differential Privacy", in Henk C. A. van Tilborg and Sushil Jajodia (eds), *Encyclopedia of Cryptography and Security*, Springer US, Boston, MA, 2011, 338–340: https://doi.org/10.1007/978-1-4419-5906-5_752.

22 Data smoothing means removing noise from a data set so that important patterns stand out.

23 Synthetic data is information generated by algorithms that is not real-world data but reflects real-world data, mathematically or statistically. See European Data Protection Supervisor (EDPS), "IPEN Webinar 2021 – 'Synthetic Data: What Use Cases as a Privacy Enhancing Technology?'", EDPS, 16 June 2021: www.edps.europa.eu/data-protection/our-work/ipen/ipen-webinar-2021-synthetic-data-what-use-cases-privacy-enhancing_en.

24 Prokopios Drogkaris and Monika Adamczyk (eds.), *Data Protection Engineering – From Theory to Practice*, European Union Agency for Cybersecurity (ENISA), 27 January 2022: www.enisa.europa.eu/publications/data-protection-engineering.

25 UN Global Pulse and Leiden University, *Big Data for Development and Humanitarian Action*, 7–9. See also Júlia Zomignani Barboza, Lina Jasmontaitė-Zaniewicz and Laurence Diver, "Aid and AI: The challenge of reconciling humanitarian principles and data protection", in *Privacy and Identity Management. Data for Better Living: AI and Privacy*, IFIP International Summer School on Privacy and Identity Management, Springer, Cham, 2020, 161–176: https://doi.org/10.1007/978-3-030-42504-3_11.

contexts. Humanitarian Organizations should therefore consider whether any data they release or information they provide using data-intensive Artificial Intelligence systems can be used, even in an aggregated form, to target the people they seek to protect. Furthermore, information on "invisible populations" can be extracted indirectly using data on different groups related to them, with potential implications in terms of discrimination or actions against minorities, even more so in case of conflicts. It is important, therefore, always to keep in mind the "big picture" of the potential implications of using data-intensive Artificial Intelligence systems in a context characterized by reduced protection systems and heightened vulnerabilities.

EXAMPLE:
Authorities might use public or published findings based on the extraction and analysis of tweets and other material on social media networks to locate the epicentre and flows of public demonstrations, and to avoid loss of human life. However, these same findings might then be used by the same authorities to identify individuals who took part in such public demonstrations (or who did not), which can have severe consequences for the identified groups of individuals.

Artificial Intelligence may involve Processing scenarios such as the following:

EXAMPLE 1: the extraction and analysis of public communications through social media, search engines or telecommunications services, as well as news sources. This can help demonstrate how methods including sentiment analysis, topic classification and network analysis can be used to support public health workers and communication campaigns.
EXAMPLE 2: the development of interactive data visualization tools during a humanitarian incident. This can help demonstrate how communications signals or satellite data could support emergency response management.
EXAMPLE 3: Analysis of messages received through a Humanitarian Organization's citizen reporting platform.
EXAMPLE 4: Analysis of social media, mobile phone network metadata and credit card data to identify individuals likely to be at risk of enforced disappearance or to locate persons unaccounted for.

Focusing on the large-scale data sets potentially used by Artificial Intelligence, the following may be relevant:
- **accessible data sets**: i.e. data sets that are already publicly available, such as public records released by governments or information people have intentionally made public in the media or on the Internet, including through social media;
- **data sets held by Humanitarian Organizations**: e.g. lists of distribution beneficiaries, patients, protected individuals, individuals reporting violations of international humanitarian law/human rights;

- **data sets held by private Third Parties**: e.g. mobile telecommunications, Internet service, banking and financial providers, financial transactions data, remote sensor data, whether aggregated/pseudonymized or not;
- **a combination or aggregation of data sets** of Humanitarian Organizations, authorities and/or corporate entities (including the organizations mentioned above).

Humanitarian Organizations may play the following roles in data Processing:
- process data held for the purposes of their respective organizations, in their capacity as Data Controllers or Joint Controllers (when determining the purposes and means of Processing jointly with other Humanitarian Organizations, public authorities and/or commercial entities);
- employ Third Parties who process data on behalf of the organization (e.g. commercial entities that use Artificial Intelligence for predictive analyses on the data held by the Humanitarian Organization and for the purposes of this organization) and act as Data Processors;
- require commercial entities that are and remain the Data Controller to carry out analyses on data for humanitarian purposes and to provide conclusions/findings to the Humanitarian Organization. Such conclusions may relate to aggregated/pseudonymized data, or data identifying individuals of possible relevance to Humanitarian Action.

17.1.3 CHALLENGES AND RISKS OF USING ARTIFICIAL INTELLIGENCE

Despite their potential, Artificial Intelligence applications carry challenges and risks. Besides data protection concerns,[26] all the above-mentioned use cases also present practical implementation challenges. For example, Artificial Intelligence-based image recognition software used to identify missing people may provide too many false positives. These false matches could not only create confusion among case workers, but also potentially give false hope to families. Other systems could be more accurate but potentially miss positive matches (known as false negatives). While false negatives may not be much of an issue in commercial applications, they can have important consequences in the humanitarian sector. If an organization misidentifies a child who has lost contact with their parents, this can cause harm to the entire family.

Artificial Intelligence can also pose risks to affected people. For instance, if Artificial Intelligence is used to identify the right target population for a particular humanitarian programme, and the solution does not make a correct identification, people who

---

26 See also Anne Meuwese, "Regulating algorithmic decision-making one case at the time: A note on the Dutch 'SyRI' judgment", *European Review of Digital Administration & Law*, Vol. 1, No. 1, 2020, pp. 209–211.

would otherwise be entitled to participate in the programme could be excluded. This has happened in practice in Sweden, where thousands of unemployed people were wrongly denied benefits by a government system that used Artificial Intelligence.[27]

Since most Humanitarian Organizations will acquire off-the-shelf solutions rather than developing their own models, there is a not-insignificant risk that algorithms could deliver unexpected or unreasonable results. This also highlights the risk of decontextualization when choosing off-the-shelf Artificial Intelligence models – where models originally used for one purpose are then reused in a different context and for a different purpose[28] – or when using models trained on historical data from a different population.[29]

In addition, vendor lock-in poses a risk because switching solutions may be costly. Organizations could also be targeted by commercial ventures that are primarily interested in gaining access to and exploiting the large data sets they hold, sometimes at great risk to the individuals and communities to whom the data belong.

Bias poses another risk to the effectiveness of Artificial Intelligence, especially in specific humanitarian contexts where it is important to use data sets fit for the intended goal. As with many other technologies, the concept of "garbage in, garbage out"[30] also applies to Artificial Intelligence, and using unfit, inaccurate or irrelevant data may affect the accuracy of the solution. This is particularly challenging for a Humanitarian Organization, as off-the-shelf algorithms will extremely rarely fit their contexts. For instance, if a Humanitarian Organization wants to develop facial recognition software to help find missing people, the training data sets will need to be sufficiently broad to ensure that racial variations in physical features are integrated to maximize the precision of the matching function.

---

[27] Tom Willis, "Sweden: Rogue Algorithm Stops Welfare Payments for up to 70,000 Unemployed", AlgorithmWatch, 25 February 2019: https://algorithmwatch.org/en/rogue-algorithm-in-sweden-stops-welfare-payments.

[28] See Robyn Caplan et al., "Algorithmic Accountability: A Primer", Data & Society, 18 April 2018, 7: https://datasociety.net/library/algorithmic-accountability-a-primer, citing the case of the PredPol algorithm, originally designed to predict earthquakes and later used to identify crime hotspots and assign police.

[29] See Council of Europe (CoE), *Guidelines on Artificial Intelligence and data protection | T-PD(2019)01*. See also Council of Europe (CoE), *Artificial Intelligence and Data Protection: Challenges and Possible Remedies | T-PD(2018)09Rev*, report on Artificial Intelligence (Strasbourg: Consultative Committee of the Convention for the Protection of Individuals with regard to Automatic Processing of Personal Data (Convention 108), 25 January 2019): https://rm.coe.int/artificial-intelligence-and-data-protection-challenges-and-possible-re/168091f8a6.

[30] According to the free online dictionary of computing (http://foldoc.org), the concept of garbage in, garbage out relates to the fact that "computers, unlike humans, will unquestioningly process nonsensical input data and produce nonsensical output". The term is also used to refer to "failures in human decision-making due to faulty, incomplete, or imprecise data".

Processing Personal Data using Artificial Intelligence also presents major challenges for Personal Data protection. When Processing large data sets for purposes other than those for which they were collected, there is a risk of violating basic notions of data protection, including purpose limitation, data minimization or data retention (i.e. keeping data only as long as necessary to fulfil the purposes of data collection).[31] In essence, large-scale data analysis thrives in open and unrestricted Processing environments while, on the other hand, Personal Data protection favours limited and well-defined Processing. Data protection thus needs to be applied in an innovative way to these technologies.[32]

The fundamental principles of data protection must be respected while performing Artificial Intelligence-based data Processing. These principles include (i) fairness and lawfulness of the Processing; (ii) transparency; (iii) purpose limitation; (iv) data minimization; (v) data quality. While some of these principles are compatible with the nature of Artificial Intelligence applications, others raise questions or conflicts.[33] Consequently, Humanitarian Organizations must be particularly careful when applying them in practice.[34]

17.2 APPLICATION OF BASIC DATA PROTECTION PRINCIPLES

Solutions that integrate or use Artificial Intelligence process large amounts of data – both personal and non-personal – in order to function properly. In this regard, it is crucial to consider that these applications can infer Personal Data from non-personal information or anonymized data. This is because Artificial Intelligence solutions are increasingly capable "of linking data or recognizing patterns of data [that] may render non-personal data identifiable".[35] This means that Artificial Intelligence can also reidentify data provided, for example, by a variety of sensors and smart devices.

---

31 See Chapter 2 – Basic principles of data protection. See also: Council of Europe (CoE), *Artificial Intelligence and Data Protection: Challenges and Possible Remedies* | T-PD(2018)09Rev.

32 See Council of Europe (CoE), *Guidelines on the protection of individuals with regard to the processing of personal data in a world of Big Data* | T-PD(2017)01; Alessandro Mantelero, "Regulating Big Data: The guidelines of the Council of Europe in the context of the European Data Protection Framework", *Computer Law & Security Review*, Vol. 33, No. 5, October 2017, pp. 584–602: www.sciencedirect.com/science/article/abs/pii/S0267364917301644?via%3Dihub; UN Global Pulse, *Guidance note on Big Data for achievement of the 2030 Agenda*, 19 August 2019: www.unglobalpulse .org/policy/privacy-and-data-protection-principles; European Data Protection Supervisor (EDPS), *Opinion 7/2015: Meeting the Challenges of Big Data*, Opinion, EDPS, Brussels, 19 November 2015, 4: www.edps.europa.eu/data-protection/our-work/publications/opinions/meeting-challenges-big-data_en.

33 See also Mantelero, *Beyond Data Human Rights, Ethical and Social Impact Assessment in AI*, chap. 1.

34 The discussion on data protection in this chapter builds on the principles set out in Part I and examines them in greater detail.

35 Centre for Information Policy Leadership, *Artificial Intelligence and Data Protection in Tension*, Artificial Intelligence and Data Protection: Delivering Sustainable AI Accountability in Practice,

An assessment of the risks of Reidentification should therefore be carried out and, when possible, the Data Subject or relevant stakeholders be informed of the results of this assessment. If there is a strong possibility of Reidentification, the analysis should not be performed, or the methodology should be adjusted.

For these reasons, the use of Anonymization as an "exit strategy" with respect to data protection obligations is not always effective. Moreover, anonymous, or anonymized data may also present technical challenges as the capacity to process may be hindered during Processing.

In addition, the accuracy of Artificial Intelligence outputs when Processing anonymized or aggregated data should be assessed. The methods and level of Anonymization or aggregation should therefore be carefully selected to minimize not only the risks of Reidentification but also to ensure that the data maintain an adequate level of quality to achieve credible results.

17.2.1 LEGAL BASES FOR PERSONAL DATA PROCESSING

When carrying out Artificial Intelligence-driven Processing operations, Humanitarian Organizations may rely on one or more of the following legal bases:[36]
- the vital interest of the Data Subject or of another person;
- the public interest, in particular based on an Organization's mandate under national or international law;
- the informed Consent of the Data Subject;
- a legitimate interest of the organization;
- the performance of a contract;
- compliance with a legal obligation.

However, the specific nature of Artificial Intelligence applications and related data Processing poses some challenges to this traditional framework, mainly in the case of individual Consent to data Processing and secondary use of collected data (i.e. data originally collected for a specific purpose and then reused for a different one, as is often the case in Artificial Intelligence given the large-scale data sets needed).

As pointed out in literature, the effectiveness of Data Subjects' Consent as a legal basis has been weakened by lengthy and technical data Processing notices, social and technical lock-ins, obscure interface design, and lack of awareness on the part of the Data Subject.[37] These developments are even more relevant in the context of

---

10 October 2018, 11: www.informationpolicycentre.com/uploads/5/7/1/0/57104281/cipl_ai_first_report_-_artificial_intelligence_and_data_protection_in_te....pdf.

36 See Chapter 3: Legal bases for Personal Data Processing.
37 For a broader analysis and refences see Alessandro Mantelero, "The future of consumer data protection in the E.U. Re-thinking the 'notice and consent' paradigm in the new era of predictive analytics",

Humanitarian Action, when Data Subjects already experience imbalances of power and other contextual needs that hamper their effective self-determination.

Moreover, Artificial Intelligence-based profiling and hidden nudging practices challenge both the idea of freedom of choice based on contractual agreement and the notion of Data Subjects' control over their personal information. Finally, the frequent complexity and obscurity of Artificial Intelligence algorithms hamper the possibilities of obtaining truly informed Consent.

Legal scholars have addressed these issues by emphasizing the role of transparency,[38] risk assessment[39] and more flexible forms of Consent, such as broad Consent[40] or dynamic Consent.[41] Although none of these solutions solve the problems affecting individual Consent, in certain contexts they may, whether alone or combined, reinforce self-determination.

Notwithstanding these unresolved critical issues in terms of theoretical framework and regulatory instruments, Consent can be a legitimate ground for the Processing data collected by a Humanitarian Organization, but also for the reuse of data collected by Third Parties for different purposes. An example in this sense is the Data Analytics offered by social media networks or mobile phone operators to assist Humanitarian Organizations which could, in some cases, be based on Consent. In such cases, the social media platform or mobile operator in question can inform Data Subjects of the intended Processing by means of a pop-up window or text message with the relevant information and provide a Consent request.

Computer Law & Security Review, Vol. 30, No. 6, 1 December 2014, pp. 643–660: https://doi.org/10.1016/j.clsr.2014.09.004.

38 See e.g.: Lilian Edwards and Michael Veale, "Slave to the algorithm: Why a right to an explanation is probably not the remedy you are looking for", *Duke Law & Technology Review*, 16, 2018 2017, pp. 18-84; Andrew Selbst and Julia Powles, "'Meaningful information' and the right to explanation", *International Data Privacy Law*, Vol. 7, No. 4, 19 December 2017, pp. 233-242: doi.org/10.1093/idpl/ipx022: https://proceedings.mlr.press/v81/selbst18a.html; Sandra Wachter, Brent Mittelstadt and Luciano Floridi, "Why a right to explanation of automated decision-making does not exist in the General Data Protection Regulation", *International Data Privacy Law*, Vol. 7, No. 2, 1 May 2017, pp. 76-99: https://doi.org/10.1093/idpl/ipx005.

39 See Council of Europe (CoE), *Guidelines on the protection of individuals with regard to the processing of personal data in a world of Big Data* | T-PD(2017)01; Mantelero, "Regulating Big Data:The guidelines of the Council of Europe in the Context of the European Data Protection Framework"; UN Global Pulse, *Guidance note on Big Data for achievement of the 2030 Agenda*; European Data Protection Supervisor (EDPS), *Opinion 7/2015: Meeting the Challenges of Big Data*.

40 Mark Sheehan, "Can broad consent be informed consent?", *Public Health Ethics*, Vol. 4, No. 3, 1 November 2011, pp. 226–235: https://doi.org/10.1093/phe/phr020.

41 Jane Kaye et al., "Dynamic consent: A patient interface for twenty-first century research networks", *European Journal of Human Genetics*, Vol. 23, No. 2, February 2015, pp. 141–146: doi.org/10.1038/ejhg.2014.71.

In order to ensure that the Data Subject receives adequate information before giving Consent, such information should include the outcome of the DPIA (if carried out)[42] and could also be provided via an interface that simulates the effects of the use of data and their potential impact on the Data Subject, in a learn-from-experience approach.[43] Data Controllers should provide Data Subjects with easy and user-friendly technical ways to withdraw their Consent and react to data Processing incompatible with the initial purposes.[44]

It is important to assess the validity of Consent even when adequate information has been provided to the Data Subjects at the time of collection and the purpose of Further Processing is compatible. This assessment should take into account the level of literacy of the Data Subject as well as the risks and harms to the Data Subjects for the Processing of their data.[45]

Without the Consent of the Data Subject, Personal Data can be processed in the vital interest of the Data Subject or of another person, i.e. where data Processing is necessary in order to protect an interest essential in the life, integrity, health, dignity and safety of the Data Subject or that of another person or group of people. Furthermore, additional legal bases, such as public interest, the legitimate interest of the organization and performance of a contract or compliance with a legal obligation may also be grounds for data Processing.

Regarding the use of vital interest as a legal basis for emergency work of Humanitarian Organizations in armed conflicts and other situations of violence, there are several cases where the Processing of data by Humanitarian Organizations is presumed to be in the vital interest of the Data Subject or another person (e.g. if data are processed in cases of Sought Persons, or if there are imminent threats against the physical and mental integrity of the persons concerned). However, the condition of vital interest may not be met when data Processing is carried out in a non-emergency situation, for instance for administrative purposes.

Humanitarian Organizations should carefully consider the existence of important public interests, which are sufficiently closely linked to Artificial Intelligence-based operations envisaged, to be used as a legal basis for Processing Personal Data. The public interest could be the appropriate legal basis for data Processing where a mandate to carry out a Humanitarian Action is established in national, regional or

---

[42] See Section 17.6: Data Protection Impact Assessment and Human Rights Impact Assessment.
[43] Council of Europe (CoE), *Guidelines on the protection of individuals with regard to the processing of personal data in a world of Big Data* | T-PD(2017)01.
[44] Ibid.
[45] UN Global Pulse, "Tools: Risks, Harms and Benefits Assessment", updated 2020: www.unglobalpulse.org/policy/risk-assessment.

international law and where no Consent was obtained and no emergency exists that could invoke vital interest as a legal basis.

Humanitarian Organizations should be aware that public interest as a legal basis for Personal Data Processing is not transferable, because it is specific to the Organization's mandate under national or international law. The conditions (if any) under which a Third Party may undertake the data analysis, including using Artificial Intelligence, on behalf of the Organization or that are applicable to International Data Sharing need to be examined separately.

Humanitarian Organizations may also process Personal Data where this is in their legitimate interest, provided that this interest is not overridden by the fundamental rights and freedoms of the Data Subject. Such legitimate interests may include Processing necessary to make their operations more effective and efficient, including facilitating logistics to enable pre-deployment of aid and staff in anticipation of Humanitarian Emergencies, where such insights could be obtained from data analysis. The use of Artificial Intelligence for administrative purposes may also fall under this category.

17.2.2 PURPOSE LIMITATION AND FURTHER PROCESSING

One of the most significant challenges in using Artificial Intelligence for humanitarian purposes is that Artificial Intelligence operations are very likely to be run on existing data sets, previously collected by the Humanitarian Organization or by Third Parties for a different purpose. The key question is, therefore, to determine whether the envisaged analysis is compatible with the original purpose of collection. If so, Artificial Intelligence operations can be carried out under the existing legal basis. If not, a new legal basis for Further Processing must be found.

In addition, applying the purpose limitation principle[46] to Artificial Intelligence may be challenging because these technologies have the capacity to process data in ways that were not originally planned, and are used to identify new patterns and inferences which are, by their nature, unknown and unexpected.

EXAMPLE:
In 2012, researchers found that when Artificial Intelligence algorithms analysed a person's Facebook "likes", with no further information from that person, the solutions could "automatically and accurately predict a range of highly sensitive personal attributes including: sexual orientation, ethnicity, religious and political views,

---

46   See Section 2.5.2 – The purpose limitation principle.

personality traits, intelligence, happiness, use of addictive substances, parental separation, age, and gender".[47] More specifically, the solution correctly discriminated "between homosexual and heterosexual men in 88% of cases, African Americans and Caucasian Americans in 95% of cases, and between Democrat and Republican in 85% of cases".[48] In this particular case, the solution was being asked to make these correlations. Yet in other situations, Artificial Intelligence solutions may draw such inferences on their own and reveal sensitive information about a person even when that was not the developer's intention.

As discussed in Chapter 2: Basic principles of data protection, at the time of collecting data the Humanitarian Organization concerned must determine and set out the specific purpose(s) for which data are processed. The specific purpose(s) should be explicit and legitimate and could include anything from restoring family links, to protecting individuals in detention, forensic activities or protecting water and habitat. The purpose of any planned analytics should be specified at the outset of data collection, and when new purposes are added this must be consistent with the data protection requirements in terms of compatible purposes and legal grounds.

Artificial Intelligence – in a similar way to big data[49] – represents a challenge for the application of the purpose limitation principle. On the one hand, analytics make it hard to identify the specific purpose of data Processing at the time of data collection and, on the other hand, Machine Learning algorithms (whose purposes are necessarily specified) may not anticipate and explain how these purposes are to be achieved. In both cases therefore transparency on the purpose and methods of data Processing may remain limited.

In addition, the purpose limitation principle should also be considered with regard to the data sets used and potential unwanted outcomes. If it is foreseen that the solution may process Personal Data in ways that are incompatible with the defined purpose or that it will reveal information or make predictions that are not desired, these factors should be taken into account when choosing the training data set and developing the model.

In these large-scale data-intensive applications, it is common to carry out Processing operations that require the data to be processed for purposes other than those for which they were initially collected. In this case of secondary use of data,

---

47 Michal Kosinski, David Stillwell and Thore Graepel, "Private traits and attributes are predictable from digital records of human behavior", *Proceedings of the National Academy of Sciences*, Vol. 110, No. 15, 11 March 2013, p. 1: https://doi.org/10.1073/pnas.1218772110.
48 Ibid.
49 See also The Norwegian Data Protection Authority, *Artificial Intelligence and Privacy*.

Humanitarian Organizations may therefore assess whether Further Processing is compatible with the purposes initially specified at the time of data collection, including where the Processing is necessary for historical, statistical or scientific purposes.[50]

In order to establish whether these operations can be considered Further Processing that is compatible with the purpose for which the data were initially collected, attention should be given to the following factors:
- any link between the purposes for which the data were collected and the purposes of the intended Further Processing;
- the situation in which the Personal Data were collected and, in particular, the relationship between Data Subjects and the Data Controller, and possible expectations of the Data Subjects;
- the nature of the Personal Data;
- the possible consequences of the intended Further Processing for Data Subjects;
- the existence of appropriate safeguards.

Based on these factors, it is possible that in several cases different humanitarian purposes are linked and considered compatible with each other. Compatibility depends on the circumstances of the case and Further Processing would not be compatible if new risks arise, or if the risks for the Data Subject outweigh the benefits of Further Processing. Further Processing would also not be compatible where Processing is potentially detrimental to the interests of the Data Subject or his/her family, in particular when there is a risk that the Processing might threaten their life, integrity, dignity, psychological or physical safety, freedom or reputation. This includes consequences such as harassment or persecution by authorities or Third Parties, judicial prosecution, social and private problems, restriction of freedom, and psychological suffering.

It should also be highlighted that some data protection regulations, such as the EU GDPR, pose restrictions to secondary uses of Personal Data but adopt specific derogations for public interest purposes, which include humanitarian purposes. In cases, where Third Party data are processed for purposes that go beyond those for which they were originally collected due to the humanitarian value in the use of the data sets, humanitarian purposes should not expose the Data Subjects to new risks or harm.

EXAMPLE 1: Data sets collected by a Humanitarian Organization while dealing with an incident, for instance in order to distribute aid, may be used at a later stage for the

---

50 See Subsection 2.5.2.1 – Further Processing.

purpose of understanding patterns of displacement and pre-deploying aid in subsequent Humanitarian Emergencies.

EXAMPLE 2: Data sets collected by a telecommunications provider in the course of providing its services to its subscribers may not be used without these subscribers' Consent in Data Analytics Processing by Humanitarian Organizations, if it can result in such individuals being profiled as potential bearers of a disease, with consequent restrictions on movement imposed by authorities. In these cases, Humanitarian Organizations and their Third Party counterparts should consider whether mitigating measures, such as data aggregation, would be sufficient to remove the risk identified.

17.2.3 FAIR AND LAWFUL PROCESSING

As is always the case with Personal Data Processing, if Personal Data will be processed within the Artificial Intelligence solution or as part of its training, a lawful process requires a legitimate legal basis for the Processing to take place. Chapter 3: Legal bases for Personal Data Processing, outlines different legal grounds and points out the limitations of using Consent as a legal basis in Humanitarian Action. Limitations to the use of Consent, in particular the possibility of withdrawing it, are also relevant to the development and improvement of Artificial Intelligence solutions.[51]

When a Humanitarian Organization develops an Artificial Intelligence-based solution, it should identify an appropriate legal basis to process Personal Data to train the algorithm to achieve a clearly defined purpose. A legal basis should also be defined for the Processing of new Personal Data to fulfil the intended objective once the system has been trained. Lastly, the organization should also identify a legal basis for Processing data to improve the model, in the case of dynamic models.

With dynamic models, including off-the-shelf solutions developed by technology companies, it is important to remember that all data fed into the system during development and application will be used to improve it. This may pose further challenges to the use of Consent, since beneficiaries might agree to having their Personal Data processed for a particular humanitarian purpose, but may not expect it to be used for the development of the Artificial Intelligence solution.[52] In such cases, if the identified legal basis for Processing is Consent, the Data Subjects should be informed, in an easy-to-understand manner, of the reasons why their data are requested, what they will be used for, and how they will influence the solution. They should also be informed of potential risks, such as Reidentification by the solution or the fact that their data could be accessed during a malicious attack.

---

51 See also above Section 17.2.1 – Legal bases for Personal Data Processing.
52 Future of Privacy Forum, *The Privacy Expert's Guide to Artificial Intelligence and Machine Learning*, 8.

In light of the above, Consent may not always be an appropriate legal basis for the use of Artificial Intelligence in the humanitarian sector. While the delivery of aid or life-saving services may mean that vital interest[53] or public interest[54] can be considered legitimate legal bases to justify the Processing of Personal Data, the development of Artificial Intelligence solutions sometimes may not. To determine whether the improvement of Artificial Intelligence solutions is acceptable under the chosen legal basis, an organization should consider whether the Further Processing for the improvement of the solution is compatible with the initial purpose for which it collected the Personal Data.

The principle of fairness[55] requires that all Processing activities respect Data Subjects' interests, and that Data Controllers take action to prevent arbitrary discrimination against individuals.[56] The issue of discriminatory bias in Artificial Intelligence is widely recognized and debated.[57]

EXAMPLE:
In a well-known example, an Artificial Intelligence solution was developed in the United States to predict reoffending rates in criminal cases, in order to help judges decide whether or not to grant bail to convicted offenders. The solution incorrectly rated black defendants as being almost twice as likely to reoffend as white defendants.[58]

To minimize the risk of discriminatory bias, it is recommended that Artificial Intelligence developers "adopt a human rights by-design approach and avoid any potential biases, including unintentional or hidden, and the risk of discrimination or other adverse impacts on the human rights and fundamental freedoms of data subjects".[59]

Bias in Artificial Intelligence solutions may stem from the use of biased data sets as training data, from systemic biases in society, or even from developers deciding

---

53 See Section 3.3 – Vital interest.
54 See Section 3.4 – Important grounds of public interest.
55 See Section 2.5.1 – The principle of the fairness and lawfulness of Processing.
56 The Norwegian Data Protection Authority, *Artificial Intelligence and Privacy*, 16.
57 Sandra Wachter, Brent Mittelstadt and Chris Russell, "Why fairness cannot be automated: Bridging the gap between EU non-discrimination law and AI", *Computer Law & Security Review*, Vol. 41 (2021), 105567.
58 Julia Angwin et al., "Machine Bias", ProPublica, 23 May 2016: www.propublica.org/article/machine-bias-risk-assessments-in-criminal-sentencing?token=p-v0T1xjfOJ8jrJHzc08UxDKSQrKgWJk.
59 Council of Europe (CoE), *Artificial Intelligence and Data Protection: Challenges and Possible Remedies* | T-PD(2018)09Rev, 2.

which features to assign more value to in each data set. Moreover, when there are historical biases in society, it may be difficult to find unbiased data to train Artificial Intelligence or it is necessary to "clean" or normalize the data sets or adopt alternative solutions such as debiased synthetic data.

More generally, to prevent bias, a model must be trained with relevant and correct data and must also learn which features to emphasize. Depending on the case, when there is a risk of arbitrary discrimination, information related to racial or ethnic origin, political opinion, religious and philosophical beliefs, sexual orientation or any other information that could be grounds for discrimination may not be processed or may be protected in a way that does not emphasize them leading to discrimination.[60]

The training data must also be fit for the purpose of the Artificial Intelligence solution. In other words, the selected data must be relevant to the task, and constant checks and updates will be required to identify inaccurate and/or corrupt data and remove them from the training data set. New data may also be added to avoid bias. It is therefore important that Humanitarian Organizations work with developers to ensure that the solution they acquire or develop is applicable or suited to the organization's needs in a particular context.

The fact that Artificial Intelligence models should not emphasize such categories of data does not mean, however, that suppressing them from the data set will necessarily eliminate the risk of bias. The system could correlate other features such as race or gender, and the model may learn to be biased based on those correlated features, which are known in this context as "proxies".[61] Moreover, since the main discriminatory feature has been removed from the data set, it might be more difficult to detect and correct the bias.

EXAMPLE:
A separate study looking at the US predictive solution discussed earlier found in almost 70 per cent of cases that the algorithm made a correct reoffending prediction despite its clear bias. In this second study, however, race was not included in the data set, highlighting "the challenge of finding a model that doesn't create a proxy for race (or other eliminated factor) – such as poverty, joblessness, and social marginalization".[62]

---

60 The Norwegian Data Protection Authority, *Artificial Intelligence and Privacy*, 16.
61 Centre for Information Policy Leadership, *Artificial Intelligence and Data Protection in Tension*, 14.
62 Future of Privacy Forum, *The Privacy Expert's Guide to Artificial Intelligence and Machine Learning*, 15.

For this reason, when choosing the training data set, an Artificial Intelligence developer – whether acting as an independent Data Controller, a Data Processor, or a joint Controller with a Humanitarian Organization – needs to assess the quality, nature and origin of the Personal Data used, and consider the potential risks to individuals and groups of using decontextualized data to create decontextualized models.[63] One way to achieve this is for Data Controllers to include, in the continuous DPIA process (see Section 17.2 – Application of basic data protection principles), "frequent assessments on the datasets they process to check for any bias", and to "develop ways to address any prejudicial elements, including any over-reliance on correlations".[64] Not taking such measures has both legal and ethical implications.

In addition, Artificial Intelligence deals with possible correlations and therefore raises concerns about data selection, representation and population estimates. Researchers should take care to understand the representativeness of the data used and report potential biases. Moreover, policymakers should be aware of potential biases and account for them when making decisions, as inaccurate and biased data could lead to harmful and unfair policy decisions.

Finally, we could also identify a procedural component of fairness, requiring that any employees, contractors or other parties involved in data Processing undergo training to educate them about these risks and the steps to be taken to mitigate them.

17.2.4 TRANSPARENCY

Alongside fairness, transparency is another crucial aspect of data protection. According to this principle, the Processing of Personal Data must be transparent[65] for the Data Subjects involved, who should receive key information concerning the Processing when their data are collected.[66]

Transparency also contributes to the application of the fairness requirement in data protection. Given the complexity of the Processing, transparency on its methodology (including where possible the algorithm) is very important, so that the rigour of the approach can be independently assessed (beyond the Data Subjects' right of information[67]) and is the main requirement to perform a meaningful risk analysis.

Transparency, however, can be a challenging principle to apply when it comes to Artificial Intelligence, since these solutions are based on advanced technology that

---

63 Council of Europe (CoE), *Artificial Intelligence and Data Protection: Challenges and Possible Remedies* | T-PD(2018)09Rev, 2.
64 Article 29 Data Protection Working Party, *Guidelines on automated individual decision-making*.
65 See Section 2.5.1 – The principle of the fairness and lawfulness of Processing.
66 See Section 2.10 – Information.
67 See Section 17.3 – Rights of Data Subjects, and Section 17.5 – International Data Sharing.

can be hard to understand and explain in lay terms.[68] Moreover, many Machine Learning models include multilayered networks in which the outputs are a result of an internal process that may not be replicated or understood mathematically even by the data scientists and the solution designers themselves.[69] This multilayered architecture is commonly known as the "black box", since it may make it impossible for those using the solution to understand how it reached a specific conclusion or prediction. In other words, the reasoning behind the functioning of these applications is in most cases not transparent or intelligible for human beings; consequently, it is difficult to assess the fairness and quality of the process.

One suggested answer to the challenge of transparency in Artificial Intelligence applications is to explain the logic behind the solutions, in other words giving information about the type of input data and the expected output, explaining the variables and their weight, or shining light on the analytics architecture. This approach, known as "interpretability", focuses on understanding the causality of a change in the input to the output, without necessarily explaining all the logic of the machine through its multiple layers. In the case of black boxes, however, achieving interpretability will often be difficult and it is important to be transparent with Data Subjects about unknowns and areas of uncertainty. Other approaches are based on selective disclosure or contractual strategies, but they also suffer some limits or cannot be generalized.[70]

Humanitarian Organizations need to work with developers on the issue of "explainability", especially when they intend to use Artificial Intelligence solutions to support decision making. They should be able to explain to Data Subjects how the solution works, what risks may arise, how the Artificial Intelligence system achieves its outcomes and what arrangements are in place for a human decision maker to review its decisions or suggestions if needed.

Finally, care should be taken in decision making about transparency if it conflicts with data sensitivity at the individual level, or when transparency in Processing could encourage circumvention of the data Processing system by malicious actors and thus bias it.

17.2.5 DATA MINIMIZATION

The data minimization principle requires organizations to limit the Processing of Personal Data to the minimum amount and extent necessary to achieve the purpose of the Processing.[71] With the use of Artificial Intelligence, however, large-scale

---

68 The Norwegian Data Protection Authority, *Artificial Intelligence and Privacy*, 19.
69 Future of Privacy Forum, *The Privacy Expert's Guide to Artificial Intelligence and Machine Learning*, 17.
70 See also Andrew D. Selbst and Solon Barocas, "The intuitive appeal of explainable machines", *Fordham Law Review*, Vol. 87, No. 3, 2019 2018, pp. 1085–1140.
71 See Section 2.5.4 – The principle of data minimization.

Processing is often required for its functioning, and moreover the search for new patterns and correlations in data sets can make it difficult to circumscribe the range of data used.[72] Moreover, training such solutions using suitably large and representative data sets is also necessary to reduce potential bias in their outcomes.[73]

Despite this tension between Artificial Intelligence and data minimization, various solutions are possible to balance the different needs. These are set out below, along with their potential limitations:

- Employing techniques that can make it harder to identify individuals through the data, such as restricting the amount and nature of the information used. This approach may not fit certain Artificial Intelligence solutions that require large amounts of data to function well. In addition, making data hard to identify does not, by itself, guarantee respect for the data minimization principle.
- Using "synthetic data" as training data. Synthetic data "is an artificial data set, including the actual data on no 'real' individuals, but which mirrors in characteristics and proportional relationships all the statistical aspects of the original dataset".[74] This is a very promising solution,[75] but it still requires real data as a starting point. It also requires more expertise from data scientists, and it may suffer from some limitations stemming from the replication process and the difficulty of ensuring accuracy when many variables and complex situations are considered.
- Adopting a progressive approach by collecting what is thought to be the minimum amount of data necessary to achieve the expected results and then testing the solution to see how it performs. After testing, more data may be added if needed, and the solution can be tested again until it achieves the desired outcomes. This approach reduces the Processing of unnecessary data and seeks to ensure that the solution is trained on the minimum possible data set, while also making Reidentification harder.

Despite the challenges associated with data minimization in Artificial Intelligence, this principle does not mean that large-scale Processing is forbidden, but rather that it poses higher risks that require appropriate security and risk-mitigation measures. Moreover, as mentioned previously, not all Artificial Intelligence solutions require large volumes of data to be accurate. Those based on reinforcement learning, for instance, can be trained with little data.

The data processed by Humanitarian Organizations should be adequate and relevant for the purposes for which they are collected and processed. This means ensuring

---

72 Centre for Information Policy Leadership, *Artificial Intelligence and Data Protection in Tension*, 14.
73 Ibid., 13.
74 Future of Privacy Forum, *The Privacy Expert's Guide to Artificial Intelligence and Machine Learning*, 8.
75 Council of Europe (CoE), *Artificial Intelligence and Data Protection: Challenges and Possible Remedies | T-PD(2018)09Rev*.

that data collection is not excessive and that the time period for which the data are stored, before being anonymized or archived, is limited to the minimum necessary. The amount of Personal Data collected and processed should, ideally, be limited to what is necessary to fulfil the specified purpose(s) of data collection, data Processing or compatible Further Processing, or to what is justified on another legal basis.

Finally, although Artificial Intelligence often requires large-scale data sets, it is always crucial to carefully design the data strategy, by keeping the contents of data sets collected by Humanitarian Organizations to the minimum necessary for the purposes of the Processing and defining the purpose of data Processing as specifically as possible. Data Controllers and, where applicable, Data Processors should carefully consider the design of their data analysis, in order to minimize the presence of redundant and marginal data.[76]

17.2.6 DATA RETENTION

Personal Data should be retained only for a defined period as necessary for the purposes for which they were collected.[77] Following the initial retention period an assessment should be made as to whether the data should be deleted or whether they should be kept for a longer period to achieve the purpose. If this Processing is performed on pre-existing data sets, as "compatible Further Processing",[78] the Processing should take place within the data retention period allowed for the purpose of initial collection. Renewal of the initial retention period, if a renewal is contemplated by the retention policy at the time of collection, can take place to enable analytics as "compatible Further Processing".

However, in the Artificial Intelligence context, a longer period for data retention may be justified when data are used to monitor the performance system[79] and prevent unexpected biases. If a model shows bias, it can be helpful to have the training data set available to investigate the potential source of the bias. During the retention period, Data Controllers must ensure that data remain updated to reduce the risk of inaccuracies.[80]

Given the variety of uses Artificial Intelligence may have in the humanitarian sector, specific retention periods should be considered in the context of each programme. In this regard, Humanitarian Organizations should consider and set an initial retention period, such as a two-year period for audit purposes. Should the data still be

---

76   Council of Europe (CoE), *Guidelines on the protection of individuals with regard to the processing of personal data in a world of Big Data* | T-PD(2017)01.
77   See Section 2.7 – Data retention.
78   See Subsection 2.5.2.1 – Further Processing.
79   Centre for Information Policy Leadership, *Artificial Intelligence and Data Protection in Tension*, 15.
80   Article 29 Data Protection Working Party, *Guidelines on automated individual decision-making*, 12.

needed after this initial period, organizations should conduct periodic assessments based on their retention needs and consider their legal basis for amending the retention period. They will also need to seek additional Consent from Data Subjects if their data are retained for longer than the duration they consented to at the point of collection.

17.2.7 DATA SECURITY

Data security[81] is an essential aspect of Artificial Intelligence solutions, particularly in the humanitarian sector. Humanitarian Organizations must be mindful of the risks that these technologies pose and implement the highest level of data security when using them. Attacks by malicious parties typically fall into one of three categories:
- **model inversion attacks**: attempts to reveal information about the training data by inverting the system's model;
- **poisoning attacks**: attempts to decrease the utility of the model;
- **backdoor attacks**: attempts to gain unauthorized access to the solution and modify it after it has been trained.

Looking specifically at model inversion, it has been demonstrated that some systems remember their training data sets. For example, if a person's face has been used to train a facial recognition system, a malicious party could query the system again and again, slowly changing the input image to reconstruct the face with sufficient precision to know that the person in question was part of the training set.[82]

Another type of deliberate attack involves adding noise to the data in order to decrease the quality of outcomes, sometimes even leading to useless results such as making wrong classifications and predictions.

All these factors mean that inadequate data security can pose significant risks for vulnerable individuals in the context of the use of Artificial Intelligence. In view of these risks, it is important to build strong and secure systems that effectively protect against unauthorized access. Pseudonymization and encryption techniques are some of the methods that can assist in this regard. While the technique of training models on encrypted data is still in its early days, static models that receive encrypted inputs and produce encrypted outputs are already commonplace, albeit with their own constraints. The use of differential privacy[83] should also be considered when training Artificial Intelligence solutions.

---

81 See Section 2.8 – Data security and Processing security.
82 Matt Fredrikson, Somesh Jha and Thomas Ristenpart, "Model inversion attacks that exploit confidence information and basic countermeasures", in *CCS'15: Proceedings of the 22nd ACM SIGSAC Conference on Computer and Communications Security*, ACM, Denver, CO, 2015, 1322–1333: doi.org/10.1145/2810103.2813677.
83 "Differentially-private algorithms are resilient to adaptive attacks that use auxiliary information. These algorithms rely on incorporating random noise into the mix so that everything an adversary receives

Finally, in considering the suitability of security measures required to protect information in Artificial Intelligence-based solutions, it is important to take into account that the outputs of the Processing may produce more Sensitive Data than the initial data sets, including individual or group profiling, and could prove harmful to the individuals concerned if they fall into the wrong hands. In this case, the Humanitarian Organization should implement adequate security measures to protect the output, which are appropriate for the risks involved.[84] Additionally, regular data security and data privacy training is essential to raise awareness of security threats and to avoid Data Breaches.

17.3 RIGHTS OF DATA SUBJECTS

Data Controllers are responsible for determining the means and purposes of the Processing and for ensuring that Data Subjects can exercise their rights.[85] Although Artificial Intelligence may make it more difficult for Data Controllers to comply with these obligations, choosing such solutions as a means to achieve a certain purpose does not excuse Data Controllers from their responsibilities. Humanitarian Organizations should therefore have procedures and systems in place to ensure that individuals can exercise their rights. At the same time, as is discussed in Section 2.11 – Rights of Data Subjects, the exercise of these rights may be limited in certain circumstances.

17.3.1 RIGHTS RELATED TO AUTOMATED DECISION MAKING

Data Subjects have the right to not be subjected to solely automated decision making, i.e. "decisions by technological means without human involvement",[86] when such decisions produce legal effects or similarly significantly affect the individual in question.

EXAMPLE:
Some examples of solely automated decision making include speeding fines imposed purely on the basis of evidence from speed cameras, automatic refusal of an online credit application or e-recruiting practices without any human intervention.[87]

---

becomes noisy and imprecise, and so it is much more difficult to breach privacy (if it is feasible at all)".
Aaruran Elamurugaiyan, "A Brief Introduction to Differential Privacy" Medium,
31 August 2018: https://medium.com/georgian-impact-blog/a-brief-introduction-to-differential-privacy-eacf8722283b.

84 See Section 17.2.7 – Data security, and Section 2.8 – Data security and Processing security.
85 See Section 2.11 – Rights of Data Subjects.
86 Council of Europe (CoE), *Artificial Intelligence and Data Protection: Challenges and Possible Remedies* | T-PD(2018)09Rev, 8.
87 Ibid.

The rationale behind this right "is driven by a concern for algorithmic bias; a worry of incorrect or unsubstantiated solely automated decisions based on inaccurate or incomplete data; and the need for individuals to have redress and the ability to contest a decision if an Artificial Intelligence system is incorrect or unfair".[88] These concerns are justified by examples such as the Swedish benefits case mentioned above, where a rogue solution meant that "thousands of unemployed people were wrongly denied benefits".[89] In Humanitarian Action, a similar problem could arise if Artificial Intelligence solutions make decisions about who receives aid or who is included in a target population for an aid programme. Beneficiaries should always have the right to have a human being oversee decisions that affect them.

It should be noted that "[t]o qualify as human involvement, the controller must ensure that any oversight of the decision is meaningful, rather than just a token gesture".[90] This is particularly important because those making decisions may blindly rely on the Artificial Intelligence solution's suggestions on the basis that mathematical algorithms are supposedly failproof. Consequently, the presence of an individual human decision maker alone is not sufficient. The decision maker must have the ability to refute the machine's decision or suggestion.[91]

On a similar note, decision makers may not fully understand how the system arrived at a particular decision or suggestion and may therefore find it difficult to assess whether it was made wrongly (see Section 17.2.4 – Transparency, above). Decision makers should always be able to examine all the facts and information from scratch and make an independent decision, without considering the Artificial Intelligence solution's outcome. This is not always straightforward, however, since an Artificial Intelligence solution is able to process much more information than a person in the same situation. Setting up a multidisciplinary team, including individuals with expertise in the sector and technology developers, may be one option in such cases.

It is possible that individuals, regardless of their level of expertise, may be reluctant to challenge an Artificial Intelligence system's automated decisions, given how accurate the technology can be. Consequently, another issue to take into account is how the human intervention would be arranged so that a review of the decision is "carried out by someone who has the appropriate authority and capability to change the decision".[92] Organizations therefore need to consider whether it would be acceptable

---

88 Centre for Information Policy Leadership, *Artificial Intelligence and Data Protection in Tension*, 16.
89 Willis, "Rogue Algorithm Stops Welfare Payments".
90 Article 29 Data Protection Working Party, *Guidelines on automated individual decision-making*, 21.
91 Council of Europe (CoE), *Artificial Intelligence and Data Protection: Challenges and Possible Remedies* | T-PD(2018)09Rev.
92 Article 29 Data Protection Working Party, *Guidelines on automated individual decision-making*, 27.

for beneficiaries to be subjected to automated decision making if they had the right to request human intervention. Here, the very case for using the technology in the first place may come under challenge.

In any case, it is essential that beneficiaries are informed about any automated decision making they are being subjected to, including the logic behind the Artificial Intelligence solution, the significance of the Processing and its envisaged consequences for them.[93] They must also be able to object to the Processing.

The rights of the Data Subjects are described in Section 2.11 – Rights of Data Subjects. The rights to information, access, correction, erasure and objection are considered crucial components of an effective data protection policy. However, Artificial Intelligence-based Processing of Personal Data poses significant challenges.

The Data Subject's exercise of the right to information about automated decision making (also relevant to the transparency principle, see Section 17.2.2 – Purpose limitation and Further Processing) is more difficult in the Artificial Intelligence context, given the complexity of such systems and how they operate. It is therefore important to explore alternative means of Artificial Intelligence transparency and consider new forms of information provision, such as the creation of public registers describing the key functions and characteristics of the most impactful systems. It may also be advisable to investigate the provision of information to representatives of potentially affected groups.

Organizations engaged in humanitarian use of Artificial Intelligence are encouraged to incorporate complaint procedures into their Personal Data Processing practices and internal data protection policies. These procedures should enable data correction and erasure. However, it should be recognized that the exercise of certain individual rights may be limited by the legal basis of the Processing. For example, requests for opt-outs by individuals may not be observed in the event of Processing undertaken under the legal basis of public interest described above.

Humanitarian Organizations need to ensure that no automated decisions are taken with regard to individuals which could lead to harm or exclusion from humanitarian programmes, without any human intervention. In practice, this means that a human being should always be the final decision maker when decisions are taken on the basis of Artificial Intelligence outputs that may have adverse effects on individuals.

---

93   Ibid., 25.

EXAMPLE
In the event of aid distribution, a decision based on output from Artificial Intelligence to prioritize a specific region or group of people (to the disadvantage of those left out of these regions or groups) should always be cross-checked and validated by a human being.

17.4 DATA CONTROLLER/DATA PROCESSOR RELATIONSHIP

Artificial Intelligence solutions tend to blur the traditional distinction between the roles of Data Controller and Data Processor, which is centred on the idea of power to control and supervise the data Processing in relation to the definition of its purposes and means. This is largely due to the fact that in the case of Artificial Intelligence solutions, providers retain important privileges as regards the organization of the service and Artificial Intelligence architecture.

17.4.1 ACCOUNTABILITY

To have a proper allocation of accountability and liability obligations, it is crucial to carefully determine which entity actually acts as Data Controller, retaining the control over personal information and a general power to manage the purposes and means of data Processing, and which processes Personal Data on behalf of the Data Controller and is therefore a Data Processor. It is also possible that more than one entity jointly determines the purposes and means of the Processing and may be considered as joint Data Controllers.

EXAMPLE 1: Humanitarian Organizations sharing data sets and undertaking Data Analytics using their own organizational resources may be considered joint Data Controllers.
EXAMPLE 2: Humanitarian Organizations sharing data sets but outsourcing the Data Analytics to a commercial service provider that will transfer the findings and keep no records for its own use will be considered joint Data Controllers, and the service provider will be considered a Data Processor.

In accordance with their different roles and respective spheres of competence, Data Controller and Data Processor are accountable for the decisions they adopt concerning data Processing. However, as explained above, Artificial Intelligence sometimes evolves in ways that cannot be fully understood by developers themselves due to the "black box" effect. This may raise questions around the concrete implementation of the accountability principle, which requires Data Controllers to comply with data protection requirements and to be in a position to demonstrate that they have taken adequate and proportionate technical and organizational measures within their respective Processing operations.[94]

17.4.2 LIABILITY

Automated decision making (see above) raises particular issues around liability. In health care, for instance, machines are often considered to be more accurate than humans in diagnosing certain diseases such as specific types of cancer, or at analysing X-ray images. For this reason, doctors may feel compelled to follow the machine's recommendation.[95] Here, it might be unclear who is responsible for the diagnosis.[96] To counterbalance this, organizations may seek to extend the product liability logic to algorithms, thereby placing the full burden of liability on the developer company (although this may be very difficult to negotiate in practice). From an ethical perspective, it is also important for Humanitarian Organizations to understand their own responsibilities when choosing to use such technology and to be accountable to beneficiaries accordingly.

In a different scenario, the performance of Artificial Intelligence systems can be significantly affected by the poor quality of data available in a given context, such as in geographic areas where the use of poor scanning technologies generates biases in image-based diagnoses. In these cases, Humanitarian Organizations must therefore carefully assess the data quality to avoid potential liability.

Some specific tools, such as a data management plan and DPIA, can contribute to better clarify the roles of different parties engaged in the Processing. Once these roles have been defined and the corresponding tasks assigned, it is important to establish which relevant contracts need to be entered into among the data Processing participants.

Data collection or International Data Sharing across Humanitarian Organizations and/or national borders and/or third (private or state) bodies should generally be covered by contractual clauses. These contracts are important and can play a key role in liability management for the following reasons:

---

[94] See Section 2.9 – The principle of accountability.
[95] Victor Demiaux and Yacine Si Abdallah, "Comment permettre à l'homme de garder la main? Les enjeux éthiques des algorithmes et de l'intelligence artificielle", French Data Protection Authority (CNIL), Paris, December 2017, 27: www.cnil.fr/sites/default/files/atoms/files/cnil_rapport_garder_la_main_web.pdf.
[96] Ibid.

- They should clearly allocate the roles between the various parties and, in particular, put them on notice as to whether they are acting as Data Controllers, Data Processors or joint controllers.
- They should contain an outline of the data protection obligations to which each party is subject. This should include the measures that the parties should take to protect Personal Data transferred across borders.
- They should contain obligations to cover data security, responses (objection or notification to the other party) in case of authorities requesting access to data, procedures for handling Data Breaches, Data Processor return/disposal of data at the end of the Processing, and staff training.
- They should also require that notice be given to the Humanitarian Organizations involved if any data are accessed without authorization.

17.5 INTERNATIONAL DATA SHARING

Personal Data and other types of data processed in Artificial Intelligence solutions often cross national borders due to the presence of international service providers and the use of cloud computing services. This leads to the application of provisions and practices relating to international cross-border data flows.[97] In this regard, attention must be paid to applicable law and jurisdiction.

International data sharing may involve several scenarios:
- Personal Data are transferred by a Humanitarian Organization (Data Controller) to Third Parties (Data Processors), either commercial entities or other Humanitarian Organizations, to be processed in its behalf, e.g. cloud computing service providers;
- Personal Data are shared among Humanitarian Organizations, public authorities and/or commercial entities (joint Data Controllers), e.g. partnership in joint actions;
- Personal Data are transferred to other Humanitarian Organizations, public authorities and/or commercial entities that autonomously process such information for their own purposes (Data Controllers).

Data protection laws restrict International Data Sharing, so Humanitarian Organizations should have mechanisms in place to provide a legal basis for it when Data Analytics are conducted, as discussed above.[98] It is essential to assess the potential data transfer risks prior to International Data Sharing, taking into account the local regulations in the country of destination, and to inform Data Subjects adequately. In case of potential risks, suitable mitigating measures can be adopted, both at contractual level

---

97 See Chapter 4: International Data Sharing.
98 See Section 17.2.1 – Legal bases for Personal Data Processing.

(e.g. contractual clauses, codes of conduct) and at technical level (e.g. data encryption, strong Pseudonymization). When the risk is high and the mitigation measures cannot reduce it, a decision should be taken to refrain from data sharing.[99]

Since in many cases International Data Sharing concerns the use of Third Party services, when Humanitarian Organizations hire Artificial Intelligence service providers, they should collect all relevant information on cross-border data transfers. In some cases, companies providing Artificial Intelligence solutions may have an incentive to use and exploit the results of the Processing of Humanitarian Organizations' data (e.g. commercial purposes, profiling). It is therefore very important that any contractual arrangements with them make it completely clear that the purpose of the Processing is and must remain exclusively humanitarian, and that the service provider keeps the humanitarian Processing segregated from its commercial activities.

If any doubts arise as to whether the service provider can or will respect this condition, the Humanitarian Organization should refrain from engaging in the Processing. This is because any Processing other than Processing exclusively for Humanitarian Action may have serious implications for Data Subjects. For example, outputs of analytics which identify categories of potential beneficiaries of Humanitarian Action may lead to consequences such as denial of credit, higher insurance premiums, stigmatization, discrimination or even persecution.

Humanitarian Organizations should also be alert to the risk that, in situations of violence or conflict, the parties involved may seek to access and use the findings of Artificial Intelligence-based analyses to gain an advantage, which would compromise the safety of the Data Subjects and the neutrality of Humanitarian Action. Consequently, in cases where the outputs are potentially sensitive, it is important to consider a scenario where Humanitarian Organizations develop their own Artificial Intelligence applications without recourse to Third Party solutions.

17.6 DATA PROTECTION IMPACT ASSESSMENT AND HUMAN RIGHTS IMPACT ASSESSMENT

Since the use of Artificial Intelligence can pose substantial data protection risks to individuals, an organization should carry out a Data Protection Impact Assessment (DPIA) before making a decision to implement such a solution.

A DPIA involves identifying, evaluating and addressing the impacts on Data Subjects and their Personal Data of a project, policy, programme or other initiative that entails

---

[99] See Chapter 4: International Data Sharing, and Section 4.4 – Mitigating the risks to the individual.

the Processing of such data.[100] It should ultimately lead to measures that avoid, minimize, transfer or share risks associated with the Processing activities. A DPIA is a continuous process and should follow a project or initiative that involves the Processing of individuals' data throughout its life cycle.

Given the limits to transparency in the use of Artificial Intelligence, publicly available DPIAs can also help increase beneficiaries' acceptance and use of Artificial Intelligence solutions by Humanitarian Organizations.

DPIAs are important tools during project design to ensure that all aspects of applicable data protection regulations and potential risks are covered.[101] DPIAs are now required in many jurisdictions and by some Humanitarian Organizations.

Apart from clarifying the details and specifications of the Processing, DPIAs should focus on the risks posed by it and on mitigating measures. These risks, according to the most relevant models of DPIA, are not limited to the right to privacy and data protection but should include risks to the rights and freedoms of natural persons.[102] In line with the by-design approach and the minimization of data Processing-related risks, DPIAs need to be conducted prior to any Artificial Intelligence-based operations and updated when Processing operation or contextual elements change.

Several risks can be considered in a DPIA including, according to the specific Processing operations, the nature of processed data, the inferences extracted using Artificial Intelligence applications, and the context where Processing is carried out. Some examples concern the risk of Reidentification of individuals of relevance for Humanitarian Action, in case of use of anonymized data or pseudonymized/aggregate results made available to Third Parties, or the risk that the results of Artificial Intelligence-based analysis performed by Humanitarian Organizations may be exploited by commercial Third Parties and/or authorities for unrelated purposes.

Further examples of risks that should be considered in the broader context of human rights protection include:
- requests to Humanitarian Organizations for specific patterns or information about certain categories of individuals by authorities or corporations that could potentially expose Data Subjects to discrimination or detrimental consequences and compromise the neutrality of Humanitarian Action;

---

100 See Chapter 5: Data Protection Impact Assessments (DPIAs).
101 See Chapter 5: Data Protection Impact Assessments (DPIAs).
102 For assessment tools specifically developed to assess the risks in Humanitarian Action, see UN Global Pulse, *Tools: Risks, Harms and Benefits Assessment*.

- access and use of the results of Artificial Intelligence-based analysis by parties in a situation of violence or conflict to gain an advantage over other stakeholders and thus compromise the safety of the Data Subjects and the neutrality of Humanitarian Action.

Finally, considering the role of Artificial Intelligence service providers in Humanitarian Action, the DPIA should also consider the risk that commercial providers may have incentives to exploit the findings of the Processing for commercial purposes, e.g. to improve their understanding of their current or potential customers or for further customer profiling.[103]

With regard to the risk identified in the DPIA, the assessment considers the likelihood and severity of potential negative impacts on Data Subjects, also considering competing rights and freedoms and legitimate interests recognized by the law. On the basis of the analysis of this potential impact, specific mitigation measures are adopted, including in the design of the used solutions, such as Anonymization techniques, privacy-enhancing technical measures, and legal and contractual obligations to prevent possible Reidentification of the persons concerned.[104]

Although DPIA has become a mandatory requirement under national and international[105] law, assessment methodologies mainly adopt a limited perspective with a main focus on Processing, task allocation, data quality and data security, without adequately considering all the human rights potentially impacted by Artificial Intelligence applications, their diversity and complexity. However, as pointed out by the UN High Commissioner for Human Rights,[106] it is necessary to adopt a broader perspective, embedding human rights in Artificial Intelligence development, deployment and use, with a comprehensive by-design approach to counter potential adverse impacts.

17.6.1 HUMAN RIGHTS IMPACT ASSESSMENT FOR ARTIFICIAL INTELLIGENCE

Human Rights Impact Assessment (HRIA) can thus guide Artificial Intelligence developers and users from the outset in the design of new Artificial Intelligence solutions, facilitating comparison between alternative design options, and following the product/ service throughout its life cycle, by using an iterative approach, based on risk assessment

---

[103] See Section 2.3: Aggregate, Pseudonymized and Anonymized data sets.
[104] Council of Europe (CoE), *Guidelines on the protection of individuals with regard to the processing of personal data in a world of Big Data* | T-PD(2017)01.
[105] Council of Europe (CoE), Convention 108; Council of Europe (CoE), Protocol Amending the Convention for the Protection of Individuals with Regard to Automatic Processing of Personal Data, para. 10.
[106] Office of the United Nations High Commissioner for Human Rights (OHCHR), *A/HRC/48/31: The Right to Privacy in the Digital Age*, report of the United Nations High Commissioner for Human Rights, UN Doc, OHCHR, 15 September 2021, www.ohchr.org/en/documents/thematic-reports/ahrc4831-right-privacy-digital-age-report-united-nations-high.

and design mitigation solutions. For these reasons, HRIA is considered the cornerstone of future Artificial Intelligence regulation at international and regional level.[107]

However, in dealing with the impact of Artificial Intelligence, traditional HRIA methodologies cannot be applied directly but must be contextualized by considering the specific nature of Artificial Intelligence. The two most relevant changes introduced in the HRIA in relation to the Artificial Intelligence context concern the *ex ante* nature of the assessment carried out and the greater focus on quantifiable risk thresholds. As for the former, an *ex ante* approach is required by the guiding role that HRIA aims to play in Artificial Intelligence project design and development, as opposed to the *ex post* evaluation centred on corrective policies that usually characterizes traditional HRIA.

Regarding the focus on risk thresholds, this is in line with the requirements emerging in the regulatory debate on Artificial Intelligence where the definition of different risk levels is crucial in the acceptability of Artificial Intelligence products and services, and directly impacts on the obligations of Artificial Intelligence manufacturers, providers and users. A quantitative dimension of assessment, in terms of ranges of risks, is therefore needed both for Artificial Intelligence design guidance and legal compliance.

Compared to the voluntary and policy-based traditional HRIA practice in the business sector, once HRIA becomes a legal tool it is no longer merely a source of recommendations for better business policy. Future Artificial Intelligence regulation will most likely bring specific legal obligations and sanctions for non-compliance in relation to risk assessment and management, as well as given risk thresholds (e.g. high risk).

17.6.2 HUMAN RIGHTS IMPACT ASSESSMENT: PHASES AND PROCEDURE

Notwithstanding these important differences impacting on the assessment methodology, the main building blocks of the assessment procedure remain the same and are similar to the phases of DPIA schemes: (i) the planning and scoping phase and (ii) the data collection and analysis phase.

The first stage deals with the definition of the HRIA target, identifying the main features of the product/service and the context in which it will be placed. There are three main areas to consider at this stage: (i) description and analysis of the type of product/service; (ii) analysis of the human rights context; (iii) identification of relevant stakeholders.

---

107 CoE (Ad Hoc Committee on Artificial Intelligence (CAHAI)) *"5th Meeting, Strasbourg, 5–7 July 2021: Abridged Meeting Report and List of Decisions"*, 7 July 2021, CAHAI(2021)10: www.coe.int/en/web/artificial-intelligence/cahai-1; European Commission, *Proposal for a Regulation of the European Parliament and of the Council Laying down Harmonised Rules on Artificial Intelligence (Artificial Intelligence Act) and Amending Certain Union Legislative Acts*, 21 April 2021, COM/2021 206 final.

The second stage focuses on relevant empirical evidence to assess the impact on human rights. Since in most cases the assessment is not based on measurable variables, the impact on rights and freedoms is necessarily the result of expert evaluation, where expert opinion relies on knowledge of case law, the literature and the legal framework. This means that it is not possible to provide a precise measurement of the expected impacts but only an assessment in terms of range of risk.

In line with risk assessment procedures, three key factors must be considered: risk identification, likelihood (L) and severity (S). With regard to the first, the focus on human rights and freedoms already defines the potentially affected categories and the case-specific analysis identifies those concretely affected, depending on the technologies used and their purposes. Since this is a rights-based model, risk concerns the prejudice to rights and freedoms, in terms of unlawful limitations and restrictions, regardless of material damage.

The expected impact of the identified risks is assessed by considering both the likelihood and the severity of the expected consequences, using a four-step scale (low, medium, high, very high) to avoid any risk of average positioning.

Likelihood is the combination of the probability of adverse consequences and the exposure (Table 17.3). The former concerns the probability that adverse consequences of a certain risk might occur (Table 17.1) and the latter the potential number of people at risk (Table 17.2). Both these variables must be assessed on a contextual basis and the engagement of relevant shareholders can be of help.

The severity of the expected consequences (Table 17.6) is estimated by considering the gravity of the prejudice in the exercise of rights and freedoms (Table 17.4) and the effort to overcome it and to reverse adverse effects (Table 17.5).

Table 17.1 Probability

Low	The risk of prejudice is improbable or highly improbable.	1
Medium	The risk may occur.	2
High	There is a high probability that the risk occurs.	3
Very high	The risk is highly likely to occur.	4

Table 17.2 Exposure

Low	Few or very few of the identified population of rights-holders are potentially affected.	1
Medium	Some of the identified populations are potentially affected.	2
High	The majority of the identified population is potentially affected.	3
Very high	Almost the entire identified population is potentially affected.	4

Table 17.3 Likelihood table (L)

		Probability			
		1	2	3	4
Exposure	1	1	2	3	4
	2	2	3	5	9
	3	3	5	9	12
	4	4	7	12	15

Likelihood	
Low	1
Medium	2
High	3
Very high	4

Table 17.4 Gravity of the prejudice

	Gravity of the prejudice	
Low	Affected individuals and groups may encounter only minor prejudices in the exercise of their rights and freedoms.	1
Medium	Affected individuals and groups may encounter significant prejudices.	2
High	Affected individuals and groups may encounter serious prejudices.	3
Very high	Affected individuals and groups may encounter serious or even irreversible prejudices.	4

Table 17.5 Effort to overcome the prejudice and to reverse adverse effects

	Effort	
Low	Suffered prejudice can be overcome without any problem (e.g. time spent amending information, annoyances, irritations, etc.).	1
Medium	Suffered prejudice can be overcome despite a few difficulties (e.g. extra costs, fear, lack of understanding, stress, minor physical ailments, etc.).	2
High	Suffered prejudice can be overcome albeit with serious difficulties (e.g. economic loss, property damage, worsening of health, etc.).	3
Very high	Suffered prejudice may not be overcome (e.g. long-term psychological or physical ailments, death, etc.).	4

Taking into consideration the L and S values, the overall impact is determined using a table (Table 17.7) where colours from lightest to darkest represent the overall impact, from lowest to highest. Once the potentially adverse impact has been assessed for each of the rights and freedoms considered, a radial graph (Graph 17.1) of the overall

Table 17.6 Severity table (S)

		Gravity			
		1	2	3	4
Effort	1	1	2	4	6
	2	2	3	5	8
	3	3	5	8	10
	4	5	8	10	12

Severity	
Low	1
Medium	2
High	3
Very high	4

Table 17.7 Overall risk impact table

		Severity [impacted right/freedom]			
		Low	Medium	High	Very high
Likelihood	Low				
	Medium				
	High				
	Very high				

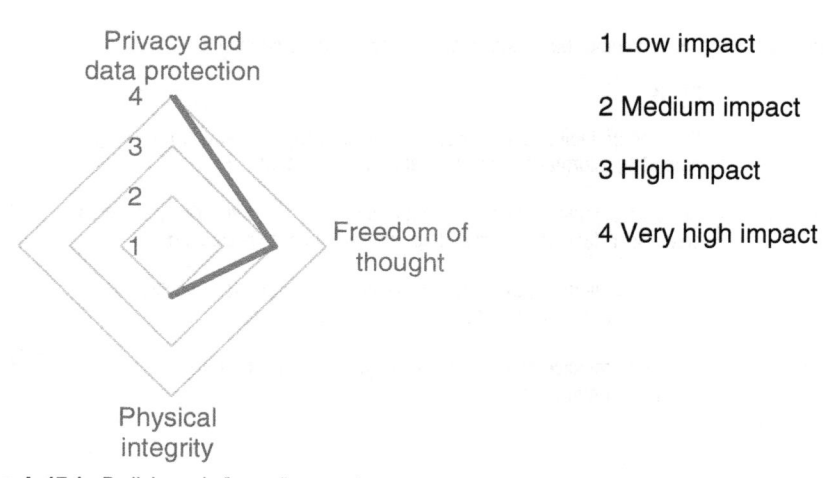

Privacy and data protection
4
3
2
1
Freedom of thought
Physical integrity

1 Low impact

2 Medium impact

3 High impact

4 Very high impact

Graph 17.1. Radial graph (impact) example

impact can be used to decide the priority of intervention in altering the characteristics of the product/service to reduce the expected adverse impacts. Factors that can exclude the risk from a legal perspective (e.g. the mandatory nature of certain impacting features) should be considered.

After the first adoption of the appropriate mitigation measures for the foreseen risks, further rounds of assessment can be conducted according to the level of residual risk and its acceptability.

17.7 DATA PROTECTION BY DESIGN AND BY DEFAULT

Data Protection by design and by default involves designing a Processing operation, programme or solution in a way that implements key data protection principles from the outset, and that provides the Data Subject with the greatest possible data protections (see Chapter 6: Designing for data protection). The key data protection principles in this sense are:
- lawfulness, fairness and transparency;
- purpose limitation;
- data minimization;
- accuracy;
- storage limitation (limited retention);
- integrity and confidentiality (security);
- accountability.

The by-design approach also represents the concrete implementation of the impact assessment concerning data Processing. The adoption of specific mitigation measures or changes to the system design are usually the main way to tackle the potential risks identified in the impact assessment.

The measures to be adopted from a data protection by design perspective are necessarily context-specific, but solutions such as synthetic data, Pseudonymization, Anonymization (where possible) and encryption techniques are frequently components of the by-design approach.

17.8 ETHICAL ISSUES AND CHALLENGES

Given the speed at which technologies are evolving, the law often lags behind major societal changes. It is therefore likely that some of the ethical issues associated with Artificial Intelligence solutions are not yet covered by existing laws. In addition, there is a sphere of social and ethical issues and values that is not reflected in legal provisions but is relevant in defining a given community's approach to the use of data-intensive Artificial Intelligence systems and their social acceptability.

When opting to develop or use Artificial Intelligence solutions, Humanitarian Organizations should of course consider whether they comply with data protection laws and data protection by design principles. Importantly, however, they should also reflect on potential adverse impacts on the ethical and social implications of the data Processing.[108] For more guidance on the topic of analysing systems, see Section 6.3.3 – Analysing purpose limitation.

Artificial Intelligence tools present many risks, such as the possibility of discriminatory bias or lack of system accuracy. Also, some developers may train systems on data obtained either illegally or through unethical methods. This is particularly worrisome when users of such platforms or services are members of vulnerable groups.

Risk assessments that go beyond traditional data protection and cover a wider range of interests, ethical standards and rights (such as the right to non-discrimination)[109] are of great importance. Societal interests and ethics are broader than law, and organizations should consider the wider contextual background, including political and cultural nuances. This makes evaluating ethical values more complex, context-dependent and comprehensive than assessing compliance with data protection laws alone.

There have been numerous attempts to define the ethical principles that apply to the development of Artificial Intelligence. Examples include the Asilomar Artificial Intelligence Principles[110] and the International Conference of Data Protection and Privacy Commissioners' *Declaration on Ethics and Data Protection in Artificial Intelligence*.[111] Academics are also conducting research into ethical issues related to Artificial Intelligence,[112] and some multinational companies are developing their own sets of ethical principles.[113]

---

108 Mantelero, *Beyond Data Human Rights, Ethical and Social Impact Assessment in AI*.
109 Ibid., chap. 2.
110 Future of Life Institute, "Asilomar AI Principles": https://futureoflife.org/ai-principles.
111 International Conference on Data Protection and Privacy Commissioners, *Declaration on Ethics and Data Protection in Artificial Intelligence*, Declaration, 40th International Conference of Data Protection and Privacy Commissioners, Brussels, Belgium, 23 October 2018: http://globalprivacyassembly.org/wp-content/uploads/2018/10/20180922_ICDPPC-40th_AI-Declaration_ADOPTED.pdf.
112 See for example the ACM conference on Fairness, Accountability and Transparency (fatconference.org), which has gained prominence in recent years.
113 Marcello Ienca and Effy Vayena, "AI ethics guidelines: European and global perspectives", in *Towards Regulation of AI Systems: Global Perspectives on the Development of a Legal Framework on Artificial Intelligence Systems Based on the Council of Europe's Standards on Human Rights, Democracy and the Rule of Law*, by Isaac Ben Israel et al., Council of Europe (CoE), 2020, 38–60: https://edoc.coe.int/en/artificial-intelligence/9656-towards-regulation-of-ai-systems.html; Thilo Hagendorff, "The ethics of AI ethics: An evaluation of guidelines", *Minds and Machines*, Vol. 30, No. 1, 1 March 2020, pp. 99–120: https://doi.org/10.1007/s11023-020-09517-8.

However, ethical assessment, like social assessment, is more complicated than that of Data Protection and Human Rights Impact Assessment. Whereas the latter refer to a well-defined benchmark, the ethical framework involves a variety of theoretical inputs on the underlying values, as well as a proliferation of guidelines, in some cases partially affected by "ethics washing" or reflecting corporate values.

Experts therefore play a crucial role in detecting, contextualizing and evaluating Artificial Intelligence solutions against existing ethical and social values. Much more than in the human rights assessment, experts are decisive in grasping the relevant community values, given their context-specific nature and, in many cases, the need for active interaction with rights-holders and stakeholders to better understand them.

Given the impact Artificial Intelligence can have, ethics committees are attracting increasing attention in Artificial Intelligence circles as they can provide valuable support to developers in designing rights-based and socially oriented algorithms.[114] In terms of the composition of such committees, where societal issues are significant, legal, ethical or sociological expertise, as well as domain-specific knowledge, will be essential. Humanitarian Organizations could therefore consider establishing an ethics committee to assist them in dealing with such issues when deploying Artificial Intelligence solutions.

To ensure compliance with legal and ethical standards, Humanitarian Organizations should consider the following two steps:
- First, they should answer the following three questions:
  1. What should actually be done?
  2. What is legally allowed?
  3. What is technically possible?
- Second, when choosing to use new technologies, they should consider the problem they are facing and whether Artificial Intelligence can help solve it by asking the questions below:
  - What problem is solved with Artificial Intelligence?
  - What problem is not solved?
  - What problem is created?
  - How does this technology perform compared with other technologies that may be less risky?

In this respect, ethical assessment also has an influence on the design of Artificial Intelligence solutions, especially with regard to acceptability of the proposed Artificial Intelligence solution. This assessment not only examines the Artificial Intelligence product/service itself but looks at a wider range of alternative

---

[114] Council of Europe (CoE), *Artificial Intelligence and Data Protection: Challenges and Possible Remedies* | T-PD(2018)09Rev, 16.

possibilities to meet identified needs, also considering solutions that are not necessarily based on Artificial Intelligence.

In this regard, the zero option (not using Artificial Intelligence) should always be kept in mind. This is particularly relevant where the use of Artificial Intelligence would be legal but not ethically acceptable. For instance, if the solution chosen by the organization is not well accepted by the intended beneficiaries of the programme, this feeling of discomfort or distrust may justify a decision not to implement the technology.

APPENDIX 1

TEMPLATE FOR A DPIA REPORT

COVER PAGE

- Data Protection Impact Assessment on [name of activity]
- Contact person, title and email address
- Date

EXECUTIVE SUMMARY

If the DPIA is more than 20 pages, it should include an executive summary. The executive summary should include details of why the DPIA was undertaken, for whom and who conducted it. The executive summary should include the key findings and principal recommendations.

INTRODUCTION AND OVERVIEW OF THE DPIA PROCESS

The introduction should outline the scope of the DPIA, when, why and for whom it was performed and by whom. It should provide some information about the activity assessed. It should introduce the methodology employed in the DPIA (e.g. the method chosen to engage stakeholders).

THRESHOLD ASSESSMENT

This section should list the questions addressed by the Humanitarian Organization to determine whether a DPIA was necessary and what should be the scale of the DPIA.

DESCRIPTION OF THE ACTIVITY OR PROJECT TO BE ASSESSED

The description of the activity to be assessed should state who is undertaking the activity and when it is to be undertaken. It should state who will be affected by the activity, and who might be interested in or affected by the activity. The description should provide contextual information about how the activity fits in with the Humanitarian Organization's other services or activities.

INFORMATION FLOWS

This section should detail (at a minimum):
- the type of data to be collected;
- whether sensitive information will be collected;

- how the data will be collected;
- for what purposes the data will be used;
- how and where the data will be stored and/or backed up;
- who will have access to the Personal Data;
- whether Personal Data will be disclosed;
- whether sensitive Personal Data will be disclosed;
- whether any data will be transferred to other organizations or countries.

COMPLIANCE WITH LAWS, REGULATIONS, CODES AND GUIDELINES

The DPIA report should identify the laws, regulations, codes of conduct and guidelines with which the activity complies or should comply. At the global level, the privacy principles listed in the ISO/IEC 29100:2011 standard of the International Organization for Standardization (ISO)[1] are useful as a reference in a DPIA. In addition, the DPIA report should state how it complies with the Humanitarian Organization's confidentiality rules and codes of conduct, and how the Humanitarian Organization monitors compliance.

STAKEHOLDER ANALYSIS

The report should identify who are the principal stakeholders interested in or affected by the data Processing and how the DPIA or the Humanitarian Organization arrived at this list.

DATA PROTECTION IMPACTS (RISKS)

This section should detail the privacy risks identified in relation to the main privacy principles found in relevant legislation and the Humanitarian Organization's confidentiality rules and codes of conduct.

RISK ASSESSMENT

This section of the report should include details of how the risks were assessed and the results of any risk assessment undertaken.

---

1   International Organization for Standardization (ISO), "ISO/IEC 29100:2011 | Information Technology – Security Techniques – Privacy Framework," 2017, www.iso.org/standard/45123.html.

ORGANIZATIONAL ISSUES

The DPIA report should include a section that describes how senior management is involved in decision making related to data protection. This should include discussion identifying any organizational issues that are directly or indirectly affected by the data Processing activity. For example, it may become apparent that the data Processing requires putting in place an organizational mechanism for ensuring accountability, i.e. that a senior manager is responsible for ensuring that the programme does not negatively affect the Humanitarian Organization or its stakeholders.

In the course of the DPIA, it may become apparent to the DPIA team that the Humanitarian Organization needs to spend more time on raising the awareness of employees about privacy and/or ethical issues, and that the Humanitarian Organization needs to mainstream data protection in the organization. The report should state what the Humanitarian Organization does now to raise employee awareness of data protection and how it could improve.

The report should state how the Humanitarian Organization identifies, investigates and responds to data protection incidents, e.g. data protection breaches, how the Humanitarian Organization decides to notify affected parties and how it seeks to learn from an incident.

This section should also describe how the Humanitarian Organization responds to requests for access to personal information or to correct or amend the information it has gathered and to whom the data are transferred and what safeguards the Humanitarian Organization insists be in place before making a transfer.

RESULTS OF THE CONSULTATION(S)

The report should specify what efforts the Humanitarian Organization has made to consult with stakeholders, to gather their views and ideas about potential data protection impacts, how they might be affected by the data Processing (positively and/or negatively) and how negative impacts could be mitigated, avoided, minimized, eliminated, transferred or accepted.

The DPIA team should specify which consultation techniques were employed (surveys, interviews, focus groups, workshops, etc.), when they were undertaken, the results of each consultation exercise and whether differences in opinion were discovered when different techniques were used.

The DPIA should state who was consulted and what information materials the Humanitarian Organization provided to stakeholders, including families of the missing.

The DPIA should state whether the consultations yielded any new findings and what efforts the Humanitarian Organization had made to take into account stakeholder views and ideas in the design of the data Processing activity.

RECOMMENDATIONS

The DPIA team should set out their recommendations for avoiding, minimizing, transferring or sharing the data protection risks. Some risks may be worth taking and, if so, the DPIA should say why. The DPIA should be clear who will bear the risk (i.e. will it be the Humanitarian Organization or stakeholders or others?). The DPIA should also set out what further work is necessary or desirable to implement its recommendations (for example, the DPIA should mention the need for independent Third Party monitoring of its recommendations.

The DPIA should also make recommendations as to whether the DPIA report should be made public. There may be circumstances where it might not be appropriate to make the DPIA or parts of it public – e.g. there may be confidentiality or security reasons. Often the report can be redacted in places and then made public or sensitive parts can be placed in a confidential appendix. Alternatively, the Humanitarian Organization could provide a summary of the DPIA report.

APPENDIX 2
WORKSHOP PARTICIPANTS

All workshops were co-organized by the Brussels Privacy Hub and the ICRC. Workshop participants included representatives of the following organizations:
- Barclays;
- Belgian Privacy Commission;
- Biometrics Institute;
- Brussels Privacy Hub;
- Canadian Red Cross;
- Cash Learning;
- Council of Europe;
- Council of the EU;
- Dalberg Data Insights;
- EFTA Surveillance Authority;
- Engine Room;
- European Commission, DG ECHO;
- European Commission, DG Justice;
- European Data Protection Supervisor;
- European UAV-Drones Area;
- Facebook;
- Fairphone;
- French Data Protection Authority;
- French-speaking Association of Personal Data Protection Authorities;
- Government of Luxembourg;
- GSMA;
- Harvard Humanitarian Initiative;
- Human Rights Watch;
- ID2020;
- International Committee of the Red Cross;
- International Federation of the Red Cross;
- International Organization for Migration;
- ITU;
- KU Leuven;
- MasterCard;
- Médecins Sans Frontières;
- Mercy Corps;
- Microsoft;
- MIT;
- Netherlands Red Cross;
- Norwegian Red Cross;
- Orange Business Services;
- Oxford University;
- Politecnico di Torino;
- Privacy International;
- Queen Mary University of London;

- Royal Military Academy Belgium;
- Ryerson University – Privacy by Design Centre of Excellence;
- Sensometrix;
- SES;
- Spanish Data Protection Agency;
- Swiss Data Protection Authority;
- Swiss Federal Institute of Technology in Lausanne;
- UN Global Pulse;
- UN Office of the Special Rapporteur on the Right to Privacy;
- United Nations High Commissioner for Refugees;
- United Nations Office for the Coordination of Humanitarian Affairs;
- University of Geneva;
- USAID;
- VIVES University College;
- Vrije Universiteit Brussel;
- World Food Programme;
- World Vision International;
- Yale University.

INDEX

Footnotes are indicated by n. after the page number, and figures by fig.

access right, 15, 38–40, 107–108, 158, 225–226, 266
accountability principle, 35, 60, 63, 151–152, 319–320
accuracy of data. *See* quality of data
adequacy findings, 61
administrative activities, data processing for, 28, 305
AI. *See* artificial intelligence
anonymization and pseudonymization
   for artificial intelligence use, 297, 301–302, 315
   before further processing, 24
   blockchain tools as pseudonymized personal data, 251–252, 261
   cash and voucher assistance beneficiaries' data, 139–140
   definitions, 18–20, 52n.12
   dimensionality problem, 85
   for drone-collected data processing, 105
   re-identification risk, 19–20, 71–72, 139–140, 297, 301–302
anonymous use of mobile messaging apps, 202–203
applicable law. *See also* international data sharing
applicable law, 20–21
artificial intelligence
   anonymized data, re-identification using, 297, 301–302
   benefits and applications, 219–220, 293, 294–295, 298
   bias problem, 296, 300–301, 309–311, 314, 316–318
      ethical assessment, 329–332
      HRIA (human rights impact assessment), 324–329
   data controller/data processor relationship, 299, 319–321
   data minimization principle, 295, 301, 312–314
   data protection by design and by default, 329
   data subjects' rights, 309–311, 316–319
   datasets used by applications, 296, 298–299, 320
   definition and functionality, 290–292
   DPIAs (data protection impact assessments) for, 296–297, 320, 322–324
   international data sharing, 320–322
   introduction to topic, 290
   legal bases for personal data processing, 302–305, 308–309, 318

purpose limitation principle and further processing, 296–297, 304, 305–308, 322
retention of data, 314–315
risks and challenges, 292–303
securitizing data, 315–316
social media data analysis using, 232–233, 235, 237, 298, 303–306
transparency principle, 304, 308–309, 311–312, 318
authenticating identities. *See* identity verification

backup procedures, 32
balancing of data rights and other interests
   confidentiality protection, 15, 39
   in emergency situations, 14–15, 17–18, 35, 44, 49
   historical record protection, 15, 26, 40–41
   human rights protection, 14–15, 54, 282
   proportionality principle, 14, 24–26, 122–123, 227–228, 264
bias problem of artificial intelligence. *See under* artificial intelligence
Big Brother Watch case, 177–178
biometrics. *See also* identity verification
   benefits and applications, 114–116
   data controller/data processor relationship, 126
   data minimization principle, 122–123, 227
   data subjects' rights, 124–125
   DPIAs (data protection impact assessments) for, 117–118, 120, 125–126
   fair and lawful use principle, 120–121
   generally, 114
   legal bases for biometric data processing, 118–120, 124
   purpose limitation principle and further processing, 121–122, 123
   retention of data, 123
   risks and challenges, 115, 116, 117–118
   securitizing data, 123–124
   sharing data, 125–126
   special protection requirements for data, 116–118, 124
   types, 115
blockchain
   applications in humanitarian sector, 219, 256–258, 267
   benefits, 250, 252–253, 255
   data controller/data processor relationship, 261–263
   data minimization principle, 263–264

blockchain (cont.)
  data protection by design and by default, 260–261, 271–272
  data subjects' rights, 265–268
  decision-making framework for deployment, 269–272
  definition and functionality, 250–253
  DPIAs (data protection impact assessments) for, 258–260, 271
  international data sharing, 268–269
  proportionality principle, 264
  retention of data, 264
  risks and challenges, 255–256
  securitizing data, 264–265
  types, 253–255
'by design' approach. *See* data protection by design

cash and voucher assistance
  beneficiaries, identity verification, 115
  benefits, 131
  blockchain technology for, 256, 257, 258, 267
  data controller/data processor relationship, 143
  data minimization principle, 139–140
  data subjects' rights, 141
  DPIAs (data protection impact assessments) for, 139, 140, 141, 143–144
  generally, 130–131
  legal bases for beneficiaries' data processing, 136–137
  personal data collected and generated via, 132–135
  purpose limitation principle and further processing, 137–139
  retention of data, 140
  risks and challenges, 131–134, 256
  securitizing data, 140–141
  sharing data, 141–143
checklists for data protection compliance, 15–16, 26–27
children, 45–48, 294–295
CISCO Tactical Operations, 278
CLOUD Act (US), 178–181, 186
cloud services
  benefits and applications, 148
  blockchain applications supported by, 264
  data controller/data processor relationship, 151–152, 154–158, 166–167
  definition, service models and infrastructure, 148, 149–151
  deletion of data, 150, 155–156, 157, 161
  DPIAs (data protection impact assessments) for, 152, 153, 156, 165–166
  fair and lawful use principle, 153
  GDPR codes of conduct, 167–168
  government access to data. *See* cloud-based data, government access
  as international data sharing, 58, 165
  legal bases for personal data processing, 152–153
  privileges and immunities, implications for, 149, 152, 157, 160–161, 166–167, 186–189
  purpose limitation principle and further processing, 153–154, 159
  risks and challenges, 148–149
  securitizing data. *See* cloud services, data security
  transparency principle, 154–155
cloud services, data security
  asset protection, 160–162
  audits and procedures for, 164–165
  data in transit protection, 160
  data subjects' rights and, 158–160, 165
  during development, 163
  governance of, 162
  identity verification, 164
  operational security, 162–163
  particular vulnerabilities, 164
  privileged data, technical security measures, 167
  responsibilities for, 156–158, 163–164
  risks related to infrastructure types, 150–151
  separation between users, 162
  staff selection and training, 163, 164–165, 167
  supply chain security, 163
cloud-based data, government access
  criminal investigation grounds, 178–184
  impacts on aid beneficiaries, 184
  impacts on humanitarian organizations, 184–186
  introduction to topic, 172–173
  legal duties generally, 173–174
  national security grounds, 174–178
  risk mitigation, 186–189
community identifiable information, 8
compliance with legal obligation (legal basis), 53–57, 284
computer security measures. *See also* cloud services, data security
computer security measures, 31–32, 34, 51–52
confidentiality duties
  cloud service providers, 157, 159, 181
  contractual duties, 31, 32–33
  data rights balanced against, 15, 39
  in emergency situations, 17–18
  health data processing, 27–28, 54, 89–90, 184
  identity verification before information disclosure, 39–40, 216
  levels of confidentiality, attribution of, 33
confirmation right, 39, 49
connectivity as aid programmes
  data controller/data processor relationship, 282–283
  DPIAs (data protection impact assessments) for, 279, 281–282

INDEX 345

examples, 277–278
international data sharing, 287
introduction to topic, 276–277
legal bases for personal data processing, 283–284
operational context, 278–279
retention of data, 286
securitizing data, 284–286
stakeholder partnerships for, 279–281
transparency principle, 286–287
consent (legal basis). *See also* information right
 for artificial intelligence use, 302–304, 308–309, 318
 for biometric data processing, 118–120, 124
 of cash and voucher assistance beneficiaries, 136–137, 258
 of children, 45–48
 of connectivity as aid beneficiaries, 283–284
 for digital identity data processing, 225, 226–227
 documentation of, 48
 for drone-collected data processing, 102, 107
 freely given, 46
 information requirements for, 36–37, 46, 48
 for international data sharing, 60
 for mobile messaging app data processing, 203, 206
 for social media data processing, 244–245
 objection right, 40, 41, 44–45, 48–49, 107
 timing of, 46
 transmission methods and modes, 46, 48
 of vulnerable adults, 45–47
 when not required, 44, 45–46, 49
 withdrawal of, 40, 49, 304
contact tracing apps. *See also* mobile messaging apps
 data minimization principle, 93
 DP3T protocol design, 81–82, 91–92
 generally, 79–81
 risks and challenges, 84–86, 88, 89–90, 92–93, 95
contingency planning, 33
contracts for data processing. *See* data controller/data processor relationship
contractual performance (legal basis), 52–53, 60, 284
correction right, 40, 207–208, 226, 266–267, 318
counter-terrorist legislation. *See* cloud-based data, government access
COVID-19 pandemic
 combating misinformation during, 234
 contact tracing apps used in. *See* contact tracing apps
criminal investigation legislation, 178–184
cross-border data sharing. *See* international data sharing
cross-functional needs assessments, 25
crowdsourcing, 108–109

data analytics. *See* artificial intelligence
data controller/data processor relationship
 artificial intelligence use, 299, 319–321
 biometric data processing, 126
 blockchain use, 261–263
 cash and voucher beneficiaries' data processing, 143
 cloud services-held data processing, 151–152, 154–158, 166–167
 connectivity as aid programmes, 282–283
 digital identity management systems, 223–224
 drone-collected data processing, 109–110
 social media data processing, 243–244
data controllers
 accountability of, 35, 60, 63, 151–152, 319–320
 data processors, distinguished from, 18, 261
 data processors, relationship with. *See* data controller/data processor relationship
 data security obligations. *See* data security
 data sharing by. *See* data sharing; international data sharing
data minimization principle. *See also* deletion of data; retention of data
 artificial intelligence use, 295, 301, 312–314
 biometric data, 122–123, 227
 blockchain use, 263–264
 cash and voucher assistance, 139–140
 cloud-based data, 155
 for data protection by design, 93–94
 digital identity management systems, 216–217, 227–228
 drone-collected data, 105–106
 generally, 25, 26–27
 mobile messaging app data, 207, 208–209
data processing principles
 accountability, 35, 60, 63, 151–152, 319–320
 data minimization. *See* data minimization principle
 data quality. *See* quality of data
 'do no harm' (precautionary principle), 24, 35, 69–70
 fair and lawful use, 21–22, 120–121, 153, 308–311
 proportionality, 14, 24–26, 122–123, 227, 264
 purpose limitation. *See* purpose limitation principle
 transparency. *See* information right
data processors
 confidentiality duties. *See* confidentiality duties
 data controllers, distinguished from, 18, 261
 data controllers, relationship with. *See* data controller/data processor relationship
 international data sharing by, 58, 63–65
 sub-processors, 18, 124, 151, 157–158, 188

data protection by design
　artificial intelligence systems, 329
　blockchain applications, 260–261, 271–272
　case study. *See* contact tracing apps
　cash and voucher assistance systems, 140–141
　data collected centrally, 93–94, fig.6.1
　data minimization principle, 93–94
　design assessment process
　　potential risks identification, 88–90
　　risks assessment, 90–93
　digital identity management systems, 222–223
　generally, 78–79
　mobile messaging apps, 210–211
　purpose limitation principle
　　purposes determination, 87, 88
　　rationale, 82–87
　　technical challenges, 94–97
　risks retention, 87–88, fig.6.2, 94–95
　'system' definition, 79
data protection impact assessments. *See* DPIAs (data protection impact assessments)
data quality. *See* quality of data
data retention or deletion. *See* deletion of data; retention of data
data security
　anonymization and pseudonymization. *See* anonymization and pseudonymization
　artificial intelligence applications, 315–316
　biometric data, 123–124
　blockchain-stored data, 264–265
　cash and voucher assistance beneficiaries' data, 140–141
　cloud-based data. *See* cloud services, data security
　for connectivity as aid programmes, 284–286
　contingency planning, 33
　data controllers' general duties, 29–31
　deletion of data. *See* deletion of data
　by design. *See* data protection by design
　digital identity data, 228–229
　drone-collected data, 106
　internal organization measures, 34–35
　international data sharing, risk mitigation, 61–63
　IT security, 31–32, 34, 51–52
　mobile messaging app data, 202–205
　physical security, 31
　social media data, 247
data security officers, 34–35
data sharing. *See also* international data sharing
　anonymized or pseudonymized data, 18–20
　biometric data, 125–126
　cash and voucher assistance beneficiaries' data, 141–143
　with cloud service providers, 159–160
　digital identity data, 220–221
　drone-collected data, 108–109
　generally, 41–43
　with government authorities. *See* government access to personal data
　with humanitarian organizations without privileges or immunities, 54–57
　information right, 42
　mobile messaging app data, 199–200, 204–205
　by social media platforms, 211, 236–238, 247
　with third parties. *See* third parties
data subjects' rights. *See also* human rights
　access, 15, 38–40, 107–108, 158, 225, 266
　artificial intelligence use and, 309–311, 316–319
　balanced against other interests. *See* balancing of data rights and other interests
　blockchain applications and, 265–268
　claims for breach of, 38
　cloud services and, 158–160, 165
　confidentiality. *See* confidentiality duties
　correction, 40, 207–208, 226, 266, 318
　digital identity management systems and, 224–226
　erasure, 40–41, 155–156, 207–208, 226, 267, 318
　information. *See* information right
　objection, 40, 41, 44–45, 48–49, 107
deceased persons, 8, 39, 49
deletion of data. *See also* data minimization principle; retention of data
　biometric data, 123
　cash and voucher assistance beneficiaries' data, 140
　cloud-based data, 150, 155–156, 157, 161
　drone-collected data, 106
　erasure right, 40–41, 155–156, 207–208, 226, 267, 318
　inaccurate data, 27
　mobile messaging app data, 201, 203–204, 207–208
　paper records destruction, 33–34
　from portable media equipment, 32, 34
　social media data, 246
　by third parties, 29, 32, 34, 140
demographically identifiable information, 8
designing systems for data protection. *See* data protection by design
detained persons, 51
differential privacy, 315–316
digital identity management systems. *See also* identity verification
　adoption of, 214, 218–219, 221–222
　data controller/data processor relationship, 223–224
　data minimization principle, 216–217, 227–228
　data subjects' rights, 224–226
　design of, 216–220, 222–223
　DPIAs (data protection impact assessments) for, 222

INDEX 347

governance of, 218
international data sharing, 229
legal bases for personal data processing, 226–227
proportionality principle, 227
purpose limitation principle, 227
retention of data, 229
scenarios of use, 220–221
securitizing data, 228
terminology, 214n.4, 215, 217
digital systems for data protection. *See* data protection by design
digitization of paper records, 33–34
disasters. *See* emergency situations
discretion, duties of. *See* confidentiality duties
disease prevention, 234, 295
'do no harm' (precautionary principle), 24, 35, 69–70
DPIAs (data protection impact assessments)
  for artificial intelligence use, 296–297, 320, 322–324
  for biometric data processing, 117–118, 120, 125–126
  for blockchain use, 258–260, 271
  for cash and voucher assistance, 138–139, 140, 141, 143–144
  for cloud services use, 152, 153, 156, 165–166
  for connectivity as aid programmes, 279, 281–282
  for digital identity management systems, 222
  DPIA report template, 333–337
  for drone operations, 110
  for mobile messaging apps use, 196, 206
  process. *See* DPIA process
  for social media use, 239–241, 247
  when appropriate, 45, 63, 66–67, 72–73
DPIA process
  (1) determining necessity for DPIA, 67
  (2) assembling DPIA team, 67–68
  (3) describing the processing of personal data, 68
  (4) consulting stakeholders, 68–69
  (5) identifying risks, 69
  (6) assessing risks, 69–70
  (7) identifying solutions, 70–72
  (8) proposing recommendations, 72
  (9) implementing recommendations, 72–73
  (10) providing expert review or audit of DPIA, 73
  (11) updating the DPIA, 73
drones/UAVs and remote sensing
  data collection and processing equipment, 98, 100
  data minimization principle, 105–106
  data subjects' rights, 106–108
  DPIAs (data protection impact assessments) for, 110
  generally, 100–101
  humanitarian action uses, 98–99
  legal bases for drone-collected data processing, 102–104, 107
  outsourced operations, 101, 109–110
  purpose limitation principle, 105
  retention of data, 106
  safety risks, 99–100, 101
  securitizing data, 106
  sharing of data, 108–109
  transparency principle, 104–107

e-evidence legislation, 183–184
email correspondence, 31
emergency situations
  balancing of data rights and other interests in, 14–15, 17–18, 35, 44, 49
  connectivity loss. *See* connectivity as aid programmes
  drone-collected data processing in, 103
  presumption of high risk in, 69–70
  social media use in, 233, 241
  vital interests in. *See* vital interests (legal basis)
Emergency Telecommunications Cluster, 277
erasure right, 40–41, 155–156, 207–208, 226, 267, 318
EU law
  on data controllership, 243–244
  GDPR (General Data Protection Regulation), 6, 78n.1, 117, 167–168, 307
  on government access to cloud-based data, 176–177, 183

Facebook
  data collection and retention by, 236, 246
  as data controller, 243–244
  data sharing by, 204, 237–238
  Facebook Connectivity initiative, 278
  Messenger and WhatsApp services. *See* mobile messaging apps
facial recognition, 100, 105, 294–295, 299, 300–301, 315
fair and lawful use principle, 21–22, 120–121, 153, 308–311
family members, data access right, 39–40
fundamental rights. *See* human rights
further processing. *See also* purpose limitation principle
  artificial intelligence use for, 304, 306–308
  of biometrics data, 121–122, 123
  of cash and voucher assistance beneficiaries' data, 138–139
  of cloud-based data, 153–154, 159
  of drone-collected data, 105
  generally, 22–24
  of mobile messaging app data, 193, 209, 210

GDPR (EU General Data Protection Regulation), 6, 78n.1, 117, 167–168, 307
Global Privacy Assembly, 4–5

government access to personal data
  cloud-based data. *See* cloud-based data, government access
  compliance with legal obligation (legal basis), 53–55, 284
  mobile messaging app data, 197, 200, 201–202, 204
  smartphone surveillance, 284–285
  social media data, 232–233, 238–239, 240, 298

health data processing, 27–28, 54, 89–90, 184
health promotion, 234, 295
historical record-keeping, 15, 26, 40–41
human rights. *See also* data subjects' rights
  artificial intelligence, bias problem, 296, 300–301, 309–311, 314, 316–318
    ethical assessment, 329–332
    HRIA (human rights impact assessment), 324–329
  data protection as human right, 7
  data rights balanced against, 14–15, 54, 282
humanitarian emergencies. *See* emergency situations
humanitarian organizations. *See also* data controllers
  campaigning and fundraising by, 232, 235–236, 244–245, 257
  compelled data disclosure, impacts on, 184–186
  legitimate interests of. *See* legitimate interest (legal basis)
  NGOs (non-governmental organizations), 18, 20–21, 277–278
  staff of. *See* staff of humanitarian organizations
  with privileges and immunities. *See* privileges and immunities

ICRC (International Committee of the Red Cross), 7, 50n.8, 189n.52, 233, 241n.46
ID2020 Alliance, 224
identity verification
  biometrics. *See* biometrics
  cash and voucher assistance beneficiaries, 115
  for cloud services access, 164
  digital systems for. *See* digital identity management systems
  facial recognition, 100, 105, 294–295, 299, 300–301, 315
  general duties of, 39–41, 216
  KYC (know your customer) obligations, 137, 142, 144, 221–222
  'legal identity' definition, 214n.4, 215
  purpose creep risk, 86, 222
  for SIM card registration, 134, 137, 142, 198, 221, 280
  social media data used for, 232–233
immunities. *See* privileges and immunities

impact assessments. *See* DPIAs (data protection impact assessments)
important grounds of public interest. *See* public interest (legal basis)
inaccurate data. *See* quality of data
inferred data. *See* non-personal data, inferences from
information right
  artificial intelligence use, 304, 308–309, 311–312, 318
  balanced against other interests, 14–15, 35
  biometric data processing, 124
  of cash or voucher assistance beneficiaries, 141
  cloud-based data processing, 154
  confirmation of data processing, 39, 49
  of connectivity as aid programme beneficiaries, 286–287
  data sharing, right to be informed, 42, 60
  digital identity data processing, 225
  drone-collected data processing, 104, 106–107
  personal data obtained from data subjects, 36–37, 46, 48
  personal data obtained from third parties, 37–38
  social media data processing, 245–246
  transmission methods and modes, 35, 39, 49–50, 107
integrity of data. *See* quality of data
International Committee of the Red Cross (ICRC), 6–7, 50n.8, 189n.52, 233, 241n.46
international data protection standards, 5–7, 21, 58
international data sharing. *See also* data sharing
  artificial intelligence use, 320–322
  basic rules, 59–60
  biometric data, 125–126
  blockchain-stored data, 268–269
  cash and voucher assistance beneficiaries' data, 142–143
  cloud services as, 58, 165
  connectivity as aid programmes and, 287
  contractual arrangements for, 61–65
  definition and scenarios, 41–42, 59
  digital identity data, 229
  drone-collected data, 109
  entities engaging in, 58–59
  legal bases for, 60–61
  mobile messaging app data, 211
  reasons for, 58
  risk mitigation, 61–63
  by social media platforms, 211, 236–238, 247
  US/UK agreement on electronic data exchange, 180–183, 188
internet connectivity. *See* connectivity as aid programmes
IT security measures. *See also* cloud services, data security
IT security measures, 31–32, 34, 51–52

INDEX

KYC (know your customer) obligations, 137, 142, 144, 221–222

legal bases for international data sharing, 60–61
legal bases for personal data processing
   alternatives to consent, when permitted, 44, 45–46, 49
   artificial intelligence use, 302–305, 308–309, 318
   biometric data processing, 118–120, 124
   cash and voucher assistance beneficiaries' data processing, 136–137
   cloud-based data processing, 152–153
   compliance with legal obligation, 53–57, 284
   connectivity as aid programmes, 283–284
   consent. *See* consent (legal basis)
   digital identity data processing, 226–227
   drone-collected data processing, 102–104, 107
   legitimate interest. *See* legitimate interest (legal basis)
   list of, 36, 44
   mobile messaging app data processing, 206–207
   performance of a contract, 52–53, 60, 284
   public interest, important grounds of. *See* public interest (legal basis)
   social media data, 244–245
   vital interests of individuals. *See* vital interests (legal basis)
legal risk assessment. *See* DPIAs (data protection impact assessments)
legitimate interest (legal basis)
   for artificial intelligence use, 305
   for biometric data processing, 120
   for cash and voucher assistance beneficiaries' data processing, 137
   for connectivity as aid programmes, 284
   for drone-collected data processing, 104
   generally, 51–52
   for international data sharing, 60

machine learning. *See* artificial intelligence
medical data processing, 27–28, 54, 89–90, 184
metadata
   of cash and voucher assistance beneficiaries, 131–135, 136, 137, 138–139, 142
   cloud-based metadata. *See* cloud-based data, government access
   connectivity as aid programmes collecting, 280, 284–286
   drone-collected, 100
   on mobile messaging apps, 193, 198–201, 203
   on social media networks, 232, 240
missing persons, 39–40, 49, 294–295, 298, 299, 300–301

mobile messaging apps. *See also* contact tracing apps; social media
   benefits and applications, 192, 193, 194–195
   data minimization principle, 207, 208–209
   data protection by design, 210–211
   data subjects' rights, 207–208
   data types collected and stored, 197–200
   definition and functionality, 194, 197
   deletion of data, 201, 203, 207–208
   DPIAs (data protection impact assessments) for, 196, 206
   international data sharing, 211
   legal bases for personal data processing, 206–207
   managing, analysing and verifying data, 209–210
   purpose limitation principle and further processing, 193, 209, 210
   risks and challenges, 192–194, 196–197
   securitizing data, 202–205
   third party data access routes, 199–202
   Whiteflag Protocol, 257–258
mobile network connectivity. *See* connectivity as aid programmes

national security legislation, 174–178
'necessary' data processing, 25, 26–27, 50–53
NGOs (non-governmental organizations), 18, 20–21, 277
non-personal data, inferences from
   anonymized data, re-identification risk, 19–20, 71–72, 139–140, 297, 301–302
   generally, 17–18, 54, 297
   social media data, 235, 241–242, 305–306

objection right, 40, 41, 44–45, 48–49, 107
once-only principle, 220
outsourced data processing. *See* data controller/data processor relationship
overriding interests. *See* balancing of data rights and other interests

paper records destruction, 33–34
passwords, 32
PATRIOT Act (US), 175–176, 177
performance of a contract (legal basis), 52–53, 60, 284
personal data processing
   anonymization and pseudonymization. *See* anonymization and pseudonymization
   definition, 16–17
   DPIA description of, 68
   further processing. *See* further processing
   for identity verification. *See* identity verification
   legal bases for. *See* legal bases for personal data processing
   parties engaged in. *See* data controllers; data processors

personal data processing (cont.)
  principles and rights. *See* data processing principles; data subjects' rights
  risk mitigation. *See* data security; DPIAs (data protection impact assessments)
  sensitive data. *See* sensitive data
  sharing of data. *See* data sharing; international data sharing
  staff members' data, 28, 53
perturbing/redacting data, 20, 39, 72
physical security of data, 31
portable media equipment, 32, 34
precautionary principle ('do no harm'), 24, 35, 69–70
principles of data protection. *See* data processing principles
prisoners, 51
privacy right. *See also* confidentiality duties
privacy right, 7
privacy-enhancing technologies. *See* data protection by design
privileges and immunities
  cash and voucher assistance provision and, 142, 143
  cloud services use and, 149, 152, 157, 160–161, 166–167, 186–189
  data protection as human right transcending, 7–8
  data sharing by protected organizations, 54–57
  data subjects' claims and, 38
  international data sharing and, 62
  standards-setting permitted by, 21, 58
processing of personal data. *See* personal data processing
proportionality principle, 14, 24–26, 122–123, 227, 264
pseudonymization. *See* anonymization and pseudonymization
public interest (legal basis)
  for artificial intelligence use, 304–305, 318
  for biometric data processing, 120
  for cash and voucher assistance beneficiaries' data processing, 137
  for connectivity as aid programmes, 283–284
  for drone-collected data processing, 103–104
  generally, 44–45, 50–51
  for international data sharing, 60
  for mobile messaging app data processing, 206–207
purpose limitation principle. *See also* further processing
  artificial intelligence use, 296–297, 305–306, 322
  biometric data processing, 121
  by design. *See* data protection by design
  cash and voucher beneficiaries' data processing, 137–138, 139
  cloud-based data processing, 153–154, 159

digital identity data processing, 227
drone-collected data processing, 105
generally, 22
mobile messaging app data processing, 209

quality of data
  artificial intelligence, bias problem, 296, 300–301, 309–311, 314, 316–318
  correction right, 40, 207–208, 226, 266, 318
  data quality principle, 27, 158–159

rape survivors, 184
rectification right, 40, 207–208, 226, 266, 318
redacting/perturbing data, 20, 39, 72
re-identification risk, 19–20, 71–72, 139–140, 297, 301–302
relatives, data access right, 39–40
remote access to computer servers, 31–32
remotely piloted aircraft systems. *See* drones/UAVs and remote sensing
retention of data. *See also* data minimization principle; deletion of data
  artificial intelligence use, 314–315
  biometric data, 123
  blockchain-stored data, 264
  cash and voucher assistance beneficiaries' data, 140
  checklist for, 26–27
  cloud-based data, 155–156
  from connectivity as aid programmes, 286
  digital identity data, 229
  drone-collected data, 106
  for historical record, 15, 26, 40–41
  initial retention period, 28–29
  mobile messaging app data, 201, 203, 207–208
  social media data, 246–247
  by third parties, 34
rights. *See* data subjects' rights; human rights
risk mitigation. *See* data security; DPIAs (data protection impact assessments)

securitizing data. *See* data security
sensitive data
  biometric data. *See* biometrics
  definition, 17
  health data, 27–28, 54, 89–90, 184
  inferred from non-personal data. *See* non-personal data, inferences from
  on portable media equipment, 32
sexual violence survivors, 184
sharing of data. *See* data sharing; international data sharing
SIM card registration duties, 134, 137, 142, 198, 221, 280
social media. *See also* mobile messaging apps
  artificial intelligence used to analyse, 232–233, 235, 237, 298, 303–306
  benefits and applications, 232, 233–234
  connectivity as aid programmes involving providers, 279

data controller/data processor relationship, 243–244
data sharing by platforms, 211, 236–238, 247
data types generated, 234–236, 240
DPIAs (data protection impact assessments) for, 239–241, 247
government access to data, 232–233, 238–239, 240, 298
legal bases for personal data processing, 244–245
retention of data, 246–247
risks and challenges, 232–233, 241–243
securitizing data, 247
transparency principle, 245–246
sought persons, 39–40, 49, 294–295, 298, 299, 300–301
staff of humanitarian organizations
confidentiality duties. See confidentiality duties
legal action, data processing for defence purposes, 52
personal data of, 28, 53
personal data processing by. See data processors
remote access to computer servers, 31–32
security of, 39
statistical disclosure control process, 71–72
sub-processors, 18, 124, 151, 157–158, 188
supply chain management, 163, 257
Swiss Blocking Statute, 188
system design for data protection. See data protection by design

tax administration, 53
telecommunications connectivity. See connectivity as aid programmes
third parties
cash and voucher assistance operatives. See cash and voucher assistance
cloud service providers. See cloud services
connectivity as aid programmes in partnership with, 279–281
deletion of data by, 29, 32, 34, 140
drone operators, 101, 109–110
government authorities. See government access to personal data
mobile messaging apps, third party data access, 199–202
personal data obtained from, 37–38
social media providers. See social media

sub-processors, 18, 124, 151, 157–158, 188
systems designers, 94
unauthorized data access by. See data security
TikTok, 234, 236, 238
transborder data sharing. See international data sharing
transparency principle. See information right
Twitter, 236, 238

UAVs (unmanned aerial vehicles). See drones/UAVs and remote sensing
UNHCR (UN High Commissioner for Refugees), 7, 245–246, 277, 286–287
United Kingdom
interception of communications legislation, 176–178
US/UK agreement on electronic data exchange, 180–183, 188
United Nations
connectivity initiatives, 277
data protection standards, 5–6, 7
privileges and immunities of, 187
United States
CLOUD Act, 178–181, 186
US/UK agreement on electronic data exchange, 180–183, 188
USA PATRIOT Act, 175–176, 177

verifying identities. See identity verification
vital interests (legal basis)
for artificial intelligence use, 304
for biometric data processing, 119–120
for cash and voucher assistance beneficiaries' data processing, 137
for cloud-based data processing, 153
for drone-collected data processing, 103
generally, 44–45, 49–50, 51
for international data sharing, 60
for mobile messaging app data processing, 206–207
voucher assistance. See cash and voucher assistance
vulnerable adults, 45–47

WhatsApp. See mobile messaging apps
Whiteflag Protocol, 257–258
withdrawal of consent for data processing, 40, 49, 304
World Medical Association International Code of Medical Ethics, 27

Milton Keynes UK
Ingram Content Group UK Ltd.
UKHW020112041124
450634UK00014B/103

9 781009 414654